An Eloquent Sufficiency

An Eloquent Sufficiency

50 writers talk about life and literature over lunch

Edited by
Susan Wyndham

The Sydney Morning Herald/Dymocks
Literary Luncheons

SMH BOOKS

A publication of SMH Books,
a publishing division of John Fairfax Publications Pty Ltd ACN 003 357 720
John Fairfax Publications is a member of Publish Australia

First published 1998

Printed by McPhersons Printing Group Pty Ltd, Victoria
Typeset by DOCUPRO, Sydney
Design: Cheryl Collins Design, Sydney

National Library of Australia Cataloguing-in-Publication data

An eloquent sufficiency: 50 writers talk about life and literature over lunch.

ISBN 1 86290 124 4.

1. Authors, Australian - 20th century. 2. Australian literature - 20th century - History and criticism. 3. Literature and society - Australia. I. Wyndham, Susan.

A820.9003

Contents

Acknowledgments	vi
Introduction	vii
Roald Dahl	1
Paul Theroux	6
Fay Weldon	12
Wilbur Smith	16
Elizabeth Jolley	22
Colleen McCullough	28
David Marr	34
James Michener	40
Jan Morris	48
Susan Faludi	52
Barry Humphries	59
Michael Caine	65
Jung Chang	70
Morris West	75
David Malouf	82
Vikram Seth	89
Blanche d'Alpuget	94
Anne Summers	99
Ranulph Fiennes	105
Frederick Forsyth	111
Kate Grenville	116
Jeffrey Archer	121
E. Annie Proulx	127
Graham Richardson	132
Maeve Binchy	137
Desmond Tutu	142
June Salter	145
Frank Moorhouse	150
Ruth Rendell	155
John Berendt	160
Judy Cassab	166
Josephine Hart	173
Gordon Chater	177
Nicholas Evans	181
Joanna Trollope	186
Melvyn Bragg	192
Bill Bryson	198
Margaret Atwood	203
Adeline Yen Mah	210
Robert Hughes	214
Tim Bowden	219
Minette Walters	225
Peter Carey	231
Frank McCourt	237
Michael Palin	243
Ruth Cracknell	248
Dickie Bird	252
David Suzuki	258
Bryce Courtenay	264
Arundhati Roy	269
Index of authors	280

Acknowledgments

Text

The talks by the following authors are published by kind permission of Random House Australia:

John Berendt, Michael Caine, Judy Cassab, Susan Faludi, Josephine Hart, David Malouf, David Marr, Colleen McCullough, James Michener, Michael Palin, Ruth Rendell.

The talk by Roald Dahl is published by kind permission of the Estate of Roald Dahl - © copyright Roald Dahl Nominee Ltd.

The other talks are published by kind permission of the authors themselves.

Photographs

The publishers would like to thank the following for permission to reproduce photographs:

Allen & Unwin Publicity Dept - for photographs of Maeve Binchy, Tim Bowden, E. Annie Proulx (photographer Jon Gilbert Fox), Vikram Seth, David Suzuki, Minette Walters (photographer Isolde Ohlbaum)

Camera Press Ltd - for photograph of Margaret Atwood (photographer Sally Soames)

Kate Grenville - for photograph of herself

Harper Collins Publicity Dept - for photographs of Jeffrey Archer, Jung Chang, Frank McCourt, June Salter, Fay Weldon, Morris West

Hodder Headline Australia Publicity Dept - for photographs of Dickie Bird, Melvyn Bragg

Penguin Books - for photographs of Elizabeth Jolley, Adeline Yen Mah

Random House Australia Publicity Dept - for photographs of John Berendt, Judy Cassab, Susan Faludi, Ranulph Fiennes, Josephine Hart, Barry Humphries, Colleen McCullough, David Malouf, David Marr, James Michener (photographer Steven Pumphrey)

Pan Macmillan Publicity Dept - for photograph of Wilbur Smith (photographer Julian Broad)

University of Queensland Press - for photograph of Peter Carey (photographer Marion Ettlinger)

All other photographs in this book are published by courtesy of the Photo Library of John Fairfax Publications Pty Ltd.

Introduction

In just a decade Sydney has become the Literary Lunch capital of the world. New York might have its author readings by the dozen and London does the grand but occasional literary banquet. Nowhere else, though, has anything on the scale of the *Sydney Morning Herald*/Dymocks Literary Luncheons, where club members and other dedicated book lovers plan their year around a program of events that combine good food, wine and company with the best local and international writers talking in the most intimate, entertaining ways about their books, their life and subjects ranging from Hollywood movies to South African politics. Who said writers were solitary souls?

The first *Herald*/Dymocks Literary Luncheon was held on December 2, 1988, with 120 people crowded into a room at the Sydney Hilton to hear Morris West talk about his latest novel, *Masterclass*. The following year there were nine lunches, including one of Roald Dahl's last public appearances before his death the following year. 'People were passionate from the start,' recalls Ian Hicks, the *Herald*'s Literary Editor at the time. 'They crammed into the Southern Cross Hotel at the Haymarket for Roald Dahl; they *insisted* on coming, even when we told them they'd be sitting behind a pillar.'

Everything grew fast. Over ten years we have had more than 200 literary lunches and dinners, gourmet and sporting lunches, evening talks and children's events. In 1998 alone there will be 40 events, and we now routinely fill hotel ballrooms with anywhere from 300 to 700 people. Most people go home with at least one signed copy of the visiting author's book. Many a writer has looked with awe at the mob gathered just to hear them speak.

Our choice of speakers has been eclectic. We've had novelists and politicians, actors and feminists, journalists and adventurers, artists and comedians, biographers and memoirists, bestsellers and prize-winners, celebrities and ordinary people with extraordinary stories to tell.

As for highlights, everyone has their own. Ian Hicks wickedly remembers introducing newspaper tycoon and then owner of the *Herald*, Conrad Black, who had written an autobiography. 'It was the only time I've had to tell the boss his book wasn't so hot.' Hicks also hosted the most dramatic of lunches, when Frank Moorhouse protested that his novel *Grand Days* had been unfairly disqualified from the Miles Franklin Award, and several members of the audience protested more loudly that they hadn't come to hear him complain, leading to an unruly debate that made some vital points about Australian culture. Moorhouse's talk is included in this collection.

For another *Herald* Literary Editor, William Fraser, 'One of the most touching was James Michener, who was very old at that stage and was a fantastic trouper.' Michener died last year, making our record of his talk in this book even more valuable.

My own memories stretch back only three years but take in meeting literary heroes such as the equally sharp-witted Margaret Atwood and E. Annie Proulx; young talent such as Booker Prize-winner Arundhati Roy; great entertainers such as the erudite Robert Hughes, the hilarious Gordon Chater and the sharp-tongued story-teller Jeffrey Archer, who returned for the fourth time this year. I introduced Archer as having become 'very rich' from his writing, which seemed to shock him, and I described Nicholas Evans (*The Horse Whisperer*) as 'spunky', which he seemed to enjoy.

I have certainly enjoyed the opportunity to straddle the line between literary critic and party host, to dine with the human beings behind the books. It may be the work that matters in the end, but in this personality-driven age a book feels enriched when we learn from the author whether he wrote it in ink or on a computer screen, how she messed up her first radio interview, and the way a small idea grew into a work of passion for both writer and reader.

These lunches have been generously supported by the *Sydney Morning Herald* and Dymocks Booksellers and by the personal energy of many people. Most of all I want to thank Judy Benson, known to club members, publishers and authors as the delightful dynamo who has run the Literary Luncheon program from its beginning. Thanks also to Judy's team of workers, to my predecessors Ian Hicks and William Fraser, to the many *Herald* and Dymocks staff who have given their time and enthusiasm; to our other sponsors, Sheaffer Pens and Mildara Blass; and to the hotels that have turned on their hospitality, in particular the Hilton, Sheraton on the Park, Wentworth and Regent.

For helping to create this book, thanks to Sarah Hodgkinson and Lisa Hunter of Fairfax Book Publishing, to eagle-eyed editor Ann Atkinson, to the designer Cheryl Collins, to my researcher Bonnie Tsui, and to all the authors who kindly agreed to share their words once again.

Most importantly, thanks to you, the people who read books. Without you there would be no literary lunches and no *Eloquent Sufficiency*. I hope you'll find great pleasure, as I did, in reliving talks in this selection you might have heard, or experiencing them for the first time in print. Lightly edited, they translate from stage to page remarkably smoothly. Run here in chronological order and including a selection of audience questions, they make fascinating literary history.

I wish I could pour you a cup of coffee or another glass of wine as you dip into the book. But please help yourself, and *bon appetit.*

Susan Wyndham
Literary Editor
The Sydney Morning Herald

Roald Dahl

Born in Wales of Norwegian parents, Dahl has delighted generations of children with his wickedly humorous and fantastic tales, *James and the Giant Peach* (1961), *Charlie and the Chocolate Factory* (1964), and *Matilda* (1988), among many others. His adult fiction tipped over into the macabre, as in his famous story collections *Someone Like You* (1954) and *Kiss Kiss* (1959), later serialised for television as *Tales of the Unexpected*. Often controversial in his private life and public opinions, he died in 1990.

3 April 1989

I've been accused of being a little bit unpleasant or prickly in some of my work, especially for children, and I've gone into it deeply on my own and done a sort of psychiatrist's job on myself and I think I've discovered the reason. The reason is that my mind was warped when I was very young by being deprived of any knowledge of sex.

I know I've made up a lot of stories in my life but what's coming now is an absolutely true story and it's not made up. It tells you what happened to me when I was at my prep school at the age of 12. This was 1928 and we were totally ignorant of the facts of life. I used to get hold of newspapers and find every photograph I could of couples getting married and I would examine them through a magnifying glass, because I'd been told that you could only have babies if you got married so I figured that something very peculiar must be happening during the ceremony. And I used to look at them through my little glass and all I could see was a chap putting a ring on her finger and I thought, well, that couldn't do it, could it? I was a very bewildered young man.

But my hopes rose during my last term at school, because on the last day of my last term I knew, as we all knew, that the leavers got a very famous and exciting lecture from the headmaster, in which all mysteries were solved and everything was explained. And on the last morning of our last term there were eight of us leavers and we were quivering with excitement as we queued up outside the headmaster's study. We filed into the sanctum and ranged ourselves around his desk in a semi-circle – I can remember it vividly, I was second from the right. And there he sat, this dangerous monster – I can see it now, his hair was slicked back with a famous hair cream that everyone used in the Twenties, which was called Anzora. Anzora masters the hair, it used to say, and we all used it and when it dried on top of your scalp, it left a hard crust, like a well-made crême brulée.

The other thing I've always remembered about him was that one of his front teeth was framed, literally framed, in gold, with a gold ring all round it, around the edge, and I wondered why he did this because the tooth itself was a horrible brown, the colour of a ginger biscuit, and it was not worth framing. And there he sat, this man, usually so fierce and confident, and this morning he was distinctly nervous. He was fiddling with a pencil. He refused to look us in the eye and one corner of his mouth was twitching.

'You boys,' he said, 'are about to leave this school and go into the dangerous world of grown-ups, I am therefore about to tell you the secret of life. Though I say it myself, few men could bring themselves to tell you what I'm going to tell you but I must do my duty and I shall not shirk it.' Well, here it comes, I thought, by golly here we go, we're going to learn it all now. He said, 'Now, listen carefully and never forget what I'm going to tell you next: each of you boys has attached to your bodies something called an organ. Thanks to the high standards of morality in this school you are totally unaware of such things as this but I expect you can guess what I'm referring to.' We stood there guessing and we got it about right actually.

He said, 'Now, here comes the vital part, and I say it again, never forget what I'm going to tell you next. This organ of yours is the exact equivalent of an electric torch and the end of the organ, as you can see from its shape, is the bulb of the torch. Now if you so much as touch that torch with one finger, or even with the tip of one finger, the torch will switch on and the bulb will light up. Never do it. Because what happens, what happens when a torch switches on and the bulb lights up? The battery runs down. And I must tell you, little boys like you have very small batteries and in no time at all you'll get so weak that your legs will go all wobbly. You certainly won't be able to play football at your next school. So never, never touch it. It's the most dangerous thing you can possibly do. That's all I have to say to you. I hope you do well at your next school. Good-bye.'

We filed out and I thought, well, by golly, if this organ of mine is so bloody dangerous, what's it for? I was a very perplexed young man of 12 years old. We went home that morning – and we were not fetched in cars like people are today. In 1928 we made our own way home. We were taken by bus to the station, that was in Weston-super-Mare, St Peters School, and I got on the train for Paddington and to celebrate my leaving this school I drank copious bottles of fizzy lemonade. By the time I got to Paddington my bladder was bursting, so I toddled along the platform with my little suitcase and found the gentlemen's lavatory and down I went, into the murky depths of this damp place, and I chose a urinal. I was just unbuttoning my flies when suddenly the headmaster's words thundered in my ear and I withdrew my hand as though there was a viper inside there. But I had to go.

So I undid them, very carefully, leaned forward with my forehead against the horrible white thing, and wiggled it out and got it done. And I wiggled it back in and did them up and just as I was stepping back I saw that now there was a man in the one next to me, a tiny little pasty-faced fellow. And I thought, well, by gosh, let's see how he does it, there must be a trick to this. So I peeped round the side and, by God, he was holding it in his fist. And I thought, well, no wonder he's a pasty-faced little runt, his battery must be absolutely flat.

And being a jolly kind little boy, I thought the least I can do is to impart to him this great secret the headmaster had just told me. And so, rather nervously, I tapped him on the elbow. He looked round and said, 'What do you want?' I said, 'Well, sir, I think I could tell you something, you know.' He said, 'You don't tell me anything, you bugger off, you horrid little boy.' And I scuttled up the steps and out and I was terrified and I was more perplexed than ever.

I got the bus across London and got to Charing Cross, where I took the next train to get home, to Bexley, Kent, and walked home from the station and said hello to my mother and sisters. And the first thing I always did when I got home from school, the greatest luxury, was to take a bath because we only had one a week and so it was a wonderful thing.

So I was lying in the bath, luxuriating, and I started washing myself and when I got to this bit, I realised I could not wash it. Life was getting difficult. But I sprinkled soap suds on it with my fingers and wiggled my hips underneath the water and wiggled my hips around and got it done more or less. And then I got out and started drying myself and I dried all of it except this bit and I thought, what do I do? So I folded the towel up and started flapping it, to make a breeze, and as I was doing that a great idea struck me, a really great idea.

One of the latest inventions in the 1920s was called the High Speed Electric Hair Dryer, a massive machine with a long aluminium barrel like a sten gun, and I knew that my older sister had just bought one of these. So I zipped along the corridor to my elder sister's room and borrowed it. Plugged it in, in the hall, pulled the trigger and dashed back to the bathroom and aimed it, and a searing blast of hot air struck me amidships but I hung on and I was dry. I stood there thinking, it's amazing because all the really great inventions of this world are usually made in extraordinary places. Newton was sitting under an apple tree when one fell on his head and we had the theory of gravity. And some Greek chap was in his bath and he watched it and

"The most difficult thing I ever found in life, when you meet someone for the first time is sizing up his character . . . The trick is to look him in the earhole."

he invented the displacement of water by a solid. And I'm told that Einstein was feeding his parrot when he thought of relativity. And I was flapping a towel at my organ and I invented the organ dryer and I was really braced by this. And as I got dressed I thought to myself, the least I can do, having invented this, is to write to the headmaster and tell him so he can incorporate it in his next end of term lecture. He might even buy one himself and save his battery from running down.

I don't want to go on about this because there were endless sequels to it and problems until suddenly I was put right, at my next school. But you have got the gist of it and what I'm trying to tell you is why my mind was warped when I was young and how the stories that come out have that nasty side to them.

As I've grown more senior, I've picked up a number of good tips and I'd like to pass this one on. The most difficult thing I ever found in life, when you meet someone for the first time, a man particularly, is sizing up his character. Is he a bounder, is he a stinker, is he a good egg or what is he? And I discovered that it's no good staring him in the eyeballs, as headmasters do to small boys – it's a myth about the eyeballs, they tell you nothing. The trick is to look him in the earhole. Either one will do because you can't look into both at the same time. Now here it is: if you see tufts of hair sprouting like grass out of his ear hole, you know the man's a bounder. I don't mean little fluffy, fluffy bits, because all men have those, I mean big tufts, as though he was growing mustard and cress in there. If you see this, you have got him weighed up.

A rich growth of hair, or pubescence, as we experts call it, indicates without doubt that the man is as randy as a rabbit and will try to roger ever girl he meets. This happens to be true, don't laugh. The first serious treatise on this subject was written by a Moroccan professor, called Professor Mohammed Ali, from the Marrakech University, and amongst many other things he described how barbers had known about this for a long, long time. Even if you go today to Trumpers in Bond Street in London to have your hair cut, at the end of it the barber will point his scissors at your ear and say, 'Do you want these removed, sir?' If you are a hirsutissimus, which is the technical word for it, you always say yes. And the problem there is that it presents a real problem for a serious investigator like me because you have got to then stand on your toes and peer deep into the auricle canal and look for tell-tale bristles and this is not easy for a short man who wants to check out a tall man unless the tall man is sitting down and hirsutissimus is never sitting down, he's always running around chasing after women, isn't he?

Let me recite to you a few tiny verses which come from a book of *Revolting Rhymes* that I've written but they've turned out as slightly more revolting than the last lot and therefore I've been told that we can not publish it as a children's book. It will be published as an adults' book, with a notice on the cover saying, 'Danger. Keep away from children' – so they'll all go and get it.

A lady whom my mother knows,
came in and took off all her clothes;
Said I, not being very old,
by golly gosh, you must be cold;
No, no, she cried, indeed I'm not,
I'm feeling devilishly hot.

My mother said, there are no joys
in ever kissing silly boys.
Just one small kiss and one small squeeze
can land you with some foul disease;
You mean from just one tiny kiss?
You know quite well my meaning, miss.
Last week when coming home from school,
I clean forgot Mum's golden rule;
I let Jim Young, that handsome louse,
steal one small kiss behind our house;
Oh, woe is me, I've paid the price,
I should have listened to advice;
My mum was right one hundred fold,
I've caught Jim's horrid runny cold!

Our gym instructress, Miss McPhee,
when gym was over said to me,
stay on, Bill Smith, I'll teach you things,
I'll make you better on the rings;
And after that we'll reinforce
your work upon the vaulting horse.
I stayed behind. She closed the door.
She had never been so kind before;
She said, so you can get it right,
I'll have to hold you very tight;
She held me here, she held me there,
by gum she held me everywhere;
She kindly taught me after that,
to wrestle with her on the mat;
She taught so many things to me,
our gym instructress Miss McPhee.

Somebody gave me a sheaf of paper here with questions on it and I was told that I ought to open them and see what people want to know. Why do you write about beastly smells, horrible, ghastly people and attractive but unwinnable women in the desert? Well, it's all a bloody silly question, isn't it? I write about horrible, ghastly people because most people are horrible and ghastly.

When will another Uncle Oswald book be published? Never, never. As you get older you get less dirty, you know.

What is your favourite chocolate? That's a good question, from Lyn Aston-Wallace, aged 27. I think it's a Dairy Milk Flake. I'll bet that you don't know when the Dairy Milk Flake was invented by Cadbury's. It was invented, strangely enough, in 1920. The history of all the great chocolates you eat is quite amazing. All of them were invented by the 1930s, every one. You know about old Doctor Peters, who first invented solid chocolate in Switzerland in 1880 and then you have got the Cadbury's bar in 1905 and then you have got the Bourneville bar. Then you have got the Dairy Milk Flake in 1920 and in 1930 you have got the Kit-Kat which Rowntrees invented.

And then came the greatest breakthrough of all in 1932 – I don't know why I'm telling you all this, you are a whole lot of grown-ups – but in 1932 a young man came from America. His father ran a tiny chocolate factory in Chicago, and his name was Mars and he made a single bar, which was called the Milky Way. His son had taken his engineering degree at Yale and he wanted to come into his dad's chocolate factory and his dad said, there's not room for the two of us in here, son, and he gave him – this is a true story – he gave him $5000 and his recipe for Milky Way and told him to go off and make his fortune.

He went to England and took his father's Milky Way and he put a thin slab of soft toffee, on top of it. Great. Then he had to work out how to make chocolate stick to soft toffee, because this is very hard to do. Cadbury's produced a thing 20 years ago called the Twirly-Wirly and all the bits of chocolate came off onto the carpet and the parents complained and they took it off. But he found the secret and he produced the Mars Bar. And this is the greatest moment, of course, in chocolate history and the year after that the Aero was invented. Then in 1936 Forest Mars came up with a second great invention. He took a little pellet of dough flavoured with vanilla and he exploded it inside a vacuum and he produced the Malteser but he made a mistake. The first time it went on the market he called it Energy Balls and everyone laughed so he changed it to the Malteser. But it has been a great bestseller ever since.

The following year you got Smarties, you got Caramellos. The 1930s was to chocolate like the Renaissance was to Italian painting. Nothing, nothing of any worth has been invented since then.

Paul Theroux

In his travel books – *The Great Railway Bazaar* (1975), *The Kingdom by the Sea* (1983), *The Happy Isles of Oceania* (1992), *The Pillars of Hercules* (1995) among others – American writer Theroux combines an elegant, personal style of reportage with sharp cultural observations that earned him the title 'the great grump of travel writing' from *Time* magazine. He is also well-known as the author of novels such as *The Mosquito Coast*, filmed by Peter Weir.

22 September 1989

I had written a lot of novels, I would say five novels, before it had even dawned on me that I could or that I should write a travel book. But one year, it was 1973, I had nothing to write. I had finished a novel and there was really nothing left. I did not have any ideas and I thought, what to do now? I was looking at a map and I thought, I will leave London, where will I go? The Orient Express – such an evocative name and would make a lovely book.

Then I saw the black line on the map that went further – Ankara, to Tabriz, to Tehran and onward to Mashhad. I thought, that is terrific. There is no trouble. You simply get on a train, when the train stops you stay a night, get on the next train and keep going. I thought I would just talk to people, write things down and let time pass and pretty soon I would end up in Saigon or Singapore or Tokyo and then go back by a different route on the Trans-Siberian. It seemed to me the simplest solution to travel – I did not even have to leave the ground. Of course as things turned out, I did leave the ground. You cannot enter Burma by road and Vietnam was at war but it seemed to me very simple, something that I could do in a matter of months and not terribly expensive.

Yet I was so very embarrassed about doing it because I thought this is not a real book. A real book is *Moby Dick* or *Great Expectations* or *The Tree of Man* or *Riders in the Chariot*, one of my favourite books. That is a real book but this is a book written by a person who has nothing to write. But I did it and it seemed to work and a few years passed, I wrote some more novels, paid some school fees or shall I say the bills rolled around again.

Bruce Chatwin was a great friend of mine and he said very kindly that *The Great Railway Bazaar* inspired him to travel. He was working at Sotheby's and he said the book triggered off his desire to quit his job and go away to Patagonia. When his book *In Patagonia* came out and I reviewed it, I said, 'This is a wonderful book but how did he get to Patagonia?' It is the secret of the book. Bruce Chatwin simply pops up in Patagonia. I didn't even know where Patagonia was. I thought it was one of these mythical places, but it turned out to be a place. It's in Argentina, as you know, and when I looked at the map I thought, there's a place you can get to without leaving the ground. I would simply leave Boston, go through the States, go through Mexico, Central America, travel straight down and do that, and so I did.

Again I had to take a few planes but basically it was a simple problem and the same with *The Kingdom by the Sea*, simply going around Britain. In any travel book the itinerary is the thing. Once you have a way of travelling, or a route, then there is no problem. Someone might say to you they are going to Perth. The first question would be, how are you going? Are you taking the train, are you going by road or are you going by plane? The way you travel around a country determines your attitude toward it, and the experiences that you are going to have.

I have taken pleasure in writing and I have tried to give it to a reader. But travel writing often still seems to me a very insufficient form, a very limp and suspect, dubious thing to do. In a travel book you sometimes wonder just why anyone bothers and what's the point of it. There are plenty of brilliant writers who have written them. Graham Greene went to Mexico for five weeks – only five weeks – and he came back and wrote *The Lawless Roads*, a wonderful travel book about Mexico, and also *The Power and the Glory*. So five weeks in Mexico and he came back with a travel book and I think one of his best novels.

"I would usually try to conceal the fact that I was just curious."

Similarly Evelyn Waugh wrote travel books and novels and many other novelists have written travel books. Dickens wrote travel as well as novels. Anthony Trollope actually came to Australia and New Zealand and wrote about it, as well as writing about 65 novels. So, many people have done it but you could ask yourself why did they or what did it add up to or did it matter? Were they paying school fees too? Does it add up to anything?

So I used to be somewhat embarrassed about it. And if someone said, 'What is the point? Why did you go there?' I would usually try to conceal the fact that I was just curious. Patagonia, lovely name. Or the Congo, think about Tarzan. I always wanted to go to the Congo. I went there and it was a very weird and wonderful place and dangerous looking. A lot of places I have gone simply because I like the sound of the name, some of them turn out to be something and others not.

The most recent travelling that I have done was in China about which I wrote *Riding the Iron Rooster*. I had gone to China strictly out of curiosity in 1979 and '80 because I was offered a free trip down the Yangtze River on a press trip. It was on a ship that had been redecorated by Chairman Mao's wife for visiting dignitaries but then no one could tell me which dignitaries had been on it.

What struck me about China was how depressing it was and how I never ever wanted to go back there. It seemed to be in the most extreme stage of poverty. It was the middle of winter and people wore the little padded jackets and hats and sort of lampshade type hats and straw sandals – they looked like Michelin men – and it seemed a very benighted place. Although no one complained about the cold, the damp, the snow, the heat. People simply worked and they talked about the Cultural Revolution which they referred to as 'the Great Proletarian Cultural Revolution which has given us so many benefits'. I thought this is an interesting place but it is not a place that I want to revisit. I also wondered if this was what the world would look like in a hundred years' time – when you have cut down all the trees, eaten all the animals and are just living on cabbages in a big, rather dusty tower block. God, I thought, this is the future for maybe half the world.

Then my brother was doing some trade with China – he is a lawyer and he made a number of visits, actually a hundred visits to China over the period from '74 to about '85. Such was the nature of his business – selling, representing companies that were making tennis shoes and bicycles and representing aircraft companies, things like that. The Chinese were trying to develop and he kept saying that China had changed. It was not the same place. I said that was impossible. I remembered the sight of an elderly woman pulling a cart loaded with iron bars, the kind of iron bars that they use in reinforced concrete. Just pulling this very, very heavy cart. She had sandals and it was muddy road and it was raining and it seemed a symbol of the old eternal China. The woman dragging this cart down a muddy lane. In 1980. And no one owned a private car. No one owned an automobile. Old cars were owned by the government.

"In the Soviet Union several housewives I met in the streets offered to make love to me if I bought them a cassette recorder."

I am sure some of you have been to China and seen that sort of thing. Not a pretty sight and yet inspiring to see people working so hard and even able to feed themselves and not dependent on another country. Anyway, my brother encouraged me to go and I went and wrote a book about it because when I saw it I thought: This is amazing! It is different. It has changed. China has actually changed. Furthermore, to take the trip to China I had gone through England, France, Germany, East Germany, Poland, the Soviet Union, down through Siberia and Mongolia and then got to Peking where I started my trip as it were. It was quite a roundabout way of starting.

In Poland people were queuing up to buy fatty

meat and just ham hocks, as we call them in the States, and in the Soviet Union several housewives I met in the streets offered to make love to me if I bought them a cassette recorder that cost them $171 – very much out of touch with market forces! In Siberia people said, 'Will you sell me your watch? Sell me your shoes, sell me your underwear?' There has got to be something wrong with a country that wants to buy your underwear. There has also got to be something wrong with a country that can get people to the moon or orbiting the Earth but they make toilet seats out of very splintery plywood.

"When the book came out, I was wondering, as I usually do, if I'd done the wrong thing once again."

But in China people were not queuing up for consumer goods, they were not queuing up for food, they seemed very much themselves. Food was available to them. Cassette recorders were available. They had more clothes than they really had any need for. The markets were crammed full. But they obviously lacked political freedom and they even said so to me. A lot of people complained about the lack of freedom or the fact they wanted to travel and they were not able to travel and I was dutifully noting things down and then the students demonstrated and there were in late '86 and '87 lots of demonstrations. I said, 'What is the problem? I do not understand what the problem is. This country has reformed.' They said, 'Yes, but not fast enough. We want better food in the cafeterias. More sexual freedom. We want to be able to publish the student newspaper. We do not want to have to get permission every time we do something.'

So I just wrote things down and I thought, this is supposed to be a jolly travel book but I will do my bit and I kept at it. Just in a rather plodding and pedestrian way, noting down the kind of details which are much too boring for a television program and would take a journalist too much time. I saw so many things that surprised me, so many things that were unexpected. And when I wrote the book it seemed to me I was writing something that I had not anticipated. I regarded writing a travel book as a bit like raking leaves – rake, rake and then you've got a pile of leaves and you scoop them up and you put them in a container, just a lot of detail.

When the book came out, people complained that I seemed rather unsympathetic to the Chinese. But I had witnessed student demonstrations, I had talked to a foreign minister who said he thought the students were the equivalent of hippy scum. He said, 'What do they know about democracy? They don't know anything, they are just privileged people.' As is the way with some reviewers, a lot of the review headings for the book were quite similar, in fact I got rather sick of looking at them. 'Cantankerous traveller rides the rails again.' 'Grouchy, grumpy, at it again.' 'Hate to get in a train with this guy.' That sort of thing.

I was a little discouraged by that because I thought I had seen something that was news. And they said, 'Very hard on the Chinese. He mentions how cruel they are.' Well, you go into a Chinese railway station and you often see a little picture, that looks like a Wanted poster – a mug shot – and in China it has a red mark over the person's face. I discovered that these portraits on the railway stations are pictures of men who have recently been executed in that town. Deng Xiao Ping had a well-worn and I think tried and true saying that goes 'Execution is the one sure means of education'. Another one of his was 'Killing a chicken to scare the monkeys'.

I mentioned this in the book and I mentioned the fact that nearly every year roughly about 3000 people are executed. The figures have been monitored by the Hoover Institution in the United States, and in an Anti-Crime campaign between '83 and '86, 10,000 were executed. This is not a horror story I am telling you, this has been going on in China for many years. Even when you ask the Chinese about execution or capital punishment they say that's the Chinese way. They say in China capital punishment is swift. Very swift. The person is shot in the back of the neck with a bullet and the family pays for the bullet, the family of the criminal pays for the bullet. The criminal might be an arsonist, a rapist, member of a secret society, not a killer in other words. He might be someone who stole a lot of money from the state government. He might be someone whose hand was in the till. He might be someone who walked off with a warehouse full of bicycles, a very anti-social crime.

When the book came out, as I said, the reviews were mixed and I was wondering, as I usually do, if I'd done the wrong thing once again. Until this June, when I felt a sense of sadness, even though it was a form of vindication. The events in Tiananmen Square didn't surprise me greatly – the response of the government, the fierceness, the late response, was appalling, but not that strange to anyone who had been in China. I felt that my book was somewhat prescient, not because I'm an old China hand but only because I am a travel writer, as well as a novelist, and because I had taken those trains in out of the way places and had noted down detail. In some cases perhaps boring detail, but it's the collection, the whole picture that a travel writer makes, that is often the heart of a country.

A travel book may be a lot of other things too. It may be a stunt or it may be an adventure, it may be a person finding themselves like Robyn Davidson taking a camel across Australia or Wilfred Thesiger taking a camel across the Empty Quarter. So travel books can also be stunts or ordeals or adventures, or they might be based on something simple like taking a train. But ultimately I think that, if the job is done properly, a kind of truth is expressed, and even though it seems to be expressed with the left hand, still the book remains the heart of the country.

! ?

SPEAKER: Does travelling as you do make writing easier?

PAUL THEROUX: Yes, I think it does, because you work on a novel for, say, a year or two and you can only write a novel really in one place. I also was working on a novel, *My Secret History*, in China and I did it on a train, it's true, but it's not the most satisfactory way of doing it. Normally if you write a novel, you sit in a room, sit at a desk, and the days pass and it's a slow accumulation of detail. I write in longhand, I don't have a computer, I've written all my books just with a pen, so it's a rather laborious process. Travelling does make writing easier because at the end of the long period of isolation when I am writing a novel, I feel like getting away, like doing something, going somewhere.

I'm not a particularly social person, not a party-goer anyway, so my idea of a good time would be to go somewhere that I am curious about. As a matter of fact I've always been curious about the northern part of Queensland and so when I finish this trip I'm going to head to Cairns and Port Douglas, taking a boat to Cooktown. I'm travelling with a collapsible kayak so I'm going to paddle around and camp.

SPEAKER: Since presumably you do not have total recall when travelling, do you make notes immediately after conversations?

PAUL THEROUX: I make notes immediately after I have a conversation. If you hold a conversation with someone, the worst thing you can do is show them a pencil. You can really strike fear into a person's heart by writing down what they say. I do not carry a tape recorder or anything like that but afterwards I write things down. If you tape record something you get a lot of extraneous material but if you take notes you write down the essential things and usually in the tone of voice, with the pronunciation the person used, to make the dialogue live. That is what novelists do and travel writers also. I take a lot of notes.

SPEAKER: Would you travel on a night train that does not have sleeping cars? New South Wales Railways are planning to discard sleeping cars on the Melbourne and Brisbane lines next year.

PAUL THEROUX: The most foolish thing any government can do is start cutting down on the railways. And I do not say that because I am a railway buff. In fact, I am not really much of a railway buff and I am fairly ignorant about the technicalities of trains. I say that because if you look at any Western country, say a country in western Europe, nearly all of them are modernising their trains. There is an item in the paper today about how the French are now developing a new high speed route in the south west. There is already one from Lyon to Paris. The Channel tunnel is going to revolutionise travel. Why are the French building this train? To compete with an internal airline. To have a train competing with an airline may seem a little strange but it is not far-fetched to think that a train could compete with, say, the trip between Melbourne and Sydney though it is quite a long distance. But it would have to be modernised.

A country that allows its infrastructure of transport to go into decline and lets people buy a lot of Japanese cars and imports oil and thinks that the future lies that way is treading the primrose path to damnation.

Fay Weldon

Weldon began her career in advertising, creating the slogan 'Go to work on an egg', moved into television, where she wrote the first episode of *Upstairs Downstairs*, and developed into a 'leftish, humanist feminist', in her own words, and the bestselling author of more than 30 fierce, funny novels about women and their relations with men and with each other. Among them: *The Lives and Loves of a She-Devil*, *The Cloning of Joanna May* and *Big Women*.

28 September 1989

I was talking to my publisher just now about a rather disgraceful episode which occurred when I was chairperson of the Booker Prize a few years back. It had seemed to me that if you were going to make a speech in public, you had better actually say something which mattered. I was, as I later found out, really expected to make a speech about Whither Literature?, which is a safe, boring thing to do and enables Booker McConnell, who runs the prize and very nobly puts up the money for all this carry on, to print the speech and give it out as a PR booklet to all its clients.

But I decided in my wisdom, or lack of it, that I would use the occasion to address the publishers about their terrible behaviour towards writers and inquire why would they not sign the Minimum Book Terms Agreement then under discussion. I had consulted the Society of Authors and the Writers' Guild and all kinds of people about the matter, and it was actually quite a serious speech, or rather polemic. I had arranged for the organisers to provide me with those devices politicians use in which the words are projected onto two glass screens which the audience can't see you are using, and so assume you're just the most fluent speaker possible.

The only thing is you don't know what you're saying because you're not working it out as you go along; you are acting and you haven't even learned the lines; you're just reading. The BBC, which were filming this occasion, were also projecting the screens. They were on a work to rule and at 10 o'clock precisely they went on strike. My speech had started as an attack, and I intended to round it off much more gently by saying, 'Nevertheless, I only say this for all our good, we're all in the same business, all on the side of books', etcetera. But the screens went blank while I was in the middle of a tirade and I couldn't think of what to do so I just said, 'Well, that's all' and sat down, without even attempting to placate anyone.

"The head of the Publishers' Association hit my agent. It was a wonderful evening."

There was an uproar, there really was an uproar, and people were hitting each other down there amongst the tuxes. The head of the Publishers' Association hit my agent. It was a wonderful evening, it really was, and yet these things do in their own way work – the relationship between publishers and writers is much better now, perhaps because, I like to think, some notice was taken on both sides as to what everybody was feeling.

I'm not going to say anything so alarming today. I suppose there always has been an element of delinquency in what writers do. Some subversion is bubbling away there or they wouldn't bother to do it at all. I began my career in a very unliterary way, in a very unrespectable way, as an advertising copywriter. I was writing television commercials – that must be about 20, 25 years ago – before it had turned into the kind of high profile profession that it has become. Which meant that I was writing the scripts as well as filming and editing and dubbing. These days teams do it.

Commercials themselves seemed a little bit strange to me, but you worked out that they were really just little stories that sold a product. A teledrama, it seemed to me, would be a longer story which sold an idea and it was on this base that I proceeded from the writing of advertising copy to writing television dramas. I then discovered that you could have more control and also more responsibility with the writing of novels and progressed to novels which in the beginning were really just novelised television drama. But then I realised there was more to it than this: proper novelists go about their business in a rather different way.

When I was in advertising, I worked on the egg campaign; indeed for a time was partly responsible for it, and coined the phrase, in those innocent days, 'Go to work on an egg'. Going to work on an egg, of course, was a socially irresponsible thing to adjure as the whole nation started eating them for breakfast and their cholesterol level must have risen appallingly – it's very hard to be harmless in this world, isn't it? But I'm never one to waste material, or to let ideas go easily and I can't help feeling when I look at this novel, *The Cloning of Joanna May*, that I am actually using the same old idea, Go to work on an egg.

We are all preoccupied these days with human eggs and male technology, and indeed human technology, and the strange paths into which this is leading us. It is about (if novels are about their plots, which I rather doubt) a woman and a divorced wife, aged about 60, a rather passive, placid person, though capable of, in her husband's eyes, gross misdemeanour on occasion, who discovers that 30 years ago her husband had her cloned.

Her husband is a very powerful magnate, runs nuclear power stations and has medical technology at his fingertips. He had her cloned when she was young and beautiful and there are now four of her, five of her in all, wandering the streets, none of them knowing their relationship with the other, the younger ones of course brought up in a newer, allegedly newer, freer age. All have been implanted as embryos in different wombs and it is my way of working out the nurture/nature debate: how much we are what we are born, how much our futures are within our control, how much we are worked upon by our education, our parents, how right we are to say, 'It's all my mother's fault', or 'It's all my school's fault', and how much in fact it is our own fate, or our own fault, which makes us what we are.

The novel is, as they say, multilayered – so many things seem to be true at the same time. There is a world which comes into my novels quite a lot, which I think is a way of looking at the world as if it were a magic place in which somehow the past, the future can be seen as well as the present. That I think is because I live near Glastonbury in England which is ancient Avalon and the source of a strange wisdom and every second house has 'Astrologer' written up outside it and every next house has 'Divination' and 'Meet yourself as you really are', 'Karmic intervention', all kinds of things, and you get to half believe the rest of the world is like this, which it is quite dangerous, I think, to assume.

I have some questions from the audience here. 'How do you coordinate raising four children and writing at the same time?' The answer is: with difficulty. 'Are the children a source of inspiration?' and the answer is of course that they are – in two ways. I think as a parent you discover your own nature. It is not until you have children that you discover how horrible you are. And if you are going to write fiction about really horrible people as I sometimes do, you present such people in the search for some kind of understanding of them. You do condemn them sometimes but on the whole I prefer to leave it to readers to condemn, or to make their own decision. I propose, I set up the situation and then hope that the reader will be sufficiently engaged to say, 'This woman is insane', or 'It's not like that', or better still, 'Yes, it is perhaps a little bit like that', and to feed back what they read into their own lives. Now, if you are going to do that, you have almost to be more horrible than your most horrible reader. You have to forgo your good opinion of yourself, you have to understand that as a human being you share the fate of all human beings as your readers do and that people are capable of truly terrible things.

"You almost have to be more horrible than your most horrible reader."

Of course, from children you also get back to the pleasure and the joy of life, the way of looking at things which constantly surprises you and you see how wise this uncluttered mind can be and so they are, I think, a source of inspiration, of knowledge and of course of frustration because you want to write and they want you to talk to them.

If you manage to organise it so that they are happily somewhere else, the cat will come and sit on your paper and they seem to have a real knack, cats, of working out how best to inconvenience you. We have quite a savage cat at home – it's quite nice really but if you try and move it, you can have quite a battle. I have found myself with this cat – there'll be the desk, there'll be my papers, I'll have a pen (I write by hand), the cat is sitting there, I try and move it and it will lift out a paw and go like that, I will lift up my finger and go like that, and we can have quite a battle. It occurs to you that you can actually pick this thing up and put it somewhere else which you do but by that time you have lost the drive and the telephone has gone and it is more fun to do something else so you do. So I'm very fond of the cat.

'How did you research life on the road with a band for your novel, *Leader of the Band*?' Well, I went on the road with a band, not for research but because my husband plays jazz trumpet and his band went down to the South of France in a terrible old minibus and I went too as a groupie. It was a wonderful and horrific trip.

'You said in an article that you are always a feminist when in Australia but not necessarily in England.' If I say I'm a feminist when I'm in England, 60 people get up and say, 'You're not, you're not'. To which I reply, 'Where are party headquarters, tell me that, where is our manifesto? By what right are you correct and not me in my attitudes?' In other words, I will say I am the only one in step and you are all out of it. It is a difficult business being a feminist.

'What are the negative aspects of the feminist movement that you indicated one does not wish to be associated with?' I don't think any – if feminism is under attack, I'm a feminist. The word gets somehow used in the wrong way, it's lost its proper meaning. To me to be a feminist is to search and work towards a world in which women are seen as people first and of a certain gender second and that is what we all, I think, work towards no matter what our differences. I wrote a novel called *Puffball* in a time when it was not the thing to suggest that women were at the mercy of their hormones at any time in their lives and when babies were somehow unfashionable. That wasn't very popular but people came around to my way of thinking and fecundity became an okay word which was something as I had four children by then.

Life of a She Devil, which has been on television here and has been filmed with Meryl Streep and Roseanne Barr, was another case in point. The first half of the book produced a kind of role model, a woman who became independent and managed to do without domesticity and helped other women become their own people; in the second half of the book, however, she turned to run for traditional cover. The film, you will be pleased to know, actually stops half way through the book, leaving the story ideologically correct.

Wilbur Smith

Smith, a former accountant, was born in Central Africa and now lives between South Africa and the Seychelles with his wife, the novelist Danielle Smith. His love of Africa, where he owns a farm and game reserve, is reflected in his fast-moving contemporary and historical novels. Since his first book *When the Lion Feeds* (1963), he has published 25 more, most of them international bestsellers, including *The Seventh Scroll* and *Birds of Prey* (1997), which took his Courtney family saga back to the swashbuckling maritime adventures of the seventeenth century.

13 August 1990

If I were asked to describe myself in two words they'd have to be 'writer African', so those are what I'm going to talk about today. In 3000 years BC in Thebes on the Nile a scribe called Amenhotep wrote a palette which is now in the Cairo Museum. On it he wrote: 'The scribe is a fortunate man. While others toil in the fields beside the Nile he sits in the temple precinct at his ease. He eats the sweetmeats of the temple sacrifice and his wives wear fine linen [he got that down right], his words endure like monuments of stone and Pharaoh smiles upon him.' When I read that, I thought to myself, come on Hotep, who are you kidding? You're talking to one of the boys now.

But the general feeling remains that a writer has a very romantic, glamorous life. So what I'm going to talk about first is some of the indignities that have been heaped upon me in my career.

My first book that was published – we don't talk about the other one – I had written out longhand and so I had about 1500 pages of foolscap covered with ballpoint pen and I needed someone to type it for me. I advertised in the paper and a lady wrote in and agreed a fee for her typing and I gave this all to her and she took it away. After a week I was keen to see it actually looking like a book so I phoned her up and said, 'How are we doing?' 'I'm going quite well,' she replied. So I said, 'What does that mean? How many pages have you finished?' She said, 'I've done 10 pages.' So I jumped on my motor cycle and went around to see her. 'What seems to be the problem?' I asked. 'No, it's no problem at all but there's so many mistakes and your grammar is awful and the funny way you put things,' she said, 'so I'm correcting the book as I go along.' That was the end of a beautiful friendship.

"It's just that the bug bites you, it itches so badly and only one thing will stop it itching and that's to scratch it with a pen."

And then came a time when I was actually published and 4000 books disappeared into limbo and I wanted to call myself a writer and I tried it a couple of times at parties. People would say, 'What do you do?' and I'd say, 'Well, I'm a writer' – panic comes over their faces. 'Oh, Wilbur who? Should we know you? What do you write?' So I gave up that and when people asked me that question, I said, 'Well, I'm in paper.' Relief, now we can talk as equals. But then came the dreadful evening where one lady wouldn't accept that as the final answer. She said, 'What kind of paper?' So I said, panicking,'Recycled paper.' So she said, 'Oh, toilet paper?' And I said, 'You've been reading my reviews.'

Then came that fateful morning when I thought I saw someone actually reading one of my books in an airport lounge at Heathrow. I just stopped dead and a chill came over me. There was a lady reading a book that could have been one of my mine, but she was holding it so I couldn't actually read the title. So I sidled across. She looked up and realised that she was being watched, so both of us looked away and she went on reading and then I dropped my pen on the floor and I crawled on my hands and knees past her. She looked at me startled but I saw it was my book she was reading. It was *When the Lion Feeds* by Wilbur Smith. Oh, it was an incredible moment. I lurked in the corner for 20 minutes watching her, seeing if she smiled, if she was getting excited by it and finally it was too much and I walked across to her and I said, 'Madam, excuse me, but that is my book you're reading.' She jumped up, put it in my hands and said, 'Oh, I'm dreadfully sorry, I just found it lying here.'

Later on I went on my first television show in America. Television there is different to here; you go on these very early morning shows and they just line up the people that are to be interviewed. In front of me there was a Maori chief and a parachutist and an artist who drew pictures with his toes. There's no preparation. They just walk you in front of the mike, you sit down, the camera goes on and they start. So when my turn came I went and sat down and the interviewer said, 'But where's your seal?' I said, 'I'm terribly sorry I didn't know they were obligatory.' He said, 'Well, if you're a seal tamer you're supposed to have your seal with you. People don't want to see you, they want to see the seal.' So I said, 'But I'm a writer.' He went pale and shouted to his producer, 'Hey, Jack, I told you, no more writers. What do you say to them?' At that moment the camera went on and he said to me, 'And so, Mr Harvey, you are a writer. Can you give us, in five words, the plot of your new book?'

I was once visiting a bookseller in the north of England and she said to me, 'Would you sign 20 or 30 books for my regular customers and I'll just send it to them and they'll be very grateful.' The sequel was, she told me later, that two weeks later she got one back from an irascible old colonel with a little note which said: 'Dear Madam, I've been dealing with you for 25 years and it's the first time you've ever sent me a defaced copy. Kindly send me a clean book.'

Later, when things started going better, I went on a show called *The Terry Wogan Show*. This is a show that nobody watches but everybody has seen and if you go on it you cannot walk down the street for three or four days afterwards; everybody accosts you. You can't ride on the bus, you can't have your hair cut, they've all seen you. So after four days of this I thought, I've got to flee the country.

Heading back to the Seychelles, in the airport lounge again, there was a character watching me from across the room who obviously recognised me. Here we go again, I thought. Finally he came across to me and said, 'I know you, don't tell me where, I never forget a face. No, don't tell me . . . IBM conference in Zurich in 1982! You're the salesman from Bermuda.' I said, 'That's me.' So we had a long conversation about IBM and he said, 'How's Jack?' and I said, 'Oh, didn't you hear, he ran away with his secretary.' 'No, not Jack!' Finally they called my flight and he said, 'So long, I'll see you in Geneva next year.' I said, 'I'll be there.'

But being a little serious for a moment, the real rewards of writing come from the fact that you spend most of your life in the company of book people, in the company of publishers, booksellers and readers. In my world people are divided into two categories, the readers and the non-readers. It's quite extraordinary how often people will come up to me and say, 'My wife reads your books but I never read.' I think, gee, you wouldn't come up to me and say you beat your wife or you never change your underwear but you come up to me and say you don't read. We can only feel sorry for you.

In my own family we had a reader and a non-reader. My father never read anything but the newspaper, he never even read my books; he made an attempt once, I must say, he was loyal. But my mother read everything. She is still alive; Dad died of boredom, he really did, but my mother will never be bored. Just before I left to come on this trip, I asked how she was and she said, 'Oh, I've just had the most wonderful book in.' She was so excited about it. And she said, 'The gift of imagination is the most precious thing that I have ever been given in my life.'

Occasionally people come to me – either a teacher or a parent – and they say, 'I just want to shake your hand. Our child would not read books and then we gave him one of your books and now he reads everything.' And I think to myself, that is a good excuse for existing, to have been able to give that gift to so many other young people and know that they will probably pass it on to their children in time.

So when people ask me why I write, the answer is not to become rich and famous – because for one thing, if you set out to try and be rich and famous when you write a book, you're going to be neither of those things. It's just that the bug bites you, it itches so badly and only one thing will stop it itching and that's to scratch it with a pen.

I've spoken about writing, now just a few words about Africa, which is the other thing that I am. Africa to me is not one place, it's a thousand places – it's the mountains, the eternal snows on Kilimanjaro, it's the coral beaches, it's the great savannas with those flat-topped acacia trees on them, it's the wild herds of game, it's the great rivers. The Nile, the Congo, Limpopo, Zambezi, even the names give me goose flesh. And in between all those wonderful things is what we call MMBA, which stands for Miles and Miles of Bloody Africa.

"My goodness, it wasn't Spotty at all, it was a big black-maned lion that had eaten Spotty and Grandpa was thrashing it."

Africa is a country of so many paradoxes and contradictions and so much beauty, so much cruelty, we could talk for a week on it and not even touch the surface. People say to me, 'Your books are very violent, very bloody', and I say, 'Well, Africa is a savage continent.' It has been in turmoil for 6000 years. Some of the most terrible things that have ever happened to mankind have happened in Africa: the slave trade was one of the great demographic experiences, an explosion, a trauma that went right through the world, when millions of people were shipped out of Africa.

It's still a country of civil war, of conflict. For instance, Angola now, with those terrible wars that rage on there; they call it the country of men with one leg because so many of them have walked onto landmines and had their legs blown off.

And then there's Grandpa's Africa. It's the Africa that I got from the stories that Grandpa used to tell me. It was the romantic Africa, the darkest Africa of Livingstone and the explorers and the prospectors. Grandpa's name was Courtney James Smith, so some of you might recognise his name. And he could tell stories that would just fascinate a small boy of 10, when I last knew him, and so I thought that I would end by telling you one of Grandpa's stories.

You must imagine me sitting there at his feet, Grandpa with his big white beard, yellow round the mouth from chew tobacco; he'd let fly at the spittoon, which was a Tate & Lyle tin, never missed. And I'd say, 'Tell me a story.' And he'd tell me a story about Spotty, his dog. Grandpa probably had 200 dogs in his lifetime and he called them all Spotty. That way he never forgot their names.

But this particular Spotty he won in a card game in Nairobi and took it back to the farm. It was a cross between a Great Dane and a boarhound and stood the size of a Shetland pony. It was the most stupid of all the Spotties; it killed the chickens, it chased the sheep, chased the cattle and it knocked over the milk pails in the dairy – it did everything wrong. Finally one morning, 1 o'clock in the morning, a bit of a moon in the sky, Grandpa woke up and Spotty was on the verandah, growling and knocking over the furniture – a terrible cavort going on on the verandah.

Grandpa had had enough of this dog by this stage so he jumped out of bed, grabbed his sjambok – a sjambok is a long whip made of hippo hide, long black whip – and went out on the verandah and laid into that dog. After about six strokes,

Spotty was growling in a funny way so Grandpa lit a match and held it up and, my goodness, it wasn't Spotty at all, it was a big black-maned lion that had eaten Spotty and Grandpa was thrashing it.

I said, 'Gramps, then what did you do?' He said, 'I ran back in the bedroom, I slammed the door and I leant against the door and I was just so relieved that I'd got away from that terrible experience. Then I felt the sjambok in my hand starting to twitch so I struck another match and I found I had a big black Momba snake by the neck.'

! ?

SPEAKER: Do you have a favourite amongst the many books that you have written?

WILBUR SMITH: Well, it's like saying to a mother of 21 children, which is your favourite? Some of them are dumb, one's got a squint and one's too short but they really all – they're all my babies. But if there's one favourite that I do have, it's the one I'm going to write next year.

SPEAKER: Do a lot of your characters come from people that you've actually met or is it mostly imagination?

WILBUR SMITH: My first characters were Sean Courtney and his brother Garrett in *When the Lion Feeds*. I suppose that in their way they were both a little bit of me. And since then there have been so many characters in my books. Some of them are straight from history, like Cecil Rhodes, John Forster, but most of the others are a mixture of the two, in varying quantities. I'll take some of the characteristics I know from one person and a bit of imagination and I put them in that big food processor in my mind and I switch it on and they get so mixed up that I don't know which is fact and which is fiction.

SPEAKER: I've read all of your books and with the Courtneys, it's just amazing the way you tie threads together, starting with Sean and Garrett, and how you were able to follow it right through to the great-great-grandson.

WILBUR SMITH: I've had to work out a family tree now because even for me it was getting slightly complicated. One of my weaknesses is chronology – my girls get married and four months later they have a baby – so if you are really very meticulous they don't all fit together exactly right in time. But they are my extended family, the people that live in my head. And so I really don't have to imagine them too much, I just turn them loose and follow them with the video camera that I've got up there between my eyes.

SPEAKER: Mr Smith, in your books you describe a lot of hunting safaris. How do you feel about safaris now, especially the organised ones?

WILBUR SMITH: This is one of the paradoxes and contradictions of Africa that I was talking about earlier on. There was a time in Africa when the hunter was totally ruthless, immoral and with no idea to the future or to consequence, but nowadays safari hunting is strictly controlled by the National Parks Department and it is an accepted fact by the leading conservationists who are all convinced that safari hunting is one of the most important tools of conservation.

I'm not talking about protectionism, I'm talking about conservation, and they all feel very strongly that it is a matter of economics now. You have an exploding peasant population, who's in direct competition with the game for space to live, and you have to compensate those people who are going to give up grazing, forests, land, to the animals.

You must understand, if I'm a black peasant living on $200 a year, I see nothing beautiful in the elephant that comes in at night and breaks down my huts and eats my mealie, or the lion that comes into the kraal and kills my goats.

The watchword now is if the game can pay, the game can stay. So safari hunting is enormously expensive. It costs, for a two-week holiday, US$50,000, and of that $25,000 goes to the central government of the country, which makes them aware of the value of the game, and $25,000, roughly, goes to the people living in that area, living in the villages, to build schools for them, to put down bore holes for their villages so they have clean water and just the basic things in life that they lack.

You must remember also that the safari hunting is so strictly controlled that no female animals, no young animals, would be touched. The safari hunter is like a farmer; you wouldn't expect a farmer to go and wipe out his whole breeding herd. So what the National Parks are trying to do is to treat the game as a renewable resource so there will always be game. The game will pay for itself. And the ones that are taken out would have to be taken out anyway because there are just too many of them.

This is the strange and odd thing. In the Kruger National Park in South Africa, they have to kill 300 to 400 elephant every year because the land is not big enough for them. In Zimbabwe they have 60,000 elephants, as we stand here at this moment, and 30,000 is considered to be a viable herd. They have to cull those elephants anyway, so if they can use the product, the ivory and the skins and the meat from the cull, to buy space for the others to survive in, this seems to be the only outlet for the game.

It's a crazy idea, I know, kill to save. I'm not talking about poaching, where it's a non-selective thing. I was in the Zambezi Valley six weeks ago, we came across a poaching line, 16 miles long, with over 3000 wire snares in it and it had killed everything that moved through. We even found an elephant that had put its trunk into a wire snare, pulled it back and the trunk was hanging by a thread of skin; it was dying of starvation and thirst because it couldn't feed itself.

This is the sort of thing that the hunters help to prevent because they act as a non-paid anti-poaching force in the area. The only reason that we caught this poacher was because I was with a hunting safari and they were there and the black rangers, the black trackers, were even more furious than we were because one of their brethren was stealing their game. So in an odd way safari hunting is one of the tools of conservation.

Elizabeth Jolley

Since moving from England to Western Australia in 1959, after training as a nurse, Jolley has become one of Australia's finest fiction writers. Although she had written since childhood, her first book, *Five Acre Virgin and Other Stories* appeared in 1976. Full of droll and understated insights into human nature, her work includes *Palomino* (1980), *Mr Scobie's Riddle* (1982), *Miss Peabody's Inheritance* (1983), *Woman in a Lampshade* (1983), *The Well* (1986), which won the Miles Franklin Award and was a 1997 film, *Cabin Fever* (1990), *Lovesong* (1997) and numerous radio plays.

19 September 1990

I've called this talk 'Chocolate Has Its Own Melancholy'. That's the title; and I have with me a chocolate frog. 'Chocolate Has Its Own Melancholy', it's a quotation – you might like to think about where it comes from.

I thought that I would look at the choice of reading matter, things that we read, because without reading the writer really can't learn how to make the best use of the techniques of writing. And there is a hint in the text of my talk to where that quotation comes from, if anybody is thinking about the chocolate frog. In fact, it is two frogs together because nowadays you can never buy one of anything, it's always two so that you pay a little bit more.

To me one of the great things about fiction writing is the chance the writer has to dwell among his characters and in his landscapes. This dwelling in the short story or the novel can be done in all sorts of ways and for today, since we are at a meal, I have brought along some food. We all know the saying, bring a plate, so often misunderstood by new arrivals in this country.

If you read some novels simply for the story-line – excuse that cliché – you might as well hang yourself. I believe this has been said in particular, quite safely, about Johnson's *Rasselas*. We can say that because he's not here, is he.

In order to dwell in the fiction while writing, and I suppose this is true of reading, we must be able to step off into the realms of imagination. In the creative state a man is taken out of himself, E.M. Forster writes; he lets down, as it were, a bucket into his subconscious and draws up something which is normally beyond his reach.

Plato, going a bit further, writes in *Aeon*:

> *The poet is a light and holy and winged thing and there is no invention in him until he is inspired and out of his sense and the mind is no longer in him. Whoever knocks at the door of poetry without the muse's frenzy, persuaded that by art alone he will be a sufficient poet, fails of perfection and the work of the sober is forthwith eclipsed by that of the frenzied.*

I think in other words we have to be mad.

A great deal can be shown about characters through all sorts of things – through music and possessions, clothes, body language and so on and I've chosen food just for the purposes of this talk, for this dwelling in the novel.

A great deal can be shown about characters through food. Amy, in Patrick White's *The Tree of Man*, longing to be closer to her son, sees his full lips bright red and glistening with mutton fat. Strindberg's Inspector of Fisheries in the little novel *The Open Sea* is silently disappointed with the tepid coffee he is given, he's ashamed of minding so much about the quality of his coffee, but in this detail the reader is able to step into his uncomfortable temporary lodgings.

Chekhov, in a short story, describes the wife of a rich merchant weeping because the jam made the previous season has not been used up before the new season's jam is made. You can just see her fury. The jam is made out of doors and the whole story, as well as the scene set for the weeping housewife, seems fragrant with boiling cherries and sugar, a contrast to the surrounding poverty.

In another story Chekhov describes a man and wife living separately in one house – actually, when you think of them living separately in one house, it's a bit like the present times when people separate. The man lives upstairs and watches his wife from a window as she comes and goes. He really can't keep away from the window, he's always there watching his wife.

There is a famine and both are involved in offering relief to the peasants, each at loggerheads with the other so they're not achieving very much.

The man decides to leave home and he goes to the station in a snowstorm. In a fit of indecision he leaves the station and makes for the house of a friend, another long journey by sledge through the cold sleet. Chekhov then describes an enormous meal which is served, first a cold dish, white sucking pig served with horseradish and sour cream, followed by a rich piping hot cabbage stew, cooked with pork and buckwheat gruel.

"If you read some novels simply for the story-line . . . you might as well hang yourself."

The host and his guests, another one having turned up, grow tipsy and become unnaturally excited. The host, in particular, gorges himself with a grunting and smacking of his lips and the meal continues. A pie is served, followed by another long interval of drinking home-made wines, followed by a stew of pigeons, a tripe dish, roast sucking pig, duck, partridge, cauliflower, fruit dumplings, curds and whey, jelly and finally pancakes and jam. I think the writer really went to town on that lot.

Our man, the one that was undecided about running away from home and has come back from the station, starts eating with relish and then finds he is munching and swallowing like a machine, smiling helplessly and tasting nothing. The hot food and the hot room make his face burn.

Outside it is still snowing, it is bitterly cold and in all the surrounding villages the people are starving and some are tearing the thatch from their hovels in order to feed their miserable animals.

It is hardly possible to do justice here to the effect the description of the eating of this huge meal has in this story (called 'My Wife' and written in 1892).

Back home in Australia, in the novel *Lilian's Story* by Kate Grenville, a writer that I admire very much, Lilian is growing up in a household governed by the obsessions of her father. Lilian, as it turns out, is the victim, along with her Aunt Kitty, of one of these obsessions, namely incest. In an all too familiar experience of childhood, that of being an eavesdropper without really meaning to be, Lilian is hiding under a sideboard during the nervous footwork of a spoken private confessional on the part of her father and silence on her mother's side. Lilian is, as always, punished. This time with a belt, singeing her skin.

In juxtaposition the author briefly shows the reader the consolations offered by Alma, the maid. Alma is on Lilian's side:

> *Here, lovey, she said and slipped a piece of cake or a handful of date slices into my hand.*

Alma comes often from the pantry with handfuls of raisins, cold pikelets, cold potatoes and pieces of pie. Lilian eats chocolates with the soft centres running down her chin. She sucks and chews on the ones with nuts. She goes on with more cold potatoes, bread and dripping, anything to keep the muscles of her face working.

Through the description of these consolations even more insight is offered and Lilian gets fat and fatter. She carries her weight about like someone else's heavy luggage.

"In the novel I have used powdered dried egg and its ability to bounce scrambled egg off the plate."

Now we'll get onto my work. My novel, *Cabin Fever*, is set during and just after World War II in England. The central character, Vera, has her baby in a small nursing home in a converted private house. Many such nursing homes existed in those days. Women then, after childbirth, had a lying-in time of about 14 days. As you can imagine, they felt as if their legs were made of jelly when they were allowed to get up. Some of us are old enough to remember that.

The story is told in the first person. Vera stays on at the nursing home as she has nowhere else to go:

> *This cheese, Sister Peters says, it's mouse-trap but it's not bad, not bad at all. She has a rabbit sitting*

on her lap. We are all, Sister Peters and her husband, Mr Hoob Peters, and me sitting by the kitchen range, eating all our cheese ration at one go. Sister Peters fancied a cheese and pickle supper. We have a whole square of cheese each and some new brown bread. I have one more week of my month, paid for by my mother, at the Hilda Street Wentworth Nursing Home.

Vera then reflects on the previous household where she had a live-in position of nursemaid and general household help during her pregnancy. The people there were both doctors. Vera looked after their two little girls, twins aged 4, pretty with blonde shining hair and a tendency to keep changing their dresses. She compares the cheese-eating habits of the Peters at the Hilda Street Nursing Home and the Wellingtons, the two doctors:

Daddy Doctor and Mummy Doctor, the Wellingtons, would never eat cheese the way we have eaten cheese this evening. Mummy Doctor would make a thin cheese sauce to pour over some boiled carrots or onions or she would mash a tablespoonful of grated cheese into a saucepan of boiled potatoes, or she would cut some cheese in thin slices, almost like paper, and toast it on very thick slices of bread. The cheese would be made to seem endless. The only trouble being that no one would know it was there at all.

Another aspect of the food shortage in the Wellington household was the sacred butter dish, a small hand-painted saucer with a square of butter sitting on it, placed on the table at meal times but always strictly avoided, everyone being careful to take a small scraping of the margarine which was also set on the table.

This was a curious wartime habit which hung on after the war in many households. You really felt you could never take any butter, both butter and margarine being served simultaneously. A horrid sort of thing to do really.

Vera has a small amount of revenge over this in the middle of a sleepless night. I will leave you to read that bit for yourselves.

The following short passage shows something of the two characters, the Peters, their marriage and of course something about HP sauce. This is at the nursing home:

One of the differences between Mr Peters and Sister Peters is that Mr Peters says an aitch with an aitch; haitch, he says when spelling Hilda Street on the phone. He likes HP sauce. Sister Peters remembers to put it out for him. She does not like it herself but puts it in her rabbit stews and her other casserole dinners, together with a big spoonful of Camp Coffee . . .

[That's not gay coffee – I don't know whether you had Camp Coffee in Australia, it's a sort of thick dark essence. My father thought it was very sophisticated to have Camp Coffee.]

. . . a big spoonful of Camp Coffee, an essence, she says, which helps to create the spectacular rich dark gravy. She says the special ingredients of the sauce, the dates, the molasses, the rye flour, the raisin, the tamarinds and the other things, must have been really hard to get during the war but the sauce, she says, never lost its piquant flavour. Not her special choice of flavour, she says, but a favourite of the mothers and of course Mr Peters.

'I'll go along with that,' Mr Peters always says whenever Sister Peters holds forth on the HP sauce.

The rationing of food during and after the war made a great difference to people. People hoarded food; they gave it away; in fact you could go visiting and give the most miserable little bit of something as a present because it was hard to get.

Throughout certain passages in the novel I have used powdered dried egg and its ability to bounce scrambled egg off the plate. There was another thing about powdered egg – people who were pregnant really couldn't face it and in the story I have a nurse who throws up at the sight of the packet. That is an autobiographical detail, if you want to know.

The nurses are obliged to carry their rations of butter, sugar and jam in little screw top jars in string bags and these details, I hope, enhance the wartime setting in the story. There was one home sister who used to judge all the nurses and their behaviour by the condition of the ration jars and in fact she wouldn't put fresh rations into jars that hadn't been washed and polished brightly.

I'm going to end with two little quotes from Chekhov and then a profound remark – a profound remark that really comes from Chekhov. One quotation, which I think is very suitable for today, is this:

> *We lunched till 7 o'clock in the evening, when the crockery was removed from the table and dinner was served.*

I think that's a wonderful picture somehow. It comes from Chekhov's story, 'The Shooting Party'. He goes on:

> *Yesterday all day long she was rubbing her eyes and breaking crockery. The day before she over-ate herself with chocolate.*

I will end by just saying this: men and women want to make some kind of performance, something beyond the eating of a lengthy meal and the washing up and the tantrum – that's not Chekhov, that's me. Chekhov has suggested that it would be a good thing, in the face of surrounding destruction, and times have not changed, if we could all leave something worthwhile to follow on after we have gone. He suggested perhaps a school or a well.

Given the steadily increasing number of street kids, children without homes, without education and without love and the many arid, famine-stricken areas in the world, perhaps we should all try to follow his suggestion.

! ?

SPEAKER: It appears that your very early life seems terribly potent to you the more you write; how important are those early years to you in your writing?

ELIZABETH JOLLEY: I think early years are important to us all at all stages but it's only as you approach 70 that they start to become more vivid. And the other thing, of course, that brings early experiences close will be the death of a father or a mother. You get a rush of memories and you no longer can report back to these two – perhaps the only two people in the whole world who really want to know how you're getting on.

Interestingly enough, I corresponded with my father up till the day he died – he was run over. When he died I hadn't seen him for about 11 years and the bereavement was curious – an intellectual bereavement because I was no longer collecting material for letters and no longer being reminded about things from before and so on. But I find that I still do in a sense talk to my mother and father in my mind, as though they are still around, because that is a very comforting thing.

I do think early memories if they can be recalled are important for the writer, together with what I think we call hindsight – is that right, hindsight? I ought to know, I tell my students about hindsight as though I understand it completely.

Looking with hindsight at something, you see a bit of a pattern and that is very useful in writing and, of course, you have a moment of awareness, of a truth of something, an autobiographical memory, to which you can then add imagination and step off into the imagination.

I could never write anything out in a purely factual way. I would be no good at reporting for a newspaper; if I reported a burglary I think my burglar would have two wooden legs and get stuck in the pantry window, that kind of thing.

SPEAKER: How did you feel about your work being rejected for 20 years?

ELIZABETH JOLLEY: I wasn't actually conscious of waiting. I didn't go and sit by the letterbox waiting for the rejections, though we did have in those years a contract postman, who was a big, fat Dutchman who used to stand in the road and shout 'Elizabeth, a parcel for you!', and it was always a rejection – which I didn't want and he thought it would be lovely to have a parcel.

It is hard to get in to start with but the thing to do is to go on writing and if people do send rejection letters or rejection slips, after you have got over the dreadful grief and you've managed to open your eyes when they're all swollen with crying, have another look at the rejection slip and see if that person has much sense and has put something that would give you a little bit of a pointer to something you may be doing or not doing.

I think you must go on writing because when you start to get things accepted, then it's one thing after another. It's as though, very fortunately, somebody happens to like what you've done, somebody else hates it but there is an opinion on it, an opinion that is public – perhaps a little book review or a little mention – and by then you must have something else to send. It's no good just sitting back and waiting to get one thing published; you just keep writing till you've got a bank of material.

SPEAKER: You obviously admire Chekhov. What Australian writers do you admire?

ELIZABETH JOLLEY: Yes, I do admire Chekhov's writing a great deal. I reread Chekhov's long and short stories. I'm very keen on reading Ibsen's plays, though I'm afraid he isn't Australian either. Of the Australian writers, I started off when I first came in 1959, I read Judah Waten's *Alien Son*, which moved me tremendously, and I read Patrick White's *The Tree of Man*, which I've re-read subsequently. It's like a great storehouse of writing – I've read all Patrick White's work and I admire it. I've read all Kate Grenville's and Helen Garner's.

Contemporary Australian fiction is very stimulating and very readable for me, I really love it. But I also like to go back and read things from earlier times. I'm one of those terrible people that read at breakfast; I have breakfast on my own anyway, so I read then. And I always read in bed at night. Often people say they haven't got time to read. Well, the thing to do is to have a proper breakfast and read then.

Colleen McCullough

McCullough was a lecturer in neurophysiology when she published her first novel, *Tim*, in 1974. Her second novel, the romantic epic of the Australian outback *The Thorn Birds* (1977), has sold more than 30 million copies and established her as one of the world's leading authors of popular fiction. From her Norfolk Island home, McCullough has turned recently to retelling the stories of ancient history in her series *The Masters of Rome* and *The Song of Troy*. Here she talks about the first book in the Roman series, *The First Man of Rome*.

26 November 1990

I am going to ask for questions later. Perhaps the best preamble for this is to tell you what it is like to write an historical novel of the kind that I've written and of which I will write five more, making six volumes on the story of the Roman Republic.

It took me 13 years to do the research. I wrote *An Indecent Obsession*, *Credo for the Third Millennium* and *Ladies of Missalonghi* while I was doing it. After *Ladies of Missalonghi* I settled down and for 12 hours a day, seven days a week, I did nothing but plod through the ancient sources and the modern historical pundits. I am now in a position to talk quite happily as a peer to professors of ancient history and sometimes do so. I now know about as much about the Roman Republic as most professors of history and more than some, as I will tell you.

I originally started out to write one novel based on the life of Julius Caesar until the research told me that this was an impossible task, firstly because Julius Caesar never put a foot wrong, including his assassination. It is very hard to write an entertaining book about somebody who never put a foot wrong; it's human frailty that interests one most. Then as I did the research I became absolutely wrapt in the story of the last 83 years of the Roman Republic. I realised that it was just the grandest and meatiest story and that history was giving me an almost unique epoch in that throughout the period there were always two men of almost equal status pitted against each other – starting with Marius and Sulla, then Pompey the Great and Julius Caesar and ending with Antony and Octavius who became the Emperor Augustus and started the emperors off.

"I discovered the source of the tall poppy syndrome was King Tarquinius Superbus, the last king of Rome."

It became apparent that I couldn't fit all this in one novel so I thought, right, it's going to be five novels. Unfortunately what I neglected to realise was that the first novel would be setting the scene and that, because it's a world completely alien to us and we know virtually nothing about it, I would have to lay in an enormous amount of background detail that to some extent will be absent from the following novels. That slowed me down somewhat and instead of covering a period of some 24 years, I only covered a period of 10 years, so that explains the extra book.

When I sat down to write the first novel in the series, *The First Man of Rome*, it was the culmination of all these years of research and a great joy. I love to write; I make no apologies about that. I realise that it's one of the reasons why nobody takes me very seriously as a writer because you're supposed to stand here and say, 'Oh, my God, it's agony! Oh, it's so hard, I don't know how I put up with it', and all the rest of it and here I stand and say, 'Ha, ha, it's wonderful. I adore every minute of it.' It doesn't matter that you give yourself a back ache and your feet and legs swell and your eyes feel like grains of sand. The important thing is that I love every minute of my job, except when you finish it and guess what? You have to go out and flog the damn thing.

That's the penance; that is your punishment for enjoying your job. This is my last gasp of a worldwide publicity tour. In America they call me 'a global author'. Isn't that a wonderful phrase? When you're a global author it means you have to do worldwide publicity tours. My primary publisher is American and always has been an American publisher for the simple reason that a geographical accident put me 69 miles from New York City at the time I wrote a book called *Tim*. So naturally one isn't going to send the book to Sydney or to London for publication. I just sent it to New York and I've been published primarily in America ever since.

The First Man of Rome was published there on 1 October, in England I think on about 26 October and, would you believe it, the Germans, the French, the Spanish and the Italians had their editions out in translation at the beginning of November so I couldn't escape. I have been on the road for 67 days. I will have flown, excluding time waiting on the ground at various gates and whatever, 66,000 kilometres or 41,300 miles. I will have spent 87 hours physically in the air. I will have caught 36 planes including two that never got off the ground. I will have stayed in 31 hotels and one private house and all of that works out to about a plane every two days except that it doesn't quite work that way because when one does the US, where I did 19 cities in three weeks, you get on a plane every single day and you fly to the next city. Somebody on Norfolk Island once said to me rather fatuously, 'Oh, isn't it lovely, you must travel just like Queen Elizabeth!' And I said, 'Bugger that for a joke, no I bloody don't.'

I did 320 interviews and God knows how you manage to make the last one as interesting as the first but that's the challenge of it, of course, and so one does the best for oneself as well as for the poor old journo who's on the asking end of things and I don't think anybody has complained that I haven't given them a good interview. But it's absolutely gruelling punishment. A publicity tour for a global author and this is my last gasp, as I said. Tomorrow morning very early I take my last plane for the time being back to Norfolk Island and, believe me, I can't wait to get there.

! ?

SPEAKER: Why do you still use a typewriter instead of a word processor?

COLLEEN McCULLOUGH: A word processor doesn't suit me at all. I think they're excellent tools for journalists and for those who write like journalists because they draft each page as they do it. I don't need a thesaurus. I can find all the words in my head and if I use one that I query, I just look it up in the dictionary. A word processor usually has an American thesaurus and I prefer to use the *Oxford Dictionary*.

Secondly, when I start a draft I just go. And my first draft is my shortest and my last draft is my longest and I just bore ahead. I do not stop and I don't worry about anything that might have been missaid or misquoted or misspelt or whatever because you're going to pick it up in a later draft. So once I start I go from page one to, in the case of the first draft of *The First Man in Rome*, about page 900 and when I'm finished I've forgotten how the hell the book started. It's what happens, it really does, and so when I reread it, it's fresh.

I put it in a drawer for six weeks and then pull it out and see it afresh and annotate it. If I was using a word processor, having annotated it and done my corrections, I would then punch a button and the machine would type a clean draft for me and that's sounds very, very attractive when you're doing your own typing, believe me. But the problem is that when I start to retype physically myself I see whole vistas that are not annotated and so I then write a bigger draft and there's a lot of stuff in it that wasn't in the previous draft nor annotated on the previous draft. So if I physically don't do my own retyping I miss that chance to rewrite and, being a perfectionist, I like to rewrite myself. Everything I do I put through five drafts at least. It used to be ten in the old days but I've got more professional. So I put it through my drafts and every bloody word I type myself, including the last draft.

SPEAKER: When you've been researching one period so long do you telescope down to that period and no other?

COLLEEN McCULLOUGH: To some extent, yes. I believe that one of the things a true historical novel should do for the reader is to live in that world. I as the writer cannot pass any kind of judgment on the thought processes, the ethics, the morals or the customs of the time. Almost all historical novelists, especially those who don't research carefully, make the mistake of passing 20th-century judgments on their characters or else you get immortal lines like the heroine saying, 'Oh, I see, all you want to do is sleep with me.' That's 20th-century thinking.

When I'm writing I think like a Roman. I know how they dress; I can smell the streets. But when I get up from the typewriter I drop it and I become the me who's got to get dinner for the old man – that's one thing about being married, it eats into your spare time.

SPEAKER: How do you know how the ordinary Roman man spoke?

COLLEEN McCULLOUGH: You do not know how the ordinary Roman man spoke because, as one eminent modern historian put it, the history of the ancient world is the history of the ruling class. We know virtually nothing about the ordinary Roman. What we do know we pick up from writings like Petronius's *Satyricon* which is too late for my period anyway but you do get little echoes that indicate that slaves were not always reverent to their masters nor were always chastised by their masters for being irreverent. You get a fair idea from Cicero also of how the ruling class felt about ordinary people and about slaves.

When you read enormously you get feelings as much from what is not said as from what is said. The other thing is that, again quoting a very eminent modern historian, the Roman proletariat is the only proletariat in the history of the world that managed to get free food and free entertainment out of its government. Now that tells you something about the Roman proletariat. Another thing is that you *cannot* think of any ancient proletariat in post-Marxist terms. That is a fatal mistake and I've seen history teachers make it. The ancient lowly were not in any way, shape or form interested in changing the way the world ran, especially politically. As long as their bellies were full they seemed to have been reasonably happy. There were no ancient great mass uprisings against the ruling class.

After that one just uses one's commonsense. I remember somebody saying to me, after I'd written *The Thorn Birds*, 'How do you know what they were talking about in Rome during World War II?' And I looked at them and said, 'Well, I imagine that they were talking just about as anybody talked during World War II, about the war.' Commonsense is one's best ally.

On the whole I tried not to go too much into the lowly. That's a trap because we don't know enough about them and I think were one to write a book about the Roman lowly then one would indeed be treading in a morass from which one couldn't extricate oneself. So I use only two or three characters and they're the only fictitious ones. Everybody else in the book is real.

SPEAKER: What is the main theme of the book?

COLLEEN McCULLOUGH: The overriding theme is the decline and fall of the Republic. Why did it happen? Why was it necessary that Rome should become an autocracy and basically an autocracy that was more or less a figurehead because the Empire was run by an enormous and rather creepy bureaucracy headed by Greek freedmen. That's not the Rome that interests me – that's the Rome that Robert Graves wrote about.

The interesting thing is that the Republic is one of the few periods of history that hasn't been, for want of a better word, done by a novelist in the English language. The Empire has been done quite a lot but the republic, never. Thornton Wilder wrote a book called *The Ides of March* which makes me tear my hair out by the roots because it's so distorted from the historical point of view that you can't read it, if you know your history. He had Caesar married to Pompeia at the time of his assassination whereas in fact he had divorced Pompeia in 63BC and later married Calpurnia. So it's a little bit inaccurate. I am a purist, you know. I would be a great Roman Republic player of Trivial Pursuit.

SPEAKER: Why do you get bad reviews in Australia?

COLLEEN McCULLOUGH: I don't know, it's probably

that everybody remembers the bad ones and nobody remembers the good ones. Believe it or not, I have occasionally been well reviewed in Australia. As I remember, John Pringle did the critique for the *Herald* of *The Thorn Birds* and it was a good review. It was the only one but on the other hand it's not a bad thing to be able to say that John Pringle gave *The Thorn Birds* a good review in the *Herald*.

One of the things that I have noticed about the bad reviews is that they weigh more against me than against my books. So maybe it's a part of the fact that I'm big and jolly and I stand up here and say I love what I do and I don't agonise and I've never walked round behind a literary critic of any nationality with a roll of toilet paper in my hand. I think sometimes that the darlings of the critics maybe do a lot of that. In America they call it brown nosing and I'm not famous for doing that.

"To be honest, I really don't give a stuff about the critics."

I think, too, there's a tall poppy syndrome here. One of the nice things about my research was that I discovered that the source of the tall poppy syndrome was King Tarquinius Superbus, the last king of Rome, who sacked a town called Gabii. He left his son there and the son sent a messenger to his father in Rome who said, 'Your son would like to know what you want to do with the outstanding men of Gabii.' For answer Tarquinius Superbus walked out into the garden and drew his sword. He said not a word and he lopped the heads off all the top poppies in the garden. The messenger scratched his head and went back to the son and said, 'I don't know what your father wants you to do, all he did was draw his sword and lop the heads off the tall poppies.' And the son promptly executed all the outstanding citizens of Gabii. He understood the message from his father and that's where the tall poppy syndrome comes from. So it's interesting that it's Roman, isn't it.

To be honest, I really don't give a stuff about the critics. I know people think that's it sheer bravado makes me say that but, honestly, it isn't. I don't lose any sleep over them. I don't read critiques either good or bad because many, many years ago when *The Thorn Birds* hit the headlines and I read some of the things, I realised it was no good for my blood pressure and no good for my ego – which according to everybody is phenomenal anyway. There's only one way that you survive as a thriving writer and that's when people buy the book and I've been very lucky, people buy my books and that really is the greatest compliment that a writer can have, not some rave review by a critic.

SPEAKER: How do you reassure yourself that, for instance, nothing is known about Julius Caesar's mother and that somebody is not going to come out of the woodwork and say, 'Well we know this and we know that'?

COLLEEN McCULLOUGH: Two ways really. Number one, to have done the reading yourself which I have done. The other thing is you always have to be prepared for somebody to say you're wrong because even when you're reading the great modern authors on history, they're not always right. Nobody is because history is open to interpretation. Provided you don't run counter to what we know of historical fact, the rest of it is up for grabs. Why did they do things? We know what they did, we rarely know why.

In Minneapolis I was very badly reviewed by a professor of history from the local university who accused me of being 200 years out of wack because of a report in the book of a feast that Sulla went to. This fellow built up his whole review around his claim that they didn't eat those kind of things in the days I was writing about and I had my eras confused and whatever. I was on radio with him. The chap who ran the radio program had deliberately invited the critic along and figured that I was going to get annihilated on the air as well as annihilated in the newspaper. But as it turned out I was right. So I had the absolutely blissful joy of demolishing this guy because that feast was based almost word for word on a fragment of Lucilius who died in 101 BC. So I knew I was right because I had found the fragment of Lucilius in my reading and this professor of history had not.

All you can do is do a really honest effort and really know your stuff and I know my stuff but it's not to say that I'm going to be 100 per cent right because nobody is. We'd have to have lived then and have put it all down on a tape recorder. I wish somebody had.

David Marr

Lawyer, journalist and author, Marr has written acclaimed biographies of the former Chief Justice Sir Garfield Barwick and the novelist Patrick White, as well as *The Ivanov Trail* on the Canberra spy scandal. After working for the *Bulletin*, the *National Times*, *Four Corners*, the ABC's *Arts Today* program, he is now a senior writer on the *Sydney Morning Herald*. Here Marr talks about *Patrick White: A Life*. He has since edited a collection of White's letters, published in 1994.

24 July 1991

I wish Patrick White was here. I miss him terribly. He would get so much fun raging against all of this. It would be some consolation to him that there are, as far as I can see, two women here today lunching in hats. He believed women should lunch in hats. But he would, I am afraid, say that all of this was a terrible waste, particularly of my time. I should be back on the streets investigating something or other. I should be writing. I should be working. We all should be working, not lunching, not congratulating one another. We certainly shouldn't be engaged in what I am doing which is going around Australia promoting a book, my book of his life. He hated book promotion. He thought it a most terribly vulgar thing. He came from an age when books sat forever on a shelf and could quietly acquire a reputation and an audience. Books – he used to tell me and thundered at everybody – find their own audience.

I wrote this book very much as a graduate of the school of the *National Times*. I spent years and years on the *National Times* researching the lives of thoroughly worthless people – people who'd stolen something or not given something or vamoosed or betrayed people or, in one way or another, done this country down. Worthwhile work I have always felt (and still do), but worthless people. When it came to me one day that there was no life of Patrick White written and I would like to read one, one of the things that immediately made me think that I might as well write one was the notion that I could now apply whatever skills I had as an investigator and as a writer to the life of somebody who was thoroughly worthwhile. So it turned out for me to be.

There is a nightmare that all biographers have which is that halfway through the writing of a biography you will discover that the subject is second-rate and a really frightful person – that in the end they are simply not worth it. I never had that with Patrick White. I found that the man's complexity – the good in the man side by side in a jumbled heap with all that was terrible – continually refreshed me. And the wisdom of the man as well which was behind the complexities of his writing and the formality of his very, very simple life. To be in contact with that wisdom and simplicity has been the greatest privilege I've had in my life.

The other great benefit of doing a biography of a writer of fiction was that it allowed me to read a lot of fiction. I blame the older generation for doing a frightful thing to people like me – telling us that we can only read novels after our chores have been done. So that every time I pick up a novel now it goes through my mind: are the paths swept, has the dog been walked? And here was a chance to treat reading fiction as *work* and I seized that.

Of course, the older generation's attitude can go to even more dangerous lengths. I had a call from my mother one day. 'Hello darling, how are you?' she said, and I said I was well. She said, 'Are you working today, dear, or just writing?' The book is not dedicated to her. The book is in fact dedicated to my father who hated the work of Patrick White; who got to the third paragraph in *Voss*, threw it across the room and said the man was a madman.

In many ways my book addresses those people who have not liked reading Patrick White and not much liked what they know about the man. I hope it is a door for them into a world which I first entered at about the age of 15, reading *Riders in the Chariot* which came out in 1962. It was a world in which I felt immediately a part; indeed it felt that this man who had never met me was writing about me and about my world and I have always had that sense from Patrick White's novels.

"His books are not, as most of our fiction writing is, various descriptions of the pursuit of love. They are the pursuit of fulfilment."

The writing of books for me has never been a matter of knowing everything and wanting to put it down between hard covers. For me it's knowing a little bit about a subject and being terribly curious to know everything. That was certainly the case with Patrick White. My curiosity went back to the time when I was a kid. I think many of us have felt this curiosity, growing up with Patrick White as if he were part of this country like one of the peaks in the Blue Mountains. He was always there, sometimes erupting, sometimes dormant, but always there on the edge of our lives. I've been pursuing my own curiosity. It is a good rule in journalism, I think, and a good rule in writing, to pursue our curiosity.

Unfortunately I knew all along that this was going to be a long book. I was for a time terrified. I would go into bookshops, seeking out biographies fatter than my own. I would fall on the thousand pages of Lawrence of Arabia with delight. To see a truly fat biography of Dickens galumph onto the market recently was tremendously reassuring. Even Simone de Beauvoir's is longer than my book. Patrick White would reassure me that it didn't matter. He would say, 'They'll read it to the end, David, for the dirt.'

White said that when he died he would be going nowhere, but would stay to haunt those places that he loved. We are reasonably safe in the Regent Hotel but unfortunately one of the places that Patrick White loved was Taylor Square. As you know, Taylor Square is a place you can go to get early copies of the papers. In a vain and impatient gesture I went up to Taylor Square on the Friday night before the reviews of the book were to appear in the *Herald* and the *Australian*. I shouldn't have done it. I know it was the kind of thing that Patrick would have disapproved of very strongly. I got out of the car, I walked up to the paper seller, I bought two copies of the papers, I was sidling back to the car. At that moment my foot was placed by an unseen force into the largest dog turd that has ever been dropped in Taylor Square. As I was balancing the papers under one arm and trying to scrape this mess off my foot with the other, I cursed and laughed that Patrick White was still around.

! ?

SPEAKER: What's at the core of all White's novels?

DAVID MARR: First let me say what it is *not* about. Most writing of fiction, particularly of novels in the English language, is about the pursuit of happiness of one form or another. White's work is not about that. White's work is about the fulfilment of our potential. It is all about what we do with what we are given. It's mostly about work and our duty to one another. One of those duties to each other is love but his books are not, as most of our fiction writing is, various descriptions of the pursuit of love. They are the pursuit of fulfilment. He's a very, very hard taskmaster, particularly on himself.

SPEAKER: Why did he hate Australia so much?

DAVID MARR: I think we have to understand that we both love and hate things at the same time. We both approve and disapprove of things at the same time. Fundamentally Patrick White adored what this country might be and adored what this country was when he was a child. He called those childhood years – running wild through the Southern Highlands and Mt Wilson and running wild around Sydney – the 'purest well' from which he as an artist must draw.

In all his raging against the failings of this country was the memory of a perfect country that he inhabited as a child and also a knowledge – a civilised and tough knowledge – of what this country might be if only we could stop accepting second best and what others tell us we ought to be. If only we could become as he said somewhere, the native and free country of the South that we might be. He hated where we fell short but he loved this country and loved what it might be.

SPEAKER: Why did he come back to Australia?

DAVID MARR: There were two reasons why he made what I think was the supremely courageous move of his life. The principal one was that he knew, as an artist, that he *had* to return: that this was the country, the society and the language that he knew. When he returned by ship he stayed for a few months working on *The Aunt's Story* in Alexandria and then caught the ship to Australia, finishing *The Aunt's Story*. At Fremantle, coming down the gangway on a hot day into a very shabby town, he looked at the people around him and was able to say to himself. 'To you I'm a stranger, but yet I know you intimately. We are in fact interchangeable.' That was the great insight of Patrick White the writer: he knew these people and that this was where he had to write. So he returned.

Many of those people who were disappearing after the war to get to Europe were sexual refugees. They were going where they could live ordinary adult lives following their own sexual proclivities and to get out of a society which was run at that time by evangelical ministers, schoolteachers and policemen. White had the self-assurance of a member of his class and the great good fortune to have Manoly Lascaris with him and that allowed him to return and lead an adult life here without any kind of fear. So there were those two things that brought him back to this country.

SPEAKER: How do you reconcile the good and the bad in him?

DAVID MARR: These two aspects of White's life are irreconcilable. They sit together in him. He recognised both though he was always happier to talk about and freer to recognise what was bad in him than what was good and out of that jumble he believed his work came. He was completely uninterested in improving himself. He would berate himself for his failings. He would regret his failings. He would whinge about himself but he believed that he had to be himself and explore that jumble of a personality in order to write - in particular to be able to write so many completely disparate characters. He felt that if he got himself together into one kind of unified reasonable human being that that would be the only character left in him and that his ability to procreate his work with this jumble of living creatures would disappear.

He absolutely refused to have any kind of psychoanalysis. He called psychoanalysis a 'dark cave' from which he might emerge having lost something and that was his talent. You would rightly call that answer evasive.

You can see an overall pattern to the good and the bad in White. He was a man who was given to rage and in that rage the poise of his character for a time was shattered. He was like a volcano that erupted and in erupting hurt a great many people. Biography is not about etiquette, it's not about berating people for their bad manners. It is about finding where, in my case, great work comes from – and it comes out of this pain and dislocation and contradiction which I hope I've been able to map in the book.

SPEAKER: What role did the Australian land play in White's work?

DAVID MARR: In Australia we have an expression 'to love the land'. It doesn't mean the landscape. It means to love the life that is lived in that landscape and White did love the landscape. All his life, when he got out into the bush, when he was west of the Blue Mountains, he would write to people and say: 'This is magnificent. I really should live here. But then I think to myself – if I lived out here I would die of bush ballads. I am a city man, give me the pavement and the crowd.' And that's what I've called the fourth section of my book: 'The Pavement and the Crowd'.

His family on the land thought that he hated it

all. They didn't see this clear dividing line between a love of the landscape and an ability to write about it in a way I think no-one else in this country is going to be able to in future. Patrick White is in many ways like a Russian novelist. He can do servants, he can do horses, he can do sheep and nobody much is going to be able to do that any more. The land permeates his work even while he made the decision that he himself was a city person.

SPEAKER: What was his attitude towards Aborigines?

DAVID MARR: White was slow to realise things. He travelled all through Hitler's Germany without really being aware that Hitler much existed. He had an affair with one of Franco's diplomats and was seduced for a time to the Fascist side. It took him time to realise the evils that were around him in the world. Once he realised, he did what he could to make up for lost time. For his lack of insight before the war he wrote *Riders in the Chariot* and *Riders in the Chariot* was one of the first novels in the English language to actually grapple with the Holocaust.

As for Aborigines, he was jackarooing for a time out at Walgett where the Aborigines lived down on the riverbank. He had no contact with them whatever. He was 45 years old before he sat at a table and had a conversation with an Aborigine. By that time he had already imagined at least a couple of them for his novels, Dubbo of course in *Riders in the Chariot* being first. He felt angry about what had happened to Aborigines. He would say that they had been robbed and that we must help them. On the other hand, he would say their behaviour is terrible and they must be reprimanded and they must stop. That attitude, which many would attack as elitist and old-fashioned, was his attitude to the end. He was always seeking to find what it was that caused these dislocations in their own behaviour and at the same time pouring money into scholarship schemes to get Aboriginal kids through secondary schools at a time when those scholarships were not being provided by the government.

White raged against this current political fashion for believing that education could be starved of money. He believed that the core of it all was good education. That's where he put his money and later on of course he became one of the chief benefactors of the Aboriginal and Islander Dance Company and one quarter of his fortune, after Manoly Lascaris's death, will go to that dance company.

SPEAKER: Did Patrick White and Janet Frame know each other?

DAVID MARR: White was an early devotee of Frame's work and wrote her a fan letter in 1962 and she replied in 1986 thanking him for his kind support. He believed that Janet Frame deserves the Nobel Prize. On one of Janet Frame's very, very rare trips to Sydney recently she rang him up and they had a short conversation on the telephone but they did not meet.

SPEAKER: Did you enjoy being with him?

DAVID MARR: A favourite time. It depended on whether I was feeling bloody or not. There were great days when I would quietly tell him something I'd discovered and I'd just love watching his face *not* change. The best times were probably at lunch after our so-called interviews had ended. Everything with White was always on the record. I had to learn about lunch. He would say, 'Would you like some lunch?' and it took me some time to realise that was not an invitation to lunch, a fact that only came home to me one day when I saw the two men actually divide up two pieces of brawn into three so that I could join them. The invitation to lunch was, 'You'll stay for lunch, won't you?'. That was a true invitation and those times were wonderful – once, of course, we'd listened to the ABC 12.30 news which you listened to in silence. At a quarter to one you could then start talking and they were the liveliest and best times and I got some of the best information from those lunches. Not, of course, taking any notes but you can always write notes afterwards.

SPEAKER: Are misfits the only people who come through in his books as totally worthwhile people?

DAVID MARR: Patrick White felt himself a member of the tribe of the afflicted people. He was afflicted by his asthma. He felt at times afflicted by homosexuality. He felt at times afflicted as a writer. He felt at times afflicted as somebody who didn't quite fit into the society around him. He saw himself as a member of this afflicted class and he had great sympathy for other members of that class and certainly those sorts of misfits get a good guernsey in his novels. But don't forget the servants. The figures of true goodness in his novels are usually servants for whom he felt grateful all his life for the simple love and comfort that they had given him through a difficult childhood and his love and sympathy for them shines through all of his books. Indeed, his core notion of love is the service of one person to another and that was the religion of love for Patrick White.

James Michener

Michener wrote his first book at the age of 40, based on his experiences during World War II. *Tales of the South Pacific*, published in 1948, won the Pulitzer Prize and became the Rodgers and Hammerstein hit musical. More than 50 million copies of his big, semidocumentary, historical novels have sold and he wrote until his death in 1997 at the age of 90. Among his titles are *Hawaii* (1959), *The Source* (1965, about Israel), *The Covenant* (1980, about South Africa) and *Caribbean* (1989).

10 January 1992

I am very glad to be here in Australia where my wife and I spent our honeymoon many years ago up on Victoria River Downs, the largest station in the world. We have been back to Australia happily many times since. This is a kind of returning home to us. At one point in my life I lived in North Sydney for six months and got to know the city well and affectionately and served with Australians in the war. I have been in all parts of your country. We spent part of our honeymoon in Broome and Derby and that teaches you something about Australia.

I am a professional writer. That is what I do. That is really all I do. When I am working I get up at 7.30 in the morning, have a very bleak breakfast because I do not want to eat too much and I go right to work and I work until 12.30 every day, 365 days a year, and the only thing that would interrupt that was once when I had a Chinese dentist and he also liked to work in the morning and not in the afternoon. We had a bit of an impasse there. But by and large I get it done in the morning or I do not get it done. I work with two fingers on an old fashioned heavy typewriter but I am not stupid because as soon as I get done I turn it over to my secretary who is a wizard on the word processor.

I have said everything important that I am going to say so we might as well get to the fun part of this. I find it most productive if we go directly into questions and answers because it is what I do best and it ensures that at least some of the things you are interested in will be dealt with because you will set the agenda and I will try to respond.

! ?

SPEAKER: I am going back to your first novel, *Tales of the South Pacific.* Is Bali Hai a real island in what is now Vanuatu?

JAMES MICHENER: Everything I write, other than my strictly non-fiction books, is fiction. I use imaginary people often based upon real people but composites, I use imaginary settings, I use imaginary historical incidents and the material I used in *South Pacific* was gleaned from my having been in the naval airforce in World War II and having served on 49 different South Pacific islands.

I really had a most comprehensive knowledge of the South Pacific and when I wanted to write my book I based it on an imaginary island which would be like Vanuatu. The island, however, that I used for Bali Hai was totally imaginary but it was located about where Aoba is now and the name comes dramatically from a little village that I found on Sterling Island in the Treasuries, a little village actually called Bali Hai, one of the ugliest, most primitive villages I ever saw anywhere. But what a lovely name.

SPEAKER: How did you feel about the film and television versions of your work?

JAMES MICHENER: Some years ago when I had nine of my books translated into other media – I now have about 15 of them – somebody asked that question and we counted up and in the motion pictures I had three tremendous successes and three complete flops and three right in the middle. In American baseball, you men in the audience will know, that averages out to .333 batting average and that will keep you in the big leagues. I have tried to remain in the big leagues all my life but believe me, when you do you are going to run into some clinkers and we all do, we are ashamed of it, we try to do better and I forget the failures and try to remember the success.

SPEAKER: Were you allowed much input into the TV series?

JAMES MICHENER: As I said, I have done about 15 translations into the other media. I have never had any input into one of them. The great successes I have had in those fields, and I have had quite a few, have largely been due to the inspired work of other people who took the work I did and digested it into their own terms and then ran with it. Also the failures often were due to them in that they ran in the wrong direction but by that time there was nothing I could do about it. No, I have not been responsible in any respect for the movies and stage plays and television shows that I have been affiliated with.

SPEAKER: Has that been by choice?

JAMES MICHENER: It has been by choice. I think my wife would fortify me in this, by saying that I tend to be off to one side. I have never played the literary game. I do not attend salons, I do not know editors and publishers, I do not go out a great deal. I am a professional workman and I want to do it my way and I work at that very diligently, so I doubt that I would have worked in Hollywood had I been invited to do so on these plays of mine. I have no talent in that field whatever and I learned that very early.

My idea of a great beginning for a play on Broadway or in London is where the butler is talking to the maid and the maid says, 'Madam has been in the Bahamas for three months now,' and then the butler says, 'Yes, and she met this dashing Italian count,' and then they discuss that for about five minutes and then one of them says, 'Aha, here's madam now'. I am not sure that I could do better than that so I leave it to other people who do know the trade.

SPEAKER: When are you going to give us a story about the incredible history of our country? And how does an aspiring young writer get to be one of your research assistants? (And I can use a word processor.)

JAMES MICHENER: The second question first. Contrary to popular belief and things I have seen in the press quite often, I do all of my research myself. I have had a fantastically strong education in the American system and in graduate school in Scotland – I went to St Andrew's University for two years. I had great teachers and I learned something. I wrote long term papers and I learned what a sentence and a paragraph were. I took courses that were essential to my growing up and then as an adult I continued my education. I made myself into a professional geographer, never had a course in college. I work constantly at my profession and I am the result of very fine schools and very fine professors.

I went to nine universities, always at somebody else's expense. I was identified early as a bright kid who got straight As in almost everything and I got a wonderful college scholarship. I was really good in sports and I think that helped but I was also very good in my studies. And from there I went to graduate school and then travelling scholarships and then a professorship at Harvard and all the rest. Always at somebody else's expense. So I have a social attitude that a lot of other writers do not have or could not have that I am constantly aware that I was able to do what I have done because of the American educational system.

"In the motion pictures I had three tremendous successes and three complete flops and three right in the middle."

I frequently say that had I been born in Yugoslavia, and that can represent quite a few other countries, under the circumstances I was and with the prospects I had I would have spent my life counting gasoline drums. In the American system they picked me up early and kept me up there. They did not want me to fall or fail and I have profited from that wonderful education so I do all my work myself.

I have an office manager, a very brilliant Englishman, who has been with me for many years as my assistant and I frequently ask him to get me a book on, say, Tennyson from the library. At the University of Texas where I work mostly there are 23 major libraries on the campus, 23. So that the probability of my asking for a book in the morning and not getting it by five o'clock in the afternoon is very remote. Almost everything I want is there.

So I ask him to find me the books I need and I do not need a biography of Tennyson, I need about six of them because I want to know what different people say. And I especially need three written within the last 10 years so that I know what current thinking is. I live that way as a researcher 365 days a year and working on these problems.

As to your first question about writing about Australia. It is perplexing to me that I have never written about either Australia which I have known well in a most friendly way or Scotland which I have known better than any of the countries I have written about. The simple answer is that sometimes you miss the right moment or you miss the right invitation or you miss the right dream at the right time and I would suppose that that accounts for the lack of my having written about Australia. But I have never written about California, I have never written about Scotland, I have never written about quite a few things that I am quite competent in because it is a tricky business to sit down one day and say for the next three years all I am going to write about is Scotland or Australia. You had better be in the right mood when that hits because that is a long assignment.

SPEAKER: I first became a fan of yours in reading *The Source*. I have always wondered: were you there, did you dig, did you see or did you just imagine?

JAMES MICHENER: I think I had better make a little statement which I think illustrates immediately what we are talking about. If something dramatic were to happen in Tibet tomorrow, I could by the end of next week make myself one of the most competent men in the English language publishing area on Tibet because I have lived in all the countries around there.

I know who was governing in India at a certain time, I know what was happening in China, I know intimately what was happening in Iran and Afghanistan and I have done work in all those fields. I have done work in the religion, with some of the languages, the art, everything. I know an intimate amount about Tibet by the accident of having done my work in the other fields.

Now, if the same thing happened or even a more important one happened in Paraguay tomorrow, how competent would I be to write about it or to get myself prepared to write about it? I have never been there, I do not know the terrain, I do not know the history, particularly I do not know the history of the surrounding countries. I do not know who fought whom when, I do not know who the dictators were in the other countries, I do not know what the pressures are. It would take me two years to become competent to write about Paraguay because I have not worked in that field.

And that is true about the whole problem of writing, that you have to start from a platform which you know something about and if you do not, then I doubt that you ever catch up. That is why travel is important to young people. That is why reading is important to young people. That is why a good education is important to young people.

In *The Source* it was an area I knew well and to which I went with the intention of writing about Istanbul, Constantinople, and the marvellous things that happened there, because I had lived greatly in the Muslim world. I had lived in every country in the world that has Islam as a major religion except Arabia. They would never let me in, but I was all prepared to go. Then we went on a trip and I saw the great crusader castles in Israel and I remember I went to see one and we went through it and everything I had learned about Istanbul came to focus there. That was the story that I was interested in and that night I sat down and wrote out the complete outline of *The Source*. So I had a long background in that area.

And then I also worked in four or five of the digs so that I really knew what archaeologists did and what their chances were and what their great triumphs and defeats were. From that I got the background material from which I could build a story about the religious genesis in that part of the world. So I think it is a classic case of the fact that I did have a long background in the germane material and then had the opportunity to do very specialised work in the job that was at hand.

SPEAKER: I wonder if you would allow me to take issue with you on one small point about never having written about Australia. I have lived in this city almost all my life and one of the things as a very young man that taught me to love and cherish this place was a quotation I read from you in an article I believe in *Holiday* magazine in 1949 in which you described flying into Sydney by night and you said the city was like a handful of jewels flung on black velvet. It has made me very happy to live here ever since.

JAMES MICHENER: I have written about Australia and very favourably many times and I have written about Australians in the goldfields and in the islands and in the war, but the big book about Australia which I should have written and probably could have written was never done for the reasons that the big book about Scotland was never done. One of the most deplorable gaps in my life is that I never wrote the big book about Islam that I am entitled to write. That would have been invaluable in recent years had I done it. I have lived all through the Islamic countries and have great respect for them. I should have written it, but you cannot do everything.

SPEAKER: Is there anywhere in the world you have not been to that you would like to go to?

JAMES MICHENER: Some years ago I was asked this question and I wrote a little essay about it. When the government asked me to go on the committee that supervised the State Department's operations in foreign broadcasting I turned in a report which the FBI demanded and they had tracked me as having worked in some 120 countries around the world. So later this magazine wanted to know were there any that I had missed and I said I was deeply disgusted with myself that I had missed three of the best: the Amazon River which is one of the world's marvels along with the Himalayas and almost as comparable in magnitude; and Peking, that great city; and the Antarctic Ocean because I had been in all the other oceans of the world and have written about them.

"I had lived in every country in the world that has Islam as a major religion except Arabia. They would never let me in."

And within two weeks President Nixon invited me to accompany him to China and I was with him on the Great Wall of China and in Peking. Then shortly after that I was invited by the Brazilian military to fly at very low level, maybe 1500 feet, along the entire length of the Amazon River. One of the most extraordinary experiences I have ever had, that great river. And as we flew down, coming in from the south with the maps I had, there were three rivers, each one bigger than the Mississippi, feeding the Amazon and I did not even know the name of one of them. South America is bigger than you and I can imagine.

But that still left the Antarctic. And on three separate occasions I have been scheduled to go to the South Pole and every one of them aborted through sometimes my fault, sometimes just chance, but if my health holds out – we have our big 85th birthday party in New York very shortly – week after that I am heading for the Antarctic so I will have 'hit for the circuit' as we say in baseball when you get a single, a double, a triple and a home in one game. That happens about once every ten years. I will have completed where I wanted to go. I have been forbidden by doctors to go to Machu Picchu in Peru but I have been right near there. It is a terribly high altitude and a lot of people have trouble there and I am not allowed to do that but I have been everywhere else.

SPEAKER: You have written about the small people in your novels. Tell us about the future of the small people in view of what has happened in the Middle East and Russia recently?

JAMES MICHENER: As someone who has written about communism in two of my books, as someone who has thought deeply about Poland and Hungary, I have been astounded by what has happened in the last two years. I can hardly believe it. I have been a warrior against communism for the last 24 years, that is what I was doing in the government, and we knew that it was in trouble, we knew that its frontiers were very fragile and that they could not depend upon Baltic states or some of the Asian states and certainly not the Ukraine or the one that borders Romania; we knew they were in trouble. But we never believed that it would happen so suddenly.

It all came to a head for me when the Hungarian Government allowed the people from East Germany to march through Hungary without any opposition and come down through that barbed-wire minefield and go into West Germany. We knew then the fate was settled and after that the collapse of the Wall and the rest came very rapidly but even those whose job it was to predict what was going to happen did not dimly realise that it was going to happen so fast.

I can only say that I have taken no pleasure in the things that have happened in this year. The fact that we went into the Gulf War and did not finish it was a great disappointment to me although I applauded President Bush in going in when he did because I was pretty sure that Saddam would have had the oilfields of all Arabia within another week had he not moved when he did.

I cannot take any pleasure in the dissolution of the Soviet empire, it is coming too fast without decisions having been made. I am very mindful of the fact that when the United States broke away from Great Britain in 1776 it was 15 years before we could sort out the pieces and start a real functioning democracy with the balance between little and big worked out and with the three branches of government worked out; it took us 15 years to do that and we are asking Russia to do it in two months and that is terrible.

I do not know what the future is there. Our crystal balls are very clouded. I am delighted with events in the last few weeks that the Asian republics, the Muslim republics, have decided to stay with the main branch of the Russian new system rather than sign up with Muslim Iran but I do not know how long they will honour that and I would expect that we can see terrible re-arrangements and trouble in Russia for the rest of this century.

The events in Yugoslavia are just heartbreaking. There is reason why those republics should be at one another's throats and I think that in the democracies there is a tragic misunderstanding right now because Serbia is in such a bad posture, bombing Dubrovnik the way it has and overriding the little towns in Croatia. But I remember a different Croatia, I remember it very well because I was dealing with it in the work I was doing in World War II. Croatia sided with Germany, Croatia was a very active member of the axis, Croatia behaved terribly to its Serbian minorities and the Jews and gipsies, Croatia was a monster in those years. Well, it has rectified itself, it is now a pretty good functioning unit. It is probably going to be a free nation but I do not forget those realities.

Nothing grieves me more than the realisation that in this year after all these years of world history and study and improvement and working toward conciliation that in Northern Ireland you can have a religious war just as you had in France 800 years ago, not a damn bit of difference; and in the Near East you are going to have another religious war just the way you had in the time of the Crusades.

We are not a perfect people we human beings, we are very flawed in many respects and history does not work always by reason. It works in very strange ways, none stranger than when I first came here to your wonderful country where I lived for about six months. It was in the days when your very able Cabinet Minister Calwell was running the White Australia Policy very vividly, very actively, it was in the papers all the time. I came to Australia with my wife and it was the first time she had been to Australia. She had to go in a little room off to one side and sign a paper to the effect that, since she was of oriental extraction (always an American citizen), she could not stay here longer than three weeks. She had to promise to get the hell out at the end of three weeks because that was the law then. That was your immigration policy. You were very eager for immigration, you welcomed graduates of Oxford and Cambridge if they were white and if they arrived on your shores with five thousand quid and you do not get too many of those immigrants.

So one sees changes. It is so hopeful to see a change in which the people of Australia faced up to realities.

"The fact that we went into the Gulf War and did not finish it was a great disappointment to me."

I will close with this. One of the most moving things I have ever seen in my life was when the first Greek planes came in, they were American and British planes but they came in from Greece bearing young women whom the Catholic priests of Greece had gone to throughout the countryside and said, 'Look, all of your men are overseas and there is this wonderful group of Greek men in Australia and they cannot find wives and we know you, you are a girl of wonderful character, your future, believe me, does not lie here in these hills of Greece, you are not going to find a husband.' They were put on board these planes and I remember flying up with some of the Greek men to Darwin. They wanted to intercept the planes there and get the first pick of the crop.

I figured they were the kind of young men I wanted to encourage and we went up there and there were two wonderful Catholic priests, Orthodox not Roman, who had arrived in their costumes and they had these 200 or 300 beautiful little girls. One saw that what was happening here was exactly what happened in the United States when all our young men went across the prairies and got into Seattle (or where Seattle now is) and suddenly found it had no women. So what did they do in about 1853, '54? They sent back to Boston. It was not Greek priests this time, but a Unitarian priest. He went to the countryside and he got all these young women in the Boston area and said, 'Now look, girls, the men have fled, some of you are not going to get married, the thing for you to do is get aboard this ship and get out to Seattle because there you are really needed.' By and large, people go where they are needed and it works out for the best when they do that.

So it is with those thoughts in mind that my wife and I come back to this beautiful country and renew acquaintances and wish you all the best of good luck.

Jan Morris

Morris's career as a travel writer began when, as James Morris, foreign correspondent for the *Times* and the *Guardian*, she joined Edmund Hillary's expedition to Mount Everest in 1953. In the 1972 book *Conundrum* she wrote about her transsexual experience. Since then her many admired books have included *Pax Britannica*, a three-volume history of the British Empire, and *Sydney*, an examination of the city's history, lifestyle and people, published in 1992.

7 April 1992

It is a dangerous moment to be a Pom returning to Sydney isn't it, even a Welsh Pom, even a Welsh republican Pom, even a Welsh republican Pom who bowls underarm. But I find it pretty unnerving always to come back to Sydney, whatever the political climate, because I never quite know what you expect of us from the other side of the world.

The first time I came was back at the beginning of the 1960s. On that occasion I used a truly marvellous range of derogatory adjectives to express my views of your city. I looked up the piece the other day and here are just a few of them, a sort of thesaurus of my original views of Sydney: unsavoury, disagreeable, hideous, crooked, plain, spurious, dull, distasteful, lumpish, cold, vacuous, pallid, frigid, aloof, steely, scornful, accusatory, sour, scornful, irritable, graceless, sleazy, mindless, crude, spiteful, twisted, peevish, unlovely and, worst of all, humdrum. It is only a short piece, but was awfully good. You hated it.

I see from my files that 20 years on I was very much more ingratiating about you and much less fun, I fear. Perhaps I learnt my lesson because your last angry letters about the first piece took five years to reach me. I still get nasty looks from people, sometimes even now; from elderly people who remember that essay. But anyway, by the early 1980s the adjectives were very different and more flowery too. Just listen to these: wake-frothed, yacht-flecked, pristine, nooky, bosky, airy, polite, handsome, glossy, cheerful, exhilarating, even innocent, even, believe it or not, demure. But here I am again and this time I have got an entire book to throw at you. You may well be wondering what on earth I am going to say this time and how can you trust me. Why should you take any notice of a writer who describes Sydney as sleazy one year and demure the next?

"It is a dangerous moment to be a Pom returning to Sydney."

I must say, incidentally, having spent a lifetime writing about other people's cities, that I still to this day think what an awful impertinence it is to come breezing in like I do, all fancy adjectives and plastic sandals, to write about places whose citizens by the nature of things know far more about them than I do myself. I blush, I really do, to think of the grievous factual errors I have made in about writing about other people's cities. I put Toronto on the wrong lake, I put Panama City on the wrong ocean, I said longitude when I meant latitude, I have had the sun set in the east. Countless times I have put north where south ought to be, and innumerable statistics I have more or less made up as I go along, or at least I have rounded them down to the nearest million or so – like anthropologists who say, oh, new set of bones, they are 50 million years old, or maybe 80 million . . .

I think that this city has changed more fundamentally during my 30 odd years' acquaintance with it than perhaps any other city in the world. More importantly, or no less importantly, I have changed. My vision and my moods have changed. What I am recording in books like these, books about cities, and books about times too, is not necessarily what is or what was, but what I see and feel and imagine. You will probably say that is all very well, but these things are abstractions, the colour blue and the meaning of truth, etc., whereas Sydney is a city. And of course you are right. Nevertheless I have always felt it to be a rather hallucinatory kind of city, full of illusions and double meanings.

I was writing an essay a few years ago about the pleasures of food, and remembering it was here in Sydney that I first realised the real pleasures of eating and drinking. I had never been very interested in food and drink until then, but one day a friend of mine here gave me lunch at his apartment overlooking the harbour. Something about the way he presented the food and the way he ate and drank it himself, something kind of sensual about it and the crusty bread and the wine and this sort of slurping, sensual way he had, suddenly made me realise what the pleasures of eating and drinking were all about.

Years afterwards I came to write about this experience, this revelatory experience, and I felt after all that time that I could still remember every single sensation of the moment. I could taste the food. I could see my friend spreading the pâté onto his crusty bread and I could see the blue of the sky and the white sails of the yachts and crowning it all: like a benediction on this moment, this important moment of my life, the sails of the Opera House. It was only then that I realised that the Opera House had not been built then. That is what I mean about a hallucinatory city.

In writing this book I was repeatedly struck by a certain sense of unreality about Sydney. In trying to evoke that sense, of course, one has to use what is really a novelist's technique, because true travel books do not deal in unrealities. Here is a little example from the book. I was trying to capture something of the festive exhibitionism, the kind of fantastic side of Sydney.

> *For most people in the world the look of Sydney is the grand slam look, the flag and fireworks look. This can certainly be magnificent. It gives you a triumphal feel as though there ought to be incidental music in the air, preferably 'Waltzing Matilda'. (What an awful thought by the way, permanent muzak of Waltzing Matilda all over the harbour, night and day.)*
>
> *Somebody once lent me five video cassettes of the Bicentennial Celebrations in 1988. I played them at high speed, fast forward, and never was there such an exhilarating succession of images. Yachts and symphony orchestras and flags and dancing Aborigines, airships, fire floats, spouting princes arriving, bands playing, vast cheering crowds, curtsies, soldiers saluting, gabbled speeches, now a wide shining shot of the harbour, now the Opera House from the air, gun salutes I think, helicopters certainly, flowers, children singing and as the day rapidly changed into night before our eyes, a violent eruption of rockets into the sky and a pyrotechnical waterfall over the lip of the bridge.*
>
> *As the city broke into a last tremendous blaze of rejoicing light they really did play 'Waltzing Matilda'.*

See what I mean? In a way that is doubly fictionalised. I was not here in 1988, I was seeing the occasion only on a video, not in fact. The video itself blurred and heightened and made it hallucinatory, in fact, and presented it not as it was, but as I chose to have imagined it. I do admit there is nothing very hallucinatory about Sydney people who strike me as rather more solid than most but in dealing with them in this book I have had to use my imagination in a different way. I have never been afraid to invent or to amalgamate people in my work, just as a novelist does in a novel. Though in these kind of books I somehow have to make it clear to the reader that they are inventions or amalgams. There are various devices that one can use for this. Sometimes I can do it just in a tone of writing, so you know you are not expected to think of the passage as being strictly true.

"I think that this city has changed more fundamentally during my 30 odd years' acquaintance with it than perhaps any other city in the world."

Sometimes I just fall into the present tense, which shows that an event cannot be true, and sometimes again I do it by inviting my reader to meet people with me at that moment. In this book I introduce the reader to a whole gallery of Sydney characters. Many of them are historically true, people out of history, and I do not play around with them at all. Some are real and quite easily identifiable people of today, but many more I have invented. We go to an imaginary dinner party, for instance, in an imaginary apartment. You know the apartment very well – everything is the newest, pictures by the figurist of the moment, furniture in the latest Slav American mode, tulips in Chinese vases, fabrics in the muted cerise flecked with green as decreed last month by *Australian Vogue.*

"You know the people there too in a way, the ones who never stop talking about real estate values."

You know the people there too in a way, the ones who never stop talking about real estate values. The ones who end up sitting in each other's laps in a far corner of the room. The one who spills his wine all over the brand new and ruinously expensive white carpet. The woman who likes to brag about her family criminal connections and colourful racing identities and the awful old harridan who is sure to be descended from the Duke of Oxford, you know them all. Yet in a way, they exist only in my own mind. They are true but they are imaginary. They are no more actual than a novelist's characters but they are not just archetypes, and they depend for their existence really upon my mood, and my tastes and prejudices. So it is, with this city as a whole, which for my purposes is only a kind of character too.

Paul Theroux once told me that he liked writing travel books – and he really does write travel books, proper travel books – because the journey itself provided him with a plot. Well, I like writing about cities because the city is its own central character, to be interpreted variously according to my own feelings and moods. I am not describing Sydney in my book as you see it or as anybody else sees it, but as I see it; and that is why it is not a travel book.

I seem to spend half my time trying to persuade people I am not a travel writer; but I seldom succeed, to tell you the truth, and I suppose I have got to live with the definition and die with it too. I know just what the little headline will say, at the bottom of a column, page 5 *Sydney Morning Herald*, when I do finally kick the bucket: 'Sex change travel writer dies.'

Susan Faludi

Faludi used her insider's experience as a Pulitzer Prize-winning journalist on the *Wall Street Journal* to investigate the use of the media to undermine the gains of the women's movement in the US with propaganda, fear and prejudice. Her 1991 book, *Backlash: The Undeclared War Against Women*, is a best-selling bible of women's studies around the world.

3 June 1992

Lately, so-called lifestyle journalists who are eager for the latest trend story have been phoning me and the few other designated feminists *du jour* and demanding to know if the backlash against women's struggle for equality is, as they put it, over. The backlash, they say, that was new last year. What is new for 1992? I told them that regrettably the backlash does not work like hemlines. But really, they insist, isn't it the Year of the Woman? The culture is positively ga-ga over women's rights, they tell me. Oh, really, I say? Sure, look at the newspapers. After Anita Hill there were all these stories on the status of feminism. In fact, two whole cover stories on the state of the women's movement in two major Sunday magazines in the US on the same weekend. Yes, I say, delicately, but both of those cover stories attacked the women's movement and called sisterhood a myth.

OK, the lifestyle journalists concede, but look at the movies. Hollywood has gone into a feminist frenzy. Take *Thelma and Louise*. Well, that's all very nice, I reply politely, but can you name any other mainstream films in which two strong, independent women are in the driver's seat and truly challenging the system? Well, no, the lifestyle journalists mumble and hurriedly move on to TV. Just look at all those strong, independent, female characters like Roseanne and Murphy Brown and Murphy Brown and Roseanne. I delicately point out that in one of the last seasons two of the 33 new prime-time shows lodged in the US featured women who so much as held jobs, much less were independent. The rest of the women were housewives, love slaves or completely invisible. And as to those two strong women, Roseanne and Murphy, they struck the American media as two too many. *Newsweek*, for instance, sounded the 'feminists are taking over the TV screens' alarms, warning that independent women were, as they put it, 'seizing control of prime time'.

OK, say the lifestyle journalists. But here is real life, dollars and cents evidence that women's status is happily improving. In the US the pay gap is narrowing in four of the eight broad occupational categories defined by the Labour Department. Yes, say I, ever the wet blanket, but it's improved literally only by pennies, and look at the reason why. The gap is shrinking primarily due to men's dropping wages, not women's fattening pay cheques. That is hardly a victory for either sex. OK, they persist, but women soon will have the upper hand in the workforce. In the future, women are projected to take about two-thirds of the new jobs created between now and the year 2000. Yes, but two-thirds of working women will wind up in these exciting new job opportunities slated to experience the greatest future growth: typing, waitressing, kitchen help and, as the US Labour Department euphemistically labels it, private household service.

So, no, we aren't post-backlash. In fact, on so many fronts, the backlash has only dug in deeper. In the US, while some people like to think things must be better for women with Ronald Reagan out of the White House, George Bush has actually vetoed more women's reproductive and women's health initiatives than Ronald Reagan – quite an achievement.

In Australia, by the way, women's political status doesn't seem to be on the ascendancy either. Your new leadership has shown little interest in advancing women's rights, unless you call a measly one-time hand out of a couple of hundred dollars for families with children a boon for feminism. Following the March elections, indeed, you now have fewer women in the Federal Parliament than in the late '80s. Each year in this supposed post-backlash era in the US and in Australia, cases of sex discrimination, pregnancy discrimination and sexual harassment have only multiplied, and at the same time government agencies charged with combating discrimination and harassment have been increasingly crippled by budget and staff cuts. So, in the United States, the Equal Employment Opportunity Commission in 1990 had a backlog of 42,000 discrimination cases. Guess how many Equal Pay Act cases the agency filed as a result in that same year? Eight.

Each year we have more women terrorised by rising and record rates of rape and sexual violence, sex-related murders, just as the government in the US has cut off funds for battered women's shelters. Each year in this post-backlash age, we have more women forced into poverty and on the streets, thanks to increasingly punitive government budget cuts that take a disproportionate toll on women, particularly single, female heads of household. And each year in the US our reproductive rights have been restricted to the point where now we are months away from a Supreme Court ruling that, barring a miracle, will destroy what remains of our tattered right to an abortion.

Something, however, has changed for women in the last year. As Anita Hill put it so succinctly and eloquently, the silence has been broken. The backlash hasn't receded, but many of us women have rediscovered our voices and with it our political outrage. We have become angry, openly angry, about the mounting attacks on the fragile gains we have made. In the US big gender gaps have surfaced at the polls as women have thrown their formidable, demographic weight behind feminist-inclined candidates. In the UK donations to women's rights groups and groups that fund female candidates have more than doubled in less than a year. Women voters angry about the Senate Judiciary Committee's shabby treatment of Anita Hill have produced surprise upset victories this year for virtually unknown feminist candidates in Senate primaries, and furious women have shown up in historic numbers, almost a million last April, at a pro-choice march, the biggest demonstration in the US capital in American history – not that you could tell by looking at the front pages of the newspapers.

But as we get more vocal, the perpetuators of the backlash have only turned up the sound on their anti-feminist broadcasts. They responded not by listening to women's rage, but by trying to drown it out with dismissive cracks and smears such as calling sexual harassment, in the words of US Senator Alan Simpson, 'a bunch of crap', or, more effectively, by simply adopting more sophisticated and insidious methods of attacking the feminist cause. The backlash, in short, hasn't gone away. It has just found new code words and whipping girls for its hostile message.

Backlash politicians, for example, have not stopped blaming independent women for the nation's woes; they have just switched scapegoats in a sense. What I mean by that is at the start of the '80s Ronald Reagan and the New Right men singled out the independent family careeress for pillory. Single, professional woman were the bad feminist witches created by the women's movement who were supposedly destroying the family, the fabric of society and even, as Ronald Reagan informed the public in one of his presidential addresses, causing the early '80s recession. Now George Bush and governors from California to New Jersey have targeted another sort of independent woman for blame. This one is on the other end of the income ladder. Now welfare mothers are said to be destroying the family, the fabric of society, and, according to George Bush, causing the late '80s recession. They are even to blame now, we are told, for the LA riots.

"Backlash politicians . . . have not stopped blaming independent women for the nation's woes."

Our legislators have decreed that these new bad girls must be punished. Cut their child support cheques by 25 per cent if they don't find a job in a few months, proposed California Governor Pete Wilson in a state with few and dwindling numbers of jobs. Deny those welfare mums the lousy few extra dollars that they would get when they have a second child: that'll show them. And don't give those teenage welfare mums any funds if they don't move back in with their parents, proposed the Governor, even if the parents happen to be abusive and violent.

In Australia, too, you have seen a subtle backlash against the single mothers. Single mothers used to be eligible for child support till their children finished their education. Now they lose it when their children turn 16, and the Liberal Party wants to cut that back to age 12. Apparently once kids reach adolescence they don't need to eat any more.

This year the backlash media, too, has not stopped bad-mouthing feminism. Like the politicians, they've simply scripted new lines. In the '80s the media kept insisting that the women's movement had alienated that mythical average women by promoting an impossible super-woman icon and pressuring all women to aspire to hard-driving business executive status. It was actually, of course, Madison Avenue and the media that invented the super-woman, but we'll put that aside for the moment.

This year the popular refrain in the press is in a way just the opposite. Now we keep hearing that the women's movement has alienated the average woman by promoting the super-victim image and pressing all women to think of themselves as victimised and weak sheep. Before feminists were cast as loud-mouthed power grabbers. Now to the press we're cry-babies wallowing in our powerlessness. Before we were too shrill. Now the all-popular adjective appearing in the press for feminists is whiny. *Forbes* magazine, that well-known feminist journal, even dubbed my book 'the whiner's bible'.

So how do we go about blowing the whistle on the backlash when the method of attack keeps shifting, when the backlash message in the media and in politicians' rhetoric is increasingly encoded and deceptive? Along these lines I thought I would offer you some brief guidelines on how to spot the backlash; what to look for when you watch TV, read the papers and, if you can stand it, listen to your campaigning politicians. If the backlash's propagators were to compose a sort of strategy manual for themselves, this is what it might say.

Backlash Rule No. 1, a sort of modified Murphy's law: If anything can go wrong it will be the fault of feminism and female independence. Among the wrongs the politicians and media pundits have pinned on feminism include teen suicides, homelessness, prostitution, homicides, and, yes, eating disorders. Or, take this Public Service anti-drug ad that has recently run on US television. A teenage boy comes home to an empty house. He turns on the answering machine to find a recording from his working mum telling him that she won't be home for dinner again and he should help himself to the prepared meal she left in the refrigerator. The bereft boy shuts off the machine and immediately proceeds to snort several lines of coke. Feminism, it seems, can lead to drug addiction.

An important corollary to Backlash Rule No. 1: Whenever possible, frame the women's movement for crimes committed by the backlash. Take the rise in rape, for example. A *Newsday* columnist blamed the feminist movement for encouraging more sexual assaults by undermining the 'old sexual mores' that supposedly kept rapists at bay.

Backlash Rule No 2: When you attack feminism always refer to scientific evidence and studies by supposed experts. Some classic examples of the strategy employed by the media in the '80s include the infamous Harvard/Yale man shortage study that turned out to be unrepresentative and hopelessly flawed. In fact, it turned out that there was a woman shortage in the prime marrying eight years; in fact, the man who did the study was himself a bachelor past 30, which may explain the whole thing. Or the *New England Journal of Medicine* Infertility Epidemic study that turned out to be based on a tiny sample of women in Paris whose husbands were totally infertile. No wonder they were having such trouble getting pregnant. In fact, it turns out that American women's infertility rates are dropping and it appears that it is men's infertility that may be rising. Or there was the New Traditionalism 'women are returning to the home' study hailed in such magazines as *Good Housekeeping*, which in fact commissioned the study. That study unfortunately, when one goes back and looks at it, turned out to say just the opposite: that women increasingly wanted to have both a family and a work life.

I would like to say that that exhausts the list of bogus studies used to support the backlash, but new samples crop up weekly. According to a study in paediatrics, the *Los Angeles Times* advised us, 'Type A babies can blame mum'. Those over-ambitious, feminist-minded career women, the story explained, 'can expect to give birth to hard-driving, intense babies who will face a higher risk of heart attacks when they grow up'. A closer look at the study, however, reveals first of all that it is based on a big sample of 36 women. And more to the point, how do we know that their babies are type A, hard-driving types? Because they responded 'vigorously', whatever that means. It turns out that all that means is that the babies cried a fair amount, a litmus test that would seem to yield a positive result for most babies.

The other example was this big story billed on the front page of Lifestyle sections just as, conveniently, the William Kennedy Smith case was going to trial. A study shows, the *San Francisco Chronicle* reported, 'Sexy clothes attract rapists'. Emancipated mums of the sexual revolution are to blame for this one. The study said that these women were encouraging their daughters to dress more immodestly. What the study actually showed, a closer look reveals, is absolutely nothing. It wasn't even a study. It was a survey sent to 250 psychiatrists. Only 33 per cent of them responded. More than 90 per cent of the respondents were men, and if the surveys results proved anything it was that sexism is alive and well among these particular male psychiatrists who hurrumped endlessly in their comments about such 'unwholesome and exhibitionist female behaviour as wearing skirts that showed the knees'.

"Male psychiatrists who hurrumped endlessly in their comments about such 'unwholesome and exhibitionist female behaviour as wearing skirts that showed the knees'."

Backlash Rule No 3: Never let the facts get in the way of a good backlash story. The backlash's propagators don't require their evidence to come from a scientific source or even from the real world. Often fiction is used to support backlash facts. *People* magazine pointed to *Fatal Attraction* as documentation that the unwed state makes women so nutty they will stalk men who spurn them. Or, more recently, in support of the ongoing denunciation of working mums who use day care, *Newsweek* and the cover story in the *Washington Times*, to name two examples, cited *The Hand that Rocks the Cradle* as their proof that families are in jeopardy when mum leaves baby in the hands of a nanny. Or *Fortune* magazine recently announced: 'More young women are dropping out of full-time work to start families.' Their evidence? If you've got any doubts, wrote the magazine, just check out your favourite romance novel emporium. They pointed to one book on the shelves there entitled *Baby Aboard*, a novel in which the heroine apparently chose housekeeping over employment. That was their only evidence of this trend.

Backlash Rule No 4: Denounce feminists for things they never did or said. This tactic is of long standing, dating back to the early days of the women's liberation movement when reporters claimed that feminists were turning off the average woman by burning their bras. In fact, feminists never did engage in lingerie pyrotechnics, unfortunately. This year the same strategy resurfaces on the opinion page of the *New York Times*. In a piece entitled 'The Backlash Myth', that informed commentator of the feminist scene, cosmetics merchant, Georgette Mosbacher, chief executive of the anti-wrinkle cream company, La Prairie, and wife of the former Commerce Secretary, tells us that women's movement leaders scared away the average woman by denying her the right to enjoy 'a perfect manicure'. When, pray tell, did feminist leaders discuss cuticle care? Last time I checked they were challenging corporate boards, not emery boards.

Backlash Rule No 5: Co-opt feminist terms to undermine women's rights and self confidence. For instance, George Bush told us he was 'empowering' women when he cut several social programs that serve women. Plastic surgeons claim to be advancing women's confidence and choices by urging women to inject their breasts with health-endangering silicone. A corollary to this rule is to claim that men are being oppressed. Australian publisher Richard Walsh claimed recently, after women protested over an issue of *People* that featured a woman in a dog collar in a doggie position on the cover, that he had been victimised by the women's complaints.

In the US, as another example, there has been a resurgence in upscale, topless bars for businessmen. The owners of these new bars, when confronted, claimed that it is actually the gals in G-strings who are abusing the men. As the owner of one such bar, called Scores – by the way he was a former investment banker – explained to the *New York Times*, 'If anyone is being exploited it's the men, the guys buying into the fantasy of "she really likes me".' Also in Australia, the Department of Health Adviser Dr Alex Proudfoot wanted women's health centres to be found in violation of the Sex Discrimination Act. They discriminated against men by giving services to women.

Backlash Rule No 6: When feminists catch you in the act of backlashing, hide behind humour. For example, at the University of California, Los Angeles, some frat boys recently put out a songbook full of lyrics urging young men to attack women with chain saws, whips and cheese graters. When challenged by the feminist group on campus, the boys responded, 'Oh, come on gals, these songs are like a joke. They shouldn't be taken seriously.'

Finally, *Backlash Rule No 7*: When all else fails, just pretend feminism is dead and maybe it will go away. This is an oldie but goodie. The first obituary for the women's liberation movement ran just a month after the movement got under way. Again, this past year, only a month after women awoke with a vengeance to the relevance of feminism following the cold shower of the Thomas–Hill Senate hearings, the press preachers hastened to read the women's movement its last rites. The *Washington Post*'s Sally Quinn issued a column entitled 'Who Killed Feminism?' – and promptly cited feminist leaders as the main executioners. *New York Times* columnist William Safire followed suit a few days later with his column 'Macho Feminism Rest in Peace'. He declared feminism a corpse and claimed that from its ashes had risen 'a new natural womanism' – i.e. women who don't talk back.

But don't fall for this desperate last-ditch backlash ploy. The polls show feminism is more alive and kicking than ever. They show that increasing majorities of women are embracing every tenet of the feminist agenda. Increasing majorities of women are calling for a strong women's movement to push for further change, and increasing majorities of women are eager to fight discrimination, sexual harassment and violence against women. Even feminism's most hostile opponents will concede that reports of the women's movement's death are greatly exaggerated.

Barry Humphries

Humphries began acting in Melbourne University revues and with the Melbourne Theatre Company, and continues a variety of acting work, but it was his creation of the Moonee Ponds housewife Edna Everage in 1956 that launched him to international fame. In the 1970s he brought his comic-strip character Barry McKenzie to the screen with director Bruce Beresford. Based in London, he and Dame Edna have returned to Australia many times with one-man/woman shows and books including his memoir, *More Please* (1992) and the autobiographical novel *Women in the Background* (1995).

6 October 1992

I came to Sydney in the mid-1950s for two reasons: one, to escape from the Olympic Games in Melbourne which had already caused a lot of havoc. Most of the interesting buildings had been pulled down because it was thought that Latvian shotputters might think Melbourne was old-fashioned. 'Old-fashioned' meant Victorian hotels and banks; and since most of the more majestic and opulent symbols of the boom period in Victoria were on street corners they were all pulled down and new things called service stations were built. But then we had service stations on the corners where all the old banks used to be and the hotels were pulled down; and when the Olympic Games happened it was suddenly discovered that there was nowhere for anyone to stay. So an advertisement appeared in the Melbourne *Herald* asking ordinary housewives if they wouldn't mind donating their sleep-out and whether or not they had accommodation on their rotary hoists for Norwegian jockstraps.

I was a student actor in a small theatre on the campus of Melbourne University and there was established Australia's first professional repertory company called the Union Theatre. The director in residence was Ray Lawler, a very unassuming little man, prematurely balding, who wore green clothes rather like a leprechaun, and who was said to be writing a play in his spare time. It was called *The Summer of the Seventeenth Doll* and became the most famous play in Australian theatrical history.

At Christmas-time, when I already could see the writing on the wall – I was going to be fired because I couldn't learn my lines and my parts, if you'll forgive me, were getting smaller and smaller, which had a lot to do with the theatrical climate of the period – I was invited to appear in the Christmas revue where all the members of the company donned their comic guise.

I said to Ray, 'Well, what will I do?' He said, 'Perhaps you could write something about the Olympic Games.' I said, 'I know nothing about sport and I'm hoping to be out of Melbourne for this event.' He said, 'You see this ad in the *Herald*? Perhaps you could play an Olympic official interviewing a housewife. We could get Zoe Caldwell or one of the actresses in the company to play the housewife; or you could play the housewife yourself.' I said, 'I doubt if I could do that'. He said, 'Well, when we were on tour you rather successfully impersonated a rather funny woman. What was her name?' I said, 'Oh, I call her Edna after someone who looked after me as a child, a very nice woman called Edna.' He said, 'Why don't you develop that character?' I said, 'You mean I could do the voice from the wings and Zoe could play Edna and she could mime to my words?' He said, 'No, no, no. See if you can get a twin-set big enough.'

Well, I asked my mother if she had any clothes that were too big for her or that she'd bought rather rashly and she did, like most women, have an enormous number of clothes that she'd bought merely because they were on sale or something like that. So I squeezed into these and I wrote a dialogue between two people, an Olympic official and a Melbourne housewife who was not very distantly related to an aunt of mine.

We did it in the revue. It was called 'The Olympic Hostess' and Edna appeared on stage. Noel Ferrier played the official and he sat there with his notebook and in minced this extremely shy woman. I came from the respectable middle-class suburb of Camberwell in Melbourne, which was rather like a cream-brick Strathfield and from which every trace of Australia had been erased. There were no gum trees; there was no buffalo grass. If

"I asked my mother if she had any clothes that were too big for her or that she'd bought rather rashly and she did, like most women, have an enormous number of clothes that she'd bought merely because they were on sale."

there had been kookaburras they would have been shot.

There were feathery silver birch trees, English lawn which at the first burst of sunshine would die. There were all kinds of English flowers and trees. To use a word of the period, in autumn the tonings were very, very attractive. People wouldn't have to go to the Dandenongs to see the autumn tints. They would just have to drive through the streets of Camberwell. It was Bournemouth in South-East Asia. It was Cheltenham in the jungle. It was the Isle of Wight and it was culturally just like that.

The Church of England reigned and so did Mr Menzies. On the top of various hills, however, the Roman Catholics had as usual constructed their idolatrous edifices. The sectarian issue was palpable. You knew a Roman Catholic because he said 'haitch' instead of 'aitch'.

The class system was very simply divided between people who had laundries and people who had wash-houses; people who had driveways and people who had sideways; people who had front porches and people who had front verandahs; people who had back gardens and people who had back yards; people who had bloody noses and people who had nose bleeds; people who had buck teeth and people whose teeth were slightly prominent; people who went to state schools and people who went to nice, private schools – which were mysteriously called public schools – which pretended to be English and had houses even though everyone went home at night except for a few spotty boarders who, smarting from parental abandonment, quietly matriculated under their desks.

But I didn't want to malign Camberwell; it might have upset my parents. So I thought that I would make Edna – and I called her Average at first until it looked too corny and we changed the 'A' to an 'E' – come from a suburb I'd never been to, as far away from Camberwell as possible, for the protection of my family's delicate feelings. I made her come from the euphoniously named suburb of Moonee Ponds, the only suburb, as far as I know, in Australia which is half-Aboriginal and half-English, 'Moonee' being a word of Aboriginal origin. I had never been there. I've only briefly been there since because they've named a street Everage Street. It turns out to have a car park on one side and a supermarket on the other.

Edna came on and was an immense hit with the audience because all she talked about was her own house. She talked about her interior arrangements, the decorations of the house, and her family, her young husband Norm who had as yet shown no signs of the urological problem which was later to make him one of the world's most celebrated prostate sufferers, and indeed the world's first recipient of a prostate transplant.

Everything was very happy in the Everage household. There was a clever son Brucie who was already engaged to the wrong woman whose name was Joylene and, since it wasn't 'Joy' but had an 'ene' on the end of it, Edna deeply suspected a New South Wales origin. Then there was Valmai who was Edna's daughter, and a young and already artistically talented son called Kenny, or Kenneth Montgomery named after General Montgomery.

Edna told the Olympic official all of this in great detail. He was unable to get a word in edgeways. It was the first of many monologues over many years. Its success astonished me, and astonished everybody, because people hadn't made jokes about venetian blinds before and no-one thought that a very popular print of a Chinese girl with a green face was very laughable.

It was perhaps not as nice as Van Gogh's *Sunflowers* which prosperous middle-class people in Australia were beginning to put on the wall; the Post-Impressionists were finding their way onto the calendars; but no-one had laughed at these things.

No-one had laughed at sand-blasted double doors between dining rooms and lounge rooms or about Genoa velvet couches, rotary hoists or Vegemite; and no one had thought lamingtons were funny before.

So there were no jokes; there was just a relentless obsession with the comforting realities of suburban life, reproduced week after week in the *Women's Weekly*, cakes and savouries all in full colour but slightly out of register so that a lovely plate of sweet corn on toast spilt over the page; and when the Melbourne *Argus* first published a portrait of the young Queen Elizabeth in colour everyone bought it. It was so badly reproduced that the Queen's lips flew up the page just like flying ducks. Everyone listened to the radio, of course, and everything seemed right with the world because we were living in the clean, hygienic, decorative world of laminex and we were writing with biros and television had been born and Graham Kennedy and Bert Newton, Princess Panda, were idolised throughout Australia.

When I was offered, after my dismissal from the Union Theatre in spite of my success in this impersonation, a job in Sydney at a theatre called the Phillip Street Theatre which was the most exciting place in the whole of Australia, I accepted immediately. I'd recently got married which I thought was a very good way of leaving home. You can't say to your parents – or you couldn't in 1956 – 'Well, I'd rather like to live somewhere else', because your parents would say, 'What's wrong with us?' or 'We've just repainted your room'. And furthermore they'd done it in the high '50s style, a tan feature wall on which I, a rather arty youth, had hung a Paul Klee reproduction and I would sit there smoking black Sobrani cigarettes and playing George Shearing records on yellow-labelled MGM 10-inch 78s, and I thought that was living, particularly if one could enjoy the occasional surreptitious sip of crème de menthe. So I thought, well, if I get married at least if they say, 'What do you want to leave home for?' I'd say, 'I have to visit my wife, you see. We actually live somewhere else now.'

So she and I came to Sydney and what a different world it was. There were people in the streets not wearing hats and suits and ties but dressed perpetually for the beach and eating out of paper bags in the Bondi tram, where the conductor, his cheeks craggy with sausage rolls and Iced Vovos, would swing along the step on the tram as it rattled on its way to that, as it seemed to me, rather bleak Pacific-side suburb. There were no trees that I could see. Everyone seemed to have a rather bleak-looking hat-rack on their small front lawns until I realised it wasn't a hat-rack at all, it was a frangipani tree and that at a certain season little white wax propellers would grow on it and it would be exquisite and exotic and very different from Melbourne.

We lived first in Kings Cross where I glimpsed my first cockroach. At first I thought it was a rather large, modern, black lacquered coffee table – until it walked away. This was at the Rembrandt Hotel in Kings Cross, now demolished and replaced by a new building which no doubt has inherited the great-grandchildren of the cockroaches that I met in 1956.

Then I'd get on the tram and we'd go to the Phillip Street Theatre in Phillip Street, which was then a very pretty, sympathetic, attractive street, not that sharp, grey chasm of office blocks that it is now. In this theatre were wonderful revues, stars like Gordon Chater and June Salter, and Max Oldaker whom I'd remembered so well from my childhood when my mother took me to see *The Desert Song* and *White Horse Inn* and *The Gondoliers*. Max would be up there, particularly in *The Desert Song* when he entered on a white horse as the Red Shadow – probably a musical comedy which could be successfully revived today.

Max was the star of the show and then it was our turn, and I did the Edna character once more and again it was a success in Sydney, which surprised me because no-one had warned me this was possible. On the contrary, I'd been told that no-one in Sydney would ever understand Edna. 'Far too Melbourne,' they said. 'They won't get the point; and anyway,' they said to me, 'people in Sydney have got a very funny sense of humour.'

So my theatrical career began. I didn't feel comfortable in Sydney because I was not by any means mature enough to be a married man and I was living in Centennial Park in a boarding house full of old and rather depressing people, itinerant people. There were loud alcoholic rows in the middle of the night – terrifying – and a communal kitchen, and Centennial Park struck me as a very bleak, depressing sort of place where one might encounter strange men with raincoats. Whenever I saw one, I avoided him, little knowing I was probably cutting Patrick White who subsequently got his own back, not just on me either. He's cut us all now, I'm afraid.

I've had to recall all of these things because a publisher gave me a sum of money to write my life story. I found things started to flood back, writing about my early life, and I called the chapters of the book after some of the titles that I'd thought I might give to the book.

'Licking the Beaters' seemed to me a good title for a book because that was the great pleasure of an Australian childhood. If you were very good your mother would hand you the rotary beater and you'd lick the beaters. Then I called another chapter 'Weatherboard Swastikas' because I remembered a holiday with my mother before my sister was unfortunately born. It wasn't that I objected to her; she was gorgeous; it was just that several months after her birth she was still there. My mother took me to Warburton, which is a very beautiful part of Victoria, and we were in a guesthouse, because they had those then. I don't think they have them now except up in Katoomba there are a few guesthouses but on the whole they're sort of geriatric hospitals and things of that kind now, with names like 'The Ritz' – 'Mummy's at The Ritz now. We must visit her one of these years.'

I remember an afternoon in 1938, which I describe in the book, when all the Australian ladies were up one end of the lounge: polished jarrah floors, cane furniture, chintz, cretonne, mallee roots blazing; outside you could see the great eucalyptus trees, the sun in the afternoon slanting past, and a strange huddle of very odd-looking people at the other end of the lounge. Who were they? They seemed to be speaking some kind of nonsense to each other. They looked very, well, slightly scared.

"[Edna's] success astonished me, and astonished everybody, because people hadn't made jokes about venetian blinds before."

A woman leant across to my mother – she was halfway through an asparagus roll. With a jerk of her head towards the strangers at the other end of the lounge, she said, 'Jews'. I looked across the teacups and there they were indeed. Another woman said, 'Look at their rings; look at their rings. That's where they keep their money.' Another woman said, 'There's no doubt about it. That Hitler had a few good ideas.' Of course, it didn't mean much to a child of four but that group of people at the other end of the lounge of the Warburton Chalet later gave Melbourne coffee and made chocolates, decent clothes and chamber music amongst a few other things.

All these things came back to me as I sat there, oddly enough, in a rented house in a slum in Beverley Hills and I started enjoying myself. Many years later I went back to Warburton and I stood on a hill so that I could look down at this guesthouse which had extended itself; it had got bigger and bigger because of families going there and it had weatherboard wings sprouting to left and right and centre and it was exactly in the shape of a swastika, nestled in the ferns and gum trees of Warburton.

I had to describe my adolescence, my youth, my early career. I got to the point where I came to Sydney and where every pay night I would go to the Astor in Macquarie Street and have a plate of spaghetti bolognaise in a smart restaurant – and spaghetti was a very smart thing to eat particularly if you could do it just using a fork and could look contemptuously at those who needed a knife and a soup spoon.

I still think of those early days in Sydney when I wander down Macquarie Street. I think there's still a restaurant in the basement of the Astor. The Phillip Street Theatre is long gone. Other theatres have taken its place; other entertainments are available, generally of the extravagant, long-running, $120-a-ticket variety which throw in a chicken-in-a-basket and a Black Forest cake and a free trip to Japan.

In writing about my own experiences I found myself writing about Australia at that time as well; and then my first trip to England and my experiences in the ice-cream factory where I had to work which was horrible at the time and terribly funny in retrospect.

At last I got the book finished up to about 20 years ago and I rang my publisher who said, 'Well, you're only a month late with it.' So I said, 'Yes, I've got up to about 1971 and I'll do the rest in another volume. I won't be doing three volumes because I'm not the Prime Minister of Australia' (understanding that Mr Hawke's biography was going to extend to about 13 volumes which puts him in the Proustian category). She said, 'You can't do that. We've printed the dust jacket and it says "Up to the present".' I said, 'So I've got three days to cover 20 years. If you notice it moves a bit fast towards the end you'll understand.' But I thought, at least that means I don't have to dwell for too long on my last marriage; but I do politely give it half a sentence – it was a kind of a sentence, come to think of it.

In writing about my life I've tried to be as frank as it's possible for a person like me to be. It may be said that autobiography is the ultimate disguise. The more you tell people the more they seem to want to know, I've found, which makes the title of the book rather apt. I asked my mother, not long before she died, what my first words were and she said, 'More, please'. I assume I was referring to breakfast; but I've always had a rather greedy appetite for life and for its pleasures and though my own life has not been a total joy I think every human life is dramatic and interesting.

Your life would be just as interesting and exciting as mine except you probably couldn't write about it as well.

Michael Caine

The title of Caine's 1992 autobiography *What's It All About?* refers to the 1966 movie *Alfie*, which brought him an Academy Award nomination for Best Actor and turned him into an international star. Born in working-class London as Maurice Micklewhite, he began his career with bit parts and minor movie and television roles. He still unashamedly takes on films if they pay well and he likes the location but, among many others, he has given outstanding performances in *Sleuth* (1972), *Educating Rita* (1983), *Mona Lisa* (1986) and *Hannah and Her Sisters* (1986), winning the Oscar for Best Supporting Actor.

28 October 1992

It's taken me 59 years to get to Australia which is a shame. I was going to come on the £10 assisted scheme but I didn't have the £10, so I never came. The first 30 years I couldn't afford to come and the next 30 years I just didn't have the time. But the closest relationship I ever had with Australia before I've actually got here now was when I was 19 and a soldier in a regiment called the Royal Fusiliers which is a British infantry regiment. The Australians had a brigade, which is three regiments, and the Australians could only manage two – the first and third RAR, which means Royal Australian Regiment, and so we Royal Fusiliers were the third one and it was there that I met my first Australians.

I don't know whether you know what an Australian infantryman was like 40 years ago, in a pub or a bar in the evening, late – but I can tell you that was another very good reason why it's taken me 59 years to get to Australia. Some of them, the really tough ones, used to say before we had a fight, 'I want to hear him speak first'.

I was kind of worried about my timing for this book. For 59 years we haven't had a recession as bad as this and I write my first book right in the middle of it. I not only write my first book right in the middle of it, I bring it out in England the same week as Madonna's book, *Sex*. I don't know whether you've seen this book – there is little writing in it. If I'd have known, I'd have had Sean Connery and Roger Moore and me in the nude. I feel it's not a level playing field. All I've got in my book is my Aunt Lil in her swimming costume in 1936 at Bognor, which is no competition.

Then I'm going to America where they have – this is non-fiction you must remember – the strangest books which are number one. You think, oh, maybe they'll bring a biography of Frank Sinatra, some great book about anybody – Einstein or Stephen Hawking's Black Hole or whatever it is – but I looked up the longest bestseller last year and it was called *How to Slim Your Thighs*. So you see my problem. And in Madonna's book, she's got things like spanking and tying up for sex, and I thought, if I write another book, I ought to know something about this at least. So I brought it up with my wife and got a very icy reception. When I read about it, it reminded me of the story of the guy who said, 'I haven't had sex in so long, I forget who gets tied up first'.

So you write a book, you run into all these troubles and then you get the press. The press in England wrote about it and I read an article saying, 'Michael Caine's outpourings of sycophancy for the Royals'. I thought wait a minute, wait a minute, I don't remember any outpourings of sycophancy for the Royal Family. So I go rushing back to the book and counted the pages and there were four out of 483 pages on incidents where I met a member of the Royal Family who I'd never met before and this was for the British press an outpouring of sycophancy.

So I'd like to say a few words about the press, as we very seldom get the chance. I'll give you a for instance. Last year I bought a little house in Beverly Hills, a little holiday home. It's nothing really grand, nothing grand at all. It would fit inside this hall. The living room would. No, it's not true. But this is, to me, how the press works. I bought this little holiday home. So then it comes out in the paper, 'Michael Caine buys Beverly Hills mansion'.

"My view of it is, how can I name-drop? I am a name."

It's not a mansion, it's a little place. Then the next day it says, 'Michael Caine is moving back to America'. Then the next day it says, 'Good riddance, Michael Caine. We don't want to see you again'. And then the next day it says, 'You should never have come back from America. We didn't want you back here anyway'. And then the Sunday paper says, 'You're a bum of an actor anyway. You're overrated, we don't need you, we don't care about you.' I'm sitting in England going, wait a minute, I just bought a little house. What the hell is going on in this country?

Another example is one of the reviews said, 'Michael Caine name-drops a lot in this book'. My view of it is, how can I name-drop? I am a name. A name-dropper is a non-entity who drops names of people he doesn't know who are celebrities. Now you can all do it without being name-droppers because you know a celebrity. You'll say, I talked with Michael Caine yesterday. I said, get off.

I've got some questions from people in the audience. 'Is it true that when you visited your childhood neighbourhood, Charlie Chaplin was also there?' Yes, as a matter of fact, that's true. I visited the old neighbourhood, it's called the Elephant and Castle. It's a district in South London. I'll give you an idea of us people from South London. The district is named after a pub and the pub was named after an inn which was named after a mistress of Charles II who died and was buried near there and she was Spanish and she was called the Infanta de Castille and my people couldn't pronounce it so they called it the Elephant and Castle. This will give you a good idea why we produce actors and not nuclear physicists.

Charlie Chaplin was there. As a matter of fact, I revisited my old home place – he was born in some streets just round behind me in a place called Kennington – and I went back twice over a period of five years and both times I saw him there. It's a complete coincidence, both times. I spoke to him once but he didn't have the foggiest idea who I was so I said, to hell with it.

'We know how deeply you love your lovely wife, but what feminine attribute in a woman do you fancy?' I think the feminine attribute in a woman that I fancy most is . . . no, I keep thinking of all sort of dirty things. I know, I know what it is – lust. I think lust is a great thing, but only with someone you know, of course. Never do it with relations. As a matter of fact, never do anything with relations.

'Are you as charming and amusing at home?' I was worried about reading this question because I was going to have to be amusing up until now for anyone to believe that I was amusing. No, I'm not as charming and as amusing at home as my public image implies. It's very difficult to be charming and amusing all day long. I can't even speak until 11 o'clock in the morning, let alone be charming and amusing. My wife's been married to me for 20 years and she's heard all my jokes and all my stories, which is why I exaggerate and lie the whole time, whenever I'm telling a story. Like now. I would be lying even more, except for the fact that she's not here.

'I really enjoyed *Hannah and Her Sisters*, I've been to see it three times. Did you enjoy doing the movie with Mia and Woody?' That was a strange thing because I wrote about doing that movie and when this terrible case with Woody and Mia came out, I had to change things. I had written that I'm married to Mia in the film and her real flat was used in the film as our flat and her real children were used as our children and her real mother, Maureen O'Sullivan, played her mother, and finally we're doing a love scene in her bed and I'm being directed by her lover, Woody, and I look up and over the other side I can see Andre Previn, her ex-husband, who had come to see the kids. It's true – you can't make stories like this up. I had to cut this down a bit about the kids and being in bed with Mia and all this. I put a line in which the lawyers cut immediately. It said, 'It all seemed very incestuous to me', and they said, 'That is out, out, out!'.

'Were you ever considered for the role of 007 and why did you not get it?' I was never considered for the role of 007. For a start, I never learned to drive a car till I was 50.

'What was Steve Martin like to work with?' He's lovely, but he's the exact opposite of what you think. He is a very quiet, very, very shy man and he's a computer expert, he never goes out. You see him in *Dirty Rotten Scoundrels* playing this nutter. It's amazing – I'm more crazy than he is.

'Which movie role of yours was your favourite?' *The Man Who Would be King*, the picture I did with Sean Connery and John Huston. John Huston was a wonderful director. He could tell you exactly what he wanted in two or three words. Some directors, when you say, 'I'm having a problem with this part', put their arm around you and say, 'Now listen, sweetie, we'll go for a walk and have an hour. Let's have lunch, break for lunch, we'll talk about it. Let's have dinner tonight, we'll shoot in the morning.' You get a lot of this in my business. I was doing the first scenes in the picture and suddenly John said, 'Cut', and I said, 'What's the matter?' I hadn't made any mistakes or said anything wrong. He said just one thing which gave me my character for the whole film: 'You can speak faster, Michael, he's an honest man.' I've been very wary of people who talk slowly ever since.

'At what age did you start acting?' I started acting at the age of three when my mother worked out this system for when the rent man came and she couldn't pay the rent. She would go down to the front door with me with her; she would stand behind it, I would open the door and say, 'Mummy's out', and slam it. That was my first. I opened the door one day to the vicar and I thought I hadn't better slam it to the vicar because I knew what a vicar was, even though I was only three, and I said, 'What do you want?', and he said, 'We want money for the church roof. The lead's gone again.' Round my way, when you ran out of money, you went on the church roof and took all the lead and sold it. Another time I opened the door and there was a Jehovah's Witness standing there and I thought it was Jesus because I'd never seen a man with a beard and he looked just like Jesus in a thing I'd seen. But I shut the door in his face anyway and my mother asked what he had wanted. I said, 'He wanted money. Well, I guess he's not Jesus then, aye?' She said, 'No'.

'When did you first take an interest in girls?' When I was three. I went to school when I was three, and every now and then we used to have medicals, the little kids. It was both sexes and we all lined up with no clothes on to be examined by the doctor. I looked around and suddenly saw this difference and there was started a lifelong interest in the opposite sex. I couldn't wait for a medical. I used to hope we'd all get sick with diarrhoea or something and we'd have to be examined, because it was three or six months between medicals.

"I was never considered for the role of 007. For a start, I never learned to drive a car till I was 50."

It's the last question, what's this? 'Let's have a comment on introducing Mia Farrow and Woody Allen.' I didn't do it. No, actually I almost did. What happened was Mia Farrow, who's a friend of mine, asked me if I knew Woody Allen and I said, 'Yes' and she said, 'Could you introduce me?' There's a restaurant, Elaine's, which is very popular with actors and writers and Woody goes there most nights. So I organised a dinner, took her up there and Woody never came. The next night I didn't invite her as she was in a show but I took another party of people up there, including Mick Jagger and Jerry Hall who had just met – this was ages ago – and we were sitting there and Woody came in and sat down and then Mia came in. She said, 'I just thought I'd pop back on the off-chance that Woody was in', and he was there and a friend of mine called Bobby Zarim, who is a great publicity man in New York, actually introduced her. So it wasn't my fault. If anybody says anything, it was Bobby Zarim, remember the name.

I was walking along the street in London the other day and an old man came along, stopped me and said, 'Are you Michael Caine?' I said, 'Yes'.

'God,' he said, 'what a pleasure. I never thought I'd be meeting you. Do you know what I'm doing, after all these years? This is a fantastic coincidence – I am just re-reading *The Ipcress File* [which is a book, a film that I was in]. That's bloody amazing. Can I say something else?' this old boy says to me. I said, 'Yes'. He said, 'I'd just like to say you're looking very well. You obviously take care of yourself,' he said. I was very complimented. I said, 'Thank you very much'. 'Yes,' he said, you lot usually let yourself go when you're through, don't you.' So just in case he was right, please buy my book.

Jung Chang

Chang burst on to the world literary scene in 1992 with the Booker-nominated *Wild Swans*, the story of three generations of Chinese women – her grandmother, her mother and herself – from the end of the Manchu dynasty to the ascension of Deng Xiaoping. While her grandmother endured the pain of footbinding, Chang became the first person from Communist China to receive a doctorate from a British university. She is now writing a biography of Mao Zedong.

25 January 1993

Wild Swans is the story of my grandmother, my mother and myself. I think our stories reflect the history of 20th-century China.

My grandmother was born in 1909. When she was two her feet were crushed and bound. Foot binding was not just to put a piece of cloth around the feet: only the big toe was allowed to grow; the other four toes and the arch were crushed under a big stone and the binding was just to stop the broken bones from recovering. So from the age of two my grandmother lived in excruciating pain. When she was 15 she was given by her father to a warlord general to be his concubine. She was married to him for six days and he then left for six years. He had many concubines dotted around China and he only visited them when he was in town. So the rest of the time my grandmother lived as a virtual prisoner in a house he bought for her, under the watchful eyes of servants.

In 1931 my mother was born. In 1932 the warlord was dying and ordered my grandmother to bring my mother to see him at his mansion at the foot of the Great Wall. As soon as my grandmother arrived, her daughter, my mother, was taken away from her because, by tradition, the blood descendant had to be raised by the proper wife, not by a concubine. My mother was not allowed to call her mother 'mother', and had to call the proper wife 'mother'.

So my grandmother realised that once the warlord died the proper wife could do anything to her – even sell her to a brothel, which was very common in those days, in which case she would never be able to see her daughter again. So my grandmother escaped with my mother with the help of another sympathetic concubine.

She went back to Manchuria and later fell in love with an elderly Manchu doctor. The doctor was a widower and had a very big extended family. His family was very against him marrying my grandmother because my grandmother had been a concubine. His eldest son was so against the marriage he shot himself in protest. But the marriage went ahead. My mother, my grandmother, and Dr Xia lived in Manchuku, under Japanese occupation.

As a child, my mother saw a lot of Japanese atrocities: once a school friend of hers – a girl of 14 – by accident stumbled into a Japanese arms depot. She was arrested, tortured and executed in front of the whole school.

In 1945 Japan surrendered. Chiang Kai-shek's Kuomintang came. My mother was very enthusiastic about them because to her, as to the people in Manchuria, the Kuomintang were the liberators. But my mother was soon disillusioned. Kuomintang rule was terribly corrupt and inefficient. Inflation was so bad that when she went to pay her school fees she had to hire a rickshaw to carry the banknotes. And in her city there were many people selling their children for food. One of the chapter headings of *Wild Swans* is 'Daughter for Sale for 10 Kilos of Rice'. My mother saw this written on the stick that was poking out of the back of the collar of a girl for sale outside her school.

So when she was 15 my mother joined the Communist underground. She was introduced to the Communist underground by a friend of hers, a girl of 17 who was being forced to marry a 12-year-old. That was the local custom – for a grown-up girl to marry a young boy in order to bring up the boy. At the time there was a civil war going on between Chiang Kai-shek's Kuomintang and Mao's Communists. The Communists were besieging Jinzhou, my mother's city. My mother smuggled military information out of her city for the Communist forces. She became a student underground leader. She was arrested at one point and was put up against the wall and the man next to her was shot dead.

"In her city there were many people selling their children for food. One of the chapter headings of Wild Swans is 'Daughter for Sale for 10 Kilos of Rice'."

My father was a Communist guerilla leader outside Jinzhou. When the Communists took her city, they met, fell in love, and got married. Soon they had to leave Jinzhou to go to Sichuan where my father came from, over a thousand miles away. My father was a senior Communist official, so he was entitled to a jeep or a horse, whichever was available. My mother was new to the revolution so she had to walk. My father wouldn't give her a lift because he regarded this as a form of nepotism – breaking the rules. So my mother suffered a miscarriage on the way.

They arrived in Sichuan and in 1952 I was born. When my mother was about to give birth to me, doctors said that it was going to be a very dangerous birth and said my mother should be transferred to another hospital in another city, where there were better doctors and better facilities. My father was the governor of the whole region. He vetoed that. He said his wife had to be treated like everybody else.

In 1953 my family had to leave my father's home town and the reason was this: my mother's party boss – a woman – fancied my father and tried to seduce him. My father turned her down; but my father knew that this woman was a vindictive character, so he was afraid that she might take revenge, particularly against my mother. My father was right: 13 years later during the Cultural Revolution this woman and her husband were appointed by Mao Zedong as the leaders of Sichuan – a province of 70 million people. And they took ruthless revenge against my parents.

In Chengdu I grew up in a very privileged environment: both my parents were senior Communist officials; my father was one of the top officials in Sichuan province; and my siblings and I all had our different wet nurses paid for by the state. We lived in a compound with armed guards and chauffeurs and cooks. I grew up taking hierarchy and privilege so much for granted that when I first arrived in England in 1978, I thought England was wonderfully classless compared to China.

Our world was also a world without any information: China was totally cut off from the outside world. When we were children, if we wouldn't eat up our food, our nursery teachers would say: 'Think of all the starving children in the capitalist world.' And foreigners were evil figures, so when the boys played their game of guerilla warfare, the baddies would have rose thorns glued onto their noses to show that they were foreigners, because foreigners have bigger and sharper noses than the Chinese. And the baddies would say 'hello' all the time because in propaganda films foreigners always said 'hello' and so we all thought 'hello' was a swear word.

When I was six years old, in 1958, Mao launched his Great Leap Forward. He had this vision that he was going to turn China into a modern power overnight and to overtake America in 10 years. How were we going to do this? Mao's answer was: 'We must produce more steel.' But instead of making investment in the proper steel industry, he ordered the whole population to take part. In every organisation in China there was a steel quota. Everybody – writers, publishers, bus conductors, government officials, doctors, teachers, housewives – everyone was organised to make steel. I was six and my major occupation was to cook steel in the school kitchen. Mountains were stripped bare of trees to provide fuel. But what was most disastrous was that peasants were ordered to stop growing crops in order to produce steel.

It was also in that year, in 1958, the Chinese countryside was organised into people's communes and the regime banned eating at home, so we all had to eat in the canteens. Peasants filed into the canteens three times a day and ate to their hearts' content, which they had never been able to do in the best climate and the best area in China. So in that one year they consumed and wasted the entire food reserve in the Chinese countryside. The result was a devastating famine between 1958 and 1961. About 30 million people died of starvation, including many of my relatives.

After the famine Mao was forced into a kind of a semi-retirement; but he was planning his come-back. In the mid-60s there was this intense personality cult of Mao. I grew up in this time. One of the chapter headings of *Wild Swans* is 'Father is Close, Mother is Close, but Neither is as Close as Chairman Mao' – that was a song every child in China learned to sing. Mao was like our God. When I was 14 I went on a pilgrimage to Peking to see him and when I didn't see him clearly, I was so heartbroken I thought of committing suicide.

Mao was then able to use this generation which was brought up in his intense personality cult and indoctrination to launch the Cultural Revolution in 1966. I was 14 then and, like literally all my urban contemporaries, I joined the Red Guards. But I left in a couple of months because the violence, the atrocities, just went against my nature.

"We all thought 'hello' was a swear word."

It was also in the Cultural Revolution that my parents became targets. My father was one of the few who stood up to Mao and protested against the Cultural Revolution. He was arrested, tortured, driven insane. He was not allowed medical treatment because he was accused of faking mental illness in order to escape his responsibility for attacking Mao.

My mother was under tremendous pressure to denounce my father: she refused. So she was made to kneel on broken glass; she was paraded on the street; she was tortured and sent to a labour camp as well. And my family was scattered. I, myself, was sent to the countryside and worked for three years as a peasant and as a barefoot doctor. A barefoot doctor was a doctor without any training, because Mao didn't like formal education and he said: 'The more books you read, the more stupid you become.'

For many years books were burned in China. There were no books, no theatre, no cinema, no museums, no sports. There was nothing. Mao wanted to keep the population idle so that they could devote themselves to his violent Cultural Revolution.

But I was able to read over a thousand books in those years in the countryside and this was because I have a very entrepreneurial brother who was a 13-year-old when the Cultural Revolution started – and he discovered a black market selling books, those books that escaped the bonfires. He bought a lot of books, foreign and Chinese classics; and he made his fortune by dealing in Mao badges. In those years, factories had to stop production to produce Mao badges; they had all styles and qualities and kinds. And so my brother became a connoisseur of Mao badges. In those years all collecting was banned: for example, collecting of stamps; nothing was allowed. But then people started to collect Mao badges and so my brother made a small fortune. And I was able to read a lot of books.

When things began to get better, in 1971, I was able to leave the countryside and become, first, a steel worker and then an electrician. Again, there was no training and I had five electric shocks within the first month.

In 1973 universities re-opened and I was able to get into university to learn English. Although English was my subject, we would be denounced for working too hard at it. So when I was reading an English book, if somebody came along, I had to quickly cover my book with a newspaper. We spent most of the time in political indoctrination sessions in the countryside, in the factories to do army training. I hated all this, of course, and I was such a lousy shot that when the result came in, everybody thought the gun barrel must be bent.

Wild Swans ends in 1978 with me leaving China. Before I went to England, I had never spoken to a foreigner, except some sailors in the port in the south where we were sent to practise our English. We would be so keen to talk to the sailors that we would grab them as soon as they came on shore; of course we had no idea what must have been on their minds. How different this must have been from their expectation of port life.

! ?

SPEAKER: How else would you have got rid of Chiang Kai-shek's Kuomintang without Chairman Mao?

JUNG CHANG: I hope my book puts the Communist regime in perspective. It's not a book with any particular ideology. I'm just telling a human story, and I don't know the answer. Mao succeeded because there was a tremendous disillusionment with the Kuomintang and my parents, who I believe were very fair and logical people, joined the Communists and to me that's the tragedy of history.

SPEAKER: Are you and your book welcome in China?

JUNG CHANG: The book is banned in China.

SPEAKER: Your mother visited you in London, how did she like the decadence of the West and is she ever likely to join you there?

JUNG CHANG: In fact, the book is the result of my mother's visit to the West, to London, in 1988. My husband and I took her out sightseeing and to restaurants and so on, but I realised that she wasn't having a fantastic time. Something was on her mind and then I realised she had really come to talk to me. She talked for six months. We travelled to all sorts of places in England and in Europe and our tourism became the backdrop of our conversation. When she left I sat down and I thought about my own life and thought this was a story worth telling. That's how I started writing this story. I don't think she would come to live with me, because she doesn't speak English and she has all her friends there. But I'm going to see her – in fact I was back every year between 1983 and 1989 to visit her and I'm going at the end of this trip.

SPEAKER: How could you possibly leave it at 1978? What happened to you after that?

JUNG CHANG: A lot has happened, of course. I remember when I first arrived at London's Heathrow Airport, I nearly walked into a men's toilet because I had no idea the figure wearing trousers on the door was supposed to be a man – women in China in those years were not allowed to wear skirts. And the man walking in ahead of me had long hair. I think also I was probably the first mainland Chinese to walk into a British pub. The Chinese translation for pub is *jiu ba*, which in those years meant somewhere terribly indecent with nude women gyrating or something. So no one dared to walk into a pub and then eventually I pushed the door open and walked in and of course found nothing of the sort. Very disappointing. Then I got a scholarship from York University in England and I did a PhD in linguistics. Since then I've been teaching and I'm still teaching at London University, supervising a course for the British Foreign Office to train the diplomats before they are stationed in China.

Morris West

The testimonial dinner at which this talk was given was intended to mark West's retirement after 40 years of writing. But three years later he returned with a literary lunch to celebrate his new novel, *Vanishing Point*, and a spiritual 'last testament', *View From a Ridge*. He was back again in 1998, aged 82, at a lunch to talk about his novel *Eminence*, which forecasts the death of the Pope, as he did accurately 35 years earlier in *The Shoes of the Fisherman*. Among almost 30 novels by this former Christian brother, Vatican insider and best-selling writer are *The Devil's Advocate* (1959), *Salamander* (1973), *Clowns of God* (1981) and *Masterclass* (1988).

2 March 1993

This is truly a valedictory occasion. I am retiring from an old and honourable profession. A teller of tales, a dealer in dreams. There's still work I want to do to set my papers in order for publication, to leave some kind of record of my works and days. To exercise from time to time my citizen's right to comment on matters of public concern but for the rest, let me say it clearly, I'm out of the game.

My readers and my friends ask me why and they have a right to an honest answer. I'm coming up to 77 years of age. I have ceased to be surprised at anything that happens in the world and a good story-teller must always be able to surprise his readers. There's another reason too; modes, manners, symbols, language itself has changed. They continue to change very quickly. I remember the agonies and the ecstasies of youth. I can no longer experience them or interpret them in the language or symbols of the young. If I tried they'd probably put me in jail.

Besides all this, the inventive imagination changes over the years to reflective reason. In short, I have come to understand the contentment of Matisse, working on his chapel, heedless of the jibes of Picasso. I have come to understand too the poignancy of Einstein's last words, 'I have no more mathematics.' So for what time is left for me I am turning to other crafts – the spoken word, the memoir, the essay. However, in *The Lovers* I have permitted myself, just one time only, the luxury of looking backwards.

My memories of Europe in the early '50s are fresh and vivid. Much of Germany was in ruins. The Iron Curtain had slammed down. Refugees were still in camps or drifting aimlessly as gipsies from one place to another in search of relatives or documents that would enable them to emigrate. My first journey was made in 1951. It was then that I began to understand that although I had been robbed – and I use the word advisedly – of my identity by the brainwashing processes then in use in religious institutions, I had been granted another. I realised that I had been educated for Europe. I was familiar with its history. I had enough of its languages to frank myself around.

The landscapes were strangely familiar. All the places mentioned in *The Lovers* I visited and later revisited many times. The name of the vessel in the book on which the love affair takes place is the *Salamanda D'Ora*, the Golden Salamanda. It was also the name of the boat I bought 20 years later. Even that has its own special significance for me because the salamanda is a fabled animal that can survive even in the hottest fire.

Of the people in the book, what can I tell you? I knew, I still know, some of the old noble families whose names have been connected with the Roman papacy for centuries – the Diosini, the Colona, the Punitelli, the Doria and so the list goes on. I could not write about them for obvious reasons. So I created one of my own from a family line which died out in 1731: the Farnese. The name is familiar to you, of course. The Villa Farnese, the Vere Julia and my Julia was resurrected from her own colourful past.

The original Julia had been mistress of the Borgia pope, Alexander the Sixth, to whom she gave three children. She was the sister of the Farnese pope, Paul the Third. According to their mood the Romans called her the Bride of Christ or the Pope's Harlot. I had always been fascinated by her story. It gave me much pleasure to adopt her into one of my own and to restore her other name, Julia la Bella. Julia the beautiful.

The decorations, the coat of arms, which you see in the book were devised for the occasion. The family of Farnese died out in 1731 so I wrote to a friend of mine, an archbishop called Bruno Bernard Heim who was the first papal legate sent by Rome to England since Elizabethan times. He's a very civilised man. He's now in retirement in Switzerland and I asked him how do we recreate the Farnese and he said, 'Ah, we have to have a postnominal word of honour. We create the Farnese from somewhere.' This man is a herald who has designed the coats of arms for four popes and God knows how many archbishops and institutions and he's one of the world's experts. So I looked through my small references on heraldry and found out that in the west of England there was a family called West. We had nothing to do with them, I promise you, unless we were as villeins or serfs or muck-rakers in the stables. So I promise you that there is no attempt to create a noble origin for ourselves. We were very humble people.

However, the symbol of that West family was a griffin, part lion, part bird, and the title which our archbishop finally gave to the family was the Farnese of Mongrifona. This which you see in front of me is the female escutcheon. The tassels and the coronet make it female and the Farnese lilies are shown but not the griffin which are only shown on the arms of the father. They're also in the book.

It was inevitable that once the book was published interviewers should ask me whether there was a portrait of my wife Joy in the book. There isn't. But the book is dedicated to her, as nearly 40 years have been. She has played so many roles in my life: lover, wife, friend, mother with my children, an indefatigable matriarch of our growing family. She has endured the worst of me without complaint and shaped the best of me.

Now, after that display of unseemly emotion, my hosts have commanded that I should tell you some stories. So I thought I would give you my list of firsts. My first Italian fairytale. When we first went to Sorrento, very poor and wondering what our future held, on the first $1500 that we ever earned from America, we were lodged in an old hotel called the Coccumella. It was an old Edwardian hotel and was called the Coccumella because underneath it there had been discovered an egg-shaped tomb of some former Etruscan.

Next door to it was a fabulous villa called the Villa of the Russian Princess. The Russian princess was actually the Princess Korsakov who was related to Rimsky-Korsakov the composer. The villa was a beautiful, Venetian-style structure that looked out over the Bay of Naples. And next door to it on the same plot was a ruin, basically an uncompleted castle which the Princess Korsakov had started to build for the imminent arrival of the Tsar Nicholas the Second who of course never arrived.

She had bored great wells down through the cliffs which were about 300 feet high there, down to the beach. She was going to put elevators in. The castle was to be a tremendous construction. She ran out of money and regrettably Tsar Nicholas the Second ran out of time. But the villa itself had two items which for us were a fairytale. You came in through the entrance and climbed a circular staircase up to the bedroom which was an enormous chamber with a tessellated floor and the moment you opened the door you thought you were walking on rose petals because from the door to the bed literally, the tiles were scattered with rose petals which spread in a great river from the door to the Princess's bed. You have to admit that's a fairytale but it doesn't finish yet.

"I have ceased to be surprised at anything that happens in the world and a good story-teller must always be able to surprise his readers."

Down below, the terrace looked over the Bay of Naples. In those days the Bay was marvellous because at night the fisher folk would be out with their little lamps fishing. There were still fish to be had in the Bay then. These little lamps were dotted about with the circle of lights round the Bay and the shadow of Vesuvius in the background. All this you could see from the bedroom but when you went down on the terrace there were a huge tree and a vast open space ringed by stone chairs in the middle of which was a single tile and in the centre of the single tile was the footprint of a ballerina's shoe – Pavlova's, she danced there. That was my first fairytale.

Now I should like to tell you about my first

banker. It is a matter of no news to you that I have been at times highly critical of our Australian banking system and some of those who ran it. I make no apologies for that because all my experience had conditioned me for that. In 1967 my wife said to me, 'You should write a novel about the Middle East; you should go there.' This was before the Six Day War. In those days you could only go into Israel either direct by sea from abroad or through the Mandelbaum Gate. I chose to go through the Mandelbaum Gate and took a ship, a little ship, from Naples to Alexandria and from Alexandria to Beirut. From Beirut later I travelled over the Anti Lebanon into Syria and then from Syria down to Jordan where I waited for three days with my second passport to go through the Mandelbaum Gate into Israel where my friends were waiting for me.

I had a number of introductions in Beirut and one of them was to a man called Bedas who had been a money changer on the docks in Beirut. He had risen to be the owner of a bank called Intra Bank, which became the second bank in Lebanon, greater than the National Bank. Bedas became the banker long before the oil crisis and handled the oil money for all the sheikhs from Saudi Arabia. Bedas made hay while the sun shone and he did it beautifully.

He used to entertain the sheikhs in a large chamber which I have seen. The centre of it was draped with silks like a desert tent and when the sheikhs came to see him and ask what was happening to their money, he would have hauled in a large trolley piled six feet high with gold bars, just to prove that their money was safe. Of course, all this was short-term money, deposited on call. Meantime Mr Bedas, like many other bankers we have heard of in our time, was borrowing short and lending long. He had set up Middle East Airlines. He had set up the great casino de Liban where you saw the best shows in the world. He owned several hotels. He bought half the docks in Marseilles. He bought a block on Fifth Avenue. He made investments in Brazil and Argentina and at one stage a man called Ludwig, the man who made his money laying pipe lines in Iraq and Syria, came along to Bedas and said, 'Bedas, you know I'd like a little share of this.' And the National Bank came along to him similarly and said, 'We'd like a little share of this.' And Bedas, suffering, as so many that we know have suffered, hubris, pride and overweening insolence said, 'No way'. So they sat in the wings and waited while he made more and more investments until he was 3 per cent liquid and then they all moved in and the short-term money moved out as indeed did Mr Bedas. My acquaintance was through his assistant manager, a young American who blamed me much later for my unseemly revelations in the book, *The Tower of Babel.*

However, Mr Bedas fled to Brazil where he had another bank and he also had another fortune stored but the gods were not to be cheated. Mr Bedas fell ill of a terminal cancer and flew to Switzerland for treatment where, while he was being treated, he bought a very expensive car. He was held up by the police one day for speeding and the policeman asked to see his passport which said that he was a Brazilian and the policeman said, 'Oh how fascinating, my family spent some time in Brazil', by which means he discovered that Mr Bedas did not speak Portuguese. They put him in jail where he died. That was my first banker.

Next I would like to tell you about my first pope. My first pope was Pope Pius the Twelfth, Papa Pacelli, who had of course held the position all through the war. He had been a papal nuncio in Germany and when I first met him which was much later in 1958, it was towards the end of his reign. I had just written *Children of the Sun* and was being presented to him in what was called a private audience. Now don't kid yourself, there's nothing really private about a private audience – unless you happen to be a statesman where you talk one on one, with a couple of monsignors standing by to translate – and don't believe all the stories they tell you about popes being multilingual. They are, but they're not inspired by the Holy Ghost and Papa Pacelli's English was somewhat difficult. His German was much better.

In those days, ladies had to wear black gloves, high-cut, long dresses which showed no ankle and gentlemen had to wear sober suits. My audience was arranged by no less a man than Big George. Big George was the late George Seabury who was six feet four and when he played ice hockey he was over seven feet. He was enormous. He was the publicity man, the public relations man, for Pan Am in Rome which meant that all the distinguished visitors who came in carrying money for the Pope, especially people like Archbishop Spellman and so on, were received at the airport and given the full treatment. George said to me, 'Do you want to see the Pope? I'll arrange it.' So it was arranged.

I would like to describe this occasion for you. First of all you went in through the Angelic Gate and then through the Court of St Damasus. You had the papal salute from the chaps with the slashed doublets and hose, the Papal Guard, and then you were taken to the first of a series of waiting rooms. There were only six of us, three men and three women. In the first chamber we were met by a monsignor. You knew a monsignor because he wore that long black cassock with red piping and he had a grave and serious air. He spoke in a kind of religious whisper as he instructed us in somewhat broken English that we must not speak to the Holy Father unless the Holy Father spoke to us.

We were all Christians and so we were expected to kneel and kiss his ring, then we might offer him, after he had spoken a few words, religious objects to bless – missals and rosary beads and so on. Above all we should comport ourselves with dignity and quiet. Then we were moved into the second room where we had two more monsignors

"So for what time is left for me I am turning to other crafts – the spoken word, the memoir, the essay."

and someone on whom I'd like you to concentrate your attention. A little man in a frock coat and striped pants. A little tubby man with his hands decently under the tails of his coat. We were shunted from one room to the other and in the fourth room, again with much whispering and arrangement, shuffling hither and yon, were made ready for the presence of His Holiness.

I have to tell you this, it is one of the minor footnotes of history. His Holiness's housekeeper at the time was a certain Suora Pasquelina, Sister Pasquelina, who was a German nun who had run his household since he had been papal legate in Germany and she ran it with very German thoroughness. Cardinals trembled. Mere archbishops went pale at the mention of her name because she had been known to send them packing and the only one who really could get past her was Spelly from New York because he always came bearing money and you'll find him in the book.

One of the tasks she performed for him in his later days, which is a task that has been performed on me and other performers, is that she applied a little touch of make-up before he went into the audience because he was a very pallid man and in those days he was getting old and was rather shrunken.

"Mr Bedas fled to Brazil where he had another bank and he also had another fortune stored but the gods were not to be cheated."

Into this holy of holies we are accompanied by the little man in the frock coat. One of the monsignors peels off and His Holiness is brought out. He was a very impressive man. He was very tall. He had that long, thin, aquiline Roman face – a very princely man. The company gave him the obeisances. He stood there, he said a few words in English and French as there were a couple of Frenchmen there. His French wasn't bad but his English was execrable. He made a few banal remarks and they were all banal, I promise you.

Finally he gave us his blessing and then the little man who had accompanied us came into his own. He alone was able to approach the sacred person of the pontiff and arrange the pontiff as he arranged us, for a photograph. He was the official photographer. We were all touched by this contact with greatness and sanctity and the papal office. His Holiness was then ushered out. One of the monsignors went with him, two remained as well as the little man. The little man then unceremoniously slung his camera round his neck, pulled out a little book of dockets and said, '6000 lire each, how many?'

To conclude, my first hero who is really an anti-hero. In old Rome there is a square which dates back to the 16th century called the Field of Flowers, the Campo di Fiori, and in the middle of that square is a brooding statue – a hooded monk with his hood drawn over his face. There are various inscriptions on the base of it, around which on some nights the market people pile their boxes and burn them.

The statue is Giordano Bruno, a wandering scholar, a fugitive monk who was burned for heresy on that spot in 1600. The statue was erected in 1889 by subscriptions from the University of Rome which was then, after the reign of Pius the Ninth, a very anti-clerical place.

This statue fascinated me. I read all I could find about Giordano Bruno. He was in the first place a Dominican monk born in Naples who fled his monastery and became a wandering scholar in the manner of the day. He went to England. He found a place in the train of Sir Philip Sidney, the poet. He probably knew Christopher Marlowe. He was not a reputable character. He was probably a spy for Walsingham. He was a dramatist. He was a poet He was to all intents and purposes a time server. That's what he was.

He went to Switzerland where he knew Calvin and also Zwingli and then went on to Venice where he became a scholar in residence in the house of Mocenigo. The Mocenigo family still lives, the present branch are old friends of ours. They live near Rome and they have told me that the Mocenigo palace in Venice, which is on the Grand Canal, is still haunted by the ghost of Giordano Bruno. When Mocenigo hired him, he hired him to teach him magic in order that he might win back the Doge's cap which his uncle had lost when he lost Cyprus to the Turks and a number of the ports of the Venetian empire. He thought he could get it back by magic.

The reason for this somewhat foolish ambition is plain because Bruno had written a book on the art of memory as well as other books on plural worlds. That in fact formed the base for one of the heresy charges against him, among others. Of course, ironically, at the moment the Vatican is helping to finance the search for other worlds, with the Vatican astronomer investigating the possibilities of other civilisations in outer space. So times change. Bruno was tried for heresy in Venice and under the torture and under the promise of future safety he recanted.

At that stage, however, Venice and Rome were very much apart and Rome was very anxious to bring them together because the ambassador from England in Venice at that time was one Sir Thomas Wootton and they thought that he might turn Venice into a Protestant republic. So a deal was made where the promise to Bruno was cancelled and he was taken to Rome where he languished in prison for another seven years and this time when they asked him to recant he refused and then they burned him. His last recorded words were, 'Gentlemen, at this moment I think that you are more afraid of me than I of you.'

I wrote a play about him which is, I still think, the best thing I've written. The point I'm trying to make is that it was the future which judged Bruno, not his first accusers. It has always been so. The works that I've written are what they have always been, hostages to fortune. Whatever the critics may say about them in praise or in blame, it is the public which will judge them as it has always done.

I make no bones about being a professional writer. That is what I do, that is what I have done. I have no regrets and I have a certain pride. I have always written the truth as I saw it. I have never prostituted my pen to base ends. I have always hated bullies: police who abuse their authority; bureaucrats who invoke petty regulations against the distressed; politicians who develop the illusion that they are our rulers instead of our servants; churchmen who dispense law instead of the charity of the gospel.

I have written about them all and the power games they play. I have also written about the unrecognised virtues of those who by a constant miracle manage to carry on their daily lives in a brutal world and still maintain the human decencies. I don't believe that virtue can be enforced by law. I don't believe that belief can be changed by force. In any community you can impose order, but you cannot impose compassion, charity, the decencies of common folk. Those who at this moment aspire to government should remember that.

What more can I say? The play is over. As dramatists go, I've been lucky enough to dictate my own curtain line. I thank you my friends, my readers, my family. We have borne each other company on the pilgrim road. I have been proud to walk it with you. Shalom, peace on your house.

David Malouf

Born in Brisbane of Lebanese and English parents, Malouf was known first as a poet and then became internationally distinguished as the author of lyrical novels about personal and national histories and mythology. Among them are *Johnno* (1975), *An Imaginary Life* (1978), *The Great World* (1990, winner of the Miles Franklin Award and Commonwealth Writers Prize), *Remembering Babylon* (1993, shortlisted for the Booker Prize and winner of the International IMPAC Dublin Literary Award), and *The Conversations at Curlow Creek* (1996).

20 April 1993

Most writers are very unwilling to come out from behind their books and appear as just themselves; not out of fear of facing their public, or in any way out of modesty – least of all out of modesty – but because they feel they are bound to be disappointing: that they can never be quite what they appear to be or what readers would like them to be from the books. A good many of us write because on the page we are in complete control. There is a chance there of getting things right; not perfect but somewhere along the way to that, whereas off the page is always a muddle. So the good news I have for you, if this turns out to be disappointing, is that unlike so much else these days, in the case of writers, what you see is *not* what you get.

Young people who want to write are usually told, and it is good advice, to write out of their experience – that only the world they know in their senses, that they know all the weights and balances of as they affect the small details of daily living, is what they will be able to make real and vivid in the minds of their readers. The only difficulty is to know where what you might want to call your experience begins and ends. Easy enough if we limit our experience to what actually happened to us: to what we have seen with our own eyes, felt with our own hands, to events we have been real witnesses of, even if we didn't stand quite at the centre of them. But is this really the sum of our experience?

Think of what happens to us when we read a book or see a film or a play and allow ourselves to be absorbed by its world, to suffer what the inhabitants of that world suffer, to learn painfully or in a burst of laughter the truths that they uncover about life and our strange part in it. Isn't that also a kind of experience? Don't the things we discover there, in our senses and on our nerves, stick in some way and change us, enlarge what we know of others and of what a thing it is to be alive? That experience comes to us in a secondary way, by our submitting ourselves to a world that is not our world and may be very far from our world but which becomes ours. So long as we are absorbed and entranced we lose ourselves in it and get back some larger self.

Experience of that kind, imagined and made real, is very much what a writer is concerned with as his daily business. And it is that kind of experience that he wants his reader to have. I am sometimes asked, for example, if some episode in *Johnno*, my first book, really happened, because the book looks like a piece of autobiography and because some of its material, but not all, really is drawn from my own background and my own life. My answer to that question is the one that I think any writer would give: yes, everything in the book really happened. If not in my actual life at least in the writing. And the truth is that at this distance I cannot always make the distinction. I cannot remember accurately which episodes in the book draw on memory and which ones I made up, because by now they both have, in my mind, the same consistency of reality, as I hope they do for the reader.

What I ask myself and want to talk about is where this capacity comes from that allows us to imagine ourselves into situations and skins that are not our own but that may become our own. A capacity that writer and reader share and on which the success of all story-telling and all of its importance to us depends.

If you think for a moment of your childhood you will admit, I think, that some of your strongest memories – memories in which as a little person you seemed to stand at the centre of a vivid world of sight and sound and smell – are ones that you don't remember at all but only heard about through that fund of household stories and reminiscences that is part of every family's history. What we take into our young and vivid imagination, through the telling, becomes an experience as real to us as if we really could recall, in all the liveliness of our five senses, that happening.

This is true, I would suggest, not only of stories of which we were the subject but of stories we hear out of the lives of our parents, our grandparents, or all those friends of the family and others who are so fond of recounting things, and which small children hear and overhear. The process of taking those stories in, of making them real to ourselves so that we can see and hear and smell what is happening in them, of grasping a phrase or a described detail and making a whole perception out of it, a whole vivid experience, is one of our earliest ways of learning about the world we are in and the imaginative process it involves is the same one we draw on as readers and even more as writers.

Writers may be, at least in one sense, no more than people who have retained more strongly than others that capacity of grasping a word or a detail, and making a whole of it; of taking what is overheard or misheard and imaginatively making of it an experience you stand at the vivid and real centre of.

We all know, if we think back a little, that childhood experience of eavesdropping, overhearing. Here is an account of it I discovered just the other day in an interview with the poet Gwen Harwood. I was particularly struck because the world she was speaking of is the same Brisbane world that I grew up in, a decade earlier than I knew it, but pretty much the same:

> *When I was small, we lived in the country, in what was then the country, in Brisbane and my friend Alice and I had a special cubby under the tank stand. It was quite a high tank stand but just right for two little girls. And my grandmother grew violets there in which lived the beautiful Queensland green frog. And they seemed to like us, we loved them and we used to sit under there, cuddling them in our hands and talking to one another and listening to the people talking up on the verandah at the back and they took no notice of us so we had a continual stream of remarkable adult conversation. We did not understand very much of what it was about. 'In labour for 16 hours' we imagined was some kind of digging.*

What that little memory points to – and I am sure we all respond to it – is how much of a child's early experience comes out of an oral world, a world of household story-telling and talk. And my guess is that this is still so, even in the age of television. Certainly, at the time Gwen Harwood is speaking of, and in my childhood a decade later, the world was almost entirely an oral one. I was made aware of this when I read some of the reviews of my novel *Harland's Half Acre* from the United States where reviewer after reviewer pointed out, perhaps because things have moved faster there, that the world the book came out of was a world in which story-telling was still the most important source of entertainment in households. And of course that was true till very lately.

My childhood was filled with overheard gossip, which I had to decode, and which became a great training in listening to what was being said beyond the words. Decode because, as in Gwen Harwood's case, some of the terms referred to facts I couldn't make sense of, but also because they were always trying to fool me – 'Careful,' they would say, 'big ears is listening' – though, like most children, I had cracked the code long before they thought I was capable of it. Beyond the gossip there were also actual stories told to me by my mother, or by our girl Cassie, while I was being bathed or having my hair combed or shelling peas or watching Cassie make pastry or being taken for a walk or while we were waiting for a bus or tram, and by my father while I was helping him with a bit of carpentry, or by workmen who came to the house and would talk to me while I hung about watching them.

"Unlike so much else these days, in the case of writers, what you see is not what you get."

So that I heard a great deal which I vividly imagined, and made part of my experience; about my mother's childhood in England, and all that life of her large family before the Great War, my father's hard boyhood, growing up as a migrant child in Brisbane after the turn of the century; from Cassie about growing up on a farm outside Harrisville; and from all those workmen and family friends about life on ships – the carpenter my father used was an old man called Pop who had been a ship's carpenter – or in the trenches of the Great War and in Paris and the Middle East.

If I am writing about almost any happening of this century, out of the world of my mother's or my father's childhood as well as my own, I feel I have access, through the senses and the feelings, to the real details of it. It is part of my experience, even though some of it took place before I was born. And the key to all that is some capacity we have to set ourselves at the centre of what we have known, in all our senses only in the hearing about it, in the telling. What I am speaking of now is what seems to me to be central to the whole business of writing and also of reading.

Imagination as I understand it is not a matter of dreaming up fantastic happenings or playing games with illusion and reality. That is more properly called invention and has to do with the active intelligence. What I am thinking of is something more inward, perhaps more naive than that, certainly more passive and dream-like and which belongs, I think, to our earliest way of dealing with the world. The ability to take one vivid detail and, by a leap of the imagination, use it as a spy hole into a whole vividly apprehended world. To pick up one gesture or a few words out of a conversation overheard and intuit from it a whole life in all its particularity, its vulnerability to pain, its joy or obsessive passions or prejudice. That is very much how the writer works. It does seem to me to be a very inward and naive and perhaps child-like way of proceeding. It is also, I think, the way that reading works for the best sort of reader.

So what about a book like *Remembering Babylon* that is set more than a century ago? There is not much possibility of my having direct contact with anyone whose experience goes back that far.

The first thing I would want to say is that this is a contemporary novel, not an historical one. It could only have been written now. If it is about anything important it is about what is important to us now, not to characters who lived and died long ago. It is about the beginnings of a question that is still with us and which we are still in the middle – I would like to say the *muddle* of: namely what this continent may make of us as we fully expose ourselves to it and take it into our imagination; how it will shape and change us.

What I have done in the book is to create – I hope with the sort of detail that will make the thing vivid and present and convincing to a reader – an extreme situation, one in which a little settlement of white Europeans comes into first contact with the land, but also with the original and natural inheritors of the land. As you see, I have gone back to the absolute beginnings. But of course it is one of the features of our history that it keeps beginning over and over in different places and in different ways, though in the same way too, wherever first settlement occurs – in this case, in North Queensland, at a time when settlement was leapfrogging up the coast so that my characters, who are somewhere up near Bowen, have maybe a hundred miles of unsettled land behind them as well as unknown miles of unsettled land ahead.

I have pushed this first contact situation to the extreme by having them confront, not an actual Aborigine, but someone who has lived with the Aborigines since he was a child and has, as it were, been born a second time among them. The anxiety he provokes has to do with the fact that they know he is white but no longer *feel* him as white, and some of them can no longer see him as white either. He has made some kind of crossing over in which his whiteness has become problematical or got lost. When people look at him, their own whiteness, the rather shaky power they feel as white and European – shaky because they are in fact in their own world poor and powerless – also becomes problematical, so that they can no longer fly to the security or the superiority of it. If, by exposing himself to this unknown land, Jemmy has been so changed, then might not that also happen, over time, to themselves and their children?

Of course, not all the characters in the settlement see this exposure to a possible redefinition and change as a threat. To some of them Jemmy is a sign, not of loss and the destruction of the white or European or civilised self, but of the power of the self to cross boundaries and break into a new dimension.

"The aim of the book is to get into the reader's head and hang on there, and to have its strongest effect, one hopes, when the reading itself is over."

The creation of such a group of people, such a little group of conflicting and contradictory views, doesn't need an historical sense but an understanding of the way people are: what moves them, worries them, drives them in some cases to vindictive anger, in other cases to compassion. It requires the same ability to imagine ourselves into other people's skin that any other sort of writing demands, the kind of capacity I have already been talking about. The historical details, which need be few, will take care of themselves. It is mostly a matter of taking away, rather than adding; of taking away all the accoutrements of our modern world while retaining all those little details of sensory life, of response, of feeling, of gesture, the nuances of relationship between people in the intimate moments of their lives, that convince us that all this is happening in a world with the density and detail of the world we see about us. That is, in the dimension of the imagination that we step into, these characters have to be recognisable as contemporaries, and their world as continuous, and not only chronologically, with our own.

But that is something that can only be proved in the reading. The reading is the reader's experience. The writer's business is to make the world he is creating as accessible, as vivid to each reader's imagination and sense, as he can manage. The aim of the book is to get into the reader's head and hang on there, and to have its strongest effect, one hopes, when the reading itself is over. It is meant to become part of each reader's real experience; to be a place they have been to where they have not been previously and had not expected to go, an experience of other people's lives that has become their experience now, and changed them, and will go on changing them, as all experience does, in ways they cannot predict and, if it has gone deep enough, in ways they may never fully measure or understand.

! ?

SPEAKER: Did you start writing from an early age?

DAVID MALOUF: I started reading from a very early age. I think that writing is not a separate thing from reading. I started reading very early and loved the actual sight of print on a page, really fell in love with print on a page, and with the kind of magic whereby that was also words, and a voice, and happenings and a whole world came off it.

So from very early on I wanted to reproduce that effect, like a lot of kids of that age. I grew up in a family where I had only a sister but we always had lots of other kids in the house and so we produced little newspapers – actually printed them, never wrote them, because that cursive script belonged to the world of school but printing the thing out belonged to a world of real things that existed outside.

So we used to make up little newspapers. We even tried to sell them to the neighbours. Inasmuch as they consisted mostly of gossip about those neighbours that we had overheard from our parents or other people, we thought we were doing them all a social service. That does say another thing, and that is that writing never seemed to me to belong to a strictly private world. It has always belonged to that community world, that world where you are trying to pass it all on to someone out there.

SPEAKER: Could you tell us what importance you place on dreams?

DAVID MALOUF: I have sometimes wanted to say that what a book is is a kind of public dreaming. Usually you begin to write a book because you pick up some fact you have heard, or the beginning of a story that in some way touches on one of your own obsessions, and a lot of the writing is an attempt to find out why it is that this particular fact, out of all the facts that you have heard, is one that you feel you have to pursue. So to that extent the writing is always very personal.

But of course when you begin then to turn that into a story, and your mind goes rather lax and passive in doing that, and you have to let fall out of your head all the things you know that will get in the way, you are in a very vulnerable state to whatever is coming up from some area underneath. So the book then does become a kind of dream spun out, and of course exposes you to all those people who love analysing dreams.

SPEAKER: Someone said to me recently that with some authors you need to read between the lines, not so much simply interpret what they say or accept what they say but look for some sort of hidden meaning.

DAVID MALOUF: I myself would want to say that what the writing is meant to do is to reveal those hidden meanings between the lines. That is, I am mostly interested, in writing, in bringing to the surface of the narrative what otherwise would go unseen or unheard or unexpressed. A lot of my characters – I am sure in ways that a lot of people don't very much like – seem as if they are always half asleep, or dreaming, or existing in some sort of world where it is not action they are concerned with but what is underneath action.

When I look at other people's writing, I sometimes get impatient if I don't know what the characters might dream about. What I mean by that is that characters who seem to have only a *social* life are characters I am never much interested in. I always want to know what is there on the page about the other dimension that we live in. And we live in that an awful lot. Not just when we are asleep. We wander around an awful lot of the time with our mind idling, which means that it is concerning itself with something other than what is strictly visible, strictly social, strictly expressible really.

SPEAKER: May I ask whom you consider to be the seminal writers who have influenced your life and, secondly, it has been said now that you are Patrick White's natural heir. Is that right?

DAVID MALOUF: I was afraid you were going to say natural *child*. Speculation about Patrick White goes on still. The interesting thing, I think, is that the writers you admire most are often not the writers you feel you could in any way emulate, or would want to, or could follow. The writer that I admire most is Balzac. I could not in a fit begin to turn myself into an Australian Balzac. In English I suppose it would be somebody like Dickens, it would be somebody like Emily Brontë, it would be somebody like Melville. I think probably *Moby Dick* is the book I have read most often in my life. I don't think any of that is very useful. It is useful to me as a reader. It is not necessarily useful to me as a writer. One of the things about Australian writing, it seems to me, at the moment, is that we have a very large number of very good writers across a very wide field, and that is how it should be. That is when writing is at its richest. I cannot believe that Patrick White will ever have an heir, or that we need one.

Vikram Seth

Seth trained as an economist and has lived in England, California and China, as well as his native India. His 1993 novel *A Suitable Boy* is a 1300-page saga of four Indian families in the 1950s. After taking him eight years to write, it was bought by publishers for $1.5 million, compared with the work of nineteenth-century writers such as Tolstoy, Balzac and Eliot, shortlisted for major prizes, and, despite its size, lovingly read by an extraordinary number of people. His previous work was *The Golden Gate*, a critically acclaimed epic poem about 1980s San Francisco. This talk took the form of an interview with Ian Hicks, then Literary Editor of the *Sydney Morning Herald*, and Andrea Stretton, then presenter of the SBS *Book Show*.

14 September 1993

IAN HICKS: When you started writing the book, did you have in mind a magnum opus of this length?

VIKRAM SETH: No, I didn't, I thought the book would be about 200 or 250 pages at the very most. I don't think anything as ludicrous as the length of this book ever entered my head and if it had I would have very summarily kicked it out. Originally it was just intended to be the love story at the core of the book, the searching for a suitable boy for Lata, this young Hindu girl in the 1950s. The first sentence of the book is, '"You too will marry a boy I choose," said Mrs Rupa Mehra firmly to her younger daughter.' That in a sense is the core of the story, the finding among suitable and unsuitable suitors of someone who suits Lata.

Mrs Rupa Mehra has other children, including the elder daughter at whose wedding this remark is made, and through that elder daughter and through her elder and younger son we enter different worlds like the Calcutta commercial set, the countryside where land reforms are taking place, the lives of courtesans and musicians and all sorts of other people. Again through Lata's own three different suitors, one of whom is a cricket-playing hunk, one of whom is a young executive in the shoe trade and one of whom is a poet who is writing an immensely long novel, we enter different worlds. So that is how the book expanded, willy nilly, and I had to decide whether to chop off these various tentacles or to allow them to remain and to somehow or the other incorporate them sensibly in the book.

IAN HICKS: What sparked the development from a simple romance to a very much longer book?

VIKRAM SETH: I think it was the characters basically. The characters at the beginning were not very solid figures in my mind, but the more clear they became the less I felt that I could just tell them that I had had enough of them and they should move off-stage now. So in a sense they insisted on remaining and I didn't have the force of will to call a closure on debate.

ANDREA STRETTON: After eight years spent with these characters, what was it like for you as a writer to, in a sense, leave them behind? It's a long time.

VIKRAM SETH: A tremendous feeling of relief. I say that not because I didn't love the characters, though I must say I loved them and was exasperated with them in equal measure. It was that it had, after all, been eight years. When I was writing *The Golden Gate*, which is an equally unlikely novel, a novel in verse, 300 pages of it, set in California, there the process took me about a year to complete and there I did feel a very deep sense of regret on parting with those characters. But in the case of *A Suitable Boy*, I knew that the sound of them would be with me or at least the resonance of them would be with me for a very long time to come. Whether or not I tried to dismiss them, they would come crowding back on me; so I felt, Thank God the opus is over and now I shall revert to my own life – or so I thought.

"I felt, Thank God the opus is over and now I shall revert to my own life – or so I thought."

IAN HICKS: How have you found that process of selling the book you spent eight years writing?

VIKRAM SETH: Writing is a very lonely process and a very internalised process and even when you are doing things that are fairly complicated analytically, you don't stop to analyse them; whereas on a tour like this, you are always asked about the process of writing and what it meant to you and how you survived it and it's a very social process. So I suppose there is a slightly schizophrenic feel to it – that is, you are giving up your solitude and whether in darkness or in light, you are quite conscious that there is an audience out there that is actually listening to you and it is almost an over-social occasion in certain respects.

However, I've been a publisher myself – for a couple of years I was an editor at Stanford University Press, a job which I had to take up when my money ran out. I was supposed to be doing economics and I was diverted into writing novels. That experience taught me that one has to promote one's book. You can't expect people to automatically hear about a brick of a book of this kind – I meant a brick in the physical sense – and to read it, to pick it up, without having something that leads them on, whether it is a review or a conversation or the recommendation of a friend. So the actual business of going into a bookstore and asking for a book is very often triggered by things other than the book itself.

ANDREA STRETTON: Vikram also has written *From Heaven Lake*, which is about his travel through Tibet and Nepal. I think that was written about 10 years ago, but it has just been republished, and of course *The Golden Gate* which was written in rhyming couplets and *Beastly Tales*. They are all so totally different – it's very hard to pinpoint you.

VIKRAM SETH: Yes, I write to keep myself interested and to express what I happen to have on my mind at that particular time rather than to be slottable into a particular niche for my publishers or even readers for that matter. I write in order to communicate but I don't necessarily fulfil expectations in that the genre I write in will be predictable even to myself. Having written a travel book, my publishers wanted me to write another travel book, and when in fact I wrote a book of poems they rejected it. So I found another publisher for that and then I showed this other publisher *The Golden Gate*, the novel in verse, and they rejected that. It has happened to me again and again, and eventually I decided that I've got to follow the muse wherever it leads me and leave questions of sales, image, marketability, etc., to one side.

When I was writing *A Suitable Boy*, I really was worried that it would never find a publisher. Because if you really want a recipe for disaster, this is it: go and write a 1349 page novel with not very much explicit sex, no foreign characters other than Indian characters, not a Raj book. Don't add a glossary, make sure it stays in the 1950s. It's so expensive to produce a book like this, and there's only a certain amount that you can reasonably expect people to pay in times like these for a novel. I think if in my case it was a measure of rashness that I didn't jump off this octopus – odd image – in the case of my publishers it was a matter of some courage to take it on.

ANDREA STRETTON: When you actually completed the manuscript, though, you did have a certain confidence that you'd written a major book?

VIKRAM SETH: Certainly major in terms of size. I did think at that time that it was good but it needed a lot of work when I had finished the first draft and I excised about 500 pages of it before I offered it to the various publishers. But I told them the book would not be slimmed any further for commercial considerations and they would have to accept that if they were going to bid for the book, then it would not be very different in size, in length, from what they in fact had been offered.

ANDREA STRETTON: No doubt most people know the story of the excitable bidding for *A Suitable Boy*. In fact the rights for US and English publishers were sold for about $1.5 million which was very high. It must have been extraordinary as an author tucked away with this book all of a sudden to see people so excited about it.

VIKRAM SETH: It was really odd, it was weird, because I had been living on very little indeed for the previous few years. I hadn't followed my profession as an economist; I was very anxious about the years to come. If I was to continue as a writer and to write the books that I usually write, books of verse and things which don't make any money at all, then I'd need some sort of patronage and I didn't see how I could possibly get it. But this book in a sense has been a funny child who supports its parent from its birth rather than vice versa.

ANDREA STRETTON: Also the excitement, not just the financial investment people were prepared to make, but the general excitement from those who were reading this book as a manuscript.

VIKRAM SETH: Yes, it is odd because when the publishers started hyping the book, it was easy enough for me to discount that. But when reviewers started saying good things about the book in strong terms then I did feel very pleased but also slightly bewildered. On one Sunday, I think the *Sunday Telegraph*, the *Observer*, the *Sunday Times* and the *Independent* all came out with reviews that I wouldn't have had the immodesty to write in my dreams. I am normally quite robust, but this notwithstanding I got a headache, I couldn't cope with it and so it had that slightly double-edged feel: is this real, and are readers going to like it, and won't there be a backlash of some kind?

IAN HICKS: Curiously though, there hasn't been a backlash. In those original set of reviews, there were comparisons to *Middlemarch* and *War and Peace*. Were you embarrassed and/or surprised at that, or did you think it wholly proper?

VIKRAM SETH: Well, I didn't think it wholly proper. On the one hand it would be extremely ungracious of me if, say, the chief fiction critic of the *Sunday Times* or the *Guardian* were to put his literary credibility on the line, to immediately turn around and try to shoot down the comparison. On the other hand, it would be really idiotic of me to let those sorts of things interpose themselves between me and the next thing I am going to write. It would leave me with this huge sense of challenge which I couldn't possibly fulfil. What you really want is the relationship between you and your characters or between you and the next line of poetry that you are writing, not some kind of shadow of an exorbitant comparison. Time is very cavalier with hype and time will tell whether the book is going to be readable even in five years time, let alone twenty.

IAN HICKS: One of the key sequences in the book, almost a non-fictional sequence, was that dealing with land reform. It was not very optimistic. Is that your view of the likely fate of land reform in India?

"If you really want a recipe for disaster . . . go and write a 1349 page novel with not very much explicit sex, no foreign characters other than Indian characters."

VIKRAM SETH: The book is set in the '50s. I didn't try to prognosticate – even though I knew what had happened later, I tried to make it seem very much of the '50s. One of the characters laughs off her daughter-in-law's suggestion that there may be a woman prime minister at some time, she laughs it off very gently and indulgently as an impossibility.

The land reforms are a very complicated issue, have been a very complicated issue. At first I thought the whole subject was a boring one. But it was crucial because it was born out of the immediate concerns of some of the characters. There's a minister of revenue in the state government and he's trying to force through land reforms just a few years after independence and these land reforms are going to deeply affect his own best friend, a

Muslim landowner, the Nawab Sahib of Baitar, and indirectly the courtesans, the retainers, the musicians who depend upon these large landowners and other wealthy patrons. But during the course of these reforms, while they are passing through the legislature, the landlords are trying to shift peasants around from field to field so that they can't claim to have tilled their particular field for any length of time.

So in the mind of this minister there is this terrible ambivalence. By trying to force through a measure that is in its own nature intended to do good, he is almost exacerbating the situation and causing hardship and grief to those people whom he is trying to help and also simultaneously injuring a friend of his. So it is a very human subject. As to what happened in the long run, it is very difficult to say. I think there were good results of that land reform in terms of productivity of the land and so on, but of course the people who were landless peasants, who couldn't claim to till anything themselves, were left out of it completely. It's a complicated issue.

IAN HICKS: I found it fascinating reading that part of the book against the background of Australia's own slow coming to terms with land reform – Aboriginal land claims after Mabo. It is a very moving part of the book but it doesn't leave you with any great sense of optimism.

VIKRAM SETH: I think it's true and the same, for instance, for the Hindu/Muslim tensions which are also implicit in the book, partly because, on the domestic level, the young cricketer whom I mentioned turns out to be Muslim, a most unsuitable boy from Mrs Rupa Mehra's point of view, but also because during those years immediately post-Partition, there was a lot of tension between the communities. Indeed, the calendar most unfortunately clicked into a situation where the Muslim month of mourning, Mohurram, coincided with the Hindu month of celebration of the Dussehra, so that led to terrible troubles in the streets. There too one asks oneself whether one ought to be optimistic. The thing is not to be optimistic but to be as realistic as you can as a writer.

SPEAKER: How was the book reviewed in India?

VIKRAM SETH: The one thing that I wanted to make absolutely sure of was that the book should be published in India before it was published anywhere else. After all it was a book about India, it was basically for an Indian audience and I wanted it to be typeset and published in India first and at a price that was at least a little more affordable in Indian terms than a foreign price would be. It was received, I think, very well by readers by and large. Considering that it is very expensive even in its present form in India compared to people's salaries, it's had a tremendous response.

The critical response has been mixed. There have been some very favourable reviews and some unfavourable reviews, in fact even some vitriolic reviews. There are two problems in India. One is that any book that is even remotely to address various issues not in a political way but through the lives of the characters is going to touch very tender nerves. The second thing is there is something of a syndrome, and I don't think it's restricted to India but I think it is true of Pakistan, of Australia, New Zealand, even Ireland, that until you are given a good puff in England or America, I think most particularly England, there's a bit of a tall or perhaps a short poppy syndrome. The problem was that the moment that the English reviewers started praising it, then I got a salvo of praise from India. But I'm rather glad that I allowed the book to follow the sun from India to England to Canada to America rather than to go in the other direction.

Blanche d'Alpuget

D'Alpuget worked as a journalist until she moved to Indonesia as a diplomat's wife and began writing books: a biography of Sir Richard Kirby in 1977, and tough novels about Australians in foreign trouble spots, such as *Monkeys in the Dark* (1980) and *Turtle Beach* (1981). *White Eye*, a novel published in 1993, deals with genetic engineering and the environment. She is now married to the former Australian prime minister Bob Hawke, the subject of her award-winning 1982 biography.

8 November 1993

A novel is really the tip of an iceberg, for the part you see, the words on the page, are but a fraction of what lies hidden beneath; a fragment of the ideas and attitudes the novelist leaves silent and invisible. A novel that is fast-paced with a strong story, as *White Eye* is, can trick the reader simply by the speed of its narrative so that she goes flying up and over the top of the iceberg and lands in the water on the other side without glimpsing that looming presence beneath the waterline.

I would say that whereas an ordinary novel sets out gradually to reveal itself, to grow in front of your eyes, as it were, a thriller is more nimble-footed. It dashes about revealing but secretly and simultaneously concealing facts and events. Thrillers are deliberately deceptive which is what makes them so much fun. I cannot speak for all thrillers but in the case of *White Eye* the deception is two-fold and I've noticed in the reviews that have been published so far that none of the reviewers have twigged to the second game in the book. I don't really want to let the cat, or as in this case the wedge-tailed eagle, out of the bag by telling you what the second game is but I'll give a hint in due course.

To change the metaphor, I'd like to take you on a tour backstage of the attitudes and the themes in this book. In writing *White Eye*, which is my first thriller, I wanted to raise questions about issues that are interesting to me and I think important and I hope you find them interesting and important too. These include questions about animals, wild animals, laboratory animals and endangered species of animals and some people, of course, include humans in all these categories – I wanted to ask questions about how we treat our native wild animals and our feral wild animals. Can we re-examine the need for tame animals in laboratories and are we aware that we treat animals like slaves?

I wanted to ask questions about sexual politics and what I see as a new misogyny arising in response to the increased power women have attained in the past 15 years. I wanted to write about love between men and women at the end of the 20th century. About injured birds and their rehabilitation. About the scientific and economic revolution caused by genetic engineering and about the horror of reform without compassion for the individual.

"I have encountered time and again this sort of despairing misanthropy."

In the past few years we have witnessed the collapse, after more than 70 years and millions of wasted lives, of a terrifying system of reform without compassion for individuals and I refer of course to communism which is now everywhere discredited, except I am told in our universities. But in the fashionable clamour to condemn communism, let us remember that communism itself springs from something mighty and wonderful in humankind – its source is intellect. But it is intellect that has been severed from connection to the heart.

At the end of the 20th century, in a desperately overcrowded world, there is a growing temptation to remedy the environmental crises we face with a new version of this intellectual reform, already known as 'lifeboat ethics'. On a lifeboat the weaklings are thrown overboard. In the early stages of planning this book I read an article in the *Sydney Morning Herald* that stimulated my imagination and also gave me the willies. It was a story about world deforestation and overpopulation. A scientist working at the Australian Museum gave this advice to the readers of the *Herald*. He said, 'If you want to help save the Brazilian rain forest, shoot a Brazilian peasant.' In other research about what might be called 'green thinking' I have encountered time and again this sort of despairing misanthropy. I am not saying the conservationists are murderers, certainly not. I am saying that zealots turn to violence easily and nature zealots or green zealots are just as much zealots as are the mindless chanting men and women who would murder Salman Rushdie.

The overt story of *White Eye* is the temptation of a scientist who is not a mad scientist as some of the reviewers are saying. He is not mad at all. He is bad but he is not mad and I think that is an important distinction. He is a scientist who is horrified by the environmental crisis and it is his temptation to turn to scientific violence for the good of the planet and of mankind. So when I say he is bad, he is also an idealist and the two things sit together, I think, in this strange creature called humankind. There were other questions in my mind when I began writing this book and they were to do with ways of life for women at the end of the 20th century after the feminist revolution which really got going and gathered a great deal of heat and steam in the 1970s.

These days young women who have inherited the blessings and the curses of that revolution of feminism frequently declare that they are not feminists. I declare that I am a feminist but feminism is one of those words like psychotherapy which means anything that the speaker wants it to mean. Feminism for me is the acknowledgment that women have as much right to freedom as men. So in this book I have written about women exercising various types of freedom. There are five main female characters: there is a mother/grandmother; there is a politician who happens to be a Senator; there is a senior bureaucrat; there is a scientist, that is the woman who has been murdered; and last there is the heroine, Diana, who is a falconer who sets her birds free.

All these women enjoy and suffer from the different types of freedom that they have. The grandmother because she is old, unimportant and what is more, black, has social freedom. She has got the freedom to be herself. Her name is Grace and she did not come by this name accidentally. The politician has the freedom to do things. The bureaucrat, *surprisingly*, has the freedom to block things. The scientist who has been murdered has exercised, to an alarming degree, sexual freedom and Diana has the freedom of the satisfaction that comes from commitment to others. Back in the 1970s when I was active in the women's movement, my friends and I naively believed that if women won the right to equal opportunity in education and in employment, if we managed to throw off the shackles of the social, legal and educational inequality that we suffered from, we would be happy. It has not turned out that way, at least not yet.

It seems to me that while women have gained the whole world, as it were, in the past 20 years they have lost not their souls, certainly not, but love. In the past two decades women have lost the love of men. The gains of feminism have been purchased at the cost of love without which life may be interesting, rewarding and exciting but it can never be joyous. It can never have the divine spark and sparkle that comes to us from love alone. It is the crushing price that has been paid by men and women of the western world. It is the price of the freedom and equality which, back in the '70s, we thought we could get for no cost. One sees the resulting bankruptcies everywhere. Distrustful, misogynist, lonely men; gross pornography; discontented, lonely women; the sexual harassment epidemic that is poisoning the atmosphere of thousands of offices and work rooms. The war of the sexes used to be a jocular term. It is not any more. The campaign that began as an uprising of the oppressed in the 1970s has now entered a guerilla warfare period which is horribly entrenched, full of ambushes and sniper fire. That, I have to say, is the bad news.

The good news is that this is a passing phase, I am certain. The fact is that as never before in history the ground has been prepared for profound, sweet, clear-eyed passion between men and women. While I was researching this book a wheat farmer in western New South Wales taught me a new meaning for the word 'scarifying'. I knew this term only in its sense of lacerating by severe criticism. All writers know that meaning. Certainly men and women have scarified each other in this sense in the past 20 years but there are other ways of scarifying, as my farmer friend told me. Scarifying is also loosening the soil for sowing seeds and it has a third meaning, which is to hasten the sprouting of seeds by making incisions in the seed coats.

What has happened in the past 20 years is that the earth of our lives has been scarified for the seeds of a new sort of love between men and women, a love that has never before been expressed for it is love between intellectual, social and legal equals. Not since history began have men and women been equal in this way, that is, as full human beings equal in the expression of their human spirit.

"As never before in history the ground has been prepared for profound, sweet, clear-eyed passion between men and women."

So the penultimate theme in this book is about love between a modern independent young woman and her male counterpart.

At this point I would like to return for a moment to the question of genetic engineering. I think when the history of the 20th century is written it will be seen as many things but one of them certainly will be the century of science. Science has created the immense wealth of this century. It has allowed humans to breed and flourish in numbers so great that now we fear that science's bag of magic tricks has been exhausted by the very population it has produced and that there is no rabbit left in the laboratory hat which can be pulled out to save the show – save the rainforest, save the rivers, save the oceans from the poisons of man.

Paradoxically, however, while science has created 20th-century society time and again, producing the food and medicines we needed to fight off death, whilst science has been our saviour, it has indeed dethroned God. Like God, science also has the power to destroy the world through nuclear warfare, through chemical warfare, through biological warfare. This power of science which once belonged to God has made *it* the great religion of our age. Like religion before it, science now reveals the wonders hidden in nature.

We are in the midst of another great revelation right now, a revolutionary revelation called genetic engineering, a revelation that will determine who is rich and who is poor, who has power and who is powerless in the 21st century. As the wealth of the 20th century was founded on pyrotechnology, that is the technology of heat and electricity, the wealth of the 21st century will be founded on biotechnology and we as individuals, as a country and as a world are quite unprepared intellectually and morally for the marvels and horrors that lie ahead of us.

A couple of weeks ago it was announced in breathless headlines that some American scientists had managed to clone human embryo cells. The news media, whose function it is to make mischief, transformed this modest event into a terrifying prospect of a cloned human, à la *Brave New World*. This media beat-up has caused fear and outrage in America, as it was intended to, with picketing of the laboratory where the cloning was being done.

But while the protest is hysterical, the protesters make some important points. They point out that genetic engineering reduces life to mere information without any intrinsic meaning and it opens the way to a world made of living designer gadgets including designer humans. What is more, there are no international laws to deal with this situation. There are international laws against dum dum bullets and mustard gas but there is no Geneva convention against, for example, re-creating Tyrannosaurus Rex. Many of the articles about the cloned human embryo cells quoted Dr Arthur Caplin who is Director of the Centre for Bioethics at the University of Minnesota. Dr Caplin said that cloning human embryos does not take a Nobel Prize team with a million-dollar lab. It is fairly simple, which is exactly how I have described another type of genetic engineering in *White Eye*. It does not take enormous amounts of money and a huge team. Dr Caplin added this warning: 'Despite the scruples of most scientists, there is no way to control or contain the technology.'

I said there were two games in this novel and I will give a hint about the second one. The poem by Yeats called 'The Second Coming' begins with the magical lines:

Turning and turning in the widening gyre
The falcon cannot hear the falconer;
Things fall apart; the centre cannot hold.

This poem was Yeats's cry of horror as he contemplated the First World War and saw what it would lead to. He used falconing gone wrong as a metaphor for man's violent desires escaping and flying out of control. Parallel to the scientific story in *White Eye* is the story of a falconer who frees her birds.

I mentioned earlier that the wedge-tailed eagle whose eyes, as it were, open the book is shot down to earth, crippled. It becomes a challenge for the main character, Diana, to train this injured eagle to fly again so she can return to her true element, the sky. This brings me to a final set of questions. What does the eagle symbolise? What was the eagle to the ancient Egyptians who painted its wings in their great sarcophagi? What was the eagle to the Aztecs?

"The wealth of the 21st century will be founded on biotechnology."

What does the eagle mean to the Hopi Indians? What does it mean to the Chinese who represent it in its esoteric form as the phoenix? What does it mean to the Indonesians who call it Garuda? What does it mean to the people of Zimbabwe who call it Chapungu? Why, according to western mythology, is an eagle the only creature whose eyes are strong enough to stare into the sun? We know perfectly well that no animal has eyes strong enough to do this. Why is the eagle the symbol of the Gospel of St John? Why in old Christian churches do you find an eagle carved on the pulpit? Surely the answer is the same universally. The eagle is one of those universal symbols recognised by all peoples of all races in all ages. For the eagle symbolises the divine spirit within humanity.

So finally I ask: are we not all of us in some respects eagles, earthbound, wing broken, but yearning for the rapture of flight?

Anne Summers

Former academic, journalist, head of the Office of the Status of Women, and publisher and editor of *Ms* magazine in the United States, Australian writer Anne Summers made her name with her 1975 feminist analysis of women's place in Australian history, *Damned Whores and God's Police*. The book was republished in 1994 with an added letter to the next generation of women, about the often forgotten struggles of 1970s feminism. Summers is now writing an autobiographical work.

24 January 1994

I want to take you for a while to a remote and distant country, a land which is vastly different from our own. It's one of that multitude of small nations we know we've heard of but can't quite recall exactly where it is. For a few minutes we will visit this land – a place where strange segregation exists between the sexes; where women are prohibited from being permanently employed as teachers or as public servants once they get married; where the night news on television is read by serious bespectacled men in suits while at the end of each bulletin a bikini-clad girl appears to talk about the weather; where women's higher pitched voices are considered to make them unsuitable for reading the news – it's thought they wouldn't sound authoritative enough and thus would not be believed; where there is no equal minimum wage so that women receive on average less than 60 per cent of what men make; where jobs are classified and advertised according to whether women or men or boys or girls can apply for them; where at parties the sexes congregate in different rooms and have such different conversations they might as well be speaking a separate language; where women are prohibited from being airline pilots because of a fear that once a month they might fly off course; where hurricanes and other natural disasters are named after women; where page 3 of the afternoon newspapers feature scantily clad girls as a daily news item; where the sounds of screams from suburban houses at night are greeted with shrugs of 'just another domestic' and largely ignored.

The country I am describing is in fact Australia – Australia as it was in 1975 when *Damned Whores and God's Police* was first published.

The process of updating and adding to that book afforded me an opportunity to revisit the Australia of the late 1960s and early 1970s and even I was struck by how vast the changes have been. The country I have just described is barely recognisable today; amazing changes have taken place. Look at the still rising participation of women in the workforce, especially of married women with young children, more than 50 per cent of whom are in some form of employment. Look at the jobs women do – piloting planes, running businesses, supervising factories, reporting on politics, heading unions, many in occupations that were simply not available to women 20 years ago.

And I'm not just talking about paid employment. I was struck by how many women were amongst the volunteer firefighters who came to New South Wales from around Australia to fight the January fires. Many of those I saw were middle aged or older as were many of the men, but that was no deterrent to their energy, their dedication, their sheer professionalism and their presence was no big deal. They were totally accepted.

In pointing to these changes, I don't want to suggest that we have solved all our problems, achieved all our goals and are living in some kind of feminist nirvana because clearly we are not. A great deal remains to be done and while we're talking about the jobs that women are now doing we should not overlook those peaks that women have still to climb. I can think of quite a few jobs a woman has yet to hold. For example, Prime Minister of Australia, Chief of the Defence Forces, CEO of a major listed corporation, chairman of a major listed corporation or even a minor one, Archbishop of Sydney or Melbourne or Brisbane or any other city. But to return to the positive, over the past week I've been interviewed at least a dozen times by hosts of radio programs around the country and I've been both astonished and gratified by the almost unbelievable change in attitude compared with the treatment I received when the book was first published.

"I can think of quite a few jobs a woman has yet to hold."

Back then I was treated with scorn or ridicule. I was patronised and mocked. Even most of the print media failed to take seriously what I was saying and the electronic media had a field day snickering snidely into their microphones at the notion that women might be demanding changes to the most fundamental order of things. Don't forget that only a few weeks earlier a newspaper had used the immortal headline 'Mum's the word as the big powwow begins' to describe the Women in Politics Conference in Canberra. No matter that much of the aggressive questioning back then concealed a certain nervousness, a dawning recognition that the old order was about to crumble and be swept away.

It was still very tough to be on the receiving end, to try and avoid sounding defensive, not to play into the interviewer's hands by becoming too aggressive. The interviews this past week could not have been more different and I should mention that almost all of them were conducted by men, many of whom were older than I am. What had changed, I realised, was that these men were acknowledging the seismic shift in gender relations of the past 20 years. What is more they were willing, even eager, to take a lead in championing those changes and in affirming that they were a good thing. One or two of them even thanked me for writing the book.

It never occurred to me when I sat for several years in the bowels of the Mitchell Library researching this book that it would become both a catalyst for change and a marker of what has in fact changed. Back then my main fear was whether or not I would be able to complete the book because it had grown so much from my original idea of a quickie text on how the Australian mateship ethos operated to the detriment of women.

The more research that I did, the more I realised how constrained Australian women had been throughout the entire period of European settlement. It very quickly became apparent that the only roles which offered women any kind of social approbation were those associated with the maternal function. The working title of the book became *God's Police* after I discovered that deliciously appropriate passage in Caroline Chisholm's 1847 pamphlet entitled 'Emigration and Transportation Relatively Considered'. In it she used the term 'God's Police' to describe what she considered to be the essential civilising agents for a rough and ready colony – wives and little children, good and virtuous women.

It is difficult to overestimate the influence that this way of thinking about women has had on the evolution of Australian society and on women themselves. It became synonymous with being Australian to believe that women were responsible for the emotional and moral wellbeing of those around them. This is what good women did, married or single. If they did not they must be bad. It also quickly became clear to me as I learnt more about our past that women had received almost as rough a deal from historians as they had from the society of the day. Most historians, be they practitioners of the traditional approach or the supposedly more radical labour historians, seemed to accept without question contemporary value judgments of women.

"It became synonymous with being Australian to believe that women were responsible for the emotional and moral wellbeing of those around them."

Nowhere was this more starkly apparent than in the writings about female convicts, almost all of whom were written off as debauched and degenerate creatures by every historian who had ever put pen to paper on the subject. No one bothered to explore first of all whether or not it was true or, if so, whether there was a reason for it. In fact the reason is plain for anyone to see who bothers to glance at the official papers of the time. It was avowed British Government policy to transport women to sexually service the men of the colony, including the male convicts.

Thus, while only men convicted of serious crimes were transported to New South Wales or

Van Diemen's Land, all women, however petty the crime, providing they were under 45 and healthy were transported to a country where, to quote a British parliamentary report on the subject, 'they were received rather as prostitutes than as servants'. Even so the women were badly outnumbered and as Governor Arthur Phillip had ignored his instructions to kidnap native women from any islands the ships of the First Fleet should visit, so these badly outnumbered women were subjected to virtual non-stop sexual abuse. For this they were condemned and in the words of Lieutenant Ralph Clark of the First Fleet 'vilified as damned whores'.

As the picture of our past became clearer to me I realised I had the material to provide an interpretation of our society which combined the classic categorisation of women in western civilisation as being either madonnas or whores with the specific story of Australia's history. I rang my publisher and asked whether he thought he could publish a book called *Damned Whores or God's Police.*

Today you might wonder whether or not there would be any doubt as it sounds such a very tame title but I should remind you that back then the shock threshold was considerably higher than it is today. It was only quite recently that the *Sydney Morning Herald* had begun to use words like pregnant and virgin, not to mention the words they use nowadays.

My book had now become a far bigger undertaking than I could have envisaged when I set out to try and explain why society treated women the way it did and why women went along with it. I was now going to try and take on the received wisdom of a number of academic disciplines, criticise most of the country's leading authors and intellectuals and generally set myself up to be pretty popular in this land that so loves tall poppies.

What I did not anticipate was that the world was ready for such a book. It came out towards the end of 1975, a year that had been designated by the United Nations as International Women's Year and a year in which Australian society and especially Australian women for the first time took a really good hard look at their lives. My book fell onto unexpectedly fertile ground.

Over the years I have had total strangers approach me and blame me for the breaking up of their marriages, just as I have had many more people write, ring or talk to me in person about how the book helped give them the courage to leave marriages or relationships in which they were unhappy. It may not surprise you to learn that the majority of the first category were men and that those in the second category were exclusively women.

It surprised me when I reread the book to realise just how much had changed and just how seriously out of date some of the contemporary chapters had become. I believe that the historical chapters still stand. Just to look at the welfare/social security area for a moment for a couple of examples. In 1975 when the book was published family allowances had yet to be introduced. There was no sole parent's pension. Single mothers were referred to as unmarried mothers, their offspring as illegitimate. It seemed to me that we should not paper over the past and I decided not to rewrite those chapters. I decided that they provided a perspective on a period in which they were written. If we constantly rewrite history to fit how we see things now, we forget how things used to be and, equally important to future scholars, how we used to see them. So I left the core of the book as it was and I have added a new beginning where I update and amplify and a new end.

All together I have added more than 30,000 words so that it is now almost like two books in one – the passionate perspective I produced 19 years ago and what I hope is an equally passionate modern addition. My new final chapter I have called 'Letter to the Next Generation'. In it I have attempted to reach out across the generational divide to talk to those young women who were born since the modern women's movement began its profound revolution and who are only dimly aware that the options and choices they now enjoy are but very recently won.

It seemed to me important that the feminists of my generation should tell our story so that a record exists of what drove us and of what we tried to do. No such link existed between us young women of 25 years ago and a previous generation of feminists and by the time we managed to find each other the gulf that separated us was simply too wide. This was brought home to me in quite dramatic fashion one day in 1974 when the phone rang and a quavering voice issued me an invitation to have afternoon tea with Ruby Rich. I was by then well into the research for this book otherwise I doubt very much if I would have known who Ruby Rich was.

Fortunately I knew by then that she had been an important pioneer of sex education. In 1926 she had cofounded the Racial Hygiene Centre of New South Wales, one of whose objects was the teaching of sex hygiene and the prevention and eradication of venereal disease and that she had spent her life working to save women from unwanted pregnancies and what we now call STDs. It was not an easy meeting. The friend who accompanied me and I made unusual concessions. We abandoned our usual jeans for frocks, a big ask in those days. We were deferential and respectful and a little awed at being in the presence of one of our forebears. Ruby Rich was in her late 90s, frail but alert and eager to give us advice, but the more than 70 years that separated us was simply too great. She could not comprehend the issues that moved us and we had little tolerance for the notions of racial purity and eugenics that marked her as a first-wave feminist.

I decided there and then that I was not going to wait until I was 98, if I live that long, to try and explain myself to 25-year-olds even though today it is rather different from the divide that separated me and Ruby Rich – at least our generations are contiguous. There is some chance of our speaking a similar language, of sharing similar values and goals and I believe the women's movement of the 1970s and '80s was one of the great social movements of our time, whose story certainly deserves to be told so that it is not forgotten.

"... let Australia evolve peacefully towards a republic that affirms the equality of women and men."

I'd like to conclude by saying that I'm grateful to Paul Keating for having brought me back to Australia a year or so ago. The experience of working in his office made these new chapters more relevant and more timely than would have been possible had I completed them as I thought that I would while still living in New York. Being back here has also made me face the fact that we as a nation are about to embark upon an important new journey as we formulate the kind of republic we wish to become. One of the important legacies of the women's movement must be that women become an integral part of that national debate.

We have a unique opportunity to build upon the progress of the past two decades by developing a vision of ourselves that embraces the absolute equality of the sexes and makes it part of the kind of nation we become. Just as the United States threw off the shackles of Britain with an affirmation that all men are created equal, more than 200 years later let Australia evolve peacefully towards a republic that affirms the equality of women and men.

SPEAKER: You wrote in your book that the family survives on the conscripted labour of women. I think society's definition of the family and women's role in maintaining it is still a problem that hasn't been solved. Would you like to comment on how far you think we've come on that subject in the last 20 years?

ANNE SUMMERS: You'll recall that in the original edition when I used the term 'the family' I put it in quote marks because I was trying to make the point that we have a sort of a notion in our heads about what the family is or at least ought to be, whereas in fact I was trying to argue that it is a social construct which has very many forms; people live in different types of family. I think that 20 years on we are more acknowledging and more tolerant of the fact that not everybody lives in a traditional nuclear form of family. In fact if you look at the statistics now only a minority of Australians still live in that way.

I think that we now acknowledge the fact that family is very much something we choose as well as what we inherit and that we make our own types of living arrangements. I think that women over the past 20 years have had to struggle very hard with the fact of what their own role should be within that construct – particularly as so many women are in the workforce and what has happened for so many women is that by taking on paid employment in addition to their family responsibilities they've simply taken on an additional job and have done two jobs instead of the one that perhaps existed in the traditional family set-up.

We use the phrase 'the double burden' to describe that situation and I think that one of the challenges over the next few years is going to be to work out how we, particularly women with children, can reconcile our working and our family lives in ways that are fair to all of us.

SPEAKER: In the book you make the comment that there is yet to be written a formal history of the women's movement in Australia. Is it likely that such a book will be written?

ANNE SUMMERS: I find it quite remarkable that we have failed to write our own history of a movement of such importance, a movement which has produced such dramatic social change and a movement which has been spearheaded by people who learnt the hard way that history belongs to those who write it and I don't understand why. It's not just true of Australia. It's true of the United States; it's true of Britain. There is no proper or current or comprehensive history of the women's movement anywhere. Compare that with, for example, labour history in this country, the number of books that have been written about conscription – there's probably 50 or 60 books on that four-year period way back in 1916 – and yet this great movement of two decades' worth of change rates a few articles and that's all.

Whether it's a matter of funding I don't know. But I hope that there is a young team of women out there or men who have the interest and the energy and perhaps they can get some publishing support. They should go round and interview people like us while we've still got our brain cells and can still remember. A lot of people have started it and no one's ever finished it. The National Library has a fantastic collection of the documents, the T-shirts, the badges, everything, but somebody has got to turn all that raw material into a living history.

Ranulph Fiennes

Britain's greatest polar traveller has led expeditions to both poles since 1969. Fiennes made the first circumnavigation of the world by the polar route on foot between 1979 and 1982. He has financed his journeys with lectures and books including *A Talent for Trouble*, *Where Soldiers Fear to Tread*, *Hell on Ice* and *Mind Over Matter*, co-authored with Michael Stroud, about the first unassisted crossing of Antarctica.

7 February 1994

I would like to talk about people who make a living or profession or career out of expeditions. There used to be a lot more than are around now. Certainly in the United Kingdom, as you are probably aware, things have changed. We used to be very good at exploring remote areas and also pretty much unbeatable at football and cricket – except in Australia.

Those three things have gone by the wayside of late and in the case of exploration there are now only six of us in Britain who make a living from doing expeditions. This is very sad and I would point the finger of blame at careers officers at schools who are so narrow-minded that they don't even offer it as an option.

There are three main questions which come to us on returning from expeditions. One of them nearly always comes from women's institutes and that is how do we go to the loo at minus 122 degrees fahrenheit. The answer to this is obviously of no relevance to you so I will not go into that one. They also ask why our toes keep falling off and not more obvious male appendages. But the main question is, of course, why do we do this for a living instead of some more easy endeavour.

I can trace my motivation back to when I was aged about one in Windsor in the United Kingdom at a time when the Germans were bombing it for no good reason and my mother got fed up with this and my father had just been killed in the war. So she moved all my sisters and me out to South Africa for 11 years without consulting us.

The educational standards over there in those days were a lot lower than they were in the United Kingdom. So when we got back, with me aged about 11 or 12, my mother wanted to educate me. The only place which would take people with such a low level was, of course, Eton College. My level was, in fact, so low that I couldn't even keep up with theirs, but for the five years I was there, there was at least boxing which didn't require too much nous and also stagopholy which is for people who have an edifice complex – people who like to climb tall buildings by night and put things on top of them.

My mother realised that if I stayed there, I was not going to be able to do the only thing which I had ever wanted to do since I was little, which was to command the Royal Scots Greys which my father had commanded when he was killed.

Unfortunately for me, in his day there were 600 grey horses and no A level exams but by the time I came along there were 60-tonne tanks and you couldn't get into Sandhurst to be an officer without these A level things. So, realising that Eton wasn't going to get them for me, my mother sent me to a college in Brighton. If you went there you definitely had your A levels when you came out the other end and I am not at all proud of having broken their record. I should explain this was not my fault, it was due to a lady at that time called Mary Quant who had just invented the world's first mini skirt and we had quite a lot of 15- and 16-year-old Norwegian girls at this college.

I failed the A levels twice. But luckily, as with most things in life, there was a sort of back door. In this case you could avoid Sandhurst by going to a place called Mons Cadet School which was a six-month boot camp and you got into the army the back way, as a second class officer, which I did. I joined the Scots Greys out in Germany, which was where all the British Army was, and there I spent five years in tanks learning how to retreat from the East German border. We never practised advancing once in five years. This tended to get tedious so when I saw a notice on the board asking for people to join a thing called the SAS I applied.

Nobody in those days knew what the SAS was. We all knew about Scandinavian Airline Services, but not SAS from a military point of view. I went over to Hereford which is where you go to get selected or in most cases not selected and there I found to my dismay about 200 soldiers trying to get in and 18 officers. All of them were built like brick houses, all of them – or a lot of them – had red berets, ex-paras, none of them came from the cavalry. They called me donkey walloper and I was secretly delighted when over the next ten days they were ruthlessly eliminated, I think because the staff were looking for people from a physical point of view, not from intellect. I was still there.

Unfortunately on the eleventh day they switched and I had to become very alert. If you had failed just one of their courses you were thrown straight out and I can remember one occasion when we were crossing the local river by night without any clothes on, for some military reason, and the next day I woke up late, very knackered. You were meant to get up at six, I woke up at about 11 o'clock and I feverishly reached for the envelope with the day's instructions at the bottom of the bed. That day we were to steal £180,000 from the local bank down in Hereford. I had Barclays, the other bloke had Lloyds.

I rushed down in civilian clothes and to my

horror the place was closed. I went around the back and the light was still on so I banged and luckily the manager came out. Very nice man, very naive and I explained to him – because truth is often the best policy – that I had been in Germany, I was trying to get into the SAS, so I had brought all my family silver and wanted somewhere secure to put it and he said, 'Well, we're extremely secure.' He showed me all these funny wiring devices and so on and I thanked him, copied everything down, carbon paper and I put my copy of the plans into the headquarters just on time.

The two of us had the rest of the day off, went up to Birmingham, saw a film, had a spaghetti dinner and I stupidly left my copy of the bank raid plans behind in the restaurant. The restaurateur, I suppose thinking he was a goody goody British citizen, told the police, gave them the copy of the plan and there was a ministerial inquiry. The whole of the Worcester and Herefordshire police had their leave stopped for the weekend in order to surround all twelve Hereford banks because I hadn't put which bank it was on the plan.

I was up before the commanding officer, a bloke called Slim, his father had been in Burma, and he said any more behaviour of this nature and I would be thrown straight out. I was quite relieved because I thought I already was, but in retrospect I think that they thought that I had left the plans in the restaurant on purpose in order to make trouble and they like that sort of person. If they had realised that I was just vague they would definitely have thrown me out. But I got the message and so I behaved very well for about six months of doing strange things in odd places.

At the end of which a friend of mine from Eton rang up. By then he was a wine salesman in the west country and he had been in a pub where he had heard the locals complaining bitterly because their village, a place called Castle Combe which had just been voted Britain's prettiest village by the Americans, had been descended on by Twentieth Century Fox in order to make a film called *Doctor Doolittle* with Rex Harrison. The villagers were trying to complain that their beautiful trout stream was being dammed up to make a lake for this film with 30-foot sandbags and concrete.

"Unfortunately the security guys had dogs all over the top of the dam, but having been at Eton he was up to this."

My friend decided to bring the outrage to the public attention by blowing up the dam the night before the film people arrived. Unfortunately the security guys had dogs all over the top of the dam, but having been at Eton he was up to this. He rented eight Alsatian bitches and put them upwind of the dam. Well, that was the plan. Something in fact went wrong with the bitches so he rang me up to ask if I would stand in. This was because he knew that I had a lot of explosives because I'd been on a course for two months where you learn to blow up as much as possible with as little as possible.

Because I was quite good at this I had a lot left over at the end of every day. It seemed pretty stupid to pass this back to the sergeant major so I put it in the boot where after two months it was full and sweating and so what better way of getting rid of it than this public-spirited gesture? Unfortunately everybody was caught. I was actually not caught in person. I had just been doing another course on escaping from dogs by night. But the car numbers were all recorded and I was put in prison. I was given six months probation and I was thrown out of the SAS back to my own regiment who were still retreating from the German border.

After yet another year of tanks and mud in Germany we saw another notice on the board which said: 'Anybody to apply to join the Sultan of Oman's forces.' They were fighting the communists coming in from the Yemen who were committing genocide amongst the Muslims that we were to work for. So, about 11 of us from the regiment went to see the colonel. I watched them all coming back out of his office looking gloomy because he had turned them down as being too valuable to the regiment, but he signed my papers instantly and I went off.

This was where I learnt to get a taste for travel in remote areas. We didn't do very well militarily in that area because when I had to leave after two and a half years we had lost 98 per cent of the entire countryside to the communists.

In the end I had to leave because of my lack of A levels and I found myself in London outside the safety of the khaki umbrella of the army. I put on my CV that I was an expert at leading free tanks in an easterly direction. There were no job offers and what could I do? I got married at the time so I needed to make a living. The only useful things the army had taught me were skiing and mountaineering and canoeing and so I thought, well, either I could be an Outward Bound instructor or start doing expeditions on a sponsorship basis.

I chose the expeditions, my wife went in with me on it and the only rule we had was that we would never pay anybody anything for anything. You may say this is scrounging. The correct terminology is sponsorship. So for about ten years we did expeditions in hot countries because that's more comfortable than in cold ones. Basically swamps and deserts and jungles and rivers – for instance up the River Nile, the longest river in the world, using a mini hovercraft. Did expeditions in British Colombia. All over the place. Twenty-four expeditions.

My literary agent is the boss of any expedition because he decides whether or not a plan on the drawing board can go ahead. It can go ahead if he can sell it to the BBC and the *Sunday Times* and so on because then you can get the sponsorship that you need. Not otherwise, and for one expedition alone we needed £29 million worth of equipment. Naturally, you end up having to do what he says and around about that time he pointed out that the public, in Europe anyway, for some obscure reason had stopped liking hot expeditions and only wanted polar ones. So, we had to go cold and my wife decided that we ought to start ambitiously by doing the first journey around the world through the poles which involved going through the North Pole, the South Pole, the Antarctic, the Arctic, the North-West passage and everywhere in between.

I didn't argue with her because I don't and I went off to do what everybody does if you're going anywhere on an expedition which is basically to find out who has been into that area before you and where they got killed so that you don't get killed in the same place. This is known as the reconnaissance stage. Normally you would go off and buy maps, but this plan of hers was 110,000 miles, which is a lot of maps. So I went to W.H. Smiths and was sponsored with a six-inch tin globe of the world in order to make a detailed route study of her proposal.

The white bits at the top and bottom were the crucial ones. Antarctica – your nextdoor neighbour – is bigger than the whole of China and India stuffed together. Far bigger than North America and yet there were only 700 people in it – and that was during the high season. Normally there were only about 200. It had only been crossed once in history under Sir Edmund Hillary, who had previously been up Mt Everest, and Dr Fuchs, the boss of the British Antarctic Survey. An enormous amount of experience and £2.5 million worth of support from their governments, and yet it still took them four years of solid planning and two years in Antarctica. Six years for just 2000 miles out of Ginny's 110,000 mile plan.

"Human beings are very badly designed for getting on with each other."

Another problem was the Arctic which, of course, is just a sea with a bit of ice floating around parts of it and this also had been crossed only once historically by Europe's greatest polar traveller, Wally Herbert, with three friends. And these four people had 29 years of previous polar experience. Ginny and I had spent an entire winter in Glasgow, but we still had a lot of polar training to put in. And before we could even get going on this we ran into three major problems.

One was the British Government who are a pain in the neck. They had never let any private expedition get to Antarctica ever and they weren't about to change their minds and they stop you finding out who the right bureaucrat is. Instead of putting 'Polar Desk' on the door it says 'Latin America Department'. We eventually ran the right man to earth, and he said that I would get his blessing on our proposal over his dead body, which I took to be a bureaucratic negative. For four years he continually shot down my letters of proposals and in fact after four years he did die and we did get to Antarctica.

The second of our problems was equipment. It took us seven years, working every day, every week, every month, without pay, to get the equipment that we needed together for nothing. We had eventually 1800 sponsors from 19 countries around the world.

The last problem was the worst – it was, of course, people. Human beings are very badly designed for getting on with each other. Basically they don't. If you put two of them into a confined space like your average home you get, at the moment, a one in three divorce rate which is just a symptom of this bad design factor. If you put them, as we would, into a 9-foot by 20-foot cardboard house in Antarctica 6000 feet above sea level, six months of total darkness without any TV, nothing except each other to look at, this is a very good test of compatibility. But if they fail it you can't get rid of them, or not by acceptable means. So, it is best to choose them very carefully before you go.

Who do you want? Who would you take if you were going to an area where for 4000 miles there's nothing. No hospital. Of course people are needed who can at least take out each other's teeth and appendix in a tent. We need people who can take carburettors to bits at minus 60 degrees with thick mitts and not fumble where a lost screw can't be replaced. People who can navigate without a compass because down in Antarctica the inconsistent variations between 18 and 110 degrees tend to make the compass unreliable. Also they must be able to map-read without a map. We had a map, of course, but it was all white and lacking in information. So, you might think that we advertised for doctors and dentists and radio operators and so on, but if you do this you get specialists and you all know what the Italian for specialist is – *prima donna*. You ask them to clean out the camp toilet and they don't like it because it's beneath them. Then I have to get a loo attendant as well.

So what we do is choose people who have no skills. They don't even need A levels and all we do require is they have to be good-natured – which is very difficult to find – and patient. Very patient indeed, almost thick. This is why we tend to look in ex-military areas for them. We ended up with 180 volunteers, we wanted about three and so we cut them down and we eventually got one who had been a Whitbread beer salesman for nine years in London and the other one had been teaching ladies how not to have their handbags stolen in supermarkets for ten years.

Their polar credentials were absent, but they had the right characters. You can't change people's characters. You can train them in skills and so the three of us became the land group to do this expedition of 110,000 miles. And we needed a radio base on the edge of the Antarctic and Arctic, which is the nastiest job of all. So I gave it to my wife Ginny. And we wanted one person who would be living with her and working with her for three years. Therefore I didn't want anybody who was physically attractive. We found a Yorkshireman but he was no good and so we ended up with Simon Grimes, now of Sydney, who was a wonderful bloke throughout the expedition. That became the manual part of the whole expedition, 48 people altogether.

During our expedition we became the first people to reach both poles, north and south, across the whole of the Antarctic, the Arctic and everywhere in between. On route we held major shows, one of which about 15 years ago was when our ship, the *Benjamin Barring*, was just opposite the Opera House for ten days and we had a wonderful turn-out there. We gained export orders for the companies that had helped us – one way of paying them back. Since then we have done another nine expeditions, mostly unsupported. We hold the world record for travel towards the North Pole without any form of support.

In 1992 I got a panic call from Charlie Burton, one of the transglobers, who asked if I realised that the Scandinavians had announced that they were going to try the first crossing of the Antarctic continent without support. I had looked at that plan 11 years previous and I knew it was not possible because the Americans and Russians had tried it using machines and found that no machine designed by man was sufficiently fuel-efficient to cross the continent without support. Huskies couldn't do it. Humans certainly couldn't do it. But because the Norwegians were trying we thought we had better go anyway and we set out in '92 and by a lot of luck and other things we finally managed to cross the continent from the Atlantic to the Pacific. We set out each towing 450 pounds. That is compared with a man's load in Scott's expedition of 250 pounds and that's why we were a lot slower.

But we did eventually make it. The scientific work is being analysed, mostly physiology, a study of slow starvation under stress. All the blood and urine samples have gone to Russian and American universities. When they are back they will be uniquely valuable to nutrition, mainly for third world countries and also for top-rate athletes. The other side of it is that we raised money. In 1986 Prince Charles, who has been patron for 20 years, asked, 'Who are we raising money for?' and I said, 'We don't.' He said, 'Well, you ought to be.' So we started and have now raised £3.2 million for the Multiple Sclerosis Society and we have built Europe's first research centre for MS in Cambridge with 12 neurologists.

Frederick Forsyth

Forsyth has written nine novels and sold 50 million copies, beginning with the brilliant thriller *The Day of the Jackal* in 1971. His early career as a journalist gave him an eye for accurate detail and some of his subject matter – in *The Dogs of War*, for example – came from his time reporting undercover in Biafra. Although he has announced his retirement many times, his latest novel, *Icon*, appeared in 1998.

24 June 1994

In the first days of 1970, I found myself destitute and without a job and without a flat and without a car and without any prospects, having prior to then been perfectly happy as a foreign correspondent for a number of newspapers and magazines and the Reuters News Agency. And being, so to speak, in extremis or de profundis, I thought, well, I had better do something. And so, like everybody else who eventually ends up writing novels I realised that all useful occupations had eluded me and there was nothing left for it but to be a writer.

So I sat down at a typewriter and I wrote a book called *The Day of the Jackal* which I thought little of at the time. Being a no-hope author I had a no-hope agent, such is the way of the world. The man couldn't sell ice cream in the Sahara, but I gave it to him anyway and went back to journalism and he duly got me four rejection slips. Well, three slips to put it bluntly and a letter. I wish I had kept the letter because it said, 'We have read this with considerable attention and we feel it has no reader interest.' And back came the manuscript.

By about September the chap said to me, 'Look, I've really got a much more promising novelist under my wing and I think we ought to sever relationships and here's your manuscript back.' So I said, 'Thank you, very much.' And I just happened to know a chap called Harold Harris who was then editorial director for Hutchinsons. I knew him socially so I went along to him and inveigled my way into his presence and said, 'Look, I know this is a bit cheeky. I've got a manuscript.' And his eyes glazed as they do. 'Oh, God, an unsolicited manuscript and he's in my office. I'll fire the secretary tomorrow.'

The reason that it had been turned down – I think – is that people had been reading the first chapter and working out that this was a book about a chap trying to shoot Charles de Gaulle and Charles de Gaulle was very much alive and in retirement in France and so what is the point because we know that it cannot work and therefore there is nothing to write about and so we will chuck it out. So they chucked it out.

This guy actually did take the trouble to go through it and he called me up on the Monday and said, 'If you'd like to be here at four o'clock we'll talk about a contract.' I thought, Wow, published! When I got there he said, 'Actually, I'd like to talk about a three-novel contract, this one and two more. Have you any other ideas in your head?' So of course, lying like a dog I said, 'Good Lord yes, oh, coming out of my ears.' 'Good,' he said, 'can I have a couple of synopses by nightfall?' So I thought, well, what do I know about? I know about France, but I can't do France again. I know Germany, been in Germany. I had attended a trial of a concentration guard once. I thought, Yes, Mossad hunting down Eichmann, sort of do a repeat of that. Do a runaway Nazi. What else do I know about? Mercenaries. I spent a bit of time in West Africa living off rice, lizards and sleeping in rain ditches and generally associating with these lumbering psychopaths. So I went back and I said, 'Look, we can do Nazis or mercenaries.' He said, 'I'll have Nazis first, and mercenaries second.' I said, 'Thanks very much.' That November de Gaulle died, poor old thing, so he never saw it.

"I realised that all useful occupations had eluded me and there was nothing left for it but to be a writer."

Let us come a little further up to date, to my book *Fist of God*. I think like most of you I sat through the Gulf War as the proverbial couch potato. There was the big screen in the corner of the room and there was the control button and I suppose we all sat and we watched the generals in their starched fatigues which had never seen desert dust, pointing to maps and saying chaps going there and there. Planes flying through the sky, flat top carriers plunging up the Gulf.

Towards the end I began to think, this is a wonderful production. I don't know whether it is Mr Turner or whether it is Warner Bros but someone is giving us a hell of a production here. I was surprised really that Tom Cruise didn't come on, supported by Gene Hackman. When finally the last image of the last carrier and the last fighter bomber and the last creased general faded from the screen I sat there and I looked at the darkened screen and I thought, Gentlemen, gentlemen, I don't believe you. It couldn't have been that easy, it couldn't have been so flawless. Wars are never flawless and then I began to ask questions. That's fatal. It comes from the journalistic background, this inability to believe a word you're told by authority – scepticism, if you wish, coupled with a bump of curiosity.

I began to think, how can it be that these American satellites – which they told us with enormous pride they'd spent billions on and were so sophisticated that they could actually read the number plate of a car in the desert from space – manage to overlook 200,000 Iraqi warriors poised on the border of Kuwait? Were we taken by surprise? And why did Ms Averil Glaspie, the American ambassador, tell Saddam Hussein to his face – and on camera – that America didn't give a toss whether he went into Kuwait or not and 48 hours later we were all consumed with moral indignation. Or were we?

And then I wondered about the brotherly ties of love and friendship that existed between the people of Kuwait and the people of Australia or anywhere else. Then I wondered about the necessity of restoring the deeply democratic Sabah regime that had just imprisoned the entire opposition. I began to wonder whether there wasn't a hidden agenda and the more I pushed and the more I shoved and the more I used my journalistic wiles to find out what really went on behind the scenes, the more it occurred to me that there were a lot of secret agendas. That it wasn't like we were told at all.

I discovered, for example, that about the spring/summer of 1990 the West generally, in the form I suppose of London and Washington and some analysts and some politicians and some generals, had become deeply perturbed by the power and the threat of the war machine that Saddam Hussein was building up or had built up ironically through purchases mainly made to him by the developed West. It was clear that he had been very close to having an atom bomb of his own. He also had awesome stocks of poison gas which we'd seen him use on the Kurds and on the Iranians. We hadn't been too fussed about the Iranians but the idea of them using it on the Brits and the Americans of course is quite unacceptable. The germ warfare program was proceeding apace.

He also had one million and a quarter men under arms and the fourth largest standing airforce in the world. I say standing because it seldom flew. I wondered whether in fact a decision had not been made that at the first conceivable and viable opportunity that war machine ought to be destroyed and wouldn't it be a juicy opportunity if he invaded Kuwait and gave us the choice and the chance to do exactly that.

I began to move towards the theory that probably that was roughly what had happened.

I decided there was a story in this war so I built this little story basically around four men, one of them a British special forces officer, Mike Martin. Mike Martin is fictional. That said, there have been expatriates born and raised for example in the Arab world who later in life have been able to pass for Arabs. I know that two SAS officers did penetrate Baghdad during the war disguised as Arabs. They were on in/out missions but they got away with it, they both returned home and they were not perceived. Therefore it seems to me feasible that you could actually find an Englishman, particularly with an Arab background and upbringing and perhaps an Indian grandmother giving him the dark complexion, who could pass among Arabs for an Arab. It's been done. After all Sir Richard Burton, I don't mean Elizabeth's ex-husband, I mean the explorer Sir Richard Burton, did make the pilgrimage to Mecca in the last century disguised as an Arab. He spoke the language so well and could pass for an Arab in his day. It has been done. It can be done.

Mike's younger brother Terry, the academic, they exist. Likewise the Iraqi colonel Badr, Osman

Badr, who had been at school in that little prep school in Baghdad back in the '50s with the English boys. The American fighter pilot is another fictional character but he is based upon an existing American fighter pilot. The fighter squadron, the 336 tactical fighter squadron, does exist. I visited with them and flew with them in Goldsboro, North Carolina. Colonel Steve Turner was indeed their commanding officer and he did tell General Horner to blow himself which is unusual but he got away with it. He actually went up from Lieutenant Colonel to Colonel which is a sign perhaps of General Chuck Horner's democratic approach to military matters. These four then are the inner core of the story and it is really about what happened to them, what they did, what they did to each other, who lived, who died and then around them is floating a peripheral ring of other sub-plots. The gun, that amazing 180-metre barrel, one-metre calibre Babylon gun, did exist. It is not fiction and the whole of the first chapter isn't fiction.

"[Saddam] had the fourth largest standing airforce in the world. I say standing because it seldom flew."

Jerry Bull, whom I met, did invent and design the Babylon gun. The trouble was he thought, because he was a dreamer, that his Babylon gun would be used for launching packages of instrumentation into space. He knew it couldn't be used as a conventional artillery piece because it couldn't move side to side or up and down. When he learned that Saddam Hussein had not a fraction of interest in science, in space, he worked out what it was really going to be used for.

Then there was the question of the isotope separation. The preparation by Saddam's scientists of the necessary quantity of bomb grade uranium 235. That's not fictional at all. There *was* the question of whether we did or didn't have an agent inside Baghdad. To this day, I can't say, Yes, we did. I think we did. I talked to the men who control that area in the CIA and SAS and they both looked benign and smiled as they do and tapped the sides of their noses and the Englishman said, 'Well, Freddy, old boy, if you want to believe it I suppose you can.' I said, 'Are you denying it?' He said, 'No.' I said, 'Are you confirming it?' 'No.'

So I think we had somebody inside Baghdad because I know we were getting information that couldn't have come from satellites and high flying aircraft and radio intercepts. There had to be somebody in there. Twice we were actually given the overnight location of Saddam Hussein. Twice we bombed those overnight locations. Twice we were wrong. He wasn't at home. And then suddenly an order came from Washington, stop immediately. Complete revocation of the order to kill Saddam Hussein. Saddam Hussein must and will live and rule Iraq. If you want to find out why, read the book.

Then Mossad, what the hell was Mossad up to? I don't believe the Israelis were sitting on their thumbs all this time and who really destroyed the Scuds in the western desert of Iraq? At the end of the war they said it was air power. Two years later the Pentagon admitted they hadn't destroyed one. By then I had already discovered it was the SAS who destroyed the Scuds, up to a hundred of them, on rolling in and out missions, lying in the desert, hiding out by day, watching by night and as these Scuds elevated themselves into fire position using TOW or MALAN anti-tank missiles to destroy them.

In an outer ring come the bits you will recognise. Schwarzkopf, of course, is there, General Chuck Horner is there, Buster Glosson and his deputy are there, Sir Peter de la Bilière is there, Maggie Thatcher, George Bush.

One last anecdote about which again you may say, how the hell did you find that out? The answer is: I'm pretty certain I'm right. I was told that I'm right and, no, I'll never be able to prove it. Why didn't Saddam Hussein ever use poison gas on the allies? He had no scruple about using it. When we burst through those sand walls into lower Kuwait and lower Iraq, row after row of Iraqi artillery pieces were found abandoned and beside them stacks, mountains of gas shells and not one had been fired. It struck me that surely some gun commander would have fired if he'd been ordered to fire. Someone who was at the meeting told me that on 7 February (at the height of the air war but before we marched on 24 February), James Baker, the American Secretary of State, told Tariq Aziz – remember him, the little dumpy fellow, the Foreign Minister of Iraq – to his face in Geneva, 'If you use poison gas against the GIs, we will nuke Baghdad', and he wasn't joking.

Kate Grenville

Grenville has given voice to some unforgettable female characters in the story collection *Bearded Ladies* and her novels *Lilian's Story*, winner of the 1984 Australian/Vogel Literary Award, and *Joan Makes History*. Another novel, *Dark Places*, took up the story of Albion Gidley Singer, the disturbing misogynist in *Lilian's Story*. Grenville lives in Sydney with her husband, the cartoonist Bruce Petty.

18 July 1994

Dark Places is a very dark book and it took me a long time to write. It's a very dark subject and those who've read it now tend to look at me as if I've been through a long, debilitating and rather unsightly illness – as if I've come out in a kind of pustular rash and now that it's finished they say, 'Are you feeling better now, dear?' I reassure them that, yes, now that I've got it out of my system I am much better, thanks.

But it's not quite true because I think writers, no matter what stage of the writing process we are at, can always find an excuse to be gloomy and pessimistic. It's part of the job description.

If you have just finished a book, as I have, you are completely convinced to the depths of your heart that you will never write another book. If by any chance you do manage to write another, naturally it won't be any good. If by any chance it's a reasonable book, it probably won't get any reviews. If it does get reviews, of course they'll be very bad reviews. If it does happen to get good reviews, it will only be because the reviewer has felt sorry for you. Naturally no-one will buy the book. If they buy it, it is only because they got your book mixed up with somebody else's. Writers can always find a reason to be pessimistic.

But there are some good bits about writing and the very best bit is standing in the shower in the morning with the steam rising up around you and in the mist your next book takes shape and it's perfect. It's wise, it's witty, it's honest, it's elegant and naturally it's going to be a best seller. The very worst bit is when you have to get out of the shower, put your clothes on and actually sit at the desk. That bit is terrible.

The other very good bit, the bit that makes up for all the years of anguish, is when you write 'Kate Grenville, July '94' in a beautiful brand-new copy of one of your books.

I think one of the problems of being a writer is that you get absolutely no feedback. It is a cliché about being a writer that you are locked in isolation. The only time writers make the paper, usually, is either if they win a prize, particularly if they're squabbling about a prize, or when they die. After all, how many times have you seen the headline 'Writer writes masterpiece' or even better 'Chapter 7 nearly finished'?

The main thing you need to become a writer, it seemed to me when I was young, was to have a very interesting list of eccentric things that you had previously done for putting on the back flap. You know the kind of thing. You can probably think of much better ones that I can. Kate Grenville perhaps taught Hindustani in Uzbekistan, sold hamsters door to door, sailed single-handed around the world in a kayak made from an old shower curtain. So my first step to becoming a writer was to be a failure at as many other jobs as possible.

My first job was with the Australia Council and I had to do things like book the Commonwealth cars and book the plane tickets and yes, Don Burrows, it was I who stuffed up your flight on 25 March 1972 and left you stranded at Mascot on a wet night, and it may be that I changed the course of Australian music forever by failing to book the Commonwealth car for Jeannie Lewis in 1973.

"My first step to becoming a writer was to be a failure at as many other jobs as possible."

When I finally decided to become a writer it was because I had been a teacher for a while and I had these terrible recurrent dreams which any teacher will recognise, I'm sure: 300 or perhaps 3000 faces are turned expectantly towards you, 3000 pens are poised and you realise you've forgotten to prepare the lecture and the only thing in your bag is a 1968 bus timetable. So when that started to happen I decided that it couldn't be worse to be a writer.

I did think, though, that there were a lot of rules about being a writer and I used to read books about what other writers said they did. I read that Camus, the French author, said you must write every day. Henry James said that you must 'observe perpetually'. Hemingway said that it was 90 per cent perspiration and 10 per cent inspiration. Flaubert said that it was necessary to be bourgeois in your life so that you could be revolutionary in your art. This was all very well and good, but none of it had anything to do with me.

My circumstances were that I had no idea what I wanted to write about, only that I thought I wanted to write. I had a husband, a household, two beautiful children and also two goldfish, a cat, two mice and about a million shiny cockroaches down in the kitchen. I would bet any money that Hemingway never had to vacuum Rice Bubbles out of the back of the couch. I'm quite sure that Flaubert never had to fish the Batman socks out of the mouse cage.

Virginia Woolf came close to it. She said: 'Every time I took up my pen to write, I found a shadow falling across my page. That shadow was the angel in the house.' I suspect that Virginia Woolf probably never had to make a birthday cake in the shape of a shark but she was getting on to the right idea. Actually the writer who really has said it, I think, is the Melbourne author, Carmel Bird. She has written several terrific books and she says in one of them: 'You can have a finished story or you can have a clean house. The choice is yours.'

"I would bet any money that Hemingway never had to vacuum Rice Bubbles out of the back of the couch."

I'd like to go one better and think that one could have stories *about* clean houses. Classics that might be written: Dickens might have written *Bleak Housework*, for example; Miles Franklin could have written *My Brilliant Housework*; Christina Stead, if she had only thought of it, would have written *The Man Who Loved Housework*; and of course Shakespeare should have written *Hamlet, Prince of Housework*.

Dark Places is not about housework, although when our eight-year-old son looked at the cover the other day and read 'Dark Places', he thought for a long time and he said, 'Is that a book about that little dark spooky bit underneath the dining room table?' I had to tell him that, no, it was not, but I think in a way he's right, because every house does have that dark, spooky bit underneath the dining room table and this book is about that dark spooky bit. This book is a sort of torch which one might shine momentarily into that dark spooky bit.

It's set in about 1900 and its hero – hero is probably not quite the right word – its protagonist, I suppose, is a man called Albion Gidley Singer. From the outside there's nothing wrong with Albion Gidley Singer at all, he is a completely solid man in his beautiful suit and his wing collar, completely full of confidence, absolutely not a flicker of doubt but, of course, inside Albion Gidley Singer is a shrivelled, shrunken, dwarfish little person, a self that has never been allowed to blossom into fulfilment. He has to cover up this little inadequate person with a show of being super confident. His daughter, a female version of himself, eventually becomes a victim of his abuse.

Dark Places is connected to *Lilian's Story* even though the two books are quite independent of each other. If you like, *Lilian's Story* is the light place and *Dark Places* obviously is the dark place and really the two go together. If you have a source of light you automatically have a shadow and I think that is really why I wrote the book. I loved writing *Lilian's Story*. Out of anything I have done, it was the book I most enjoyed writing. It was a pleasure to be living in the persona of that character but I was aware when I was writing it that there was another side to the story and much though I did not want to write it I could not leave it alone. It was like a scab that I had to keep scratching at.

The shadow had to be written about. I had to go in there and explore it and that is why I have taken on the somewhat unpalatable task of exploring not just what Lilian's father did to her but the much more difficult and, I think, interesting question of why. Child abuse is all around us. Every morning in the *Herald* there is some new example of, usually, men taking their children off and shooting them and then themselves, and stories of sexual abuse. It is not only *out there*, though. I think it is within us too. I do not think any of us would be honest if we said that there was not a dark place inside us. The thing about those dark places is that if you ignore them and turn away they get bigger and darker and scarier.

Writing this book was a very scary process at times and I kept putting it aside and trying to pretend that I did not have to write it. But once I had actually got myself to the end of it, I felt like somebody who had been in a very dark room fighting some nasty, scaly, slimy wild creature and when I finally finished the book and could flick the light on I found that in fact it was just a tiny little, rather repellent but not actually all that frightening bit of slime. I think that most of us can understand Albion's problem which is that he feels that the real self is not going to be acceptable and that therefore he has to manufacture a mask and the mask is the only thing he dares to show to the world. Of course, what that means is that inside, that real person becomes more and more frightened of revealing himself and I think that fear very quickly turns to hatred and cruelty towards the outside, people around him.

I have often been asked why I had to write it in the first person. One answer is that if I had not got in there and told it from the first person I would not have felt that I was telling the truth about it. Albion does not think he is a monster. *We* all do, but he does not think he is a monster. He has perfectly good reasons for doing all the things he does. The other thing, of course, is that first person allows it to be funny. The joke in this book is that Albion does not get the joke. In *Lilian's Story* I think the reader was laughing with Lilian but with this book the humour is in the gap between Albion's perception of things and our perception. We can see how grotesque he is and he cannot.

"I do not think any of us would be honest if we said that there was not a dark place inside us."

It is a sort of 3-D. It would be interesting to know what this book would be like if in fact instead of being *Dark Places* by Kate Grenville, it was *Dark Places* by, say, Frank Moorhouse or Rodney Hall or Peter Carey. One would read the whole book differently, I think, and I suspect in fact that only a woman has the freedom to write this kind of book which is a parody of something which a man perhaps could not find the distance from, but maybe I am wrong.

When I was writing it, it seemed to me that it would be very difficult to sustain a whole book in the voice of a man and it surprised me how easily it flowed out. I began to wonder whether I was some kind of verbal transvestite that a male voice came so extraordinarily easy to me. But when I thought about it I realised that actually women are bilingual. We are all bilingual, I think, because as women together, we have our own sort of language, we have our own kind of patois like a lot of oppressed classes of people, which is slightly foreign to men. We can also, of course, fluently speak manspeak when we have to function in the world. So in fact it was not that difficult for me to slip into malespeak for this book. The male voice I think is still the overwhelming one in our culture. It is the primary one. The female voice is always the secondary one, the aberration. In a way the hard thing for a woman writer, I think, is to find her female voice and to write truly out of that because that female voice often does not take the form of a logical sequence of ideas. So in fact it was almost frighteningly easy to become a man for this book.

Just before I gave this book to the publisher, the night before, I had a very vivid dream. I was standing beside a very deep, swiftly flowing, clear river and I was holding the manuscript of this book, 300 or 400 pages of typescript, and as I stood there they started to fall out of my hands into the water and be swept inexorably away. I was absolutely terrified. 'I'm not ready to let it go!' I plunged in after it, plunged in up to my shoulders in the water but the more I plunged, each page dived further down as if they deliberately wanted to get away from me. It was a very panicky dream but when I woke up I realised that in the dream I had gone through some rite of passage and I was now prepared for the book to be launched, as it were, on the stream.

#!?

SPEAKER: How do you write? Do you sit down and work regularly or do you wait for the muse?

KATE GRENVILLE: The muse is a very infrequent visitor at our house. It probably visits the other end of the house where my husband is doing drawings but it does not often visit my room. We have two young children so, much as I would love to work 9 to 5 Monday to Friday, that has not been possible until really this year because they have been too young. So I write when I can.

Elizabeth Jolley said that she mastered 'the art of the little note' by which she meant that little thing scribbled on the back of an envelope or the back of the Woolies' docket. I also, like Elizabeth Jolley, now have a huge drawer bulging with dockets from Woolies on which I have written moments of inspiration, unfortunately usually illegible.

I usually begin by writing by hand because I am often embarrassed by what I write the first time. It just looks so stupid and feeble that I prefer to write it by hand because only I can read my own handwriting and even that only sometimes. But then I type it into the computer and it suddenly gets that very official public look but that is the point at which I can tinker around with it. I generally write a lot of drafts. I am not one of those people who can get it right first time. For *Dark Places* I was up to draft 20 when I had that dream of letting it go by the side of the river. I think with *Lilian's Story* I wrote about 12 drafts. So I just fit it in whenever I can really and I am looking forward to the next few years because now that the children are at school I will be able to work more regularly.

Jeffrey Archer

Britain's youngest Member of Parliament was forced to resign when a company he had invested in went bust. Lord Archer's first novel, *Not a Penny More, Not a Penny Less* (1976), was about four men who were swindled out of £400,000 and devised a scheme to get it back. The book sold 2 million copies and was the first of Archer's string of international bestsellers, including *Kane and Abel* (1979) and *The Fourth Estate* (1996). In 1998 he published *The Eleventh Commandment* and was planning to run for Mayor of London.

23 August 1994

I thought I would talk to you about the process of writing which came to me very late in life, late in the sense that most writers believe from a very young age that they are going to be writers and they believe that that is their destiny and that is how they will spend their entire life. I believed that I was going to be a prime minister and captain of the England cricket team. But having failed at both and left the House of Commons after five years, facing bankruptcy I began writing.

The surprising thing about a first book is that it is almost the easiest one to write, because you do not have any knowledge. It is a little like marathon running. It may surprise you to know that the New York marathon has been won on two occasions by men who have never run the marathon before and neither men ever won a marathon again. It is because once you have been through the process, you know what agony it is and you are much more frightened the second time than you were the first time as a total innocent.

As a first author, when you sit down to write you simply pick up the pen, paper, typewriter, computer, or whatever it might be, and just get on with it and pray; whereas the second time you know what hell it was and how hard it was to achieve what you did. Many people come to me and say, 'Jeffrey, I have finished my book', and I always ask them, 'How many drafts have you written?' and they say, 'What do you mean, I have written my draft and I finished it.' The average world-class writer does 10 to 15 drafts of a book. In my own case they are, every one of them, handwritten. There's no short cut.

I remember once in a restaurant in London I was going over to my table in the corner and I passed a table where there was a man sitting with a girl half his age who certainly was not his daughter and I remember as I passed the table he said, 'I bet Jeffrey Archer's knocked off another book this weekend.' I wanted to say to him but did not, if it was that easy, why don't you do it? What I want to get over is that it's very, very hard work.

You must not get depressed if you write a first book and don't succeed. I had 17 people turn down my first book, *Not a Penny More, Not a Penny Less*, and the eighteenth publisher, Jonathan Cape, gave me an advance of £3000. After a year's work, £3000 is not exactly a lot to live off.

The truth is that most first novels are lucky to sell 2000 copies. Publishers buy a first novel because they believe there will be a second one and a third one and a fourth one and therefore they will eventually gain back the investment they have put into the first book. But in my case they did not believe that. They thought *Not A Penny More, Not A Penny Less* was a one-off and that I would return to politics and that I would never write again. That first book in Britain sold 3000 copies which included 600 in Australia and 200 in New Zealand which will give you a rough idea of the sort of mass market I was meeting. There are more people in this room than bought my first novel in Australia.

I had written my second book, *Shall We Tell the President?*, when a lady from the Collins publishing house called Susan Watt, a very distinguished editor, said to me, 'Jeffrey, you are not a writer, you are a storyteller and you must sit down and write a story, it doesn't matter where it goes, just write a story.' I didn't really know what she meant but I sat down and wrote *Kane and Abel* and that was staggering because – I can tell you the figures, I dare to say them out loud now – my first book in Britain sold 3000 copies hardback, my second book in Britain sold 8000 hardback and my third book in Britain sold 158,000 in hardback. It can happen that way – *Kane and Abel* just went berserk in both the United States and Britain.

I had sold *Shall We Tell the President?* for $200,000 and at that time when I was penniless, absolutely stony broke, it was everything to me, and I signed a clause in the contract that said I had to sell the next book for $200,000 if they wanted it. Now, is that not weird? The reason I did that was because the head of the publishing house in America was such a nice man and had stood by me when I was down and paid the $200,000 and believed in me, so I let him have an option for $200,000 and he got the sack two weeks before I presented the book.

It being the United States, the new man was determined to have nothing to do with any authors. He turned down the option for $200,000; it sold four weeks later for $3,700,000. He also got the sack. The under-bidder was a lovely publishing house in the United States called Random House and the chairman was Larry Hughes, a really glorious man, and he under-bid. He rang me that evening at the hotel I was staying in and said, 'Jeffrey, I just want to tell you, a year today this book will be number 1 in every country on earth and I should have bid $4,000,000 but of course I could not risk it.' I have written several books since – and now the latest one, twelve short stories, *Twelve Red Herrings*.

I now have to put an asterisk by my short stories to show when they are real because the ones that I've picked up going around the world people don't believe and you have got to actually put an asterisk. The only three I have made up are totally believable; the nine with asterisks by them you are just not going to believe. In fact the second one, 'Cheap at Half the Price', the story of a lady who decides to con – that is the only word I can use – her husband and her lover into buying a $1,000,000 necklace, is true and when people tell me what an amazing story it is, I say you could not make it up.

When I arrived in the United States for my third book, I had never been able to get on a big program. In the United States you have got to get on to the *Today Show* or *Good Morning America* or the third one which is on CBS. If you do not get on one of them that you are dead. If you get on the *Today Show*, not only will you pick up every big show in Chicago, Los Angeles, Cleveland, Ohio, San Francisco, anywhere you are, it is also a farcical fact that you will hit as many people in three minutes as you will if you had gone to every other show in the United States.

"There are more people in this room than bought my first novel in Australia."

If you are a world famous author it is easy, but if you are unknown, what a struggle it is. Finally, I think more because I had nearly gone bankrupt and because I had been a Member of Parliament, they agreed to put me on the morning segment between 7.24 and 7.30, six minutes, but they told me I had to share it with two other people, so we would get two minutes each and the people I was to share it with were to be Billy Carter and Mickey Mouse.

Mickey Mouse was celebrating his fiftieth birthday and Billy Carter was launching Billy's Beers, so I arrive at the studio, got my best suit on, best shirt, new tie, the whole thing. I am all ready and I know that I have got to get in a mention of *Kane and Abel, Kane and Abel, Kane and Abel*, I have got to get it and millions of people must know about it by the end – *Kane and Abel, Kane and Abel*, I have got to get this in.

So we go into the green room, the three of us and the guy comes in and says, 'Okay, we'll be doing Mr Carter first, then we will be straight into Mickey Mouse and then we will be doing Mr Author, no, no, no, Archer, you are doing this religious book, *Kane and Abel*.' I knew it was not going to be a good day. 'I just have to tell you, Jeffrey, Jeff, can I call you Jeff, I just have to tell you, Jeff, that nobody has read it but we hear it is great.' I'm now holding my breath.

On goes Billy Carter and to do him justice he was very good on selling the beers, but there was a problem. He took two minutes and fifty seconds to sell the bloody beers, so we are now down to three minutes and ten seconds and on goes Mickey Mouse. I have to tell you, in all my years in politics and in books, I have dealt with some professionals, but Mickey Mouse is a pro and he took two minutes and twenty seconds.

The other tradition in the United States which is a tricky one is you do not actually meet the person who is interviewing you until you sit down. So if you have known them for years and got on with them for years that is fine, but I had never seen this guy, David Hartman, I had never seen him in my life, so I went in and sat down and I had got 50 seconds.

I had not learnt by then – my God, it taught me – to ignore the question and give the answer you want. He said, 'How very nice to meet you.' 'Thank you,' I said – 15 seconds. 'Are you enjoying this visit to New York?' 'Yes, I am' – 30 seconds. I got off the screen 50 seconds later and never mentioned the name of the book because he had not read it and did not want to admit it.

Now if he were to say to me 'Have you had a good trip?', I would say 'Yes, and one of the most pleasurable things was that as I flew over I noticed a lot of people on the plane reading *Kane and Abel* and I know how much you enjoyed it. Let us see you deny you even read it, you bastard.' But I was naive in those days and my publicity lady was not exactly pleased with me when I got back in the 72-foot hired limousine to take me off to Chicago and do an afternoon radio show. The book went to number 1 in three weeks. The American people, God bless them, being a little more intelligent than the *Today* program, very kindly put it to number 1 and it is an irony of that country that when I arrived in Los Angeles it was number 1 and the *Today Show* rang up.

You have got to believe this story. All three morning programs rang up and said, we want him to fly back, we will give him the whole six minute section, certainly. That is fine, we accept that, they love people who are at number 1, but I love the way the *Today* program said, 'Of course, Jeffrey will come to us because we gave him such a good start to get him to number 1.'

In this country television hosts do meet you before and I wish to pay tribute to one who was extremely kind to me when I was unknown and did read *Kane and Abel* and did believe in it, actually read *Not A Penny More, Not A Penny Less* and did believe in it. That was Mike Walsh, who was very kind to me over many years and indeed launched me in Australia in that sense.

I got a shock with him, because I was over here for a book later than *Kane and Abel*, it could have been *The Prodigal Daughter* or *First Among Equals*, and he had already agreed to have me on the show, he very kindly had me on every time I came over. This time it was to be Malcolm Fraser, Ella Fitzgerald and myself and I was to go on first, Ella Fitzgerald second and the former Prime Minister was to go on third. I'm innocently driving around in the car in the afternoon, signing books, and it was announced on the radio that Mike Walsh's show had been axed. Very unusually they were allowing him to do his last show and he rang me up and said, 'I am switching the order, I am putting Mr Fraser first, then Ella Fitzgerald, I am going to do you last.' He allowed me to do the last

"The guy comes in and says, 'Okay, we'll be doing Mr Carter first, then we will be straight into Mickey Mouse and then we will be doing Mr Author, no, no, no, Archer."

ever interview. I cancelled everything that afternoon and prepared because I knew more people would be watching the *Mike Walsh Show* that night than had probably ever watched it in the past and indeed it was a very dramatic occasion because as you can imagine he was very worked up. I would like to pay tribute to him and what a very fine television broadcaster he was.

I go back to the point I made at the beginning about drafts, for anyone who imagines it's easy to write a book. Also, I'd like to talk just for a moment about the discipline. I'm very much a lark and my wife's an owl. I like to rise at 5 and start at 6 and I write from 6 o'clock until 8 and take a two-hour break. I write from 10 until 12 and take a two-hour break; from 2 until 4 and take a two-hour break; and from 6 until 8, have a light supper and go to bed by 9.30–10.

The first draft I write – handwritten – is probably 2000 words, that will be in the first two hours and that is the only original writing of the day. I then put the 2000 words – which is probably ten pages, eight pages – on large Oxford pads and I rewrite straightaway, and that eight pages probably becomes 14, but takes two sessions. That 14 pages is handed to a typist who types it during my two hours off and it's back on my table for the last session. And then I rewrite it with a pencil – I go over the typewritten script with a pencil – and then I have what I call a third draft, which is handed in to her, she types it, and it's put on one side and I never look at it again until I've got the whole book finished. So when I've got the whole book finished – which will take six weeks, about 40–42 days – I then have the third draft in typewritten form. And then I will take, probably, a two-month break and go back to it for the fourth draft, again, with pencil on the typewritten script done by my secretary. The last novel, *Honour Among Thieves*, was 17 drafts over a period of two years, taking just over 1500 hours.

The reason I know the hours is because so many people have asked me how long does it take. My wife bought me an hour eggtimer because it's very easy to kid yourself. If you're doing 6 to 8, 10 to 12, 2 to 4, 6 to 8, it's very easy to start at quarter past 6 and very easy to end at quarter to 8, which is half an hour cheating. And if you do that four times a day, it's two hours. If you do it seven days a week, it's 14 hours and if you do it for a month, it can be 40 to 50 hours; you kid yourself. Whereas if you look at the egg timer, it says, oh, no, Jeffrey, you've still got another 30 minutes to go. And the egg timer is a very good discipline because very few people actually start bang on the first minute. I sometimes go to two hours five, two hours six and I sometimes end at 1.55. I find I can't actually concentrate, flat out, on original work for more than two hours. My wife, God bless her, can do four or five hours, but I can't.

! ?

SPEAKER: Lord Archer, in your latest book you have an unusual dedication to Chris, Carol and Alison. Can you tell me about this?

JEFFREY ARCHER: Every author has the privilege of dedicating their book to whomever they like. All people waste their money when they have a lot of it, some get dancing girls, others get yachts, some get planes. I buy art – I'm art mad – and I've been a collector now for 25 years and I have 400 or 500 paintings. And I might say I've had the very great privilege to buy several pictures here because of a quite outstanding art dealer you have in this country – I think one of the best in the world – Philip Bacon of the Bacon Galleries in Brisbane. He is quite one of the finest men I have ever met in my life and he's also one of the best dealers I've ever met in my life. I have an Arthur Boyd, a Ken Done and three Glovers, thanks to him. They've taken 20 years of collecting.

The book is dedicated to Chris, Carol and Alison. Chris Beetles of the Chris Beetles Gallery, Alison who's his assistant, and Carol who's his wife, and it's a thank-you to them for all their kindness over the years helping me with my collection. And one of the stories, 'Not For Sale', is loosely based on something Christopher told me and the hero in it – if he's a hero – is loosely based on Chris himself.

SPEAKER: I'm a monarchist but a lot of people feel that Australia should become a republic. What would you say Australia ought to do?

JEFFREY ARCHER: It's a tradition in politics, and rightly so, that you do not when visiting another country talk about their political system or their political beliefs. I think this is a correct procedure. I believe the Australian people have every right to make whatever decision they wish to make on this subject. Naturally you will find that there are a lot of people in Great Britain who would be disappointed – that won't surprise you – but it has got nothing to do with me or them. The decision will always be yours.

E. Annie Proulx

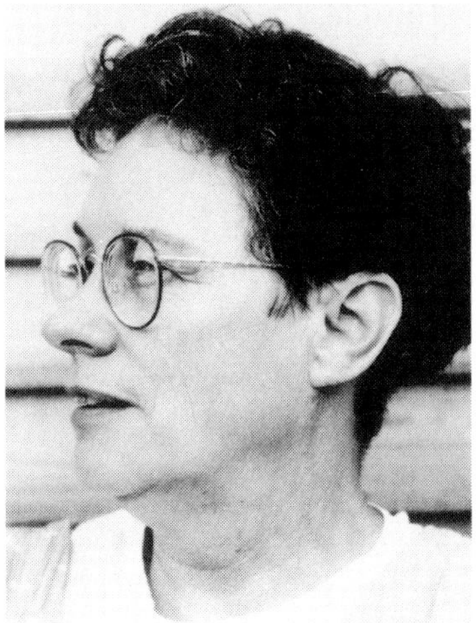

After a career as a freelance journalist, Proulx emerged in middle age, in 1992, as author of *Postcards*, described by a critic as coming close to being 'the great American novel'. *The Shipping News*, about a misfit newspaper reporter in an eccentric Newfoundland fishing village, won the 1994 Pulitzer Prize and National Book Award, and was an international bestseller. *Accordion Crimes* followed, telling stories of American immigrants and continuing Proulx's fascination with her country's history, landscape and earthy characters.

19 October 1994

It was six or seven years ago that I first went to Newfoundland on a fishing trip and I went with my friend, Tom. A few minutes after we landed at Port aux Basques, we were on our way up the only paved road, heading east on the Great Northern Peninsula through mountains that still had snow in midsummer. The place, Newfoundland, in just a few minutes on the island, seized me in a visual, bodily way. It was a very, very intense physical reaction to this bony, unutterably beautiful and narrow coastline. The weather was frightful. Cold, rainy, sleet-rattled, fog-bound, scraped by relentless winds.

The wind never stopped. It rattled the little aluminium tabs on the tent until we couldn't sleep at night. Then when it finally did suddenly stop we prayed for it to start again and blow away the incredible clouds of mosquitoes and black flies that came swooping down. I understand there are a few different varieties of flies in Australia. So far I haven't made their acquaintance. I hear that's probably a good thing. Somewhere I have read that black flies can exsanguinate a human adult in 23 minutes.

To escape the savage insects Tom and I would crawl into our tents at sunset which happens at around 10.30 pm at that latitude. One night I fell asleep and I slept very well but in the morning my friend Tom was haggard and red-eyed and he snarled at me, 'For God's sake, didn't you hear me shouting at you last night?' I had not. He pointed mutely to our wannigan, that's our cook box with all the bacon and eggs in it. There was a mess with coffee grounds, and olive oil and crackers and cheese all mixed into a rough paste along with gravel and twigs. 'It was a bear,' he said. 'A big lousy bear. He came all around the tents and then he went for the food. I tried to drive him off by shining the flashlight in his eyes but I think it just helped him make his selection.'

This trip went from bad to worse. I wanted to explore and talk to people and see everything there was to see. Tom wanted to fish. We were both covered with dots of blood and itchy bumps from the hundreds of insect bites and the weather kept shifting between heavy rain that went on for days and heavy fog that erased your hand before your face. And everywhere we went we got into great conversations with people and there was always a mug of tea and a slab of fresh baked bread.

One evening Tom and I went on the bay to fish for Arctic char. They were just starting their spawning run from the sea into the rivers. The mosquitoes were unbelievable. Although the flash of a leaping char encouraged us, we caught nothing, nothing at all. We were peering overboard, admiring, through 30 feet of crystal and icy water, the carpet of flounder below when a man in a rubber dinghy came up to us and began to talk about oil furnaces. He was a furnace salesman, the most determined salesman I have ever met. He gripped the gunwales of our canoe with a great heavy hand and began to talk of warmth and central heating. We tried to get away. He followed. We paddled towards the rocks and he came with us. We rushed for the shore, hauled out the canoe and began hauling it onto the truck. He was at our side. We started the truck and tried to escape. He clutched at the window. He thrust brochures at us, 'Look, look!' he shouted as we drove away. 'You've got to buy a furnace. This is how I makes my living.' But we did not. I learned later that we had done the unforgivable.

"The place, Newfoundland, in just a few minutes on the island, seized me in a visual, bodily way."

Tom wanted to go home. He was cold, he was tired, he was depressed, he caught neither salmon nor char. I wanted to stay. I loved the place. I probably would have bought that furnace. But I went home and I worked on my first novel, *Postcards*. Two years passed by and I went back alone. I was beginning to think about *The Shipping News* at this point and I had made some arrangements by mail to stay at a bed and breakfast called the Valhalla Lodge at the tip of the Great Northern Peninsula not far from the Viking site, the little settlement of 1000 years ago.

After three days of hard driving and ferry rides I pulled up at the door and I got out. A woman came rushing down the steps and she seized my hand. 'Let me show you the furnace,' she said. I'm not one to ignore rural folk traditions and so I followed her into a low cellar carved out of solid rock and there I was introduced to a huge and ancient oil furnace covered with buttons, flanges, switches and dials. I thought I knew who had sold it to her. 'This here's the on switch and you've got to get down and creep to get to the pilot lights, see the wind blows them out and you get in there and you turn out that one and that one over to the right and pull this little red cord see, and then down here is where you refix it but the ignition button resets it up front.' And so forth. 'Now I'll show you the towels,' she said and we went back upstairs.

"There I was, a complete stranger running a bed and breakfast in northern Newfoundland, 15 minutes after I'd arrived."

I saw the towels, the sheets, the cupboards, the pancake griddle, the freezer full of partridge berries. She showed me how to take credit card impressions with a little machine and where the good lace tablecloth was kept and then she turned to me and said, 'All right, my dear, I'm away to Goose Bay then and I'll be back in two weeks' time. When you run out of milk there's a woman up the road keeps goats.' And she was gone. There I was, a complete stranger running a bed and breakfast in northern Newfoundland, 15 minutes after I'd arrived.

The furnace did go out and I got it going again. I ran out of milk and I found the goat woman and I learned first-hand that cooperation and help freely given is what makes life possible in the tiny fishing outports of this bleak and savage coast. A place where you could trust people, even strangers, with everything you have. When the furnace salesman had come up to us in the water he was sure of a sale. He'd never seen us before. We probably didn't have a furnace, we said so right away. We had to have one. We'd broken the code. We didn't buy a furnace.

I learned better in the following years because I went back up to Newfoundland, eight or nine times, staying a month or six weeks in different places, almost all on the Great Northern Peninsula while I was working on *The Shipping News* and I learned that you do buy a furnace if somebody has to sell it to you.

! ?

SPEAKER: What are the main issues you face in the process of writing?

ANNIE PROULX: At this point I have only one main issue that I face and that's time. I was halfway through a book when things began raining down on me and it's been lying neglected for over a year in a corner. I have a number of books jammed into a corner of my head and I'm trying hard to get them down on paper. As to the actual process itself, early in the morning usually before light. My house is heated with a wood stove so I crank up the fire when it's a cold day, make a pot of coffee and sit down and write by hand until about 11 in the morning and in the afternoon I often put what I've written in the morning on the computer and I keep doing this essentially until the book is done. Meanwhile making revisions as I go. So I just keep on with it for months and months until it's all finished.

SPEAKER: What do you read for enjoyment?

ANNIE PROULX: Everything. I'm an omnivorous reader. I have a severe reading habit. I have a book-buying habit. I have got at least one suitcase filled with books so far since I've been in Australia.

I read a lot of science and technology. I read a tremendous amount of travel. I read oddities that I'm always picking up. I'm very fond of dictionaries. And while I was working on *The Shipping News* I had the great good fortune to discover one of the most incredible works of scholarship of our century, the *Dictionary of Newfoundland English* compiled and edited by George M. Story, W.J. Kirwin and J.D.A. Widdowson. A huge and marvellous book that is as enjoyable to read as a novel and I highly recommend it.

I am often asked for the names of my favourite writers. I started to make a list one time and I got to 60 names and I was only in the Bs so I knew I was in trouble. I will say that the books of Patrick White have excited me intellectually for years. I think he's one of the finest writers that has ever put pen to paper and I really don't care if he was disagreeable as a human being. He was a fantastic writer.

SPEAKER: The structure of *Postcards* is particularly interesting to me and I wondered whether you started off with that structure or whether that developed in the work?

ANNIE PROULX: I did start off with it. I had it very much in mind. The structure came at the same time as the title and I think a writer has something of a responsibility to try new things and to perhaps go out on a limb with structure and to experiment and I've done that with both of these books. I'm trying something new with one I'm working on now. So, yes, it was an experiment really.

SPEAKER: Could you tell me the significance of the white dog in *The Shipping News* and was *The Ashley Book of Knots* a book that you did come across?

ANNIE PROULX: *The Ashley Book of Knots* is another splendid book. It was written by Mr Ashley in 1944. He was a marine painter and a knot fiend – he literally could not control himself when he saw new knots. He once lunged across the counter at the butcher shop and clutched at the butcher, demanding that the butcher retie the knot he had just tied. It was a new butcher's knot that had never been seen before on the face of this earth and the startled butcher did comply while Mr Ashley sketched it.

But *The Ashley Book of Knots* which has been republished is a compendium, a history and an instruction book of, I think, roughly 5000 knots of every possible kind. Not only maritime knots but many, many others. Every occupation is in there and it too is a delight to read. I think I was struck by one particular knot and I wanted very badly to use it in *The Shipping News* but could not figure out how and that is the knot that you tie when you want to carry a cow on a pole.

As to the significance of the white dog, I'd rather not say. I'd rather not talk about what something means or what it signifies or what it symbolises because I think when a book is finished, when the author is done with the manuscript and it goes off to the publisher and the publisher takes over and then it's out there, then it becomes the reader's book and what the reader sees and feels and how the reader interprets it is the reality rather than what the writer thought he or she was doing. So it's more important what *you* think the white dog is than what I think.

SPEAKER: Did you have a publisher before *The Shipping News*?

ANNIE PROULX: Yes, I was in the very odd position which doesn't happen to many writers, of having a publisher for my first novel before I even thought of the novel. It was quite backwards. It was when the collection of short stories was done. There was a clause added to the contract that I would write a novel and I thought it was very amusing, had no intention of it. Didn't think of myself as a novel writer. So I did it backwards.

SPEAKER: I noticed in *Postcards* that all the postcards have the same postage stamp on the postcard.

ANNIE PROULX: Not my fault. I spent a week, a full week trying to track down the change of postage amounts for that book and spent many, many dusty hours with postal manuals and finally got the thing sorted out. They really worked quite well because for a long time they were one cent and then they'd be rapidly changing and escalating and zooming ever upward and it gave a kind of breathless pace to the last part of the novel that I quite liked, these changing denominations; but the publisher thought it was too difficult to put different numbers on these, even though they were all marked on the manuscript. So I'm sorry, just a generic postage stamp went on. I really feel very badly about that and it hasn't been corrected in any of the subsequent editions.

Graham Richardson

Richardson's long and controversial political career has taken him from back-room power in the Right wing of the NSW Labor Party to senior minister in the Federal Labor Government under Bob Hawke and Paul Keating to executive, journalist and columnist with Kerry Packer's media group, and now to mayor of the 2000 Olympics Athletes Village. His 1995 autobiography, *Whatever It Takes*, was followed by a somewhat different story in investigative journalist Marian Wilkinson's 1996 book about Richardson and the ALP, *The Fixer*.

9 November 1994

In the Labor Party there has never been a dull moment. For me those interesting times began as a child when I had a father who was deeply involved in Labor politics as the secretary of a trade union where war was a constant part of life. It was in the days when communists and DLP teams ran in elections. In his case, the only time ever they had a unity ticket between the Communist Party and the DLP to defeat him, they failed. In all of those times I learned a lot. The kind of lessons that he gave me were not the normal lessons that fathers give sons. They were not about how to fish or how to throw the ball. They were things like, 'You will know your friends – they are the ones who vote for you when you are wrong.' They were things like, 'Anyone who will rat on you once will rat on you twice.' They ran to things like, 'Know your weaknesses as well as your strengths because in politics ambition often outweighs talent.' I've seen a lot of that over the course of the last 20 years.

From a background where Labor politics was just heaped upon you, where Labor values reeked through the house, then you could not turn out much differently than the way I did. You grow up knowing, not believing but knowing, that there is only one true path and it is the one trod by the Labor Party. You grow up knowing that Labor has to be in government because there are millions of people out there who cannot always fend for themselves. They needed to be there.

"They were political killers and the Young Labor Council of the day was certainly a killing ground."

So, you say to yourself, if I can do anything to help along Labor to gain power and keep out the bad guys, I will. I can remember going along to a party meeting in 1968 and listening to a lot of my colleagues passionately defend the Russian invasion of Czechoslovakia. I suppose as a young 17- or 18-year-old I had never actually heard murder defended before and I certainly had not heard it defended with passion, so I knew that in my own party there were serious, often far too obvious weaknesses that had kept us out of government for a long time. So, there was a twofold task: to make sure the Labor Party was fit to govern and then to make sure it did and so I joined Young Labor.

I watched people like Keating and Brereton. You learnt a lot from them. I think Brereton would have been about 22 when he told me that you will know how many you were going to get in the ballot when you look at the number who promised to vote for you on the heads of their children and deduct 20 per cent. All those years on, that is pretty well a dead set formula that works every time. I watched those sorts of people. They were political killers and the Young Labor Council of the day was certainly a killing ground but what it did do was teach – you got a grounding in how to handle yourself in public life.

At that stage, at the age of 22, I had never lived under a Labor government. I had been born when Chifley lost and I had sat there with my parents election night after election night, feeling all bitter and twisted as we failed again and again but, of course, we deserved to. If you look at the record in the '50s and '60s, how many people really wanted to vote for the Labor Party led by Evatt and Calwell? These were not people to inspire but they were occasionally people to fear and fear Australia did. Also in terms of competence, we were not there either. You know, they had better people during the '50s and '60s and the sad thing for the great Gough Whitlam when he won in 1972 was that there was an awful lot of people who had served time for 25 years in opposition whom he inherited as cabinet members.

A lot of them were not up to it but we remember Gough with great affection. He was God. This extraordinary white-haired figure who led us from nowhere to somewhere. We did not quite know where for a few years but we realised it was better than the nowhere at which we had been and he was the first one we had who had great visions. He could look around and he could see in areas like education and health that there were grand deeds still to be done that most Australian politicians had not dreamed of doing and he set about doing them. But, of course, he had a couple of problems, three probably.

The first was that he only wanted to talk to people who were as intelligent as he was and there were not many of them, so he could not have many conversations. Then, secondly, he was not very interested in economics so he gave it to Jim Cairns and, thirdly, and above all else, for all his greatness and for all his vision, he was a lousy manager. He did not know how to handle people and in your leader you always need someone who can handle people and so Gough failed and at the end of 1975 we had a defeat most of us will never forget.

It was not ended, of course, by Kerr although Labor liked to kid itself that it was – the sacking may well have been a disgrace but it did not matter when an election was going to come, Australia was determined to get rid of us and when the chance came, they did. They deserted us in droves and we were in the wilderness but I was always lucky and luck prevailed, in two ways: John Ducker had a fight with the incumbent secretary of the party and got rid of him and I was lucky enough for him to choose me as the replacement. I know there was a democratic ballot but I think it had more to do with the nod from Ducker than anything else.

We were great believers in guided democracy – it had a lot of advantages over the other kinds so I became secretary of the party at the same time as Neville Wran won and there I watched the master, the best. No one could pick the public mood like Neville Wran could pick it and Labor then went through a number of years in New South Wales where we reached ridiculous heights. The idea of us winning the seat of Manly is actually quite preposterous – even the seat north of it we won. These were crazy places for Labor to win but we won them because we had in Wran the kind of leader that no one could resist.

I envied Wran. He was sort of good looking, smooth and suave. He actually spoke the same as I did, swore more than I did and everyone thought he was terrific. That is an art and if I could ever find out how to do that I would be a very successful fellow. That was important, that period, because it gave Labor some hope. During that time I had begun life as a party official and in 1972 was Bob Hawke's driver.

I can remember one occasion when we went out to Macquarie University which was just being built and only had a handful of students and a young overweight bearded student whose name was John Faulkner who is now our Minister for Environment and Sport met us on the lawn where he had organised for the students to assemble and Hawkey addressed them. It was all over in half an hour, 40 minutes, whatever, and I knew that it was some three hours before our next appointment which was at the Epping Railway Station – politics was never very glamorous – and so I did not know what to do with Hawkey but I had read about him so I took him to the pub – the El Rancho at Ryde.

I took him into the saloon bar – for two reasons. It had carpets and women. It was therefore a step up from anything else. We had only been there for a moment when he decided he did not like that very much, he wanted to go into the public bar. It was there I saw what I think for the best part of 20 years was a kind of extraordinary love affair between him and Australians – for three hours he held court there in the public bar and he spoke to all those who dug the ditches and built the houses and delivered the mail.

They were not big time. They had on the blue singlets. They were just your average workers but they loved him. Importantly enough, he loved them and the kind of conversation you could see develop, which got a little rowdy during the course of the afternoon as more beers were consumed. Everyone loved Bob Hawke, everyone, and it did not matter whether you took him to the board rooms – and I took him to lots of those – or whether he stood there talking to workers in a pub.

I knew when it came to the end of the '70s and into the early '80s, when Labor had to make a comeback, when Whitlam had stayed one election too long, that we had to have Hawke as leader and that meant getting rid of Bill Hayden. I have great regard for Bill. I did not then and it all boiled down to the fact that with Bill you might win, with Hawke you could not possibly lose and for a party who had been, by that stage of the game, out of office for something like 28 years out of 31, what were you supposed to do?

There was only one answer – you had to get Hawke into the leadership and a number of us over the course of some months in 1982 worked pretty hard on that. A lot of people in the Labor Party wanted to keep him out. The Left certainly wanted to keep him out. They did not want to have a bar of him but you understood that.

They regarded him as a rat. They had got him up as president of the ACTU. He had left them. They were angry. They were hurt. He had referred to them as a telephone box minority. It did not matter what the people thought and most of them came from safe seats so the people did not count and they stuck with Hayden not because he was Hayden but because he was not Bob Hawke. But inevitably you started to get the few cracks in the dam. You work on the cracks. You keep prising them a little bit more open every day and, finally, we had Bob Hawke as leader and, of course, we then had an unprecedented period of success for the Labor Party. I saw myself as an instrument to help us get there and then to stay there.

Hawke was a phenomenon and none of us should forget it, even now when some relationships are strained and a lot of people in the Labor Party are angry with him – that will pass because we did not have anyone else win four on the trot. We probably will not again and when you get someone who is that good, you ought to cling to them even if sometimes you might be disappointed in what they do. Nonetheless you also have to be able to tell them when their time is up and in the book I explained that in 1990 Hawke and I had a very serious row and I acknowledged base motives. I swore revenge. I said, 'I will get this bastard. I will do whatever it takes.'

"By 1991 it was time to tap Bob Hawke on the shoulder."

[One reason was that Hawke] would not give me the job I wanted and after the 1990 election I thought I was entitled to ask for a job and get it. Remember in that election we got 39 per cent of the vote, our lowest since the Second World War, and we won – we won on a preference strategy which I do not think it is too big-headed of me to say was mine. So I thought I would be king of the kids for a while but I was not and I was a very unhappy little fella and then he offered me the job in London to get rid of me altogether because leaders never like alternate power sources.

I got summonsed to the oval office to be told I was Minister for Defence. Now, I had never shown the slightest interest in defence, not the slightest. Never spoken in one debate but I thought, okay, I will take it, and I can remember after the discussion with Hawke walking down the corridor and having his media chief, Colin Parkes, salute me and say, 'Good morning, Admiral' and I thought, well, I have made it, have I not? An hour later I was out of the job and back in Social Security because that is how long it took Robert Ray to tell Hawke where to stick the offer of Social Security and it had come back to me because at the end of the day

I was the Labor loyalist, the bloke who would cop it. Hawke knew that and he was right but all of that made me very, very angry and I do concede in the book that I wanted revenge, but then I got over it.

By 1991 it was time to tap Bob Hawke on the shoulder. It was time because we were 25 points behind in the polls. We were drifting. We had no response. After the first challenge it got worse, not better. If you remember when *Fightback* came out, we had no response at all. John Kerin held a press conference where he could not remember some economic terms. Brian Howe had one where he gave a set of figures for which he had to apologise and then he walked into a cupboard. I gave one where I did my best to try and put a hole in *Fightback* as far as Social Security was concerned but no one was interested and they were not interested because Hewson was about to slaughter Labor. We thought so. The Liberals thought so, and the press gallery certainly thought so.

We were in all sorts of strife and most of us figured if you are going to go down, you want to go down fighting. But with Hawke that was not going to happen and so we looked at Paul Keating who was, of course, the only truly warrior statesman that Australia has had. He loved a brawl but he was a genuine statesmen. Keating was amazing. He is an extraordinary figure.

You know he left school after his Intermediate Certificate and studied at night for the Leaving. He never got a university degree but I would challenge anyone to find an Australian who knows more about economics than Keating because he has an IQ that is extraordinary – you have to, by the way, to be a Prime Minister. Just remember that a lot of bright people become senior ministers but getting over the detail of one portfolio is tough, over 30 it is bloody near impossible. That requires a special mind which Keating always had, but Keating also had a temper, an enormous temper, and over the course of the years he and I have had more fights than you have had literary lunches. Indeed, we had a couple of classics.

"Paul Keating was, of course, the only truly warrior statesman that Australia has had."

We did not speak for 12 months in 1986 and we often had little periods of a week or so when one or the other would sulk. In 1988 when I would not support him for Prime Minister he sulked for quite a while. That was when I got recorded on a telephone conversation with him where he was giving vent to what he thought of Hawke. As I say in the book, I do not remember all of it but 'envious little turd' does spring to mind.

So, this was a relationship which had a few problems and there was no joy [when we succeeded in getting Hawke replaced by Keating]. When we won, after all the difficult times that a challenge brings you, there was no look of triumph on the face of the winners. In fact, most of them were crying, most of them were shedding tears, because getting rid of a Labor icon ain't fun. It is one of the more unpleasant bits of parliamentary business but, in my view, leaders are there to win it for you. If they will not go nicely, you tear them down because no individual can ever place themselves in front of the party effort.

Maeve Binchy

After years as a teacher, a travel writer and a columnist for the *Irish Times*, Binchy turned her sense of humour and her eye for the poignant details of human experience to fiction. Britain's top-selling woman author in 1995, she has written a number of internationally loved novels, including *Echoes* (1985) and *Circle of Friends*, (1990) which were both made into hit films, *The Glass Lake* (1994) and short story collections such as *London Transports*, *The Lilac Bus* and *The Return Journey*.

11 November 1994

I'm here to talk about my book, *The Glass Lake*. Like all my books, it's set in the 1950s and '60s and, like all my books, its heroine Kit McMahon was born in 1940. This comes as no surprise to anybody who knows me because I was born in 1940 and it means the absolute minimum of research. I don't have to look up what kind of clothes people wore when they were 17, I know every song that was on the hit parade in 1956, I know how much a lipstick cost, I know what kind of clothes we bought and I know the kind of way we felt. I grew up, like Kit McMahon from *The Glass Lake*, in a country where the angelus rang at 12 o'clock and it rang at 6 o'clock and I thought this happened all over the world because how else would they know it was time for lunch and time for tea? I didn't believe that these were kind of very special things in Ireland at all.

Like Kit McMahon in the book, I also thought a lot of things, simple, innocent things, which I discovered later on in life were not true. For example, I always thought the Pope was at my parents' wedding – I thought that 'til I was about 15 – because of a thing called a papal blessing. A papal blessing, as those of you who were brought up in

"My father was a lawyer and he said, 'Maeve, don't put a real person in a book or we'll lose the house and everything belonging to it'."

the Catholic faith might remember, was a picture of the Pope which usually hung over your parents' bed and it said, whatever your parents' names were, Mary and John for instance, prostrate themselves at the feet of Your Holiness.

My parents had never been to Rome, so I thought they must have prostrated themselves at the wedding but, I thought, I never saw him in the wedding photographs – big sepia wedding photographs of 1939 and there was no sign of the Pope in it – so I thought he must have gone early before breakfast, back on the boat to Rome. I wrote all this in the book. I don't write about other people, I only write about myself and my own little weaknesses and follies and I make myself marvellous in the books; I always make myself much nicer.

In *Echoes* I made myself the teacher Angela O'Hara. She was a much nicer teacher than I was. I was a teacher looking at my watch wondering when it was time to go out and meet fellas and have a drink and all the rest of it but Angela O'Hara was a saintly teacher who just was wonderful and looked after the poor and the needy and helped them study for scholarships. This is the great thing about writing fiction, you can actually make people into the kind of people you'd like to be but I never put another person, a real person, in my books – for a very good reason. My father was a lawyer and he said, 'Maeve, don't put a real person in a book or we'll lose the house and everything belonging to it.' I have written 11 books now and nobody has ever identified themselves or seen themselves in the book which is great.

But what I do remember and put in are the kind of feelings that children have and their hopes and their dreams. I remember very well being a child. I'm 54 years of age now and I feel I'm still about 17 and one day I'm going to grow up and everything's going to happen. I don't realise that it's nearly all over. I think that one day I'm going to grow up and it'll all be there but I feel very much – I think being a teacher was part of it – the hopes and dreams of young women particularly and their ambitions and also their sensitivities and their real embarrassment if anything is different. In *The Glass Lake* Kit's mother is different to everybody else's mother and I've based this on a characteristic of my own mother. I had a marvellous mother. I came from a very, very happy family. My father was a barrister and my mother was a nurse before she was married and, of course, in those days you didn't ever continue your job after you were married because it meant that your husband couldn't support you; the whole thing was very old-fashioned.

My mother was a marvellous woman. She was a big, jolly woman and if she laughed in Sydney I'd swear you'd hear her in Melbourne. She had a laugh that you could hear around corners and around streets. She was very big and wore fur coats. She was so kind and interested in everybody. She smoked Gold Flake cigarettes non-stop. She was constantly getting involved in people's lives which I hated and when you were on the bus it wasn't the person beside you that you had to talk to, my mother talked to the entire bus. I wished when she came to the school concerts – she was so nice, I didn't appreciate it then – I wished that she could have kept quiet and she could've been in the background and worn a twinset and pearls.

One Christmas Eve I remember particularly well. My mother took me shopping and I was 15. We went to a market in Dublin where the traders were selling and calling out their wares and my mother started to talk to this woman and the woman started telling my mother about her husband who was in jail and her son who was no good and my mother took up a fruit and vegetable crate and sat on it in her fur coat and she started to smoke. I was so ashamed in case any of the girls from my posh convent school would see me and my mother smoking with a street trader and crying – because my mother started to cry over this woman's sadnesses. I was so ashamed I had to go and hide and the only place to hide was a butcher's shop. I went into a carcass of meat to hide, a terrible big lamb or ox or something was hanging up there, and I can remember the smell of it to this day and that was 1955.

I think back now, what a pity that I wasn't able to say enough to my mother, how much she gave me. She gave me all the self-confidence I have now to sit in front of a whole group of strangers in Sydney and tell you all these stories of my background, she gave me a lack of self-consciousness. We were the luckiest four children in the world because we didn't have great wealth even though my father was a lawyer. Everything was spent on our education and we didn't have a glamorous house and we never went anywhere posh but we had confidence because my parents thought all their little geese were swans.

In the book Kit McMahon has a mother who is different to everyone. Now, I didn't make her mother like my mother. Her mother was different in another way. The beautiful Helen McMahon lived in a small village in Ireland and was married to the man who ran the chemist shop. She walked down by the lake every night hitting at the reeds and the bushes and her face was sad and when they saw her, when she didn't know they were looking at her, people saw that she was crying and Kit, like every sensitive 13-year-old, knew that there was something wrong and something different about her mother.

"Barbara Bush said '. . . I just cannot believe we seem to have had exactly the same childhood. How could this be?'"

This is the point of the book, it's a mother/daughter story in a sense. She knows something is awful and then one night – and this is not giving the plot away – one dark and stormy night there's a boat found upside down on the lake and Kit's mother has disappeared and it's the kind of thing she was dreading all her life.

I can't write about real places and apparently since *The Glass Lake* has been published there have been an awful lot of people looking for Loch Glass and wanting to see it and they keep saying 'But you know where it is, it's near the big lake and it must be there', and the tourist people are saying,

'Would you once in your life write about a real place and we can all send people there and they'll be happy.' It's an imaginary place.

I assume the reason people like the books is because you'll find human life is there and human experiences. The time I wrote about was very safe because marriages never ended, maybe they should've ended, some of them were bad marriages but they didn't end. So people felt secure. Very often people didn't emigrate unless they had to so people stayed at home and they wrote to their emigrant sons and daughters and prayed that they'd come home. There used to be Emigrant Sunday where we all prayed for the emigrants. I remember thinking the emigrants were having a much better time wherever they were, with us all praying for them like mad in Ireland.

I would love to say this is not name-dropping but of course it is; I went to see Barbara Bush in the White House amongst one of my other casual outings for lunch one day. Barbara Bush was on the *Oprah Winfrey Show* and she was asked who's her favourite author and she said me and Oprah Winfrey naturally said, 'Maeve who?', because she'd never heard of me. So I wrote to Barbara Bush and said, 'Thank you very much', and we were invited, Gordon and myself, to the White House for lunch. Barbara Bush said a great sentence to me which gave me huge confidence which was, 'I was brought up as a Presbyterian in New England and you were brought up as a Roman Catholic in Ireland and I just cannot believe we seem to have had exactly the same childhood. How could this be?' And I said to her, 'I get letters from Greeks and Italians', and the rest of it. I suppose being a teacher or something, I must know what children are like and I just know the vulnerability of children and the hopes they have and the dreams and especially teenage girls; when their own mothers hate them I love teenage girls.

"People say to me, particularly in America, thank you very, very much for not putting sex and violence in your books."

I don't put any sex and violence in my books for a very good reason. Violence I would be just frightened of myself so there's no point in my trying to write it. If it was sex that I knew about, I would feel it was a betrayal of those limited number of people with whom I have had sex. If it was sex that was fantasy, I would be so embarrassed to write my fantasies because I could imagine people saying, well, get her! chandeliers and coffee tables no less! So I don't put any sex and violence in the books. To my great delight and pleasure this has not affected their sales at all; in fact, oddly enough, it has made people more comfortable about buying the books because there's not all this terrible thrusting and plunging and all the rest of it as there is in a lot of other people's books. Very often at book signings, people say to me, particularly in America, thank you very, very much for not putting sex and violence in your books. Thanks to my late mother, I am not a person at a loss for a word but I just don't know what to say. Do you say, you're welcome, because the Americans are very courteous? A friend of mine told me what I should really say is, oh, no, no, sex and violence, there's too much of that in my private life, I want a bit of escapism – which is quite a good idea.

In my other life before I was a novelist, I had two jobs: I was a teacher and I was a journalist. A teacher is always a teacher. So I want to say to anybody in this room who would like to write that there is a very simple solution, just listen to teacher: it only takes seven months to write a book, you write 10 pages a week for 30 weeks, that's 300 pages and then you have your book finished. It may not be published and it may not be good but it is finished and you are not like all the people who say, I could write a book, or, I will write a book, I must write a book; it's finished.

The other job I had was being a journalist. I am still a columnist in the *Irish Times*. I joined it in 1968 and I became the women's editor, a very, very unlikely choice. I knew nothing about cooking, so I employed a wonderful woman called Theodora Fitzgibbon to do the cookery. Theodora once sent a recipe for a lot of veal dishes and there was veal in casserole and there was osso bucco and so on. So I thought I must go through my file of pictures and I found a big picture of a casserole dish with knives and forks sticking out of it and I typed underneath it, 'Veal casserole excellent for a winter evening'. Then I put the page down and I went home. My father and I had our supper and then we looked at the 9 o'clock news on television and I saw a sight on the news that made my blood run cold. I saw Dr Christiaan Barnard from South Africa getting off a plane and I suddenly remembered where I had seen that picture before. It was not a veal casserole, it was open heart surgery. What I had thought were knives and forks were clamps and forceps and I said to my father, 'Oh my God, I have put this awful picture in for the cookery page,' and my father, the lawyer, said, 'Admit nothing'.

But I rang the editor, it was now about ten past nine, I could hear his teeth grinding on the phone, and I said, 'Mr Gageby, we can't possibly run that picture because actually it's not a picture of veal, it's open heart surgery.' 'This is very serious,' he said, 'come in here at once.' When I arrived, he said to me, his face grim and white, 'We're going to be the only paper in the world prosecuted for cannibalism.' The time was ticking, ticking away, and so I had to find another picture of exactly the same size. Eventually we found a picture of an egg in an eggcup and I typed underneath it, 'Why be content with a boiled egg on a winter's evening?'

I knew then that there was always a way on a page that you could fill in something, that the words could be written, whatever they were, they could be written at any time. Theodora rang me the next morning and said, 'You didn't actually kill yourself, darling, with the picture, did you,' and I said, 'I nearly did'.

Desmond Tutu

Archbishop of Cape Town, South Africa, for ten years, Tutu helped to end apartheid in his country in 1994. A man of great spirit and joy, and a Nobel Prize winner in 1984 for his human rights work, he helped coordinate the political struggle while black leaders like Nelson Mandela were in prison. His most powerful speeches, sermons and letters are collected in his 1994 book, *The Rainbow People of God*.

8 December 1994

This new South Africa is an incredible miracle. On the eve of our election we were all apprehensive about what was likely to be happening. We all believed that we were on the brink of a civil war, that we were going to be overwhelmed by bloodshed, a blood bath, veritably, and of course it did not happen that way at all. We had this incredible experience in our election – those long lines of people waiting to go into the polling booth should have been a disaster, but a kind of alchemy took place because instead of people being disgruntled and made mad by having to wait for so long, those queues turned out to be providential.

South Africans discovered one another. They discovered that they were compatriots, the scales fell from their eyes and they discovered that it was in fact true that race was an utter, utter irrelevance in saying anything of significance about anyone. They discovered a black mother wants a nice home, a good school, a safe environment for her children. A white mother wants the same. It was just an incredible, incredible thing. Clearly, of course, you could see that we had not been over-smart – it ought to have been as obvious as a pikestaff that people are people because they are people.

We are often told the story of how, when God created human beings out of dust, He created them and then put them into an oven, because you fire them like you fire bricks in a kiln. God got busy with many another thing and forgot that He had put the first lot into the oven. When He came and rushed to open the oven, well, it was burnt to cinders and they say this is how black people came about. Then God put a second lot into the oven and this time He was over-anxious and opened the oven too quickly and this lot was underdone – this is how white people came about, so the story goes.

The point of the story is, what of any significance would skin colour tell us about anybody? I often tell the story of imagining how, instead of skin colour, you chose something else arbitrarily. For example, since I have a large nose, supposing you said a large nose was what gave people their importance and their significance. Imagine instead of having signs like they used to have in South Africa 'Whites Only' you had something like 'Large Noses Only'. If you went looking for a loo and it said 'Large Noses Only', if you had a small nose you would be somewhat inconvenienced.

We had this extraordinary thing that happened and it can only have been because it was of God's doing. It could not have been our accomplishment. But, of course, God is a God who is always waiting on human partners to assist Him in whatever enterprise He undertakes. St Augustine says something quite beautiful: without God we cannot, without us God will not.

Yes, this miracle of the new South Africa, the democratic South Africa, has happened but it could not have occurred without very, very considerable assistance from splendid people like yourselves. I went round many parts of the world asking for help from the international community. 'Please assist us. We want to destroy an evil system. We want to destroy it relatively peacefully and we believe that sanctions are the last option that we have of a non-violent strategy.' In some places we met with resistance but by and large the response was magnificent. In this country particularly the sports boycott hit sports-mad South African whites on an exposed nerve end. The sports boycott made a huge impact psychologically. And now here we are with this incredible thing – we have a new President, democratically elected, the first such for South Africa and he happens to be the best President the world has just now.

This miracle in part has happened because of you; it has happened because of God. It has happened also because of someone like F. W. de Klerk. He may in fact have thought genuinely that apartheid is something that is totally unacceptable ethically, politically, economically and so on, or it may have been for other reasons, it does not matter. He needed to have been very courageous to have announced the kind of initiative that he did announce in Parliament on the 2nd of February, 1990.

When I sat in front of the television and heard him make those announcements I was pinching myself. I was saying somebody is going to wake you up, man. Somebody is going to wake you up and you are going to awaken to the nightmare that is apartheid. De Klerk richly deserves the accolade the international community gave when he received the Nobel Peace Prize together with Nelson Mandela.

But I want you to know too one other reason why we have to doff our hats to de Klerk. It has never been easy to step down from being the first fiddle to, say, being the second fiddle. It is very, very difficult. It is infinitely more difficult to have done what he did, which was to step down not just from being one to two but from being one to three because he is the second Deputy President of South Africa.

We have been blessed with a remarkable person in Nelson, someone who has a remarkable magnanimity and has not a stitch of bitterness, it seems, in him. He has had a remarkable capacity to forgive even his worst enemies – almost all his worst enemies are now eating out of his hand.

Have you ever heard of a country that has three national anthems? Have you heard of a country that has 11 official languages? Ours has, because of the effort to counter what apartheid sought to do.

"It ought to have been as obvious as a pikestaff that people are people because they are people."

Apartheid sought to alienate, to separate, to break apart. The question at home is how inclusive can we become? How can we embrace as many of the people of this country as possible? It is wonderful to have, not just as a figurehead but as a focus, this person of whom every part of the world seems to want to have a piece.

I recall long before April the 27th of this year a young man who had been banned, whose wife had been banned, who had been detained without trial and was tortured, said to me, 'Father, you know when they are applying their third degree methods on you, you look on them and you say, "By the way, these are God's children, they need us to help them recover the humanity they have lost".'

There is this capacity because amongst Africans there is a thing called 'ubuntu'. Ubuntu is the essence of being human – when you recognise that my humanity is caught up in your humanity. We say a person is a person through other persons. Unlike Descartes who said, 'I think therefore I am', we say, 'I am because I belong, I participate'. Anger and resentment and the desire to revenge are corrosive of community and when I demean you inexorably I demean myself. I am lessened by the extent to which you are lessened.

Who would have thought South Africa could be held up as a symbol of unity, of reconciliation? Who could ever have thought that we would be able to be, as somebody said, the flavour of the month? We who were the universal pariah, rightly so. God is going to be able to say to Bosnia, to Rwanda, 'Just look at them. You know South Africa? Yes? Well, they had a nightmare there – apartheid. It has ended. Your nightmare, Bosnia, Rwanda, Somalia, Liberia, will end. They had a problem there which the world designated an intractable problem. It has been solved and look at how they have solved it. Your problem – no problem anywhere in the world – can ever again be said to be an intractable problem.'

So, improbable as it is, we are going to be a paradigm, a symbol of hope in a world that is hungry for some success story. Here is a good story – apartheid has ended and we are making this transition from repression to democracy, from ethnocracy to democracy. We are making it. You can make it and God is saying, 'Hey, are they not something! Just look at what can be accomplished.'

June Salter

Salter's acting career began in Sydney radio in the 1950s, moving into the Phillip Street revues and innumerable performances in television series such as *Certain Women* and *A Country Practice*, and theatre, where she created a one-woman 'autobiographical musical memoir' called *Legends* in 1992. This great Australian actress produced another memoir, this time written, with *A Pinch of Salt* in 1995.

6 June 1995

In my career I've been everything, my dears –
I've been everything.
Vaudevillian, a comic, I can sing.
Review and drama, tap, buck and wing.
Interviews, TV soaps,
You name it, I know all the ropes.
Channel 2 and 7, and 9 and 10,
Phillip Street revues again, again and again and again.
The Bull 'n' Bush, the Tivoli, Mavis Bramston of fame,
I've done it all, I know my game
but no-one seems to remember my name.
I've been called a legend, a veteran, an icon, a star,
a national treasure, Alan Jones went too far.
But please don't call me Jill
and I'm not June Bronhill,
I'm not Gwennie Plumb or Rowena,
but as a bitch I'd be meaner.
I'm not Creyton or Slater,
Ruth Cracknell or Chater,
I'm not Janet or Julie or Jane.
I'm Salter, not SAWlter
c'mon now, don't falter.
June Salter's my very own name
and you can take that with a pinch of salt.

When I did my one woman show at the Tilbury backed by my musical director Mr Wynton Prisk I had that song or that piece composed for me and in fact my friend Gwen Friend wrote the lyrics and my dear maestro Tommy Tycho wrote the music. There was a particular reason for it being written. We, in this profession that I love so much, get to be well known by the public and it is very gratifying, very flattering when people want to come up and speak to you and congratulate you and say how much they enjoy your work. They say the most flattering, lovely things and swear their devotion to you for ever and then as they are going they call you by somebody else's name. It is not their fault; I think they just get a bit nervous and then you say, no, that is not me and they say, yes it is, and I say no, no, and they argue with you. They actually argue with you.

"You have no idea the accolades I get for my brilliant performance in 'Mother and Son'. I should be so lucky!"

You have no idea the accolades I get for my brilliant performance in *Mother and Son*. I should be so lucky! And I don't think I look a bit like Garry McDonald anyway. But I think the most classic example of mistaken identity was many years ago when I was doing a drug relief concert and Bobby Limb was compering. It was just before a federal election and the guest of honour that night was the leader of the opposition and his wife. After the show we were all lined up backstage to be presented to the Australian royalty and himself came along and Bobby introduced us all, that was fine. Then his lady wife came along and Bobby went to introduce me and she said, 'There's no need to introduce me to this girl.' I was a girl then. She said, 'I have followed her career for years, ever since she started and I think she's absolutely superb.' I said thank you very much and she continued to say, 'You know what I enjoyed most of all, out of anything that you have done? *I Do, I Do*.' I said, 'That wasn't me, it was Jill Perryman.' She looked at me from a great height and said,'Well, who are you?'. That is a true story and Mrs Whitlam is aware of it and has rectified it ever since.

I came into this profession via radio which is possibly the best training ground that any young actor or actress can have and unfortunately for the youngsters coming into the business today that amount of radio is not there. There's a part of my book about Mr Frank Strain, the former TV producer, entrepreneur, whom I met about 12 months after I had come into the industry. I was at a party at a friend's place. I made some lovely friends in the first 12 months and this was at the place of a wonderful actor named Kevin Brennan. As was my wont I used to sit at the piano and play and sing and I was doing just this, this particular night, and suddenly there was a great roar of people saying, oh Frankie, come and sing, come and do something for us, oh yes, clap, clap.

So I got up from the piano presuming that this gentleman was going to play for himself and he just put his hand on my shoulder and said, 'Can you play "Some Enchanted Evening"?'. So I played for him and he was wonderful. Afterwards he said to me, 'You know, Junie, at the moment I am a talent scout for 2GB for a show called *The President Hour* which is hosted by that gracious lady Miss Gladys Moncrieff and compered by a young actor named John Meillon. Seeing you here tonight playing and singing, I think it would do you the world of good if you went down and auditioned. You may not even get chosen to go on air but you can never have too many strings to your bow. So go down, it would be good experience for you.'

"They said, 'You could not possibly sing that, it is far too risqué. It is bordering on smut actually'."

So, down I went to 2GB and they got me to the piano and asked what I was going to sing. I sang a few bars of a song called 'I'm A Big Girl Now'. I only got as far as, 'I'm a big girl now. I wanted to be treated like a big girl now. When daddy tells those certain jokes it isn't fair. He tells me I'm too young and makes me take the air and I could tell a couple that would curl his hair', and they said 'Stop!'. I asked what was wrong. They said, 'You could not possibly sing that, it is far too risqué. No, no, it is bordering on smut actually.' I said I had been doing songs like this since I was 12 years old and I didn't know there was anything wrong with it. So I did another couple and they kept saying no, no, no. But finally they said, all right you can do that, and they passed me and said that I could do it on air. In those days, which was about 1953, the censorship laws on radio were very, very stringent, not like what we're subjected to now. Anyway, I did this song, so you be the judge.

A man showed me a diamond clear.
He said it's yours if you kiss me, dear.
Oh tell me, is there anything wrong in that?
I kissed him once and he asked for more.
The next thing I had the jewellery store.
Oh tell me, is there anything wrong in that?
I took my mother driving on that very same day
and she said, dear, you must return this Rolls right away.
But the funniest thing you'd never guess.
I've forgotten his name and his address.
So tell me, is there anything wrong in that?

Evidently after that went to air the switchboard lit up with people saying how dare that young girl sing such a filthy, revolting song. I have been doing it ever since actually. But they were great days. They really were. From then on I have had the most marvellous 43 years in this profession, going from radio to television and my beloved stage. Then, when I did my one-woman show a couple of years ago at the Tilbury, that was another departure. I hadn't done anything like that on my own but it was a great experience and I loved every minute of it and without my dear Wynton I don't know what I would have done.

! ?

SPEAKER: How did you come to be able to produce such an extraordinary amount of detail over such a long period?

JUNE SALTER: When I was first asked to write this book I thought it sounded like a lovely idea. I had never kept any diaries when I was small. In fact, I had never kept any diaries at all. I thought I would get over the childhood part and my growing up part and then I would have my press cuttings and so that would be all right. So I started to write from when I could remember and it all unfolded like a film in front of me. You say there is a lot of detail – 'it is far *too much* detail,' I was told, far too many names that I mentioned. Angus & Robertson contracted me to write 60,000 words and I nearly fainted dead away. I thought there is no way I can write 60,000 words. So I started off in longhand. (Jeffrey Archer and I have got that in common!) I had not worked for 12 months, but the minute I was asked to write it, work came in. So it was written sporadically over about 17 months. I just kept on writing and writing and writing and then I finally took it in to Miss Alison Pressley at Angus & Robertson's and she was very complimentary about it. She said, 'We will have to edit it though,' and I said, 'I am sure you will.' She said, 'Yes, you wrote 120,000 words.' I said, 'I was not counting.' 'No, but the computer found that out, you see.' So I thought, I don't know what I can do about this. They gave me four consecutive editors, each one of whom suddenly was appointed to another job, another department. One even went overseas. I am not sure that the other one didn't get pregnant.

Nobody wanted to touch this book and I didn't blame them – 60,000 words is a lot of words to get out. So you can see how much detail I went into but finally Bronwyn Sweeney was appointed as my fifth editor and what that girl has done I think is just absolutely miraculous except that I kept on saying, no, I want that bit back in. Andrew Olle said to me this morning, 'How can we believe that that is all true?' I said, 'Believe me, I am a very truthful person.' He said, 'Have you got that sort of memory?' I said, 'For 43 years I have been working on my memory on stage. So I have got a good memory and I do remember those things.'

SPEAKER: In your career what would you say was the most demanding role you have ever played?

JUNE SALTER: Queen Mary in *Crown Matrimonial.* There was a lot of words, and it is sometimes easier to play a fictitious character than it is to portray somebody who has lived and was so well known and so incredible a person as Queen Mary. Not only that, to get her hourglass figure I was wearing very heavy padding and we toured up north into a lot of regional places. There was no airconditioning. I think after about six months I came back home about two and a half stones lighter. It was all very demanding in the fact that Queen Mary could not show any emotion and there were a lot of times in that play where I really had to hold myself together, particularly at the end of the second act when Bertie, King George VI, comes in and says that he has been named king. As he is leaving the room his mother turns around and just says 'Bertie!'. He says, 'Yes, Mama'. And all the audience saw was my back – Queen Mary making a deep curtsy to her son. I was glad that I was not facing the audience because it was the most emotional moment.

It was also demanding working with John Hamblin. I mean, John Hamblin is the dearest, sweetest most gorgeous man in the world but he is a devil to work with – as you might know if you have seen all the tricks he gets up to in *Playschool.* There were two occasions of, again, trying to hold emotions, but this time laughter. He had a speech at one stage when he is talking about Wallis Simpson and his mother and it is a very, very serious part. He says to his mother, 'Mama, I'm a man as well as a king and I must marry Wallis Simpson.' This day at a matinee he said, 'Mama, I am a man as well as a woman and I must marry Baldwin.' I knew we had about four minutes left before the curtain came down and it was the longest four minutes of my life. On the same day later on, he had to say (and this was not his fault), 'What would you do if you were to ever meet her, Mama?'. And a lady from the audience called out, 'Chop off 'er 'ead!'.

SPEAKER: When you do stage work are you ever nervous?

JUNE SALTER: Always. It doesn't matter what I do, whether it is television or stage or standing up in front of all these people here. You stand in the wings and you say, please God, put your hand in mine, guide and guard me and let me not forget the words. Then the minute you get on that stage there is a rush of adrenalin when you feel that contact with an audience and then it settles down. But I think the day I stand in the wings or anywhere and I can honestly say I am not nervous, I will go home and shut the door and give it away.

Frank Moorhouse

Since his first collection of stories, *Futility and Other Animals* (1969), Moorhouse has been known as the Australian master of the 'discontinuous narrative' and the quintessential Balmain writer. Sexually explicit, satirical and often autobiographical, his books include *The Americans, Baby* (1972), *Conference-ville* (1976), *The Coca-Cola Kid* (1985), *Forty-Seventeen* (1988) and *Grand Days* (1994). Although about an Australian woman working for the League of Nations in Geneva, *Grand Days* was disqualified from the Miles Franklin Award because set overseas.

27 September 1995

Until recently I lived in France for four years and my new book, *Loose Living*, is a humorous expression of that experience. I have been thinking how I'm the victim of being a person who wrote *Grand Days* which was an attempt at a chronicle of Australian diplomacy or the beginning of Australian diplomacy internationally at Geneva. I'm interested that as an author I'm caught in a remarkable diplomatic row between France and Australia. I have *Loose Living* which is set in France coming out in Australia at a time when the two countries are at each other's throats and I have *Grand Days* coming out in a French translation in Paris this year to a hostile French audience; a monumental act of publishing bad timing for me. I only hope my readers rise above the issue.

Until my period in France I had spent most of my life living in Australia. In fact, I spent a huge amount of it, it seems to me, a lot of the time out in 'the bush'. Not only backpacking in the bush but also working in the bush, editing small town newspapers and such. So I spent about 50 years of my life in Australia. It was therefore something of a shock that my last book, *Grand Days*, was rejected last year by the most Australian of prizes, the Miles

Franklin. The judges refused to consider it because they felt it was un-Australian.

I come before you today following on yet another crisis in the history of the Miles Franklin award – we have the poor old Miles Franklin prize having a rough time with the Demidenko affair. Having been the author of a book that was rejected by the Miles Franklin one year and then seeing the Demidenko affair burst into flame the following year, I found myself making a rather fascinating analysis about returning from France to Australia. What is going on here? What does this mean, that my book was rejected and that this book turns out to be a hoax? Because the judges do not, of course, enter into public discourse about their reasons, we can only surmise. I think they've been rather cowardly in not entering into public discussion because I think that their dilemmas represent some wider dilemmas and turmoil in the Australian community. I want to talk about that.

This is what I surmise is going on. For a while, when my book was rejected by the Miles Franklin, I was rung by newspapers and other people who wanted me to talk about it. I found I had very little to say because I was perplexed and bewildered and I considered taking court action because it seemed that there was something untoward and something perhaps illegal in their action. I didn't pursue that course. I think now, having had time to reflect on it and having had a look at the Demidenko affair, that the judges were struggling with various mutations of what used to be called the cultural cringe and I don't think they knew that they were infected.

I will discuss the mutations later, but it seemed the original decision to exclude *Grand Days* was because it wasn't Australian enough. It was a desire to promote that rapidly fading, bucolic concept of a pastoral Australia, perhaps in the tradition of Miles Franklin, that the judges felt that they should be very careful to exclude any whiff of cosmopolitanism and especially to exclude an author who might appear to be turning his or her back on his native country.

In *Grand Days* we have a character called Edith Campbell Berry who goes to Geneva to join the League of Nations in 1920 and is consciously trying to be an internationalist in both the political and cultural sense. She is striving to become cosmopolitan, she is trying to refashion herself as an Australian but also represents Australia in its attempts to come to terms with the wider world and to become a nation state. The deeper irony, of course, is that the book is also concerned with borders and identity and the meaning of borders, national and other borders, as a way of framing one's identity. So in many ways the irony rebounds in the decision of the Miles Franklin judges.

It was well known that I had been living in France, this was part of the pre-publicity and many of my friends thought that I may be going to stay forever in France. After all, years had gone by, I had gone for six months and it was now four years.

Naturally the Miles Franklin judges would have had a picture of me living in a chateau having fine dinners, enjoying the finer things of life, writing this book and probably felt that I didn't deserve to be rewarded in any way back in this country, that I had become some sort of cultural treason.

Then the Miles Franklin judges, with the Demidenko affair, had another author context come down on top of them; this is a woman masquerading as a Ukrainian writing a book about very tragic and historically crucial times in the history of the Ukraine. She adopts the persona of a Ukrainian, and the judges of the Miles Franklin, having learned the lesson that whatever an Australian does is Australian, decide to go further and decide that anything whatsoever published in this country can now be awarded the Miles Franklin prize.

I notice that some of the commentators on the

"The judges were struggling with various mutations of what used to be called the cultural cringe and I don't think they knew that they were infected."

Demidenko affair raised the possibility that multicultural art has now become fashionable and that they were caught up in the fashion of multiculturalism. Even if that were the case, we have quite a remarkably destabilised and erratic set of judgments by the same judges in both cases, veering from a cultural cringe, as I surmise, to a multicultural cringe. But it then occurred to me that the way they were behaving also said something about the way we are behaving out in the wider community and certain turmoil about the question of multiculturalism and old-style, mainstream culture.

We may have to step back from the Miles Franklin committee of judges and look at the huge amount of correspondence to the newspapers, the huge amount of controversy over both the decisions, to see exactly why the footing is so insecure here and why this could have happened, what it means to be an Australian writer. It seems to connect with other things that have come my way since returning to Australia, other pieces of evidence that I am gradually starting to see fit a pattern and I do believe there are certain cultural or intellectual viruses which are currently plaguing us to a degree, one of which I thought we had eradicated.

The concept of the cultural cringe in its crude version, I think that has gone. It is attributed to the critic A.A. Phillips, who said in 1950 that:

> *Above our writers and other artists looms the intimidating mass of Anglo-Saxon culture. Such a situation almost inevitably produces the characteristic Australian cultural cringe.*

This was the problem of being an artist in a small, provincial country a long way from the main centres, trying to produce art in the traditions of the English language and of course the international standards that we inherited. I don't think any longer we are awed into silence because we belong to the great English language culture, in fact the opposite seems to be the case.

However, I think we have shrugged that off only to be caught by other strains of the virus and it is very hard to be aware that we have it. The first piece of evidence that came to me was three young writers, all of whom are living overseas, have rung me or written to me about whether they should continue to live overseas or not. I don't know why they ask me, someone who has some confusions of his own, but these were writers of the younger generation asking me about the cultural cringe and whether they would be punished or whether their creativity would dry up because they found that they preferred to live elsewhere than Australia.

For a number of years the writers of my generation said that we were the first generation to decide to live in Australia. The writers and a lot of artists of the generation before myself went to live overseas, Miles Franklin included. Patrick White was in a great dilemma about whether to return to Australia after the Second World War and did. But many of his age, his peer group, stayed away, many of the important ones. So then my generation came along, said no, we are staying here, we may travel a lot but we're not going away to live our lives out in other countries.

"I had become some sort of cultural treason."

But I now realise that at present a significant number of young Australian writers and thinkers are living away and coming to me with this query about whether they should or should not do this, writers such as Joanna Murray-Smith, Catharine Lumby, Susan Johnson. And of course Peter Carey has gone to New York, Lily Brett lives in New York, the winner of this year's New South Wales literary prize, and there is quite a group now, the American group, representing some of the very best of our young talent. There is a definite uneasiness among these young writers about whether they have global aspirations and from which part of the world they should launch their careers.

Of course, Australian film directors, most of whom now make films for American companies, suffer this dilemma but are considered to be contaminated by their involvement with the more dynamic and more heavily invested American film industry. I don't see any of them worrying very much about it.

Phillips himself pronounced the cultural cringe dead in 1983. It is time, he said, to accord the phrase decent burial before the smell of the corpse gets too high. I think he would be amazed at the variants of the cultural cringe that do exist and were he alive today he would be surprised just how smelly the corpse sometimes can be.

I want to quote some more examples. One specimen is from the *Sydney Morning Herald*, where a columnist was commenting on the absence of David Malouf from a literary award presentation. She said, 'The author is currently sojourning in his Tuscan home.' I focused on this little sentence. I liked the use of the words 'currently' and 'sojourning'. They are what I would consider to be wink words – nudge, nudge, wink words – used to suggest that David Malouf of course is pursuing a leisurely occupation in foreign parts, free of any considerations about what might be happening back here in his home country. Then the delightful use of the words 'Tuscan home' implicates David in an offence. The word Tuscan is redolent, of course, with exotic superiority and isn't Australia the only home that one can have?

This leads to a rage that I think shows up in my next specimen, an advertisement for the Australia Council Creative Arts Fellowships which have been changed recently to specify that the recipient 'must spend most of their time in Australia'. So now, if you are going to get any funding, there's no way you're going to go over and have the good life in France, forget it.

! ?

SPEAKER: Excuse me, Frank, surely I'm not the only one . . . I don't want to hear about your disappointment over *Grand Days*. I came to your last luncheon, I bought your book, suffered as you did when you didn't win the prize, but I feel we don't want to hear it going on. If you're not happy to be in Australia . . .

FRANK MOORHOUSE: I would read this as touching a nerve. First of all, I want to say that I live here and I've lived here 50 years, and I have to say this is just ridiculous. I think what I was doing was teasing out and analysing some interesting examples of things that are going on in Australian cultural life which reflect in such things as the Miles Franklin but I accept your complaints that I have somehow lost your interest. It is certainly not a whinge; it's simply a piece of analysis that probably does, as I think this interruption has shown, touch a nerve.

Virtually coming to the end of this analysis anyway, I feel like some of the famous expatriates like Robert Hughes and Clive James and Germaine Greer. Not like Peter Allen who, every time he came here, was asked to sing, 'Wherever I wander, wherever I roam, I still call Australia home', but I will sing that at the end of this talk. The other expatriates, of course, have to say Australia has changed so much since they left it, it's not the same place they fled, the restaurants are really first class.

SPEAKER: You're here to talk about *Loose Living.* We don't want to hear about the Demidenko affair, we know all about the Demidenko affair.

FRANK MOORHOUSE: When you do buy or read a copy of *Loose Living*, it may I hope become apparent what I was talking about was connected to the book. The book is a parody of both the French nationality and certain conceptions of the Australian nationality and it involves good-humoured parody about these questions. I felt that talking about the decisions of the Miles Franklin and other little bits of evidence pointed up very clearly – some of the reaction today did too – that in fact these are tender spots.

SPEAKER: I still want you to autograph the book.

FRANK MOORHOUSE: Thank you. *Loose Living* was written while I was in France doing *Grand Days.* It is narrated by an Australian writer who is discovering the various ways of the French and becomes involved with an aristocratic duke who is in a bad state of moral and mental health. So the narrator is introduced to what is perhaps a vision of old France, of grand baronial dinners and various other sorts of lifestyles which contrast very much with his own very humble upbringing but when you read the book you'll see that he involves himself in turning various tables.

SPEAKER: Are we the only country with this problem?

FRANK MOORHOUSE: No, in fact that is very interesting. The variations that I'm talking about have been found, for instance, throughout Russian history, prerevolutionary and revolutionary, a total preoccupation with who was Russian, who was deserting Russia. Being a cosmopolitan was considered in Russia both under the old regime and the new regime to be an offence and there was an attempt to make sure that writers stayed in native Russia and wrote about the Russian peasants. It affected the United States, especially the painters, right up until after the Second World War. America invented the whole concept of un-American activities. Certainly other countries have a problem with it.

SPEAKER: Some of us have enjoyed hearing your views on something that has challenged the thinking and the responses of a lot of people. It's something that we won't get an easy answer to, but it's something that all people should consider as we move forward. We all have a responsibility, we can't just say the decisions are made by that group of people and that's it and then burrow away and make comments among our own friends. If the decisions matter to us and if our writers matter to us, if we nurture them and then they respond in the way that they do, we're grateful, some of us, that we're able to hear your views and thank you very much for being so honest with us.

Ruth Rendell

Creator of the long-lived Inspector Reginald Wexford and author of more than 50 crime novels, Rendell is also known as Barbara Vine, author of a darker line of psychological thrillers, such as *A Dark Adapted Eye* (1986) and *A Fatal Inversion* (1987). With many of her books successfully adapted for television, and numerous crime writing awards, she is one of the most popular authors in the genre.

11 October 1995

Some 32 years ago I went on a holiday trip to Ireland with my husband, my little boy and a friend of his, touring around in a car, and we went to County Wexford. It did not mean very much to me at the time except that I had never been there before. In the next few months after I came home, I thought I would write a detective story to see if I could do it.

I had read a lot of detective stories and I was quite interested to see if I could create the kind of thing that I had so much enjoyed. I did not make very elaborate plans for it. I never thought it would be published. I had a plot which I thought was quite original and new and indeed rather shocking and advanced for its time, as it proved to be. It would not be now. I had to have a detective but at that time the detective and his sidekick, his assistant, seemed to be far less important than the characters and the plot so I made my detective, as I began to write, a sort of amalgam of other people's detectives.

I had been reading at the time the novels of an American crime writer called Hillary Waugh, a series of crime novels featuring a detective, a chief of police, in a small New England town. It was this character who contributed very much to the character of the man who was going to be Wexford. And there were also other detectives who contributed to him, notably Maigret in the Simenon novels and one or two others from the 1930s such as Sir Henry Merivale and so on. And even perhaps a detective in the novels of A.E.W. Mason whose name is Hanaud in *At the Villa Rose* and *The House of the Arrow*. So all these characteristics went into Wexford. I created a sidekick for him and called him Burden and I cannot remember why I did that. I just picked it out of the air or perhaps out of the telephone directory. But Wexford was born like that and he was given this name because I had just been to Ireland.

Well, they had to do their stuff in some town in England and I called it Kingsmarkham. This was because my son, who was a little boy at school at that time, had a close friend whose name was Keith Markham. I wanted to make this sound like a very English country town. I needed a prefix and it was going to be Bishops or Kings; it ended up Kings. These things are so much a matter of chance. I put these people in this town and at that time Wexford did not have a Christian or given name, Burden did.

So the book was written. It was typed by me on an old typewriter – I had an old-fashioned typewriter – on foolscap paper, single spacing. When I wanted to change bits – I was living in some straitened circumstances; I could not have afforded to go out buying paper ad lib – I cut off bits of a page and stuck it onto the next page. It did not look very nice.

A year later or more I decided that I had written enough books and I would send one to a publisher. I had written about six or seven novels by then and done nothing with them. My husband was working for the *Daily Mail* in London at the time and he asked the book page editor what I should do. He suggested that I might send it to Hutchinson who were then an independent publisher but are now part of Random House, who are still my publishers. They did not take this manuscript but they were quite encouraging. Had I done anything else? What I had done, of course, was the book with Wexford it and Burden and Kings Markham called *From Doon with Death* which was the first Wexford book.

I sent it to them in that state: single spacing, on foolscap, chopped around, glued together, stuck with cellotape. And now if people write to me and ask me how they should prepare a manuscript and how they should write I tell them: double spacing, as beautifully typed as you can manage, even possibly bound. I do produce, I think, quite good-looking manuscripts myself. But then, when it was most important really for me to produce a nice-looking manuscript, that was what it was like. However, they did publish it and that was Wexford.

My publishers lost this very, very small book. About 50,000 titles were published annually in 1964. And it was lost, of course, it disappeared. I did have one or two nice reviews for it. My publishers gave me an advance of £75 which was a pretty small sum even in 1964. However, in the following year an American publisher took that book and gave me 15 times as much as an advance. I could not live by writing then, on that. I think it has got better. But that was not my aim and it never has been, really.

After that, I realised that I must write more Wexford books and I did. When I saw that I was stuck with this character and that I might be stuck with him for years. I decided that I had better change him. In the next book he got a first name. He got a wife. And since he was talking to somebody who asked him if he had any children he replied, 'I have two girls.' I did not think much about that. It just seemed to happen. Well, they had to have names. His wife had to have a name and I called her Dora. I knew a woman called Dora so I called her that, not a name I like. I had to name the girls. For some reason – the reason is now lost in the mists of time – I called the girls Sylvia and Sheila, again not names I particularly like. But I always answer my inquiries on this score by saying, well, Wexford likes them. Then he had to have a name. I named him after my favourite uncle. His name is Reginald and that is Wexford's name.

"I found I could not change him. As I wrote the next couple of books he reverted to type and I was stuck with the straitlaced Michael Burden."

So by this time I had quite a family for Wexford and I had this place he lived in. By the way, I based Kingsmarkham on the town of Midhurst in Sussex in southern England where I had lived for a time as a child. I later rather regretted this because I do not live there. I live in a very different type of countryside and very different architecture and whenever I write a Wexford I have to go down to Sussex and check it all out. But it was too late to do anything about it by then. This is what happens when you do not make plans for the future because you do not think there is a future. You just write and you are stuck with all this stuff.

So I wrote more Wexford books. I wrote a book called *No More Dying Then* in which Burden, who is very happily married with two children, loses his wife; she dies. I did not think much about it at the time. Sometimes it reminds me of those lines from *King Lear*: 'As flies to wanton boys, are we to the gods; they kill us for their sport.' And so I kill people like that in my book. I killed this poor woman because I thought she was rather dull. Just like that. I also killed poor Jean Burden for the dramatic effect of having Burden in deepest mourning and frightful misery for the whole of this book.

By this time I had come into the '70s and I had never heard a great deal of response to my books. I had not had very much fan mail at that time though they sold rather well. I did not think about Wexford and Burden as having any impact on a public. But one or two policemen told me that they did not think Burden, so prudish, so straitlaced, so disapproving, could have been a real policeman because no real policeman would survive in the sordid world in which the police lived.

So I was a bit chastened and I thought, well, I will change him. I will make him more broadminded and he does have a love affair, something of a consolation for his widowerhood. But I found I could not change him. As I wrote the next couple of books he reverted to type and I was stuck with the straitlaced Michael Burden.

Then I was speaking at a meeting of library users somewhere in East Anglia and again a policeman in the audience said, 'I really think Burden is too disapproving and too censorious to be a real policeman.' I told how I had tried to change him and could not. After that a woman came up to me very timidly when I was signing books and said, 'I would like to tell you that I think your Burden is true to life because he's just like my husband and my husband is a detective inspector.' So I felt vindicated.

Wexford did not change much, but he began to gather a larger extended family. He acquired a nephew who was quite an important detective superintendent in London. I was living in Chelsea at the time and I was very taken with the river there and Chelsea Reach and the statue of Sir or Saint Thomas More according to your religious persuasion; so was Wexford. I thought, well, Wexford had better have a minor illness and go to London to recuperate and while he is there assist his nephew in some case which is much too complicated for the metropolitan police to solve but Wexford will manage to do it. So I took him to London and he also lost a lot of weight.

Both in my mind and in print in the books I had constructed a picture of what Wexford looked like physically. He was going to be very big and tall and coarse and at one time and sporadically ever since, I'm sorry to say, overweight. And I saw his face as being very fair and with sparse fair hair and very pale blue eyes. I described him, I think, several times as an ugly man. His younger daughter is very beautiful and she is described as being like him. And I think we all know what it is like for somebody who is quite, let us say, plain-faced themselves nevertheless to have a beautiful child who looks like them.

Sometime in the middle of the '70s I was sitting up in bed, in a country cottage I had at the time, reading a book – what else? – and my son walked into the bedroom eating a plate of fish and chips and said, 'Mother, has it occurred to you that Wexford is your father?' He was doing a psychology course at the time and was very Freudian. I said that I did not think it was true. But I do believe now that perhaps all women writers who have or have had a good relationship with their fathers, when they are creating a senior character, a character of some authority who is an older man, they do put a lot of their fathers into him and perhaps I did. I also put quite a lot of myself into Wexford. I am not sure if I put anybody else in but who knows? These things are picked up along the way.

"My son walked into the bedroom eating a plate of fish and chips and said, 'Mother, has it occurred to you that Wexford is your father?'"

By the '80s Wexford had acquired two grandsons. When I began he was 52 years old. Now that was almost too old to be a policeman at all. But you must remember that I did not know there would ever be any more. I did not know it would ever be published, let alone that it would ever come to television. So at some time I made a more or less conscious decision that, whereas I would try to make my Wexford books very topical, to give portraits always of the contemporary scene, I would never allow Wexford or Burden or their families to grow any older. So we have all aged but not Wexford and he remains like a character in Greek myth, perpetually, if not young, middle-aged and he will not grow any older. I will not say he will never die but he will only die with his creator. And by the time, of course, that his creator and he die, he will be very, very much younger than his creator and probably young enough by then to be her son – not my father but my son.

It was in the early '80s that the first mention was made of Wexford coming to television. But, as is always the case, the people who run television were very cautious. It is a cautious medium, a lot is at risk and it hung fire for a very long time. I am often asked if I had anybody in mind to play the part. I really never did. When I saw the rushes of the first production that was made which was *Wolf to the Slaughter* – the third Wexford book – I was rather taken aback to see George Baker in the lead role because he was so unlike my idea of Wexford. He was a handsome man, dark, very big, of course, and tall and that was right, whereas the actor who played Burden was perfect – it was as if my Burden had been made flesh. It was almost an uncanny thing to see such perfect casting.

Very soon after that I began to love George and I thought he was perfect. If Wexford had not looked like that, perhaps Wexford ought to have looked like that and he began to look like that for me. So although I have never written a word, a line, a word that was designed for television, that changed because I knew it would be adapted to television, I do, when I am writing about Wexford, see George's face in my mind's eye.

The Wexfords should have been shot in Sussex but the studios where they are made are in Portsmouth and so therefore they were made not in Sussex but in Hampshire in the New Forest and the town of Kingsmarkham is Romsey in Hampshire. Romsey is now becoming Wexfordised – it is just beginning to have the Wexford cafe and the Wexford garage. Some of the residents like this and some do not but you cannot hope to please everyone.

By the '90s they were running out of Wexford novels and short stories to televise. If I were to do nothing but write Wexfords there might be enough but I am very anxious not to write the same book twice. They have made them all and now they are making some of my other books under the title *The Ruth Rendell Mysteries*. I think they are very well made but a lot of audiences at home are very disappointed because Wexford did not appear on cue.

However, in 1991 I wrote a book called *Kissing the Gunner's Daughter* which was made for television and was successful. And then the rumour – not started by me – went round that I was going to kill Wexford and I denied it very resolutely. I can assure you it will never happen. As I have said already, Wexford dies with me. Then I had what I hope is a happy idea and it seems to have been – it has gone down well in England – that I would use Wexford, the Wexford books, to air some ideas I have about desirable social change and showing up some social evils. It is too strong to call it a political platform, but the aim is to show up some of these things and in so doing expand Wexford so that he is always growing and changing.

So in this new book, *Simisola*, Wexford examines unemployment and racism – the question of racism has only just come to a little place like Kingsmarkham – and domestic slavery. It is a state-of-Britain novel. It almost revolutionised my writing of Wexford and I thought, I have something new to handle here, something to help the expansion of Wexford's character, and I will do it again.

When I write another Wexford, which will probably be started at any rate at the end of next year, I will write again about some social evil and possible change. I think that in doing so – as in *Simisola* – I will not lose what I hope are rich and interesting characters nor, of course, an exciting and suspenseful theme.

John Berendt

A former New York magazine editor and *Esquire* columnist, Berendt fell in love with Savannah, Georgia, during his travels around the United States, and moved there to write *Midnight in the Garden of Good and Evil*, a true murder story and a vivid portrait of a Southern society. Published in 1994, the book has been on the *New York Times* bestseller list longer than any other, is an international success, and was filmed by Clint Eastwood.

16 October 1995

I am a Northerner who has written a book about the South. In America, a lot of people think that that is unnecessary, arrogant and redundant and all those terrible things, because Southerners are so good at doing it themselves. And that is true. But there I was a journalist, a magazine journalist; I had begun to tire of the monthly column for which I would dig not too deeply into a subject, write something very clever and then on to something else the next month.

I wanted to get into something in a deeper sort of way; you can only do that by writing a book. I had never written a book; I wondered if I could. I stumbled on Savannah, as I described in the book, in 1982, on a whim trip, because it was cheaper than having an expensive meal in New York. I fell in love with Savannah. I went back to New York and was involved in various projects and three years later, in thinking over likely topics, I thought, what about Savannah? I knew about the murder case before I went down there in 1985 to write the book, so I knew I had that to work with. In the book it comes somewhat later. That was a major piece of licence.

I went back to Savannah with my belongings

and I moved there from New York. I kept my New York apartment but I took another one in Savannah and for five years I lived there, researching, mixing, writing this book. In 1990 I went back to New York and for two more years I worked on it and then sold it.

When I went down in 1985 to write the book, I went to see a woman I had seen on my first trip, Mary Hardy; she is in the second chapter of my book – the woman who took me out to the graveyard to Conrad Aiken's bench. I told Mary Hardy that I was going to write a book about Savannah. Her response surprised me. She said, 'I should tell you that as far as Savannah is concerned, being a writer and being from New York is a deadly combination.' She meant that no one would trust me.

Fortunately she was wrong; people did talk to me. But she was on to something very real and, for want of a better expression, I would call it the Civil War factor. As a Northerner living in New York City, I had not thought that it would still be going strong in the South but it does. In my book there is a scene in which Joe Odom – who is my alter ego in Savannah and who constantly comments on my progress through Savannah – and I were on the roof of his house watching the St Patrick's Day parade.

As a group of marchers came into the square below, they were dressed in grey as Southern soldiers, their Civil War outfit, and they were marching in front of a wagon with low sides. From the roof, I could see in the wagon itself the lifeless form of a Union soldier in blue, lying there with blood on him and if you had been standing on the street as most people along the route were, you could not have seen this soldier, so it was a rather striking example, I thought, of the lingering resentment in the South toward the North. I had not known that it still existed. And Joe Odom, this man whose house I was standing on the roof of, once introduced me to a friend of his, to a woman who owns a lot of Piggly Wigglies. (Piggly Wigglies are grocery stores in the South.)

He said, 'I'd like you to meet Johnny B, John Berendt'. He called me Johnny B. 'He's a good yankee,' he said. And this woman said, 'How could he be? He's not dead yet.' It is not only the Civil War that creates this feeling. There is a famous essay by H.L. Mencken called 'The Sahara of the Beaux Arts'; it is a classic of the form. He wrote it in 1917 and he tore the South apart for being a cultural wasteland. He said such things as: 'There are single acres in Europe with more first-rate men in them than the whole of the South of the United States, south of the Potomac.'

"All fiction or literature in order to be good should be regional."

And that was one of the nicer things he said. 'Today,' he said, 'you will not find a single Southern poet above the rank of neighbourhood rhymester. You will not find a single prose writer who can actually write.' And at the time he may have had a point but shortly after that the South underwent an enormous renaissance in letters starting with the fugitive poets in Nashville: Alan Tate, John Crow-Ransom, Robert Penn Warren and then later, William Faulkner, Tom Wolfe, Tennessee Williams, Truman Capote, Reynolds Price. Dozens of Southern writers. This was pointed out some years later to H.L. Mencken, who said, 'Well, see what I did? Got 'em going.'

What is it about the South, we often wonder, that makes it such a romantic place, that has, in

> **"The people I found are just the typical people: a man who walks an invisible dog; a man who wears makeup on one eye . . ."**

fact, fostered this literary revolution? Perhaps it can be seen in something that Flannery O'Connor once said. She was in a bookshop and she saw a shelf full of new young writers and she said, 'You know what's the matter with them? They're not from anywhere.' And she had a point. Flannery O'Connor was from the South, from Georgia, and was actually born in Savannah. She was very much from the South. She made the point that all fiction or literature in order to be good should be regional. 'It should come from a place where there is a shared sense of history, or shared values. Somewhere where there is homogeneity. An alikeness,' she said.

Tennessee Williams said that Southerners have a humorous and colourful way of talking. They are much more lyrical than Northern people in their everyday speech and he said that the Southern temperament incorporates a love of folly and fantasy and it may well be that that is what I found in the South that was so appealing. Because everywhere I went people did tell stories; and in my book you will see that I adapted this story-telling technique to my own writing.

In the South you are the accumulation of everything you have done and everything your family has ever done. In the North, you can remake yourself any day of the week; you are forgiving of somebody new, but not in the South. You cannot escape your past, it trails behind you and this is reflected in the way people speak. For instance, in the North I might say something like, 'Before going out, Mrs Jones put on her coat.' That would never do in the South where you would say, 'Before going out Mrs Jones put on the coat her third husband gave her before he committed suicide.' You might never know any more about the third husband or the first two or anything about the coat but you know a whole lot more about Mrs Jones than you would in the North.

Savannah is an isolated city on the Georgia coast, isolated by geography because it is surrounded by the ocean and pine woods and marshes, but also isolated by choice. They do not want to have anything to do with the outside world except for travellers who want to come and spend some money and leave.

For some reason, Savannah seems to foster eccentric characters. This is true all over the South, in fact. One of the favourite pastimes of Southerners is to gossip and you do not gossip about trees or buildings, you gossip about other people. So when you talk about a person it is so much better if they have done outlandish things, ridiculous things; it makes the talk so much more fun.

The people I found are just the typical people: a man who walks an invisible dog; a man who wears makeup on one eye, all these for good reasons, of course; a black drag queen, the Lady Chablis; a voodoo priestess who goes into the graveyard, the garden as she calls it, at midnight to put a curse on the District Attorney or anything you might pay her $25 for and in the meantime she asks her old man, the dead one, to give her a number she can play and make some money, and never gets it. There is one who knows the words and music to 6000 songs, Emma Kelly, whom Johnny Mercer named 'the lady of 6000 songs' after he tested her memory and estimated that that was how many songs she knew. And the ladies of the married women's card club who, once a month, play cards, and it is a ritual that does not exist anywhere else in the South even. People in Savannah have sometimes said to me – they love the book in Savannah, by the way – but some people have said, 'Well, these aren't typical people. Why did I choose only eccentrics? God knows if there were only eccentrics, chaos would reign and the Savannah water supply would be poisoned,' etcetera.

Not to compare myself to Flannery O'Connor, but she pointed out that she wrote about grotesque people. Robert Penn Warren went further, saying, 'Yes, you should write about grotesque people.' A writer does not do his community any good by praising it. You write about people who are somehow off because it draws the reader's attention, it is dramatic to do that; and in writing about unusual people, you really comment about usual people. And it is a dramatic way to do it. People in my book have the same problems, come up against the same forces that people who are not so eccentric face and, in a way, it is a comment on the average person.

So, you find in Southern literature a tendency to write about 'the grotesque', the unusual, the eccentric and I am comfortable doing that because I dote on these people as well. I am drawn to eccentrics. Tennessee Williams was accused of exaggerating and he said, 'I'm a dramatist, not a sociologist.' What I'm writing about is human nature and I do this as a journalist; I wrote the book in the form of a novel but I am a journalist. I spent the first year interviewing people. I have hundreds of hours of tapes and I have thousands of pages of notes.

My book is not, strictly speaking, a novel created out of my head; it is a reporting job in which every sentence in it has something that relates to notes I took somewhere of a conversation, of hours in the library, whatever. In one interview, a question was thrown at me. Janet Malcolm is an American who wrote a piece, a very famous piece in the *New Yorker*, criticising the book *Fatal Vision* about Jeffrey McDonald who was tried for the murder of his family. And there were charges and counter-charges that the author had somehow skewed the writing and slanted things and Janet Malcolm, in tearing him apart in the *New Yorker*, wrote the following lines:

> *Every journalist who is not too stupid or too full of himself to notice what is going on, knows what he does is morally indefensible. He is a confidence man, preying on people's vanity, ignorance or loneliness, gaining their trust and betraying them without remorse.*

I was being interviewed. This was thrown at me and she said, 'What do you think of this?' And I read it twice to give myself time. I had read the piece; I had read these lines before, but never applied them to myself, but I said, 'I take issue with only one word: "Betray". I didn't betray any of my subjects. However, I did go into an interview with some preconceived notions, that is true.' Usually when I went to see somebody in Savannah, I had already heard a story that I wanted to hear more about from this person directly and very often I would steer the conversation around to that subject and most of the time I never had to ask the question, the answer came tumbling out.

So I said, 'I do manipulate my subjects but I don't think I betray them.' That was my immediate answer, my clever way of getting out of it and I had to think on this more deeply. And Janet Malcolm, of course, does have a point because somebody being interviewed is apt to say something absolutely marvellous. I would be a fool to say, 'Oh, that's wonderful. Now I can use you to represent stupidity and vanity in Savannah.' You do not do that. But you do think to yourself, that's terrific. So maybe in a sense you do betray your subject as a journalist.

Anyway, here I was in Savannah, a magazine editor who had decided to write a book. But, after five years, there was no book. It was 1990, no book. Where was it? Rumours circulated that I was not writing one, that I had become one of Savannah's many eccentrics and that my quirk was that I was pretending to write a book. Let us humour John Berendt. Let him come over, give him drinks, talk to him, but there is no book. Then in January 1993, word got out that, indeed, Random House had bought a book I had written about Savannah and it would be published in January 1994. Panic struck Savannah! What have we told him? Am I in the book?

Would people ever want to come to Savannah? John Berendt was writing about a murder, about a man with poison to kill everybody, about a black drag queen, about all these strange people he seemed to find so interesting. What is going to happen? The book came out in January of 1994 and a vast sigh of relief was heard in Savannah because the book is a very affectionate portrait of the city, even though it is about a murder and about strange people and odd doings. And because it is such a love note to the city, tourism has, indeed, increased by about 50 per cent. That was a year ago. The Georgia Department of Trade and Tourism announced that tourism was up 50 per cent. That alone meant that over the course of the year Savannah took in an additional $100 million.

! ?

SPEAKER: I would like to know what you did to establish yourself as an eccentric. As you say, you are only allowed stay in Savannah for a brief time if you are not an eccentric.

JOHN BERENDT: I took an apartment – that impressed people in Savannah. A lot of reporters, doing travel articles, would come in with a pad and pencil in hand and demand answers and have to catch the plane out the next day. I moved there. They liked that, a sort of commitment; they saw me jogging in the park, they saw me in my broken-down car. They saw me everywhere, and they got used to me and they liked the fact that I was willing to cast my lot with them for a certain amount of time. I did not behave in any eccentric manner but, as I said, they began to think I was only kidding about the book.

SPEAKER: Did the structure of the book give you any initial problems?

JOHN BERENDT: Structure was everything. I knew I had certain elements: I loved Savannah, the city itself; the murder case was, of course, a major element; but so were a variety of people I met, whom I wanted to pull into the story. So I started writing chapters as if they were magazine profiles: one about Chablis, one about Emma Kelly, the lady of 6000 songs, one about Lee Adler, the historic preservationist and the real task was to pull those stories together so that it all seemed like one big story. And there is a subtitle in this book. The title is long enough, but I added three more words that are on the inside: 'A Savannah Story'. Not stories. Story.

In order to make all of this diverse material seem like one story, I had to structure it in a way that pulled it together. There were certain unifying elements. Savannah was one of them; all the things happened in Savannah. My being the narrator was another. All of these things happened in front of me or were told to me. Joe Odom, a character in the book, was yet another element of glue because he kept reappearing and commenting on my progress through Savannah as if it all were one story. I knew about the murder before I started and I could have started with the murder or with the murder having already happened but I decided I would introduce people to Savannah first so that they got to know the city and the people who lived there.

Then, having met all the whole cast, the murder would happen; it happens in the middle of the book. It happens pretty far on; it was a bit dicey. I wanted to move it closer to the front but I could not. So I introduce everybody first, the murder happens and then the story takes a more linear form but the structure was absolutely everything, a major thing to work out. As a matter of fact, two months before I was finished, I took chapter number nine and made it chapter number one. I started originally with chapter number two which is my entrance into Savannah and how I got to know Savannah, my first stay there years before I started to do the book. It was nice but not very dramatic.

So I took the evening at Mercer House and put it first and I think it made all the difference because you get a sense of what the book is going to be like. Then I could afford, in chapter two, to look back into how I first came to Savannah. The structure is absolutely everything.

Judy Cassab

One of Australia's most admired contemporary painters, Cassab published her *Diaries* of 40 years in 1995. A dramatic and optimistic memoir, it won the Kibble Award for women's 'life writing'. Born in Vienna of Hungarian parents, Cassab and her family survived German occupation and immigrated to Australia in 1951. She has shown her work in dozens of solo exhibitions, twice won the Archibald Prize, and received the CBE and Order of Australia.

13 November 1995

It feels strange to be a speaker at a literary lunch, firstly because I don't think of myself as a writer; I'm a painter. True, I began keeping a diary when I was 12 and have continued to record my life ever since. I have 35 handwritten volumes which are locked in a cupboard. It's the only place in the house which I lock. My husband, Jansci, has never seen them nor has anyone else. I certainly never intended publishing them.

The second reason why it is strange is because I'm used to expressing my thoughts with a brush. When I turned 70 my friends Bernie and Barbara Leser invited us for dinner. Bernie asked, 'Judy, when are you going to do something about your diaries?' 'When I'm old,' I answered aggressively. A few minutes later I realised: I am old.

Bernie started the ball rolling. I have had the diaries typed into nine volumes. The National Library of Canberra first asked me for them. I feel relief that they are now safe just in case our flat burns down. I don't feel anxious about the paintings. I can always paint others. It's different with the diaries. I lost the first 11 years of my diaries when they were left in my childhood home in Beregsvász and perished during the war. I lost everything else there but objects, even beautiful objects, are replaceable. One can never recapture a 12-year-old self.

But to return to the typed volumes: there are 1600 pages and Bernie suggested that it be cut down to a more manageable 500. Who will do that? My friend Elizabeth Riddell did, a labour of love.

I no longer possess the diary from my 18th year either but I can tell you how I met my husband Jansci. After matriculation I participated in a debating scene. He was among the adults in the audience, sitting with a familiar friend named Feri. He was 36 years old, double my age, but, as he later assured me, this would diminish with every passing year. Jansci had remained a bachelor; no friend or family member had succeeded in marrying him off. So when I sat down after debating he said to Feri, 'See that girl? That's the one I want to marry.' Feri introduced us and I fell for him just as he fell for me.

Jansci, a chemical engineer, was the director of a brewery in Podhering near a town called Munkác. The brewery was owned by Count Schönborn an aristocrat whose ancestral castle, Schönborn, near Vienna, had 300 rooms resplendent with masterpieces, Rembrandts, Rubens, Grecos, and the like; but the count mostly preferred to live in Beregvár, another smaller castle in the forest near the brewery.

When Jansci proposed three weeks after our first meeting I told him I loved him but could only marry him if he promised he would always let me remain a painter. How he kept that promise is a golden thread all through our long marriage. He started right away. 'You are very young,' he told me. 'I want you to go to Prague and study painting for a year before you marry me. I don't want you to say in five years, "Oh, if only I could have studied".' By sending me away he really chained me. I pined and longed for him and after my lessons I had a regular cry.

Hitler's tanks roaring into Prague cut that year short. I saw a never-ending multitude of them occupying the city and I knew I had to get home fast. After long hours of standing in a queue at the German Embassy waiting for travel papers, a voice boomed out, 'Jews to the end of the queue'. It was the first time in my life that I was not a girl, not a woman, not a human being, but a Jew. It took three days to get that paper stamped and two days on slow trains to get home.

Jansci and I married in 1939. Someone asked him why he hadn't married 10 years before. 'How could I?' he answered, 'she was only eight.' Two years later Jansci was sent to a forced labour camp, and we knew that we would not be allowed any contact. So before he left we chose a star on which to meet. We both kept this nightly appointment. Jansci says it kept him alive.

We had one meeting after he had been gone a year. A visiting corporal told me that Jansci's group would be travelling through Beregszász coming from Poland going to Russia. A friend, whose husband was on the same train, and I spent the whole day at the railway station not knowing the arrival time because it was a military train. It was January, freezing cold.

The train came at 3 am and stopped for only a few minutes. We raced towards the cattle wagons where our men shouted out names. We reached up our arms and they grabbed us and lifted us into the crowded space. The train moved on. There was a wooden crate in the centre on which stood a square of plum jam and a flickering candle. By the time day dawned we were near the Russian border at Volóc and then the train slowed; we jumped into the snow.

Most young husbands begged their wives to stay home with mother. Jansci told me, 'If this has to happen to us at least take the opportunity; go to Budapest and study painting', so I did. By great good luck my teacher was Aurél Bernát, a fine artist.

"I told him I loved him but could only marry him if he promised he would always let me remain a painter."

On my first day we were given the task of drawing an old woman's hands with charcoal. Bernát thought mine was the best drawing in the class and he asked me if I worked with oils. I certainly did although there was no-one to teach me in Beregszász, no gallery, only postcards my parents bought in Italy. My teacher said, 'Bring in a painting tomorrow.' I brought a portrait of a blonde with bare shoulders and a fox fur. Bernát was speechless. Finally he declared, 'It's awful!'. I fell into a cellar of despair. 'Why, but why?' 'Because it's kitsch.' At the time I did not understand.

Bernát continued to break down my skill. He told me to work with pastels, a medium I had not used before. He wanted me to draw without so much as a single glance at the paper. The loops and curves I discovered surprised me. 'It's your subconscious,' he said. He advised me to stop painting portraits for a while. 'Do landscapes; do still lifes.'

Then Jansci came back. One of the very few that lived through the slave labour camps, he witnessed whole communities executed by the SS. He told me the tragedy of the Jews is that they cling together and so are much more easily rounded up, like sheep. We lived together in Budapest but before long we heard that the Jews in Beregszász were now in ghettos.

In the middle of May, my mother, grandmother, my uncle, my stepfather, Jansci's mother, brother and his family, were all deported. Witnesses saw our family being herded into cattle trains, 80 locked in a wagon with only a bucket of water, no food. Our friend Feri, the one who had introduced us, went to his office, carefully placed his yellow star on his desk and shot himself.

Jansci made me take the yellow star off. I shed my old self and became Maria Koperdak, my maid. I took a job in a pharmaceutical factory and Jansci chose to live in a Jewish house. We no longer had any open contact. Once we met on the street and we passed one another like strangers for he wore the yellow star and I didn't.

I compelled my body to work the eight hours every day and I kept trying to work out where the Allies were. Refugees poured into Budapest from Transylvania. In October the governor announced on the radio that the Russians were only 60 kilometres from the capital. He had decided that, instead of having the city shot to pieces, we would surrender.

Oh, the joy! I was on the way to the Jewish house when I met Jansci who flew to me, his eyes brimming over, and a complete stranger came running towards Jansci, embraced him and with the same movement tore the yellow star off his coat. The euphoria lasted all day. However, towards evening the radio began playing German marches. Rumours had it that the Nazi group now occupied the radio station. They had shot the announcer and commandeered the microphone. There had been a coup.

Immediately the Nazis began evacuating the Jews from the Jewish houses. I asked the military commandant in the factory to help me get my husband out. He escorted us to my uncle Gyuszi's flat which he shared with his Gentile girlfriend, Manyi. She was already hiding a mother and a child and welcomed Jansci. The next day Jansci decided to move into the ghetto. He thought it would be better than this furtive existence. It was like a melodrama. I declared, 'If you go into the ghetto, so do I.'

Then the doorbell rang and Kati and Fritzi, his oldest friends, fell into an embrace. Kati was an actress and Fritzi a film director. 'Thank God we have found you. We have looked for you everywhere in Budapest and now you are coming with us and we will hide you.' 'You are mad,' he answered. 'Don't you know that those who are hiding Jews are being shot too?' 'For God's sake,' said Kati, 'what are friends for?' And so we took Jansci to Róna Ucca in Zugló.

He spent three months there. Whenever a stranger came to the door he hid in a wardrobe. Not only did Kati and Fritzi risk their lives, they also risked their family who had escaped from Debrecen before the Russians occupied it. They became subterranean creatures. The siege of Budapest was on.

Most people were afraid. I felt fear only when the bombing stopped. Electricity, gas and water supplies ceased. We started to ration food. I tried not to think whether Jansci had survived the bombs locked in the wardrobe in Zugló. When some horses were shot we ran out with kitchen knives and cut their flesh; it was a feast. And when the first Russian entered our cellar Jansci was with him. Zugló had been taken 11 days before the Russians reached us. Jansci moved with them, wanting to reach me and take me back to Zugló before the looting and the raping began.

In February we left Zugló and moved back to the city. We lived in a lawyer's office we shared with four other families. The windows were shot out and it was bitterly cold. The desk was our bed and we took the velvet drapes off the windows and used them as blankets.

"May 1959 brought me my first sight of Alice Springs. I knew at once how important the moment was – a recognition that now I knew why we had to immigrate to Australia."

In March transports started. The crowd shoved in through windows; others sat on the roof of the train. When we arrived in Beregszász I could not grasp reality. After Budapest's burning houses and dead bodies these houses were untouched. It seemed that every stone and blade of grass screamed in our ears, 'Nothing has happened, nothing has changed'; but the soul of the town was missing.

I met people I knew who had returned from concentration camps like skeletons. For the first time I heard of the crematoriums and how, to the tune of Dr Mengele's 'J'Attendrai', Jews were selected to be gassed to death.

We went back to Budapest. My two children were born there. When I found I was expecting our first child we moved to a one-room flat which had no glass in the windows but we did have Pergamen paper. We also had an iron stove; the pipe stuck through our paper window. Since Beregszász was now part of Soviet Russia there wasn't anything I could have saved from our old house. Basics like cups and saucers or blankets and pillows, I borrowed all these from a friend.

Then there was a miracle. Jansci made his first business trip since the war to Vienna. He went with the brewery truck. I was still worrying about nappies and towels for the baby which were unobtainable in Budapest. The next evening the doorbell rang and there stood the driver of the truck with two large suitcases. 'Your husband sent these from Vienna,' he said; and when I opened the first one I saw baby shirts, nappies and towels and realised that these used to be mine. When my parents separated in 1929 I knew my mother had left a lot of things in Vienna but I had not given them a thought in all those years. I regarded this as a parcel from Anyu, my mother from up there. When Jansci returned he had a rational explanation for my miracle. His former boss, the Count Schönborn, had taken them out of storage and placed them in the cellar of his house in the Renngasse.

We spent four more years in Hungary. In 1949 we finally made the decision to emigrate. We spent a year in Vienna and another one in Salzburg waiting for our permits. We came to Australia in 1951 with our two boys. One was six years old, the other was four. We stayed at a boarding house in Bondi. The four of us shared one room and I shared a gas stove with eight other Hungarian refugee women. We arrived without English or money but I did have a letter of introduction to a man by the name of Charles Lloyd Jones. When I asked our landlord who this Charles Lloyd Jones actually was he thought I suffered from delusions of grandeur.

I contacted Charles and he told me he was being painted by an artist called Dobell. I didn't know who Dobell was. However, he commissioned me to paint his wife. When his son, the young Charles, came to pick me up from the boarding house in a Rolls Royce all my neighbours hung out of the window in disbelief.

In 1955 I won two prizes, the Perth prize, and later the *Women's Weekly* prize with a portrait of Judy Barraclough. I won it again the following year with a portrait of Elaine Haxton. At this stage of our new life in Australia painting was still considered a hobby. People used to ask me, 'And what do you do?' 'I paint,' I answered. 'Yes, yes, but what do you do?' It was so obvious that something one did not make a living at could not be classified as work. So, in order to make a living I began teaching, but we struggled.

Jansci insisted that we not touch the money I had won in prizes. 'It is your going away money,' he said. When the time came for me to travel, it was the studying time I couldn't have because of the war. London was my last stop. Judy Barraclough's friend, the famous model Barbara Goalen, sat for a portrait. It was seen by her neighbour Peter Thorneycroft, Chancellor of the Exchequer who had just resigned. He rang and commissioned me to do a portrait of him. He said, 'I have time now, you see, as I am unemployed.' I also painted Hugh Gaitskell, Leader of the Opposition.

By the time I left for home, I had several commissions which I did not have time to do, but for which I returned a year later. I took it into my head to get an exhibition in London. It seemed sheer lunacy, but I took along a portfolio of my work. Harry Miller of the Redfern Gallery which was booked up for six years sent me to the Crane

Kalman Gallery. He added, 'It is a heart breaking business this, but what do you expect? Painters wait years and years and you want to do it in a month.'

Andreas Kalman had already told me on the phone that he was booked up for years, but was willing to have a look at my work. So, it happened. 'Are you from Budapest?' 'No, from Beregszász.' 'I am from Mátészalka,' he said. 'I have been to Mátészalka once and I was invited for dinner to a chemist whose name was Kálmán,' I said. 'He was my father.' We were both so delighted about this (his whole family also perished), that since he liked my paintings he arranged with me a show in October 1959.

May 1959 brought me my first sight of Alice Springs. I knew at once how important the moment was – a recognition that now I knew why we had to immigrate to Australia. I felt like Ali Baba discovering the treasure cave. I felt greedy, I wanted it all. I began 14 pictures in a week. I have never experienced such colour. It was like a physical force hitting not only from front but sideways and from the back as well. At that time Ayers Rock only had one place to stay, a shed with a barrel on the roof to catch the rainwater if it rained and a tap for showering. The sheets we slept on were flown on a little plane to Alice Springs to be washed. The rock was a wonder like the Taj Mahal, indescribable. Full with legends, caves, murals, bones. My show at the Crane Kalman Gallery in London opened. I exhibited mostly the Alice Spring paintings and did well. There were good reviews in the *Times,* the *Observer* and others.

A painting of a woman's head was bought by a director of the Orient Line. He took it to his office where Sir Colin Anderson saw it. He was not only chairman of the Orient Line, but also chairman of the Tate Gallery. He said, 'If this girl could get a likeness she would be just right to paint Princess Alexandra who will launch our new ship the *Oriana.*' They went to the gallery and saw photographs of my London portraits. 'Could you undertake such a commission?' asked Sir Colin. My fare would be paid, of course. Only one thing: it is a secret. Talking about it would jeopardise the whole project. So I walked away, stunned, as if I had a bomb in my handbag.

"I do not start on a white ground, I start on a colour that I imagine is the person's colour."

In 1960 in early March a letter advised me that Her Majesty the Queen had allowed me to use the yellow drawing room at Buckingham Palace as a studio. In the palace my canvas looked like a green man from Mars, but I kept imagining the portrait for a ship rather than a palace. Meanwhile under my window there was the Changing of the Guard. 'Are you sure the six sittings will be enough?' asked the secretary. 'I think so,' I said. 'It's just that we have to vacate the yellow drawing room by the 22nd of April because on the 23rd General de Gaulle is moving in.' All these things were very strange as I tried to look at them from Beregszász and my childhood.

It was the beginning of an exciting phase of my life when I had enough commissions in England to keep me busy for two months each year. At home someone was teasing Jansci. 'How can you let your wife go to London for two months every year?' His answer was, 'You know, I prefer to have a happy wife for ten months a year than a frustrated one for twelve.' It is just part of the golden thread that I told you about.

! ?

SPEAKER: One of the things that you are famed for in your portraits is your psychological insight into the people you paint and I wondered how you get that.

JUDY CASSAB: I must tell you that it is purely intuition. So much so that I rely on it and I do not even want to know anything about the person. I do not read up. I do not look at *Who's Who*. I do not want to see a photograph. After I have seen the person once I decide what colour she or he is going to be and I put that acrylic wash over the canvas. So I do not start on a white ground, I start on a colour that I imagine is the person's colour. As I put the brush on the canvas I can already see the portrait in the mottled surface. It is there. I only have to work to get it out.

The best photograph, which is also an art form, is one moment of a life. In the portraits I paint one eye as it smiles in one sitting and on the next sitting maybe we talk about something sad so the other eye becomes a sad eye and like this hundreds of expressions accumulate on the face. It is not detectable immediately, but living with it, it certainly has a life of its own. This is something a photograph cannot do, nor does it happen in real life. Therefore I believe a good portrait transcends reality.

Josephine Hart

Irish-born Hart worked in magazine publishing, produced West End plays and presented a television book show before her husband, the international advertising figure Maurice Saatchi, helped persuade her to write fiction. The first thing she wrote was the opening chapter of *Damage* (1991), which was called 'a chilling implacable work of the erotic imagination', and became a bestseller and a Hollywood movie. Fascinated by sex, death and dark emotions, she followed up with *Sin* (1992) and *Oblivion* (1995), the latter about the effect of a young woman's death on her husband and mother.

13 March 1996

I'm sometimes asked why I set these dark tales within a family. Well, I reply, it was ever thus. If we go back to the beginning of literature, the story of Oedipus could, in the terminology of our times, be described as taking place within the first seriously dysfunctional family. Medea, who as we all know murdered her children so that her husband could not have them, is possibly the first child custody case!

The power of the family to mould us is always considered a positive power but we must face the possibility that it can painfully contribute to the negative aspects of our lives. 'Home,' T S Eliot wrote, 'is where we start from.' And he goes on to say 'we shall not cease from exploration/ and the end of all our exploring/ will be to arrive where we started/ and know the place for the first time.' And I think that's an extraordinary summary of the journey of life.

I started my journey in a very small town in Ireland called Mullingar – in Gaelic Muilean Cear – the crooked mill. I was born into a society of 7000 people, 98 per cent of whom believed exactly the same thing. The basic tenets were never questioned. Since that structure existed in every town and village in Ireland you will have some understanding of how on occasions we can be so passionately and consummately wrong.

From my father I developed a deep love of poetry. Initially he bribed me to learn lines by heart. The cost in those days was a packet of Rolos. I try the same with my children. I bribe them with computer games – sadly even poetry is subject to inflation. When I was 12 I went away to a very strict convent run by a French order of nuns, the Louis Order. These women were utterly dedicated to academic excellence. We got up at 6.30 in the morning, attended daily Latin mass, had probably two three-quarter-hour breaks during the day and went silently to bed at 9 o'clock. They were high-minded about life and work and determined to make us follow the most demanding path. Though this convent, Carrickmacross, was situated in a town even smaller than Mullingar, these nuns used to say to us in all seriousness, 'Wherever you go in the world, girls, always remember people will point you out and say "That's a Louis girl"!' Well, I'm a Louis girl, for better or worse.

I was a very focused young girl at boarding school. I had made up my mind that I was going to be an actress and a writer, depending on which world recognised my abilities fastest. But fate stepped in (three of my siblings died by the time I was 17) and I withdrew, not only from any idea of art but almost from any idea of a future in which I could live creatively. For a long period of time, I in a sense closed down the shutters in order to grieve privately with my family.

Finally, I left Ireland and went to London. Tremulously, I dabbled a little in the outskirts of acting but when offered the chance to apply for a scholarship to the Central School of Music and Drama, I turned it down. It was as though, finally and formally, I applied my will to the redirection of my life. I entered the business world and began a career in magazine publishing.

"I write in order to elicit terror and pity and then catharsis."

However, without wanting to sound like Joan of Arc, the voices in my head, in a sense, continued. They battled to have their story told. I refused to listen and continued with my publishing career. I believed that running 17 magazines would, by dint of exhaustion, kill them off. When this did not succeed, I started a company called Gallery Poets, to produce in London theatres and galleries the work of great poets, read by actors. Still the characters and stories in my head remained. I then developed Gallery Poets into a theatre production company.

In the months before I actually finally sat down and wrote *Damage* I had become what my husband described as a 'whirling dervish' of activity. I was a mother of a small child of four or five and of a child of twelve. I was still involved in publishing, though less actively. I was running Gallery Poets. I had two plays on in the West End, one *The Black Prince* by Iris Murdoch, the other Noel Coward's only tragedy, *The Vortex*. I mention this because it's rarely performed and is a masterpiece. It was at this moment that I decided to say yes to a 20-week program called *Books by My Bedside* which involved me reading five books every weekend in order to interview writers on the books they were reading.

The fact that I thought this was a perfectly sane way to live says a lot for the power of will. It also says a lot for the remarkable patience of my family.

Finally, through various sets of accidents – though of course Freud will tell you there is no such thing as an accident – I did sit down and start to write *Damage*.

In 1990 it was sent to Carmen Callil, head of Chatto, and to Sony Mehta, head of Knopf. Their reaction was astonishing. Though I didn't know it at the time, *Damage* had taken on a life of its own. At the end of that year, I had the ultimate New Year's Eve phone call. My agent Ed Victor rang, as I believed, to wish me a Happy New Year. Instead he said, 'How would you feel if I told you that Louis Malle wanted to make a film of *Damage*?' Louis Malle had been given the manuscript by Ed – remember this was before the book was published – and it had caught his imagination. Over time, I was to find out that the film of *Damage* had a life and force of its own. Having succumbed to writing and found that I was not as fragile as I had originally considered, I then wrote *Sin* and *Oblivion*.

"Though it is expressed physically, erotic obsession is driven by psychological attraction."

People ask me why I write. I write in order to elicit terror and pity and then catharsis. Like the ancient Greeks. I believe that having elicited terror and pity in your reader, you can then resolve these emotions.

Though I have been very grateful for the success that I've had, these are very unfashionable books. Many people hate them. They are extreme books and they elicit extreme emotions. The message of my books is, I suppose, 'this is possible, these things are possible, ignore this possibility at your peril'.

There is such a thing in life as moral luck. It's not my word, again it's one of the Greeks, Aristotle. Before we rush to condemn those who are in extreme states, whether through grief or desire, understand that condemnation is often predicated on the fact of inexperience.

Few good people willingly undertake the destruction of those around them. My first book, *Damage*, is about the fall of a man who is very good. It is not the story of the fall of a rake. The central character, who is never named, becomes erotically obsessed with his son's fiancee, Anna. Erotic obsession, which is different to lust, is a drive towards unity. Lust is driven by the eye, towards pleasure. Though it is expressed physically, erotic obsession is driven by psychological attraction. The following is an excerpt from *Damage* in which the main character is looking back on his life before his fatal meeting with Anna.

> *Had I died at fifty, I would have been a doctor, and an established politician, though not a household name. One who had made a contribution, and was much loved by his sorrowing wife, Ingrid, and by his children, Martin and Sally. My funeral would have been well attended by those who had gone further in life than I, and who therefore honoured my memory by their presence. And by those who believed they had loved the private man, and by their tears gave testimony to his existence. It would have been the funeral of an above-average man, more generously endowed with the world's blessings than most. A man who, at the comparatively early age of fifty, had ended his journey. A journey which certainly would have led to some greater honour and achievement, had it continued. But I did not die in my fiftieth year.*

> *There are few who know me now who do not regard that as a tragedy.*

Sin is about the power of envy which again I believe often begins in the family. Parents are unwise to ignore its destructive potential. After *Sin* was published, I had many letters from readers who told me that for years they seriously nursed a hatred for their siblings and on a number of occasions considered ways to harm them. *Sin* also deals with the desire of those who are good to ignore the reality of evil. Because of that, the innocent often collude in their own destruction. Ruth is the main protagonist in *Sin*. She says. 'I was exposed too early to goodness and I never recovered'. She is electively evil, seductively evil – I don't mean just in the sexual sense:

> *I chose my habit. I had, you understand, no grand schemes. For I was not ambitious. I did not need public applause. I was spiritual by nature. A spiritual, malevolent creature. There are, I believe, many of us about.*

Elizabeth, the object of Ruth's envy about which she has some inkling, refuses to see its dangers and therefore does not protect her child – and this failure has devastating consequences. The belief that evil does not exist is a particularly modern misunderstanding, and a very dangerous one.

Oblivion is about grief. Grief has, I believe, a moral landscape. It is the area where you are most cruelly tested, for you must make a decision to continue with life. Those who are parents are tested more fiercely than anyone else which is why, statistically, so many families are ripped apart by grief – divorce often follows tragedy. It seems to me that those who have been fiercely tested in the fire and have come through have a duty to show to others that life is possible, which is why I wrote *Oblivion*. *Oblivion* contrasts the lyrical grief of a young man whose wife has died with the almost insane, grieving rage of his mother-in-law as she watches him move on in life and, in moving on, push her daughter further to oblivion. The young widower comes in contact with a brilliant and manipulative playwright, and through his involvement with her establishes a new philosophy. She tells him:

> *You know, Mr Bolton, death's a double dealer. First he deals us our mortal death, and then our real death, oblivion, when we are finally forgotten . . . it is in the acknowledgment of the truth of our journey's end, not just death, but oblivion, that happiness lies. Happiness is a decision, Mr Bolton. Make it. And don't cry.*

Gordon Chater

British-born Chater came to Australia at the end of his Royal Navy service in 1946 and stayed as a much-loved comedian and serious actor. He began in radio and the Phillip Street revues, went on to television in *The Mavis Bramston Show* and *My Name's McGooley, What's Yours?*, and travelled to London and America with Steve J. Spears's one-man play, *The Elocution of Benjamin Franklin*. Having retired to the Gold Coast, he published his memoir, *(The Almost Late) Gordon Chater*, in 1996.

19 April 1996

It is wonderful to see how many people remember the shows that I have been in. The young ones do not and a lot of people have never heard of me. Living where I do in southern Queensland, I travel by taxi now when I go into Southport or to the doctor which seems to be every other day and more than one taxi driver greets me by saying, 'I thought you died years ago', which is of course part of the reason for The Almost Late Gordon Chater in the title of my book. There has been a slight drama because I have had rather a bad attack of what I am ailing from and I thought the title might have to be changed.

I must tell you my favourite cab story. I got into the cab and, as I hope to be a friendly person, I said to the driver something like, it is a nice warm day, and he looked at me and said, 'Yes it is. With a voice like that you ought to be on radio', so I said, 'Well, as a matter of fact, I was once on radio. I was in a session for three years with a very, very dear friend of mine called Gwenny Plumb, *Charlie and Pussy*.' He replied, 'Do not kid me, no, no, that was Gordon Chater, no, no.' He went on, 'With a voice like that, why did you not try telly, you would be all right on television' and I said,

'Well, as a matter of fact, I have been on television. Are you old enough to remember the *Mavis Bramston Show*?' 'Oh, Mavis Bramston, oh, gee, never missed it, we laughed, laughed, me and the wife wet ourselves,' he said. 'Well, I was Gordon Chater on the television.' 'No, no, you are kidding.' So then I went on about McGooley and the same thing and as we drove up to the apartment where I live, he said 'Ha, ha, ha, been trying tell me all the time, Gordon Chater, ha, ha, no telly star would travel in a cab and live at Labrador.'

I am going to talk now about my book. It has quite an interesting story. I had not worked for the ABC for 23 years, when a certain Ian Knight from the ABC asked me if I would do, for nothing, something called *A Life*. I am not very good at doing things for nothing, so I said, 'Oh, it is very nice of you to ask me to do that, but I do think, you know, there should be a fee, it is going to take a bit of time and one thing and another', and he said, 'Oh, well, if you do not want to be in the same series as Weary Dunlop and Dame Joan Sutherland I can understand that.' So I said I would do it and he turned out to be one of the most articulate, charming men that it has been my privilege to meet in my business and a wonderful director and producer and he came and we made *A Life*.

My family were happy to have it, jollier for them to have *A Life* than some rather boring ashes and an urn. Then out of the blue the biggest parcel of books arrived which I had not ordered, and at the bottom of it was a letter from Transworld Publications and a letter from my dear friend Judith Curr saying, have you ever thought of writing your autobiography?

My reply was, 'If I have an incentive, yes.' That is the accountant in me. (My father was an accountant, and he said, 'If you become an actor you will end up in the gutter.') So my wonderful, wonderful agent, Hilary Linstead, met with Judith Curr and shortly I was astonished to hear that if I signed a contract there would be a cheque and on delivery of the first script there would be a cheque, it went on and on and on.

I had never written a book before in my life, but I had written a lot of letters. So I informed my niece and nephew and friends that I had signed a contract to write a book and very luckily, thank God and very flatteringly, they had kept my letters. I was sent over 600 letters which I had written since 1945, I think, which helped me to remember a few things, so then I had to think very seriously about the process of writing a book.

I remembered that all the great writers always tell you in their autobiographies that the only way to write is to sit there for six hours and if the muse does not happen do not worry, get up and sit there again tomorrow for six hours. I was always fascinated by Compton Mackenzie, who had a beautiful home in the Hebrides and he had this wonderful writing room with the greatest view that you could imagine, looking out on to the Atlantic, and he promptly built a wall against the window so that he could not see it. So I duly thought, now, we must discipline ourselves and we must think about it and I sat down one morning, having got the chores done and tidied up a bit because I am a bit of a fusspot really and I like the ship to be ready for rounds, as we used to say in the Navy. I sat down at 7 o'clock and for four months wrote a thousand words every day, I honed them as much as I could and sent the first 25 pages to my editor who by this time I knew on the phone and who had become such a friend, Howard Gelman.

Howard was very gracious in receiving the 25 pages and I said to him, 'Please, you are my editor, you know all about publishing and writing, I do not. Please give me guidance', and he said in that soft and wonderful American accent, 'Just send another 25 pages.' Then the most tremendous shock happened – I got a cheque in the mail which I could not believe and I had thought in the contract that to deliver the script meant the whole script, but it did not, it meant the moment you deliver some script you get some money. So I could not wait to send another 25 pages.

"I got on the turps in Singapore and got on the wrong ship and said, 'When do we get to Shanghai?'. The sailor said, 'Shanghai, mate, you are going to effing Fremantle'."

I wrote 450 pages and that was in four months which I always compare with having a baby because you have the post-natal syndrome afterwards, or rehearsing a play and going through eight months of previews. It was not until long after I realised why Howard Gelman had said to send another 25 pages. He said, in the course of a conversation when we were in the middle of editing, 'Oh, it is such a luxury to have 150 pages to cut.'

So if there is a sequel, it is going to be called *What the Bastards Cut*. But seriously, I want to say this: in the theatre I have had the greatest luck to have been directed by Rodney Fisher, by Richard Wherrett, by Edgar Metcalfe, in America by well-known Ben Levitt and well-known Michael Lindsay Hogg and Michael Moriarty and if one gets good notices, which I have had fortunately for some things, it is due in my humble estimation, very largely to the director.

In publishing, Howard is a director par excellence. He has done such a good job on the book that even I find it readable. I think it has a certain interest – coming to Australia by mistake because I had hoped to go to Shanghai to see where my mother was born and I got on the turps in Singapore and got on the wrong ship and said, 'When do we get to Shanghai?' and the sailor said, 'Shanghai, mate, you are going to effing Fremantle.' But that was wonderful because all my life I had heard my father say, 'If I had my life over again I would go to Australia' and I am celebrating my fiftieth year here this year.

One of the exciting things about Australia, which does not happen in many other countries except possibly America, is that from the time I got here, almost penniless with £70 severance pay, it took me 18 years from 1946 to 1964 to average the basic wage, but during that time I was constantly helped, encouraged by everybody I can think of, and people wanted me to like Australia.

It has been a varied life. I have been lucky to work with Simon Phillips as a director, with wonderful Dame Crackers, I always call her Dame Crackers, Ruth Cracknell, who I have known longer than she likes to let me know. Although I have worked for many wonderful men in this business including Wilton Morley and Jimmy Oswin who was in charge of Channel 7, an amazing man, creating Mavis Bramston and so on, it is curiously enough the women in my life in Australia who have done more for me than I can ever count. Starting with, from day one, darling Thelma Scott and

Gwenny Plumb. Their kindness, their wanting me to enjoy Australia and their concern with my pennies and how little I had was simply marvellous.

Gwenny did the most extraordinary thing when I was in America waiting for my green card to be allowed to work there. The one thing we had never discussed in our lives (and we discussed practically everything on that radio thing and also in private) was our financial situation. I was waiting for the green card to come through, knowing it was coming through in five or six months and I was all right for money, and I opened a letter one morning, this is her generosity, not only to me but to thousands of people: 'I know you must be zilch as far as the money goes, here is a cheque for US$5000.'

I would like to finish by quoting the very last line of my book, which is, 'I have quoted contemporaries, but thanks to Australia and Australians I am now going to misquote the Bard and say Now is the Winter of My Content.'

! ?

SPEAKER: Is revue dead or is it going to come again and if so, when?

GORDON CHATER: That is up to people prepared to do it. There is still a lot of revue in New York and in London. It has to be extremely witty, very well written, brilliantly choreographed, but I do not think revue will ever end, it has gone in circles since the eighteenth century. I do understand that the ABC are doing something called *Good News Week* which is a satirical show in the form of a revue. Mind you, with all the brilliant comic talent in this country at this moment, I cannot understand why people do not sit down and create a revue either for the theatre or a contemporary version of the *Mavis Bramston Show*. It could easily be done, but unfortunately television is largely run by accountants, who have about as much wit and humour as a dead mullet. Thank God I don't have to earn my living on television any more. It can be done – I would like to think, I would love to see Max Gillies in a revue. And one of the greatest and funniest impersonations I have ever seen in my life is Gerry Connolly doing Paul Keating. Then you have got four women in this country who should have something written for them – four women on television who make me laugh, tears fall down my face, are Jean Turner, Gene Reilly, Magda Subianski and Marge Downey. I think they are absolutely without parallel and Marge Downey doing Jana Wendt is just about as funny as you can get.

Nicholas Evans

Struggling as a film-maker in London, Evans took a trip across the American south-west, which inspired his first novel, *The Horse Whisperer*. With the story of a romance between a Montana cowboy and a New York magazine editor half-written, he sold it for a record $4 million. Published in 1995, it became an international bestseller and a movie starring and directed by Robert Redford.

4 September 1996

The Horse Whisperer is not a horse story but a human story. It is the story of a high-powered businesswoman who has grown up in many different places all over the world and is somehow unrooted. She has an only child, a daughter, who is horribly injured in an accident when a truck runs into her and the horse she's riding.

In the terrible aftermath of the accident, everybody, including several vets, tells the mother that the badly injured horse should be put down. But she insists on keeping the horse alive, sensing that there is some sort of connection between her daughter's survival and the horse's survival, indeed, the survival of the whole family.

After a time, with her daughter's psychological and physical recovery stalled, the woman seeks help for the horse and hears about a man in Montana who has a special gift with damaged horses. She drags her reluctant daughter and the horse out to find this man and in one way or another all their lives are transformed by their journey.

I first heard about horse whisperers about three years ago when I was staying with a friend in the far south-west of England on Dartmoor, famous for its wild horses and prison (in which he does not live). While I was on Dartmoor my friend introduced me to a blacksmith, who told a very simple account of a horse whisperer he'd once encountered. I've always loved horses but I had never heard this term before and my ears pricked up because it had a kind of mystical ring to it.

The blacksmith gave me an eye-witness account of something which had happened about ten years earlier, involving a woman who lived in his village whose daughter had a lovely, friendly, never-do-anything-wrong pony. The family had had to move away from the village for about a year and when they returned the horse, who had been stabled elsewhere, was absolutely unrecognisable. From the quiet, gentle pony they'd left, it had been transformed into a demented, fierce creature so full of fear that it was actually dangerous to go anywhere near it.

"I had found that the horse-whispering gift is ancient."

Somebody in the village told the family of a local whisperer. In fact, he was an itinerant who passed through that part of Devon a couple of times a year. So they got in touch with him and he came to see this horse and in the course of an afternoon, so Robbie, the blacksmith, told me, transformed the horse back to what it had always been, a gentle, lovely creature.

Something about this story made me shiver. I just knew there was something there that could be the centre of a story.

For a while before I was told this story I had been, as a film-maker, thinking of writing a screenplay. I had never wanted to write a novel before, but I'd wanted to write a screenplay, a kind of epic love story set in the American west. I had been a sucker for these sorts of stories since I was a kid and long before I ever visited the US. As quite a small child I used to devour westerns.

So, though I didn't have a story, nor any characters in mind, I just wanted to write a contemporary love story set in the American west and there, in Dartmoor, three years ago, I was handed the basis of the story on a plate. Also, for some strange reason, I knew immediately that it was a novel, not a film.

But, at the time I was, as I said, a film-maker, having produced a feature film and several TV things, and I had decided that the next feature film I did I was going to direct. I had a bee in my bonnet and instead of doing what I'd always done and producing it, I was determined to go for broke and direct it. And in the process I became broke, seriously broke. The manager of the bank that was financing this folly would come and have increasingly frequent meetings with me and ask how the film was coming along and I would come up with all these increasingly fatuous reasons why it was not, including, I heard myself say one day, we are postponing it till the autumn because the light is better.

In March 1994 the company that was going to finance the film pulled out and the whole thing suddenly collapsed. The result was that I hit rock bottom and I had, it seems to me now, a sort of mid-life crisis. For the first time in my life I felt a total failure. I did not know how I was going to support my family. I did not know what I could do. I really was in a mess.

Meanwhile, I had been reading all this stuff about horse whisperers and had become obsessed by their stories. I had found that the horse-whispering gift is ancient and, though it hasn't been much documented, my guess is that there have been horse whisperers from the first time that horses and humans got together. Certainly horses have been around on this planet long before humankind and early humans hunted horses for their meat, as documented by cave paintings. Somebody at some stage – and my guess is that it was a woman because the men were all too busy hunting – made this great leap of imagination that if you harnessed horses' power you could actually hunt other animals more effectively.

So this fragile alliance between horse and humankind was born and I have always thought it must have been, for the horse anyway, like suddenly getting asked to come to bed by Hannibal Lecter. You would keep your eyes open, wouldn't you?

In the Middle Ages there were horse whisperers in all parts of the world. I found several references in Europe that were cloaked in magic and folklore and even witchcraft. There were whisperers burnt at the stake as witches because in those days if you had a horse that was behaving in a crazy way, it was said that the devil was in it. Those with the gift of taking the devil out of a horse must therefore, by definition, have something a little devilish about them.

Now in the spring of 1994, when I hit rock bottom, any sane person, I suppose, would have gone and got a job somewhere, which is certainly what my wife expected me to do. Instead I bought myself a ticket, or rather my bank, unknowingly, bought me a ticket to the west of the United States where I spent the spring of that year travelling around New Mexico, California, Wyoming and finally Montana and meeting, among many other people, three horse whisperers. They do not call themselves that but that is what they are.

The oldest of the whisperers I met was a man in central California called Tom Dorrance. Tom is about the most spiritual man I have ever met. He is little, about five foot two, bow-legged, with a face like a kind of wrinkled walnut and these funny little piercing blue eyes coming out from it. I have not told Robert Redford, incidentally, that Tom was partly the model for the character he is playing in the film. I made my character a little taller and a little younger.

Tom Dorrance, like all great gurus and teachers, does not answer your questions when you ask him one, instead he asks you a question. When I was with him I started to understand a little bit about what was happening with the whispering and I really identified with the damaged, traumatised animals that were being brought to his place. I knew who they were because in a way I felt like that myself. I was in a mess and therefore quite raw and open to what was going on.

One day at Tom's place, a six-year-old Morgan horse was brought along from about 400 miles away – which was why I made Pilgrim, the horse in my story, a Morgan. As this horse was being brought up the driveway you could have heard it kicking and screaming half a mile away, maybe more. And when it got off the trailer it really could have killed anyone who had had the stupidity to go up to it. By the end of that very day that same horse was walking in a straight line down the middle of Tom's arena as sloppy as a labrador. Anybody could have gone up to it, anybody could have ridden it. It was the most miraculous thing I had seen in my life.

But like all the best magic it was *real.*

As I drove around those vast, lonely landscapes in my little rented car, playing all kinds of music, the story was taking shape in my head.

I was lucky enough to realise that my story was not just about horses but it was also, and much more importantly, about human beings and about how we have this wonderful and very special capacity to use our brains. This allows us to get lost in life, clouded by ambition, career, paying the mortgage, the bank manager, and in that process we forget, very often, how to be human.

Tom Dorrance looked at the horse running round the arena that day and said, 'That horse has just forgotten how to be a horse.' And it seemed to me that is what the story I wrote should be about, about how people have somehow forgotten how to be human.

"Like all the best magic it was real."

On my first night back in England after this extraordinary trip I had a dream. I told my daughter about it. She was then 12 years old and a great dreamer – she loved to come down in the morning and discuss her vivid dreams. I dreamed I was sitting on the top of a mountain and I was sitting on the edge of a precipice and below me were clouds and I was fishing through the clouds with a fishing rod. Somehow I knew there was a lake below and that in this lake were some great fish but I could not see anything at all. After I finished telling my daughter this, she said, with all the wisdom of a 12-year-old, 'Oh, that's easy. You've got this great story and you don't know if you can tell it.' And she was absolutely right.

I sat down that day and started to write and in the course of that summer, June, July and August, I wrote the first half of *The Horse Whisperer*. Then, at the end of August, with the bank manager banging on the door louder and louder, I stopped, because it seemed to me that I should get real and go out and get a job. So I went out and I started hustling for some television work which I had vowed I would not do (I was only making movies, you know, now). But I went out and was prepared to take anything.

I also had the great good sense or luck to show the 200 pages I'd written plus a synopsis of the rest of it to a very dear friend of mine called Caradoc King, who is a literary agent. Caradoc was one of the few people outside my family whom I had told I was trying to write a book. I didn't want to fail too visibly, you know. So Caradoc read it and he said it was 'fine'. And that, if you are English, can cover a whole spectrum from 'fine' to 'completely bloody awful'.

He said that if I needed money (he was being rhetorical) he could try sending what I'd written out as it was to the six main UK publishers. So, on the eve of the Frankfurt Book Fair, where publishers convene from all over the world to talk about books, find the next new thing, do deals and so on, he sent this book, this half book, and the synopsis out to the six publishers as they set off for Frankfurt. And one of them, Ursula Mackenzie, took it to read on the plane.

Ursula phoned up on Monday and made an offer which, as Caradoc told me about it, had me singing my way down the garden path. Until he said, 'And I've turned it down.' I said, 'What? You must be absolutely mad.' And he said, 'No, I think something is happening.' And, indeed, it was. Over the next few days, in Frankfurt, every major publisher in the world managed to get hold of a copy of my half manuscript. We did not give it to anyone. They just got it: begged, stole, borrowed. And somebody, some dear anonymous person whom I have never met, faxed it also to Paramount Studios in Hollywood. Two hundred pages plus a 12-page synopsis – I'm glad it was not my fax machine.

By the end of this amazing week absolutely surreal offers were coming in and we were sitting, my family and I, in our kitchen in London with our mouths hanging open. Eventually there came a time when this feeding frenzy in Hollywood was drawing to a close and the publishing deals had all been done, and I still could not believe what was happening. I was told that three Hollywood mega-moguls, to whom it had boiled down by that time, would phone me. The money was all agreed but I had to choose between the producer of *Batman*, the producer of *Forrest Gump* and Robert Redford, who by then had the backing of Hollywood Pictures. And these are people whose 18th assistant gopher would not have returned my calls a week before.

As soon as Robert Redford started speaking to me I just listened. I knew it should be he who did this story for the screen. I have always thought he had a special thing about him and loved his film *A River Runs Through It*, which has quite a spiritual thing about it. He said he felt this way about *The Horse Whisperer* too, that there was something there that was a bit different.

So after all the excitement all I had to do was finish the book. Even close friends have said that this must have been a terribly difficult thing for me but actually it never was because I had been doing something that I did not think had any value at all, had lost faith in it, and suddenly I had this amazing vote of confidence. Finishing that book was the most exhilarating time of my creative life.

I am terribly superstitious. I became completely convinced that I was going to die before I could finish this book. We even had a plan worked out, Jenny, my wife, and I, that if I did die she should not tell anyone, just put me in the freezer and when my publishers phoned up she would have to tell them, 'He's too busy.' Happily I did finish it and the last year has been an astonishing time for me and one of great joy and exhilaration. And in the aftermath lots of people have said, 'Oh, how clever Nick Evans was. He got the formula for the bestseller and sat down and put all these ingredients into it.' As you know, it was never anything like that because there is no formula. Readers are too clever to be fooled by formulas.

I get people asking me for advice about writing, and the only piece of advice I can give is that if you feel passionately about something, go with it and follow your heart and tell something that moves you as best you can. That is all I did and I was lucky to stumble across this extraordinary phenomenon which has this other thing floating above it.

People have asked me: what is it about *The Horse Whisperer* that has made it touch so many people's hearts? When I was writing it, I was very aware that there were two things going on. I was following this literal trail where everything had to be plausible and make sense in ordinary everyday terms. But if I looked out of the corner of my eye there was another thing going on too, a more mythic, ancient story that I knew the literal story had to be in accord with and in which Tom Booker, the horse whisperer, was a kind of shaman figure. Whether it is because we are told about such characters in the very first fairy tales that we hear as children or not, I do not know. I think that they are somehow *in* us, these stories. There are some stories that we *know* about.

The second thing is that the book comes at a time when there is great uncertainty in the world and materialism dominates everything. There is a great questing going on for something else, for some other meaning in life. And this story is about the power of love, about how, even when the most terrible darkness and suffering and pain surrounds us, love (and I do not mean romantic love, I mean the love of one creature for another, be it a horse, a human or whatever) can pull us through. And in that process, through that pain which is actually probably necessary, we can find more out about ourselves and about the important things in life.

So that is the story of *The Horse Whisperer.*

Joanna Trollope

After writing a number of historical novels as Caroline Harvey, Trollope became famous under her own name with her first contemporary novel, *The Choir*, published in 1987 and later adapted for BBC TV. Her realistic portrayals of middle-class English family life in novels including *The Best of Friends* (1995), *Next of Kin* (1996) and *Other People's Children* (1998), have brought her comparisons with Jane Austen and worldwide popularity. She has also written about Victorian women in the British Empire in *Brittania's Daughters*.

24 September 1996

I want to talk a little bit about the revival of the traditional novel. I have not done it; I am just part of it. Maybe 10 years ago, we felt very admiringly about, say, a literary writer like Salman Rushdie. Then along came Vikram Seth who is a deeply traditional novelist and we fell upon *A Suitable Boy*, didn't we? Why did we fall upon *A Suitable Boy*? Why did we all buy *Midnight's Children* and various other things and read 10 pages and then think, I will wait until I am ill to finish this. Because with Vikram, we were *living* with these people, weren't we?

The traditional novel is, of course, where the novel began. It is not terribly old – 300 years compared to drama which is a couple of thousand, but the traditional novel is our lives. It does not matter whether it is set in the 18th century or the 19th century. People continue to want the same things out of life. Our social mores may change, our feelings about various aspects of human nature may change. We may eat different food at different times of day. We may wear different clothes. But we still are looking for the bluebird of happiness. We are still looking for a satisfaction in life. We still want to get to the pearly gates and feel you can say with a clear conscience to Saint Peter that you actually did achieve something. This is just human.

I do think the traditional novel understands this completely. The traditional novel admires story. You see, the literary novel despises story – narrative, it is felt, is for children. The traditional novel loves character; it loves the recognisableness of character. But most of all, the traditional novel loves the sort of moral dilemma that we all get ourselves into and have done down the centuries. I am afraid happiness does not make for very page-turning fiction. We have to read about trouble, that is what keeps the tension in a book.

"The literary novel despises story – narrative, it is felt, is for children."

By the way, I am not a descendant of Anthony Trollope. I come from the same family, but I come from a below-the-salt-trade branch. The Trollopes mostly come from Lincolnshire and my lot set off from Lincolnshire in the 18th century to go to London to make a little money. In fact, you have the distinction of having Anthony Trollope's only living direct descendants here in Sydney. In fact, you have the mother of his great, great grandsons here in this room for this lunch. We have Lady Trollope with us which is wonderful.

So, Anthony, I think, would be thrilled. His descendants here are descended from his second son Fred who came out to New South Wales to be a sheep farmer. As a very young man, 18 or 19, he farmed up at Grenfell. I am afraid he made rather a bog of it and had to be rescued by his father but it was a robust ambition.

Anthony wrote a curious autobiography. It is quite an eccentric book and it was not really a success. It did not really help his novels after his death because he persisted in regarding novel writing as a rather workmanlike thing. He kept on comparing it to a cobbler mending boots and the chattering classes of the day wanted something slightly more ethereal and intellectual as an approach to novel writing. He said some wonderful things in this book, one of which I tremendously share, which is that he was not interested in writing about the great passionate landscape. His great concern was to chronicle those little daily lacerations upon the spirit. Isn't that brilliant? Commuting, domestic life, the school run – all those little things that seem to chip away at your inner self. The other thing he said was that nobody gets in closer to a reader than a novelist and this, of course, is entirely true. This is exactly what the traditional novel does.

You know that phrase, to curl up with a book? There you are alone with a book. You can confide in it. There is somebody else on those pages who suffers exactly the sensations you are suffering for the moment and you know how easy it is to feel you are the only person in the world who is jealous, frustrated, suicidal, whatever it is, and there is a book to comfort you. So, I think that is part of the reason [for my current popularity].

I think, too, it may be that my books are right for now. I think I am at that wonderful moment when what I want to say is what you, bless your hearts, want to hear. There is a sort of affinity in it. I think if I had been published in the '80s, when we were all shopping for happiness in our power suits, it would not have worked at all. The books would have been too reflective, too sober, but the '90s have made us all rather thoughtful, haven't they? The approach of the millennium is a daunting business.

We are going to want to have a nice clean

sheet to write on and that has made everybody rather go back to what they have got at home, i.e. their relationships, and because I love chronicling relationships, it is a very good moment in time for my books to gain a bit of visibility.

I have to put this visibility in context. I have been well known for really no time at all. It really dates from the paperback of *The Rector's Wife* in England who (I always talk of her as 'her' in an affectionate way because she dealt with the overdraft so I have a very soft spot for her) came out in July 1992. It was not very long before that that I had been in Marks and Spencer for a very good reason. You know that the whole of the United Kingdom is socked and knickered by Marks and Spencers. I had gone in for that purpose but I also had to go in to buy a few copies of my own book.

I used to write early historical fiction as Joanna Trollope and then I had to invent this lady called Caroline Harvey. She was invented to write some romantic fiction to make a barrister out of our eldest daughter. I created the name from my Trollope grandparents' christian names put together. So she has a sort of validity. She is rather a different animal altogether. Her sense of humour I sometimes worry about but, anyway, Marks and Spencer had commissioned a few of us to write novels. They thought they would have a go at selling paperback fiction and I had written them a novel called *Legacy of Love* by Miss Harvey and they gave me almost no author copies.

So off I went with my wire basket of socks and knickers and I bought six copies of myself and took them to the cash desk. I am only telling you this story so that you can see that popularity is a small and selective business as well as very fragile. I put the basket down next to the till and the woman on the till said to me, 'Oh, you've got a lot of those.' I thought, shall I say anything? I thought, nothing ventured, nothing gained, look at Jeffrey Archer. (My mother would so disapprove of making fun of other people. Anyway, she is not here to hear me.) I said to her, 'Well, actually, I wrote this book' and she looked at me pityingly and she said, 'Oh, yes, dear, and I'm the Queen of England.'

The Best of Friends is the paperback I am really here to promote. The emotional situation that lies at the heart of this novel is a long look at a platonic friendship between a man and a woman that has gone on for years and years. I chose friendship because I think it has got a peculiar intensity now.

We are all scattered over the world, aren't we? Some of us may, of course, leave home for the precise reason that we wish to get *away* from our loving families. Others, once away, find that there is a draught. We are used to a landscape of people quite close to us. Half a world away, we have not got family any more so we make a kind of substitute family out of friends – which is fine, but it places a tremendous burden on those friendships. It makes them inevitably extremely intense and you compound that with the kind of friendships that feminism insists upon, the sisterhood, and you can see that it is potentially an extremely explosive and therefore ideal situation plot for a novel.

"The whole of the United Kingdom is socked and knickered by Marks and Spencers."

The Best of Friends has another theme which is the consequences for teenagers of arbitrary adult decisions in their lives. The adults in their lives decide to stop going to work and go back to college or leave each other or depart to live in New Zealand and the children are not old enough yet to protest about this. They have to go along as baggage and I wanted to look at those sort of decisions made by middle-aged people from young eyes, self-absorbed young eyes.

This novel is set in the Midlands in England. I never choose a real place. When I am finding place names I go through my very battered old *Readers' Digest* gazetteer and I pick out tiny villages in the middle of nowhere and give their names to my imaginary places and sure as hell there is a reader who lives in one of those villages who writes immediately and indignantly to tell me it is not at all like that, it is lovely. I have said on several occasions that the imaginary place in *The Best of Friends* called Whittingbourne is in the Midlands. I often say it is one of those really dismal towns not far from Birmingham and then you will find six people in the audience were all born in Birmingham and feel a passionate nostalgia for it.

In this town there are two families that I am concerned with. One family has three generations: a grandmother, middle-aged parents in their early '40s and a teenage daughter. In the other family, there are a couple in their early 40s and three teenage boys. The husband in the couple who have one daughter is an antique dealer called Fergus Bedford. He changed his name from being Leslie when he became the fine art dealer because he thought it was not classy enough. You can imagine the sort of man he is and he is married to Gina and Gina is small and dark and pretty and emotional and musical and neurotic and Fergus leaves her quite soon after the beginning of the book.

I will not tell you for whom or where he goes. You can discover that for yourselves but Fergus leaves her and Gina does this thing that a lot of us have either done or had done unto us. She turns to her best friend for comfort. You know this thing, don't you, of having someone crying in the spare room for days and days or sitting at your kitchen table crying into endless mugs of coffee and then your children come down and say, 'Mum, is she staying the weekend?' and you realise that this very painful but interminable round of complaint has gone on too long.

Gina's best friend is Lawrence. They were at school together in Whittingbourne when they were adolescents. They have been friends all these years but never boyfriend and girlfriend and Gina turns to Lawrence who is married to Hilary. Hilary is quite brisk. Hilary is the sort of person who is very sorry for you for about 10 minutes while you tell her the first time and then she suggests that you might just pick yourself up and get on with your life. There is a wonderful Alan Ayckbourn play called *The Bed Before Yesterday* which opens with a man lying in bed with a bad back and his wife standing by the bed and he is groaning and she is just standing there with her arms folded. After a bit he says, 'I don't really understand why you aren't sorry for me' and she says, 'Because I was born with a very small stock of sympathy and you've had it all.'

Well, that is rather Hilary. Hilary and Lawrence have three sons, three teenage sons and they also run a hotel called the Bee House, a small hotel, and they live in a flat on the top of it and Hilary runs the hotel. Hilary looks after troublesome guests, laundry, bookings, staff, all that kind of thing because Lawrence is the chef and as we know, chefs have to be allowed to be creative, not be interrupted with problems like blocked lavatories. After about three weeks of having Gina in their spare room, Hilary has had enough. And if you want to know what happens next, you know what you have to do.

SPEAKER: I have been intrigued in some of your novels to find that you do seem to, I do not know if despise is too strong a word, but you do seem to have a downer on the church. Is it just the church or is it Christianity in general? Is it the Church of England?

JOANNA TROLLOPE: This is a wonderful question. I was born in my grandfather's rectory in the Cotswolds. My grandmother was a very fascinating, very talented, and luckily extremely indiscreet rector's wife and I was very conscious from an early age of the loneliness and frustration she felt in her position. I also have to say I was born quietly into the Church of England. I remain a devoted member of it and a Christian but the thing is, once you are inside a family, you feel perfectly free to make fun of it and that is what I am doing. I was thrilled to hear that the Bishop of Dunedin in New Zealand, who is a woman, has made *The Rector's Wife* required diocese reading which I think is an accolade beyond all.

SPEAKER: I was interested in hearing your interview where you seemed to say you were not so pleased with the BBC production of *The Choir.*

JOANNA TROLLOPE: Yes, that is perfectly true. The director rewrote most of the original script. The original scripts were very pacey and quick and funny and tense and he – I am afraid the BBC had found him lying about in middle Hollywood or something – was not a Christian and was full of very exaggerated ideas about the church. He declined to go to a single service in Gloucester Cathedral throughout the filming and he rewrote most of the script as he thought it should be. We felt that the result was confusing and slow and very sentimental which I was sorry about.

There were various things that I liked very much about it. The little boy and the organist I thought were marvellous but there is something about putting actors into dog collars, isn't there? They lose their heads. James Fox, who is a fascinating man, a devout Christian and a terribly good actor, suddenly turned into this creature with a poker up his bottom instead of being what I had wanted to show in the book, which was a *real* human being who is also a priest and who felt himself to have been let down by the awfulness of humanity. I just was rather sad.

I felt it was average, rather like those school reports that had 'Could do better' written at the bottom. But the music was lovely.

SPEAKER: I was very interested in your comments on the desire people have at the moment to read a good story when they pick up a novel. I am the President of the Jane Austen Society of Australia and I think we have really seen that desire coming through with the great interest in Jane Austen's novels this year. But she tells a wonderful story and I can really see that reflected in the interests that people have had in reading your books; that people want to have a good story with recognisably human characters. You have a wonderful line in your book, I think it is *The Men and the Girls*, where you describe one of the husbands as being the sort of man who is always leaning against the one cupboard in the kitchen that you want to get to. I feel that is something that Jane Austen would have related to.

JOANNA TROLLOPE: That is a compliment I don't deserve, but thank you very much indeed. All the same, I think this has opened up something very interesting which is that narrative need not be action, it need not be boy's own adventure. We can have narratives of the heart, can we not? And that is really what Jane Austen is so brilliant at. We want to know how these emotional situations are going to be resolved. This is really what concerns all of us. The great story in all our lives is our own story. I do not think there is such a thing as an ordinary life. Our lives might look awfully ordinary to someone else from the outside looking in, but we living them know that they are like the last act of *Hamlet*.

SPEAKER: Your men are just as real and strong as your women, but have you found that men are appreciative and read your books as I think they do well to do?

JOANNA TROLLOPE: It is so funny the number of women who have said to me, 'I just left it by his bed with the page turned down saying "You could do with reading that".' About a third of the letters I get are from men. I have to say a lot of them start by saying, 'Just happened to pick up my wife's copy.' But in fact one of the best was from an old boy of 94 who wrote to me saying it was such a relief to read fiction in which men were allowed to have emotions too. And I thought how admirable because after all he had obviously grown up in a generation where emotion was absolutely forbidden, so good for him.

I have been marketed as a women's writer. I think I feel that I am a people's writer. Men in England, and I imagine quite a lot of men in Australia, are a bit shifty about reading fiction or being seen to read fiction. You can read political biography and SAS thrillers and things, but are you going to be seen carrying a book about feelings round with you? But I have been terribly heartened by the letters I have had – very, very eloquent and a lot of them full of relief. So keep at it, boys, they are meant for you as well.

Melvyn Bragg

Bragg is best known as the flamboyant interviewer and presenter of BBC-TV's arts program, *The South Bank Show*. He is also a successful screenwriter, biographer of the explorer Richard Burton and prolific author of novels, including *Credo*, an epic tale set in the Dark Ages in Britain and Ireland.

14 October 1996

Credo is set in that period after the more-or-less mythic King Arthur, who, if he existed at all and there's only the slightest evidence, existed up in the northwest of England and the border with Scotland – that is the latest evidence – there in that Solway Firth area, up on the border lands, northwest/southwest. Between that period when the Romans had left – the Romans left in 410 – and the period of King Alfred, the only king in British history called 'The Great', in that period between there, the Dark Ages, that's where the book is set.

What I want to do is to ask myself three questions and answer them. It's the best way to be able to answer questions if you set them for yourself. And I have asked myself three tremendously difficult questions: What's the story? Why did I set it in the Dark Ages? And why did I particularly want to write it?

The basic story, although there are many, many characters in it, is the story of two people. One is a historical figure called Bega, who was a young Irish princess. It was a time of divided kingdoms – we're talking about Britain at a time when there would have been about 12 kingdoms. So if I stumble over words like England, Scotland, Ireland, Wales, it's because they simply did not exist. There were small tribes warring against each other or peoples fighting against each other.

Bega was born in the west of Ireland in the Galway, brought up there by a tremendous, terrible warlord of a father, who wanted her to marry someone she did not want to marry, and she somehow got out of his clutches – this is recorded – somehow got herself right across Ireland. She then got herself across what is now the Irish Sea to the north-west part of England, went up the coast, through one or two places – St Bee's Head is named after her, St Bega's Head – one or two churches, and made a settlement somewhere in North Cumberland, and somehow got an education and became a miracle worker and until the 14th century miracles were worked in her name. That was Bega. That's my main protagonist.

My second protagonist is a man called Padric, who's an invented figure. In the afterword I point out who are real historical figures and who aren't. This is a historical fiction, not a history book. Padric is in my book the son of one of the few remaining British royal houses – the British were on the retreat then, very much on the retreat. He would have been sent from the family to Ireland for his education. Ireland at that time was the salvation of the western world. It was the great cultured place. It had not been invaded by the Romans; it had grown its own way. It was a centre of scholarship. It had great monasteries, as we would call them now, and so on. He would have been sent there for his education, and as part of his pay-back with this family, he would have had to act as a tutor. And so he went to this chieftain, he got his education – he would already have been trained as a warrior – and he would teach the young children there, one of whom was Bega. He came with her on that escape and they came across together.

The novel follows 40 years in their lives. Bega took me into one area, he took me into another. This is the second half of the 7th century I'm writing about where Bede, who writes well about it, gives me a lot of clues. Bega took me into the fantastic area of the fundamentalist but benign and extraordinary power of the Celtic saints. They're the most extraordinary people that I have ever come across: utterly fearless – men and women. The 7th century and the early 8th century is the only time in British history where there are more women saints than men by a great number. They had come largely out of Ireland, they'd go up to the north of Scotland – Iona, what is now Scotland – and come down into the north of England, north-east, down to Whitby, down to York and then go over into the Continent, and eventually they recivilised the court of Charlemagne. They were extraordinary people, driven by a tremendous faith. And mostly they were martyred. Most of them were tortured, most of them assassinated – they were going into pagan kingdoms.

Bega brings me into touch with Hilda, one of the great women of the Dark Ages, a noblewoman who founded an abbey at Whitby and trained five bishops, who then worked for her all over Europe. She takes me into all that great reach of scholarship and religion which went from nothing, as it were, at the beginning of the 6th century to almost everything at the end of it.

She takes me into Saint Cuthbert – whom I initially wanted to write about – who was the most powerful of the medieval saints in the whole of Europe, who ended his life on a tiny island, a tenth the size of this room, battered by huge seas in the North Sea, a tiny rock, and kings would come to him for his advice before they took any big decisions. He figures in the book.

She also takes me into the idea of fundamentalism, the idea of a relationship with God, and the idea of somebody who looked on the entire world as being moved by God: everything that happened, everything that moved, everything was decided by this invisible God.

"The Celtic saints. They're the most extraordinary people that I have ever come across: utterly fearless – men and women."

And she also takes me into the rivalry of the other creeds, because at the beginning of the 7th century Christianity was just one of many. I have a Celtic priestess who was extremely powerful, the same age as Bega, and they live about a mile away from each other and fight – not literally, of course, but argue right the way through these years. Different ways to approach problems: whether it's prayer or practicality; whether it's animism and so on. So Bega takes me into all that. Takes me into the Synod of Whitby, that great conference when the Romans came back again. The Romans had been in Britain for 400 years and they came back again with their church to re-attack and re-organise. And now they've come back again, you could say, for the third time with a treaty!

Padric takes me to the warrior society. We're talking about a time of savagery, which we know very well about in this century – neck-and-neck for the Dark Ages, there isn't much in it, is there, really, when you come to think of it? Padric takes me into a warrior society, a society where noblemen – it was usually noblemen or it could have been strapping lads from the serf classes, the servant classes even – were actually fed more. They were bred, they were horsed, they were armoured, they were succoured to do one thing – and that was to kill. He takes me into that extraordinary society of battles and war which is part of our past.

He also takes me into something that began to matter very much to me when I started to write – because a book is something you discover about yourself and you write more about it the more you discover. He took me into the survival of the British. He took me into the way the British did survive in that century, and I give him a hand in it.

Why did I choose the Dark Ages? Well, usually when people speak to you about novels they'll say it's mulching around and it came out of the mulch – and that's more or less what happens. It's like a lot of aeroplanes, to use another metaphor, circling in the airport and eventually one gets called in and that the one you do. If you start writing at an early age, which I did, there's always things buzzing around and something then crops up when you have finished one or the other. But this had a beginning. This had a specific beginning when I was 18 and went to university. I'd come from a very small town in the north of England of 5000 people. I was born in 1939.

There were two or three things about it that became background for this book that might interest you. Firstly, it was a very Christian and church-run town – they're not the same thing. Everybody joined in the fact that it was church-run, partly because the churches didn't charge you anything, it was all free. I went to the Anglican church. And I've got a photograph of the Anglican church choir in 1948 and there are 60 people in that choir – including two uncles and an aunt, a guy who was going to be an uncle and a cousin of my lot, to start with. Sixty, in that choir of one church.

There was a Catholic church – St Cuthbert's, funnily enough – which had the first nunnery in England since the Reformation. There was a big Congregational church, which my mother and father went to. I couldn't quite work out why they went there, and I never really asked. And underneath the Congregational church was a big hall where we used to do massively exciting things like spinning the plate and pea-and-pie supper, bring your own knife and fork, that kind of thing.

There was a Methodist church, there was a Wesleyan church, there was a primitive Methodist church known as the Quaker meeting house, there was a Salvation Mission, there was the Salvation Army – and there was something that happened at the bottom of Union Street on a Saturday night that I never got to the bottom of.

But the fact is that the churches ran the town, especially for kids, especially after the Second World War when the men came back and they wanted to give the kids a break, so they gave their time which is the best thing they could possibly have given us. The Anglicans in the AYPA, we went hiking, of course, singing songs. The Methodists had the first table tennis table. It goes without saying that the nuns ran the best dances. And you went to the Salvation Army to do things like prick bits of cardboard and hold them up to the light and hope it looked like a peacock, and you sang songs like 'I'm bobbin', bobbin', bobbin', like a tiny little robin'. So the churches ran the town. It was a church culture.

Secondly, scholarship was important to me, as part of that generation. My father had passed two scholarships. He was from a family of nine and his father was a coalminer and then a farm labourer. And he passed a very big scholarship for the village schools in the northwest of England when he was 12. He was to go to a public school but he couldn't take it up because they hadn't any money. He left school when he was 14 and went straight down to the pits. My mother left school when she was 14 on a Friday, on a Monday morning biked 11 miles to a local biscuit factory to start working there. They had rotten jobs but they made the best of it. I think I'm probably the first member of my family to have had a job he liked as distinct from a job he had to do.

"At school, the Dark Ages had been one wet Wednesday afternoon."

I stayed on at school because my dad and mum were very nice about it and the history teacher, Mr James, thought that it was worth keeping me on. Mr James suggested that I try for Oxford, this mythical place. All I knew about Oxford was what I'd read in *Jude the Obscure* by Thomas Hardy. It was a place that tried to keep out people like me. And it succeeded with Jude the Obscure, who knew a damn sight more than I did. But I got there. So scholarship mattered to me.

And also what mattered to me was the north of England because I'd knocked about a bit when I was a kid on school holidays. You had all this time free while your friends were working. And I went up to Iona which was a very wonderful place. And I'd gone across the Roman wall, which was quite near us; it's a three-day walk across the old wall. I'd gone with my first girlfriend actually, telling my parents that it was really very important for me as a historian to go along the Roman wall – and they bought that. What was utterly remarkable was that her parents bought it as well.

I went to Oxford and it was awesome. And it's important to remember and to credit the things that really strike you. There were these magnificent places. I'd go into the library – Queen's College Library – which was full of thousands of leather-bound volumes with gilt on. I'd never seen two books like that, never mind thousands. But what was more remarkable was a young man, rather like me, not noticeably different, was just taking them down and opening them and reading them and he wasn't getting arrested: in other words, this was what happened in this place. I was prepared to be massively impressed.

My first tutor taught about the Dark Ages. At school, the Dark Ages had been one wet Wednesday afternoon: the Romans left – Alfred – you know about the burning of the cakes – Edward the Confessor was a very good man – 1066, right. You had 600 years packed into 35 drizzling minutes; 600 years – and, in my view, the fundamental key part of British history – away like that. The tutor taught me about the Dark Ages and it was about these Celtic monks and saints. And it was about the fight for Britain. And it was about places like Iona and the Roman wall and Lindisfarne I'd been to. And it was about scholarship surviving. Point nought, nought, nought, dot one per cent of people could even read at the beginning of that century. At the end of this century we produced our first great British work of art, the *Lindisfarne Gospels*, which are jewelled and beautiful paintings and lovely calligraphy – and they're books. They're about reading and writing.

So this was an enormous revelation to me and I have wanted to write about it ever since. There were three things happening there that deeply interested me and still do – and they're all to do with survival. Things do disappear, cultures disappear, libraries disappear, civilisations virtually disappear. And at that time scholarship was hanging by a thread, Christianity was hanging by a thread, and Britain was hanging by a thread.

The British Celts had been there before the Romans, they'd survived the Romans. The Teutonic tribes came in at the end of the 6th century and early in the 7th, and they tried to exterminate them. And they damn nearly succeeded. And there was one battle in 685 just across the border – fully recorded, one of the few things fully recorded in that century – where the British collected themselves and in their battle, extraordinarily like the Battle of Agincourt and extraordinarily like the Battle of Britain, the few Britons against enormous odds, beat them and circled them, did that wonderful encircling movement that Hannibal described as 'the greatest thing you could do in battle', crowded them into the hills, and exterminated them. Took masses of them as slaves, took all their booty. This is well recorded. And from then on, said Bede, writing 40 years later, 'the future of the British people was assured'. And the Brits and those who came in began to thatch and that's the basis of what we are. That's where we started. The Vikings came in later, the Angles, the Normans put the marzipan on us and so on. But that was the thatch: that great British adventure which went through Britain, it went overseas, Australia, Canada, America. That's the thatch, that's the survival – and it was touch and go and that fascinated me.

How did I get to write this particular story? Well, again, I went back to when I was young. I tried to write about Cuthbert; but there was too much known about Cuthbert. There's a window in York Minster with 76 panels devoted to the life of Cuthbert. There's too much for a novelist, it's too much. I wanted somebody where I just had a few things. I wanted a lot of black holes and a lot that I could make up. After all, that's what I'm supposed to do.

We used to bike up to a particular lake and row down it. When you're looking across the lake – it's still there, it's precisely the same – there's this tiny church across the lake. And I wondered what the church was. Was it a church that had been with a village and the village was destroyed? Because there was no sign of any houses. Was it a church that belonged to a big house in the woods? There was a big house in the woods but the church didn't belong to it and the church had preceded it all because the church had a 7th-century, 8th-century foundation. What was it? Well, I found out it was a church dedicated to St Bega, it was a church where this young woman had made her settlement and from there she'd worked the miracles. Because it was proximate to where I lived, because it began to beguile my imagination, because I went there again and again, because nearby were the woods where you could take your kids, I went in that church and read about her there and started to sketch things out and that's where it started, Bega's story. In one sense a remote time, in another sense, I think, with its faith and its ferocity and its startling figures, sometimes terrible figures, very like what we have now.

One of the things I have always liked about novels was that they were supposed to bring the news. Well, this is the news of the 7th century – a little bit late, but I suspect still news.

Bill Bryson

In his first book, *The Lost Continent* in (1990), Bryson told the hilarious story of a road trip across the United States, rediscovering his own country. He followed that with equally funny and popular books on Europe, *Neither Here Nor There* (1991), and Britain, *Notes from a Small Island* (1995). He has also written several studies of the oddities of the English language, including *Made in America* and *Mother Tongue*.

29 October 1996

I am particularly glad to be in Sydney because it's rapidly becoming my favourite city in the entire world. But I have another reason for being pleased to be here and that's because I'm hoping that we might have a small laugh this afternoon. I've been living back in the United States for the last 18 months so I could really do with a good laugh. It would be completely wrong to suggest that Americans have no sense of humour; that's untrue but they have a completely different sense of humour.

What I really miss is that sense of irony and appreciation of understatement that just doesn't seem to click over there. I keep having this brought home to me by encounters I have with my next-door neighbour. He is a very, very nice man. Just to give you an example: the other week I came out the back door and he had had a tree fall down in his back garden. He was cutting it up into smaller pieces and loading it on to the roof of his car in order to cart it away and it was all dangling down over the sides. I said, 'Oh, I see you're camouflaging your car.' He said, 'No, I had a tree fall down and I'm . . . ' Now it has become kind of an obsession with me, I can't stop saying these things to him.

I lived for 20 years in England. I didn't realise it at the time but I left just as I was beginning to understand the place. Perhaps it's not so hard for Australians but for Americans Britain is an immensely confusing and idiosyncratic country. It is after all a nation where you go 'up' to reach the downs; where they have a constitutional form of government but no written constitution; where a person who flashes his car headlights at you may be saying, 'Please pass in front of me, I'm happy to give way', or may equally be saying, 'How dare you pass in front of me, you prat, I'm so angry I'm going to flash my headlights at you'; and above all where people who enthusiastically say to you, 'You must come for the weekend, do bring the children', will be appalled if you actually do.

I'm immensely proud that I know how to ride an English train and that I could get on the right train about 95 times out of 100 which I think is a pretty fair proportion all things considered. I'm proud that I can successfully erect an English deck chair, that I know you must warm the teapot before you put in the tea bags, that I understand what the letters LBW and GPO mean, that I am acquainted with Poppy Day and Morecambe and Wise and pork pies and a great deal else. It took me a long time to learn all these things and now that I can no longer put them to regular use I find that I miss them immensely.

It is a funny thing because when I lived in Britain I never missed America at all. That was, I suppose, because everything I could want from America was already in Britain: American movies, American television programs, American sport and news, American food. Sadly, it doesn't always work the other way around. I'm not exaggerating when I suggest that the United States has a somewhat insular attitude towards world news. I am sure it has not escaped your notice that we Americans are not, to put it charitably, closely acquainted with Australian affairs. Probably not one American in ten thousand could name the Australian prime minister.

"We Americans are not, to put it charitably, closely acquainted with Australian affairs."

I understand if you feel some sense of personal grievance over this but I assure you that we are indiscriminate in our ignorance, we don't know anything about anyone. I had this brought home to me on a somewhat more personal level a few months ago when *Notes from a Small Island* was published in America and the American publishers asked me to provide a glossary to explain all the quaint, exotic and arcane terms I used in the book. Among the terms I had to define for an American audience were bank holiday, dirty weekend, Christmas cracker, doner kebab, greengrocer, pork pie, motorway, railway cutting, serviettes, Tesco's, jumper, Port-a-Cabin and George Formby.

Incidentally, I was rather pleased with my definition for doner kebab. I said it was a:

> *Sandwich-type snack concocted from a sort of pita bread into which is inserted processed meat distantly related to lamb which becomes mysteriously appealing after seven or eight pints of beer.*

There were about 90 of these terms all together, all of them raised as queries by a young, well-educated and clearly quite bright copy editor in New York. Afterwards I had a careful look at them all and I calculated that even before I went to

Britain I knew at least 40 of them from just reading English mystery novels and hearing Beatles lyrics and that sort of thing. Most of the rest I think I could have figured out. I believe at the very least that I could have deduced that steak and kidney pudding is not a dessert – and I am from Iowa.

"There is a kind of wonderful grossness about the American experience which I find simultaneously appalling and enthralling."

There is a phenomenon known as the dumbing-down of America and it really is quite profoundly noticeable nearly everywhere these days. A few years ago, an organisation called the National Endowment for the Humanities tested 8000 American high school seniors and found that a very large number of them didn't know anything: two-thirds had no idea when the US Civil War took place or which president penned the Gettysburg Address; roughly, the same proportion could not identify Josef Stalin, Winston Churchill or Charles de Gaulle; a third thought that Franklin Roosevelt was president during the Vietnam War and that Columbus sailed to America after 1750; 42 per cent – this is my favourite – couldn't name a single country in Asia.

It sometimes feels as if nearly the whole nation has taken Nitol or something and that the effects haven't quite worn off. For instance, I was watching something on television recently called the Weather Channel and the weather man brightly said: 'And in Albany today they had 12 inches of snow, that's about a foot.' This isn't just some curious aberration; it happens all the time and it's really beginning to get on my nerves.

I was recently on a flight with Continental Airlines, and goodness knows why, but I was reading that letter from the president that you get at the front of every airline magazine – the one that explains how they're constantly striving to improve services, evidently, in this case, by making everyone fly through New York. This one was about how they had just conducted an exhaustive survey of their customers to find out their needs. What the customers wanted, according to the solemn prose of Mr Gordon Bethune, the chairman and chief executive officer, was:

> *A clean, safe and reliable airline that took them where they wanted to go, on time, and with their luggage.*

On the other hand, I have to say, there are many really, really good things about America. There is, for one thing, the wealth of choice. America is quite sumptuously over-endowed with almost everything and it's hard not to be captivated by that. Just last week I was in our local supermarket, standing there, trying to remember what it was I'd been sent to get, and I noticed that this particular store stocked eight different varieties of incontinence nappy for grown-ups. Everywhere I turned in the supermarket there was this same dazzling variety of choice for everything, from toothpaste to washing powders to mouth washes and shampoos. There is, in short, a kind of wonderful grossness about the American experience which I find simultaneously appalling and enthralling.

There is a great deal – a very great deal – about living in America that is wonderful: people are friendly – unbelievably friendly – and their attitudes are refreshingly upbeat; my children are growing up in a society in which it is assumed that they have a useful future; health care is stupefyingly expensive but excellent; where we live there is virtually no crime; our local university, Dartmouth, is a private and very exclusive institution and yet it actively encourages townspeople to use its facilities, swim in its pool, read in its library, attend its plays and film seasons; all of which provides a highly refreshing contrast to our experience in England.

So for all these reasons, good and bad, I'm convinced that moving to America was the best thing we ever did. I've always felt exceptionally lucky to have got to live in two countries and experience two cultures and I am delighted to see my children enjoying that same advantage, but at a much earlier age. I genuinely hope that one day they and my wife will also, as I do, miss the shipping forecasts and Benny Hill and brown sauce and all the rest of it and let me go back to England, but worse things could happen than spending the rest of my life in the United States. There is, at the very least, a certain comfort in knowing that I shall be well fixed for incontinence nappies.

! ?

SPEAKER: Have you ever had to explain cricket to Americans?

BILL BRYSON: No, no, I never have. I tried really hard in the two decades that I was in Britain to become a cricket enthusiast and I did get as far as the point of being able to watch the edited highlights, when they compress the day's play down to 45 minutes, and so you don't have the people rubbing the ball down their trousers. And I thought, speed it up a little and this isn't a bad game.

SPEAKER: You're obviously an expert on train travel. Have you ever managed to fathom out the mysteries of European train timetables?

BILL BRYSON: I wrote about that at some length in *Neither Here Nor There* because I was fascinated. I do love train timetables and things like that. I haven't really got anything to say beyond that except that they are fascinating, just the detail. I think with any trip the planning is 80 per cent of the pleasure and the reading of the train timetables is 80 per cent of the pleasure of the planning. I may be alone in this view.

SPEAKER: How many Australians told you that 'dag' was a proper word?

BILL BRYSON: I'd better explain the background to this: I wrote in *Made in America* that the Pennsylvania Dutch have a word for the little things that dangle down at the backside of sheep and get caught in their hair – the little bits of turds, to put it into its crudest term – and that, as far as I knew, these were the only people in the world who had a term for this. Of course, I immediately got letters from 87,000 people in Australia and New Zealand telling me about dags. So I'd like to take this opportunity to thank the nation for helping me.

SPEAKER: Given the marvellous insights in *Mother Tongue* and *Made in America*, how do you think the English language should be taught and is there any value in teaching grammar?

BILL BRYSON: That's a very good question – and I don't know. I don't even know any more where I stand on this language. On the one hand, you have to accept that English is a dynamic language and that it's always changing. One of the glories of the

English language is that we've never had an academy to try and regulate it or freeze it.

On the other hand, I think there's a certain virtue in traditional features of the language – to preserve a distinction between 'imply' and 'infer' and things like that. I think they're important distinctions. And I think teaching kids grammar is something to do with the basis of the language, there is value in that. However, I feel the idea of making them spend a lot of time in parsing sentences, etc., rather than just learning the joy in using the language and its facility and capacity for being used expressively, is probably a waste of time or not the best use of time. I've always felt that you can use the English language well and enjoy it without particularly understanding the grammatical complexities of it, in the same way that you can drive an automobile well without understanding the complexities of an internal combustion engine.

SPEAKER: Having read *Made in America*, I'm amazed at the amount of research you must have had to have done to write it.

BILL BRYSON: Writing *Made in America*, which is a kind of a popular history of the United States and particularly focused on the American language, the American version of English and all those words that have come into the English language from America, was a wonderful experience. I set off to write a more or less straightforward book looking at the history of American words and where they came from. But I found that you couldn't just talk about that. You couldn't talk about, say, 'hamburger', without also talking about virtually the whole of American culture, popular culture: why Americans eat hamburgers; why they invented that kind of a food; and why it took off there in such a big way. 'Hamburger', by the way is a mysterious word because it doesn't come from Hamburg, Germany, and it's obviously never had ham in it; nobody really knows where this word comes from.

I found that with every single thing I looked at that – you couldn't differentiate the linguistic history of America from the cultural, popular history of America. And once I realised that, I started writing a completely different kind of book. The research for it was a wonderfully self-indulgent exercise. I did most of the research at Drake University Library in Des Moines, my home town, for two years because I could stay at my mother's house and it didn't cost me anything, and also because it's a wonderful library and none of the books had ever been touched – this college in Des Moines is not noted for academic standards, but has a wonderful, wonderful library. I would go in and think, oh, today, I think I'll look into freeways, the history of freeways, and then I'd get bored with that and I'd decide to go and read about, say, the Hershey Bar or something else. A lot of the time I was just ranging around and it's quite interesting how often I came across things that proved to be useful in a totally serendipitous way.

Margaret Atwood

The work of Canada's most accomplished novelist, poet and essayist reflects her childhood love of Quebec's wilderness and her wry feminist intellect. Atwood has won many literary awards and has been shortlisted three times for the Booker Prize – for *The Handmaid's Tale* (1986), *Cat's Eye* (1989) and her most recent novel, *Alias Grace* (1997), based on the true story of a servant woman jailed for murdering her employer and his mistress.

11 March 1997

Instead of going into great detail about *Alias Grace*, I thought I would go into some of my own background and how I came to know some things about daily life in the 19th century that I was able to use in the book.

In fact, I partly grew up in it. I spent a large part of my earlier childhood in the north woods of Canada because my father was a research entomologist and that meant he was in the woods at the times when insects could be expected to be chewing trees. We usually went up north just about the time the ice was going out, which would be in April, and then we went back to the city about the time the ice started to come in again, which would be November. So all of that middle part of the year we spent in the woods without any running water or electricity or movie theatres or television – which had barely been invented then anyway. We did have a radio but we couldn't pick up much on it except thunderstorms.

So I was familiar with the routines associated with wood stoves – cutting the wood, splitting the wood, stacking the wood, lighting the stove, dealing with the smoke that belched out – and all of those other aspects of 19th-century home life, such as outhouses and how you got the water and especially the laundry.

Grace Marks does quite a bit of laundry in this book. She's very concerned with cleanliness and I based this on a comment which she made. She said, or is said to have said, when James McDermott stated he was about to murder Nancy, 'Don't do it in this room, you'll get blood on the carpet.' When I read that, I thought there speaks somebody who had to do a lot of laundry and scrub the floors. We did our laundry similarly to the way Grace would have done it – except in the 19th century they tended to actually boil the clothes while we would heat the water on the stove and then pour it into the zinc tub. We had a scrub board and we had Sunlight soap, the yellow kind in bars. When I had become an older child, it was my job to do a certain amount of the laundry and it was actually quite fun. There is nothing like a laundry hung out on the line to dry – not at all the same as laundry done in a dryer.

My father's family lived in rural Nova Scotia in an area where they hadn't yet put in electricity and telephones and when I visited there as a child I again saw a 19th-century household in full swing. Our own household was a bush household – the cabin, the lake, the fish, etc. My father's parents' household was the full thing – the house with the attic, the root cellar, the smokehouse, the pig raised every year and then done in and preserved. They had the kitchen garden and the outhouse and the quilts. They had the parlour organ which fascinated me as a child and they had another parlour organ which didn't work any more and was in the attic and had bats in it, which was even more interesting.

They made their own butter. I used to watch my grandmother making the butter and they did have something Grace wouldn't have had – a manually-operated cream separator. They had a wood stove to end all wood stoves. It had a huge amount of chrome on it and would have dated from probably the 1910s or so. It had warming ovens and water heaters and about eight lids that you could cook on and the kind of food they ate was still 19th-century food.

The breakfasts were enormous because you did the chores and then you had breakfast; then you did more chores and then you had the midday meal; and then you did more chores and then you had supper. The breakfasts all had big hams and meat – the 19th century loved meat, especially in North America where they could get lots of it. This is why in the novel they're always eating meat. One of the famous parts of the trial was when the butcher who used to go the house testified that he found it very suspicious that Grace told him that they didn't want any fresh meat that week because they always had meat.

When I was in my 30s we lived on a farm north of Toronto for about eight years. The house on the farm had been built in 1837. In other words, it would have been about the same vintage as the house that Mr Kinnear lived in, though his would have been a bit grander. So I was familiar with the layout of that sort of house – a big pantry, a central staircase, a front parlour, a back parlour, a summer kitchen and a winter kitchen. This is what people had in Ontario before the days of air-conditioning – they had two kitchens because it was too hot in the house if you turned the stove on in the summer; so there was a summer kitchen that was removed from the rest of the house.

These were some of the things that I had in the back of my head when I was trying to deal with Grace Marks's daily life. The other thing I had in the back of my head was Victorian literature. Many years ago when I was a graduate student my field was Victorian literature and I was particularly interested in the bits that you don't usually get to study in school. Indeed I still have a little collection of somewhat odd Victorian books. I have one called *Little Graves*. It's quite a small book and it contains nothing but poems about dead children. In that age when almost every family experienced the death of a child, there was a market for such books.

I also have several books about the woman question which was a very hot topic then – the true sphere of women, what women should be doing.

"I still have a little collection of somewhat odd Victorian books. I have one called 'Little Graves'. It's quite a small book and it contains nothing but poems about dead children."

One of my favourites is called *The True Glory of Women*. It has a beautiful peacock design on the cover. Inside it describes 'the true glory of women' as nursing the sick, staying home, raising children and doing a great deal of needlework. If you did these things, you would be respected; if you did other things, you would not be respected. There was an ongoing argument in the 19th century about whether women should be educated or not. Those against it felt that if women were educated, too much of their energy would go into their brains instead of where it should be, which was in their capacity to bear children; and then if their brains got too big, the other parts would shrink proportionately and it would not be at all good for the future of the human race to have women with great big heads and little, tiny hips.

I was very interested in these outlooks and in costume generally – how dress influenced people and how it would actually force their bodies into different positions. So long before I wrote this book I was collecting history of clothing books which are filled with fascinating details such as when underpants came in and the attitudes towards them and the big corset debate. There was a huge corset debate raging in the 19th century. Some people felt that women's bodies were by nature so rubbery and inclined to droop that they had to have corsets just to hold them in place otherwise they wouldn't be able to stand up; others felt that in fact having these corsets weakened women and prevented them from developing the muscles that were necessary to keep them upright; not to mention the effects of tight-lacing. Some women had ribs removed to make their waists smaller and pregnancy complications were common.

Look at any 19th-century fashionplate and you can see that the women's body is actually constructed from the undergarments out. You can't wear those dresses without putting on a tight corset, the kind seen in *Gone with the Wind*, when Scarlett is holding onto the bedpost and Mammy is pulling the strings. This is why fainting was such an item. Women fainted a lot because they couldn't breathe.

I was also interested for a long time in people's attitude towards women who wrote. It was sort of all right to write novels. Writing poetry was thought to be really an aberration; only men were considered to have the intellectual capacity to write poetry. It was quite daring, it was considered a higher art form. There were a couple of women who made a great success of it – notably Mrs Browning. But in general, novels were more acceptable then poetry and especially novels of an improving kind. *Uncle Tom's Cabin* was very approved of. It had a moral direction to it.

I'll tell you about how I came to write about Grace Marks. I knew a little bit about Susanna Moodie even before my 19th-century studies. In fact I'd been fascinated by her name as a child. I had her book at home and her name printed on the spine had two big round Os in the middle of it and so did mine, so that caught my attention at once. Later at school we had readers and mostly there were dead English writers in them but occasionally, just for a change, there were some dead Canadians. You didn't actually have to be a man to be a writer, there were some dead English women for which I've always been quite grateful and Susanna Moodie's bit in the school reader was about her log cabin burning down in the middle of winter. I identified with that. I'd lived in a cabin, I'd seen chimney fires. I could picture the possibilities.

Then I forgot all about her, I went to school, I grew up. But when I was at graduate school, I dreamt that I had written an opera about Susanna Moodie. It only had one person in it – her. I was interested in why I would have had such a dream so I went to the library to read her books. She was an English gentlewoman who went to Canada with her impractical husband in the mistaken belief that the family fortunes would be improved. They thought they were going to the Niagara Peninsula where there were grapes and cows and something more like England or the South of France. But the piece of land they got was in the rocky, swampy, bear-filled, mosquito-infested part and she was not at all prepared for this. She was not a very practical person. So she had a dreadful time and she wrote a book called *Roughing It in the Bush* in which she told all the other English gentlefolk not to go to this dreadful place, that Canada was suitable for peasants because they could handle it but not for more refined persons such as herself. This book made a hit in England but was not popular in Canada. People didn't like to think that they were peasants, I suppose.

"I would start about 6 o'clock, have anxiety attacks and sharpen pencils for two hours or so, and after that time I would either write or give it up and go to a movie."

She then wrote another book, *Life in the Clearings*, more or less to repair the damage and to show that there was civilisation of a sort. She went round to places like Niagara Falls and the penitentiary – a mark of civilisation that they had one. At the penitentiary she saw Grace Marks. Everybody knew about Grace so Susanna Moodie wrote her up. But she wrote from memory and her memory wasn't very good. She got a lot wrong. Then off she went to the lunatic asylum – another mark of civilisation

– and there was Grace Marks in the lunatic asylum again; she'd been transferred. Susanna Moodie ended her account by saying perhaps the poor girl was deranged all along and this would account for her participation in this shocking affair and she would be forgiven in the afterlife because she wasn't in control of herself. I read that in the '60s and I believed it because it was labelled 'non-fiction' and I was young.

I then wrote a little television play based on Moodie's version. I did leave out one bit – Susanna Moodie has the two criminals cutting up the body of Nancy Montgomery into four pieces before hiding it under a washtub and I thought this was unlikely. Firstly, they didn't have chainsaws in those days and I couldn't quite imagine what they would have used – a saw perhaps. Secondly, I didn't see why they would bother and especially I didn't see why it would be four pieces. Where would you make the cut? Any sensible person would take the legs off, arms off, head off and that's more than four. I couldn't quite see them doing it right down the middle. In fact that detail came from Susanna Moodie's literary imagination. She must have been thinking of 'drawn and quartered'.

So I did the television play and then I forgot about it after a failed attempt to turn it into a stage play. About 15 years later, I was sitting in a hotel room in Zurich and back into my head came the scene in the cellar, more or less the one that's at the beginning of the book now. So I thought this must be Grace Marks come back again and it was. This time I went off to the archives and tried to find the contemporary accounts of the story. It was a bit difficult at first because Susanna got the place and the names wrong but finally, thanks to the wonders of modern technology, we put Grace Marks into the computer and up came the newspaper story. It turned out to have happened in 1843 in Richmond Hill. Then we got hold of all of the newspapers that we could and we went off to the Kingston Penitentiary and looked in their archives, and to the lunatic asylum and looked in theirs. It turned out to have been a much more problematic and indeed a more interesting story, although less theatrical, than the one Susanna Moodie had told.

There were many different opinions about what had actually happened and especially there were many different opinions about the character of Grace Marks. One version had a demonic, sullen, manipulative, evil girl; another one a really quite amiable person, weak and easily led, who had only run away with James McDermott out of fear of her own life. There's something to that – if you were in a lonely farmhouse with two dead bodies and the man who had done them in, you'd be inclined to do what he said, at least till you got to a more populated area. So that's what she did and my story really comes out of the discrepancies, the different versions, the fact that this was a very politicised case. Tory Conservatives were against Grace, reformed Methodists tended to be for her, or at least to feel that though it was regrettable she shouldn't get a life sentence. That's how the book came about.

! ?

SPEAKER: Most of your characters right through have been what might be conventionally called stroppy women, people who challenge society. I wonder how you see the future for 'positive' stroppy women, given that in the so-called developing countries, there's an increasing move to conservatism and in the third world, the issue of women doesn't seem to have arisen at all.

MARGARET ATWOOD: I think it actually has arisen quite a lot and that people know by now that about the only way you can really deal with population explosion is by educating women. It seems to be the one factor that really does have an effect. Educating women and improving standards of health, so that instead of having 12 kids to secure their future, hoping that maybe five of them might live, people have fewer children with a better chance each.

I think the one huge problem facing the world as a whole right now is the doubling and redoubling of population. It is a limited planet. There is only so much room on it. We've already obliterated a huge number of other species and if we don't pay attention, we're going to start in on one another pretty soon; in fact we already have in some parts of the world. Giving women control over their own reproduction seems to be about the only way that really works.

This is not a 'feminist' statement, it's just observation. By the way, I have no objection at all to being called a feminist, as long as people define their terms. If it means somebody that believes that women are human beings, I'm all for it. If it means somebody who believes that every single woman is better than every single man, I'm against it simply on the basis of observation. I don't think it's an anti-woman statement to say that it's possible for women to do bad things. They wouldn't be human unless it were possible and they wouldn't have free choice unless it were possible. If they were programmed to be angels, they shouldn't get any points for being good. It's the Lizzie Borden defence. Lizzie Borden got off because it was the end of the 19th century and there was an agenda. The word had gone about that it was not possible for a woman to have given her mother 40 whacks and when she saw what she had done, to have given her father 41. It was thought to be impossible and so she got off on the superior woman defence. I think anybody reading the facts of the case remains in little doubt. You'll be happy to know, by the way, that Lizzie Borden's home in Fall River, Massachusetts, is now a bed and breakfast where you get, with your bedtime hot milk, little hatchet-shaped cookies.

SPEAKER: What are you working on at the moment? And how do you balance the time you have at home writing with time that you might spend doing promotional work like this?

MARGARET ATWOOD: I never discuss work-in-progress with anybody at all because if I do tell and then change my mind, one of you is bound to remember and ask about it later. Also I'm superstitious about it. If you talk about it, you dissipate the energy that you need to actually write the thing.

I confine promotional work to a block of time. I'm off limits while I'm writing. I have a very wonderful assistant who also has a wonderful assistant and they help with promotion. Our web page is also of great assistance. We put everything there that you might possibly want to know so that now you don't need to write us in order to ask, you can look it up on the web page.

Family matters do affect when you write, how long and what times of day, etc. I used to be a night writer because I had a day job. I would start about 6 o'clock, have anxiety attacks and sharpen pencils for two hours or so, and after that time I would either write or give it up and go to a movie. When I had a family I had to give up the night writing because small children wake up early in the morning. I also had to condense the anxiety attacks down to about 10 minutes of sheer panic to make more writing time. For a while my writing time coincided with school hours. I would start feverishly at 9 in the morning, break for lunch and go back at it at about 1.30 in the afternoon and finish at 3.30. I did that for quite a while until my child reached the stage of finding other people more interesting than she found me. This happens for a while when they are teenagers.

Now I start probably about 9.30 or 10 in the morning and I'm eminently interruptable. I always have been interrupted and it doesn't seem to bother me. If you wait for the perfect time and place that will never happen.

SPEAKER: When I was living in Canada during the premiership of Pierre Trudeau, I noticed there was a marked discrepancy between your use of language which is very imaginative, very colourful, and the use of the language by Canadians in the newspapers, which was very bland. I'd like to know your comments on that.

MARGARET ATWOOD: Newspapers do write differently to novelists and poets because they are supposed to be reporting objective truth. Usually you will find a columnist or two in any newspaper who uses more colourful language. But there was also a kind of dress code of language, certain words that you weren't supposed to use, and this still pertains to a certain extent with the *New York Times*.

I reviewed John Updike's *The Witches of Eastwick* for that paper and I ran into some difficulties. The book deals quite a lot with bodily functions and they would accept virtually none of the words that deal with these functions. They wouldn't accept 'pee', 'piss', 'urine' and I finally ended up with 'bodily fluids'. They said, 'This is a family newspaper'.

I think that dress code has been broken to a certain extent in the English press, probably in the Australian one and somewhat in the Canadian one. The holdouts seem to be the American papers, oddly enough. 'Sweat' was recently banned from the story of a friend of mine. For a long time, the *New Yorker* would not publish any story that had sex, violence or bodily functions in it, which was why it had, for many years, stories about people going for walks in the snow. Remember those? And having thoughts – they did that a lot.

But we actually broke that barrier. In fact, it was broken partly with a story of mine about a hairball that a woman has removed from herself. The male editor said, 'Margaret, you have such a baroque and gothic imagination to have made up this ovarian cyst that has hair and teeth in it', and I said, 'Well actually, Bob, I didn't make it up. Women have these quite a lot.' He said, 'You can't be serious.' I said, 'Go to the office and ask three women and see if they either have had or know somebody who has had this particular item removed.' He came back and said, 'You were right, but why didn't I know about this before?' and I said, 'It just goes to show you that there are still some things that are not discussed at the dinner table.'

SPEAKER: Did you have any books rejected before you were published?

MARGARET ATWOOD: Yes, certainly. I submitted a book of poetry probably every year for about six years when I was young and stupid and they all got rejected but I just kept doing it. I have an unpublished first novel, written in my early 20s, which was rejected by everybody, probably just as well, although it has 'promise' and it was ahead of its time. It ends with the protagonist, who is female, trying to decide whether to push the male protagonist off a roof and it was not taken well by the publishing industry at that time. In fact, I got taken out to lunch by a very nice man who said, 'This is a very good book. Could you consider changing the ending?' and I said, 'No, I could not consider it'. He leaned across the table and patted my hand – this was in the days when you could do that without being charged – and said sympathetically, 'Is there anything we can do?' I had the horrifying thought that he had identified me with the central character. That was the first time that happened but it certainly has not been the last.

Adeline Yen Mah

Yen Mah's 1997 best-selling autobiography, *Falling Leaves*, tells the tragic story of the youngest child born to a wealthy family in northern China in 1938, and her mistreatment by a cruel stepmother. The book is also a dramatic history of China in the 20th century, through British and French control, Japanese occupation, Communism and the Tiananmen Square protest in 1989.

8 May 1997

When I was a child growing up in Shanghai and Hong Kong I don't recall opening my mouth once to volunteer a spontaneous remark during any of the meal times I shared with my parents. So for me to be able to stand before you today and tell you everything I repressed and dared not say as a child is indeed a fantasy come true and a great honour.

The title of my book, *Falling Leaves*, comes from a Chinese proverb 'luo ye gui gen' which means 'falling leaves return to their roots'. The proverb tells us that as we get older we tend to go back to our beginnings.

It also symbolises the return of the wandering child to her ancestral home, as well as overseas Chinese going back to China or for that matter any ethnic group returning to the country of their origins. To us Chinese this proverb is of special significance in 1997 because of the return of Hong Kong to China on July 1st of this Year of the Ox.

Falling Leaves tells my true story, the story of one unwanted daughter in a Chinese family growing up in 20th-century China. It is a book that I have dreamt of writing for a very long time. I know very well that in revealing my past I have broken many taboos entrenched in Chinese society for the last 2500 years, ever since the time of Confucius.

Confucius had decreed that women should always remain submissive, silent and invisible. Between birth and marriage she should obey her father. After marriage she should obey her husband and when she is widowed she must obey her son. Confucius had also proclaimed that only uneducated women were virtuous. For over 2000 years Chinese women were barred from entering the imperial examinations which were the only route to becoming a magistrate. Many girls were deliberately prevented by their own parents from learning to read or write.

"Chinese women were routinely and deliberately crippled for life in order to become desirable sex objects."

For about 1000 years, ever since the Tang Dynasty, Chinese women's feet were bound from the age of three. My grandmother was told that this was a sign of beauty and femininity, much admired by men. Her feet had been tightly wrapped in bandages from infancy to prevent growth and she wore those bandages throughout the course of her life, even during the heat of sweltering summers. When she walked she swayed and stumbled as if her feet had been partially amputated. In short, Chinese women were routinely and deliberately crippled for life in order to become desirable sex objects. This barbaric practice only ended in 1911 when Sun Yat-sen toppled the Manchu empire.

As a child walking to and from school in the streets of Shanghai during the 1940s, I often saw infants wrapped in newspapers left in doorways to die. Everyone knew the victims were invariably girl babies because even the poorest Chinese parents always found a way to house and feed their sons. Interestingly, I am reading a book at present called *China in the Sixteenth Century*. It was written by an Italian Jesuit priest called Matteo Ricci who lived in China for over 20 years during the Ming Dynasty and died in 1610 in Beijing.

In his book he reported that in some provinces a prevailing custom of dealing with unwanted infant daughters was to drown them. This was done not only by the very poor, but also by those who were not abjectly poor, for fear that the time might come when they would not be able to care for their children. Thus ironically they were acting cruelly in an effort to be considerate - thinking that they were doing their daughters a benefit by murdering them. This horrific practice was carried out quite openly and with general public knowledge.

China has come a long way since the time of Ricci. But even today in the new territories of prosperous Hong Kong, daughters are still being traditionally left out of their parents' wills so that all the land and property are inherited only by the sons. This discriminatory procedure is perpetrated not only by the fathers who are partial towards their sons, but equally by the mothers against their own daughters.

Recently one of my relatives said to me that lots of Chinese women have had it much worse than I. Compared to them my life has not been so terrible. After all, every day millions of Chinese girls are neglected and some are even sold into prostitution or abandoned. I replied that this submissive silence is exactly what I wish to alter. How can change come about when no one speaks out?

My mother died of puerperal fever two weeks after my birth and I was punished by my family all my life because of this. My father remarried a beautiful Eurasian woman, half French and half Chinese, whom we called Niang. There were seven children in our family. Five from father's first wife and two from our stepmother. My only friend was my Aunt Baba, the oldest sister of my father. She was also despised because she was a spinster and financially dependent upon my father. During my miserable childhood days in Shanghai when I sat late at night on the top stair of the second floor landing waiting for my Aunt Baba to come home from her mah-jong games, I used to weave fantastic stories in my head to take myself away from the awful reality of my daily existence and dream of a time when I could blurt out to the whole world all that was buried inside of me.

"The approach of the 21st century seems to be ushering in an era where money is everything."

From the earliest years to which my memory reaches I was treated with contempt by my parents and siblings. *Falling Leaves* describes the striving of children for the love of their parents. In so doing it dares to tell the truth about the actual inner workings of a Chinese family. I have been accused of showing disrespect towards my dead parents in revealing them as they were without caution or restraint. I have been told that it is unseemly to cast aspersions on the integrity of one's own parents, even if they are dead and buried. Presumably this is a legacy of ancestor worship. There is an ancient Chinese saying that family ugliness should never be revealed in public.

Writing my book has helped me explore and understand the complexities and ambiguities of my own emotions about my past. I believe that in order to solve a problem that problem has first to be laid out in the open. I wish to recount my denigration, the pitiless denigration of one unloved and motherless child within my own family in the hope that other women will be encouraged to emerge from their passivity and victimisation. I hope that after reading *Falling Leaves* at least some parents, especially Chinese parents, will sit up, take notice and treat all their children with equal affection, attention and justice.

We live in a sadly empty and increasingly materialistic environment. The approach of the 21st century seems to be ushering in an era where money is everything. Many have no beliefs and no quest except the acquisition of cash. People such as my grandfather and my aunt Baba, who held concepts like honesty, loyalty, principles and honour, are viewed not with respect and admiration, but often regarded with ridicule and contempt. In China the term 'lao shi' which during my childhood used to describe a person who is truthful and good, now means someone who is simple-minded, naive and easily taken in. This new definition is actually in the *Concise Chinese English Dictionary* printed by the Oxford University Press in 1994. It is a sad commentary on our modern times that honesty is now viewed as stupidity.

My stepmother Niang, who always called herself French even though she was actually half French and half Chinese, wrote her will in such a way as to cause maximum strife and discord between my siblings and me. As my brother James pointed out to me, if I challenged her will in a courtroom I would be carrying out her wishes. Besides, even if I were to win a large settlement after a long legal battle, it would have been a hollow and negative victory because money was not the issue or my motivation. My aunt Baba had always taught me that unjust punishment often incurs a special type of suffering which could become ultimately redemptive and inspirational to the victim. I wanted to harness my outrage and my sorrow into doing something positive. The result is *Falling Leaves.*

Books are catalysts for personal change. I realised this very early on in life when I was a child still in primary school in Shanghai. I hope that my book will reach out to many readers all over the world, especially to those who have been rejected or unwanted or felt downtrodden as a child.

Though I don't like to think about it, I am 59 years old and in the last third of my life. Holding *Falling Leaves* in my hand, I have the curious thought that should I die tomorrow I should still be content because my book will live after me. On my tombstone I would like my epitaph to read: 'Here lies Adeline Yen Mah, author of *Falling Leaves*. She was Chinese and she dared to tell the truth about her family.' Hopefully all this will not happen in the too immediate future. It gives me enormous satisfaction to think that after I am gone perhaps my book might still change some lives and leave a tiny mark behind so that other unwanted children, maybe a hundred years from now, will be encouraged.

After all, I have always believed that one single positive dream is more important than a thousand negative realities.

SPEAKER: I'm curious to know the reaction of your brothers and sister to the book.

ADELINE YEN MAH: All autobiographies are difficult because of the reaction that you might receive from your relatives and I have disguised all their names because I don't want to hurt them unnecessarily and their names are irrelevant. I heard from my half-sister Susan who is a very prominent socialite in Hong Kong - her husband is probably one of the richest men in Hong Kong, if not the world. She was not happy but actually I think she comes out best in the book. She is a very brave person who told my stepmother, who was her mother, exactly how she felt about her and broke away many years ago - something that I myself could never do.

But we are talking about her mother and she felt that essentially now everybody in Hong Kong would know how her mother was. She also asked me why I did not confront my stepmother when she was alive and I told her that even though I knew that Niang was neither kind nor good I wanted her approval and her love all my life, even on her deathbed. I could not have written this because I knew I would have hurt her and all my life I did not want to hurt her - I could only write *Falling Leaves* after she was dead.

Robert Hughes

The expatriate Australian art critic for *Time* magazine in New York for almost 30 years, Hughes has also made his mark with knowledgable, rhetorically powerful books and television series on art and history: *The Shock of the New* (1981), *The Fatal Shore* (1986), *Barcelona* (1992), *The Culture of Complaint* (1993) and his survey of American art history and the way it reflects society's changes, *American Visions* (1997). He is now filming a series about Australia.

18 June 1997

This has been a long strange trip. *The Shock of the New* went out on television and as a book in 1981 when we were all teenagers. Afterwards, I thought maybe there's some other television series I could do and it was obvious the story of American art in some shape or form was an ideal televisual subject and also might not be without interest as a book as well.

So filled with that sort of ersatz confidence that one gets having been puffed up by a series that got some very decent reviews, I went along to people at the BBC and said, hey, let's do American art. The BBC at the time was entering a phase where all the more gifted and proactive younger directors felt that MTV was the wave of the future, therefore the idea of a lengthy didactic mini-series had the same ontological status as a herbivorous dinosaur: it wasn't going to get an audience.

So I went to PBS and PBS said, we think that's a wonderful visionary idea, why don't you go out and raise the money and we'd be happy to produce it. And so I went out, naively thinking it might be possible to raise the money, and I then spent a weird couple of years distractedly kissing arse in the boardrooms of various American corporations.

Finally, just as I was about in despair, the BBC decided to relent and so we were given the green light exactly 12 years after I had produced the first set of synopses for this series and away we went.

From the outset it was quite clear that you couldn't do a full formal history of American art on television. We decided that instead we would try and give it some kind of narrative form by rephrasing the subject, as it were, so that we were not asking what is the total sum of everything Americans have done in the visual arts, but rather putting the question of what can we tell about Americans from the things that they've made and what can we say about American dreams, hopes, fantasies, ideals, fears, etc. from the visual images that Americans have created.

This again produced a considerable problem because, in fact, the most powerful and world-encircling cultural phenomenon in America in the last half century at least has been its popular culture – its music, its films, its television, etc. and these are the things that have really gone burning out on the world and left an indelible American imprint on them. The art, at least until after the 1950s, considerably less so. In an ideal world, I would have loved to quote extensively from American films, say from the films of John Ford, when talking about the imagery and mythology of the wilderness in American painting and other visual arts, but this proved to be impossible because our budget just didn't run to it.

People, PBS people particularly, who are used to working on very small budgets, would ask what the budget of *American Visions* was and I would say $4.5 million, which sounds like a fairly impressive amount of money but actually it would buy you approximately two minutes and ten seconds of a movie like *Waterworld* and it boils down to about $500,000 a program – $500,000 US admittedly but when film companies want to charge you $20,000 a second for a quote from 'She Wore a Yellow Ribbon', then it becomes manifestly impossible.

Nevertheless, I think that we did have some success in a couple of things – first of all, in suggesting something of the extraordinary breadth of American culture since the time of the arrival of the Spaniards in the 16th century and also perhaps in tracing some of the long strands that go on in it.

"From the mid–18th century onwards, America was capable of throwing up, and with increasing frequency, really remarkable artists."

When I first arrived in America in 1970 clutching my bags of potpourri from the Farmacia di Santa Maria Novella which nearly got me arrested because it was assumed to be some other kind of herbal mixture, at the time that I first got there, it was widely assumed, not by foreigners but by Americans, that American art did not really get serious until after the Second World War – that it did this trick that we always want Australian culture to do, coming of age round about 1950, and that the achievement of people like Pollock and Rothko and de Kooning represented a kind of American maturity which the products of earlier American painters lacked.

It had always seemed to me that this was absolutely and categorically wrong. Not quite from the beginnings but certainly from the mid–18th century onwards, America was capable of throwing up, and with increasing frequency, really remarkable artists. You think of Benjamin West and John Singleton Copley in the 1760s and then that strain of pragmatic realism that develops out of Copley, that strongly American empirical grain strand that goes on to give us people like Audubon and Thomas Aikens and Winslow Homer and so on through to Stuart Davis – the achievement of these artists was no way inferior and in some cases actually perhaps even better than that of the abstract expressionists.

So therefore I wanted to emphasise American achievements in earlier periods. Of course, this has been taken by some of my American critics as an infallible sign of reactionary conservatism but I believe it to be true.

The second aim was to trace long strands, as it were, in American cultural attitudes. We have in America a culture which is more preoccupied with religion than any other culture in the developed West – 95 per cent of Americans, according to the latest and doubtless unreliable polls, say that they believe in a personal god and in a heaven and a hell in which they will be either punished or rewarded after death. Yet, despite this lengthy religious obsession, America has never produced a great religious art. It has produced almost nothing of that kind. The reason is to be sought way back at the foundation, in puritanism, in descendants of the people who had combined to almost annihilate the last vestiges of religious medieval culture in England and who now came to the United States and, finding to their disappointment that there were no stained glass windows there to smash, proceeded to confine their attentions to the American Indian.

But this odd combination of theophanic desires together with a hatred of the icon doesn't just die with puritanism, it goes right through to conceptual art and the puritan preference for the logos over the image still leaves its imprints on the present, as for instance in American minimalism.

The first great American art is really 19th-century landscape and it's a particularly American kind of landscape, it's got none of the elements of pessimism and despair that you get in European Romanticism. You cannot imagine an American Goya. It is a landscape which is the direct sign, or so it was believed, of the action of God in the world. It is God's fingerprint, it is benign. The further you go out into it, the happier and the freer you become. It is not at all like Australian landscape where traditionally the further you go into it the deader you become.

The lucky thing for me was that, having finished and more or less wrapped up the series, I then had to do the book. I will not go into the various psychic convulsions which attended this – it was a fairly rough year. But at the end of it, it enabled me to put back a ton of stuff that I had left out of the series and to enrich the argument.

"Before anything else I am a Sydney boy rather than a New York one."

I do not make any claims for *American Visions* as formal history. I would like you to think of it more as an extended essay in which I try to put together stuff which has struck me, admittedly from an Australian and an outsider angle, as remarkable about the American polity and American fantasy about that polity and about American reactions to the landscape and so on, seen within the context of their expression as art.

I don't believe that I could have written this book unless I had lived in America for the last half of my life. At the same time I don't believe I could have written it if I had been an American. There is a certain virtue to outsidership and before anything else I am a Sydney boy rather than a New York one. There is a kind of scepticism, a natural scepticism which we Australians carry with us as part of our birthright as a result of not having been told from the beginning that we were the product of God's own country. To bring one position to bear upon the other was part of the inevitable process of writing this book and I hope it worked out okay – I think it did.

! ?

SPEAKER: We have heard a lot of the critic Clement Greenberg and his tremendous influence on the American art. As you are unmistakably the best-known art critic today, can you give us some idea how much influence an art critic has today and how much also the critic is responsible for the decline of contemporary art?

ROBERT HUGHES: Greenberg is obviously a critic with whom I don't have an awful lot in common. We belong to different generations but Greenberg had certain enormous strengths, he had a really nutcracking power of visual analysis and also at the time that he was working the New York art world – which meant the American art world – essentially was a lot smaller than it is today. It was a small room in which you could reach out and touch more or less with both hands.

Also, the society in general was somewhat, though not very, hostile to modern art. Greenberg rather exaggeratedly said, taking the toll of the artist of the abstract expressionist generation, 'What can 20 people do against 140 million?' The answer is, of course, that they were very rapidly accepted and went on to become multi-millionaires even if posthumously. Greenberg had a tremendous power of consistency, he also had a function as a sort of shrink to these artists because he knew them all and he had a very rigid Hegelian notion of the inevitable progress of art history – he really thought that no figurative painting could possibly take its place in the future in that history.

There was a direction in which you went and that direction was going to be abstract whether the artist liked it or not so you either got on the historical bus or else you were left behind in the dust. It was possible to argue this belief in the 1940s and perhaps even in the early 1950s but I don't believe for a second that it is possible to argue it now. Indeed, the truth is that critics, like uranium isotopes, have a half-life, they emit protons for a while and then they turn into lead. I think I can say this without in any way suggesting that I don't have the utmost respect for Greenberg. But we didn't like one another – he used to say, 'Hughes has a bad eye', as though I suffered from some permanent case of ophthalmia, but the truth is we were just interested in different things.

I am much more interested in the symbology, the historical attachments of the works of art, whereas Greenberg was purely about form. Everybody has their own prejudice.

You couldn't have a Greenberg today because you couldn't have somebody who exercised that degree of power and control over an art world of the size that it now is.

SPEAKER: On a more personal note, do you paint, draw, sculpt, other than in words?

ROBERT HUGHES: No, I do highly expressive telephone pad doodles which I do not save for posterity. I used to be a painter, I used to do rather bad purplish de Koonings in my younger days. The only thing I do in that direction now is when I go down to Mexico looking at Mayan ruins or along the coast of Turkey looking at Greek ones, I like to take a sketch book and watercolours like Aunt Matilda on her folding canvas stool in the piazza – not because I have any illusions of these taking their place alongside the works of Piranesi but it's just that if you draw something, no matter how badly, you remember it.

SPEAKER: You are a carpenter?

ROBERT HUGHES: Yes, I've got a barn in New York, upstairs is my writing room and downstairs is a woodworking shop adorned with all sorts of fantastic machinery. I've put together a collection of power tools over the years. So when I run out of steam on a paragraph I go downstairs and chop a few dovetails and having screwed those up I come back upstairs and do what I really ought to be doing.

SPEAKER: Do you have any comments on Australian Aboriginal art?

ROBERT HUGHES: Not as many as I would like to have because the whole contemporary Aboriginal Australian art movement and its promotion – I use the world neutrally – took place a long time after I left Australia. Although I've seen a certain amount – before I left of course I had seen quite a lot of classical or early bark paintings – I'm not really sufficiently informed about what has taken place in modern Australian Aboriginal art to be able to do anything other than express my respect for it. Were I writing the book that I wrote all those years ago when I was 23 or 24, *The Art of Australia*, obviously it would have a very different content now, because I don't think there's a single Aboriginal artist other than Albert Namatjira, and he disparagingly referred to, in the whole of that book. I couldn't revise it, I'd have to rewrite it from the ground up and Aboriginal art is one of the reasons why.

SPEAKER: Do you see today in modern American art or perhaps in Australian art a desire to re-create some kind of religious consciousness?

ROBERT HUGHES: Yes, there always is, it's a constant component of American modernism, I believe.

SPEAKER: And do you see at all that this might be a kind of false consciousness, a kind of trendy, faddy sort of thing?

ROBERT HUGHES: Good God, all you have to do is go to Santa Fe and look at those interminable, ghastly sculptures of Great Chief Thunderbottom adoring the spirits of his dead ancestors in the sky to realise that spirituality in America is an industry. Everything is industrialised and especially spirituality.

SPEAKER: Is there some other way to make modern art, which I felt you were somewhat disenchanted with at the end of *American Visions*?

ROBERT HUGHES: I don't have a prescription for that because in order to change art at all you have to be an artist, not a critic. All we critics can do is make guesses and I hope recognise that something is going on that is worthwhile and be right about it, but it is not within the power of a critic to lay down prescriptions and proscriptions about what direction art should take. I think that American art, like a lot of art elsewhere, has been considerably damaged and weakened by its recoil both from the nature of the artwork as a real thing rather than as simply a sort of philosophical proposition in a real world and from its craft aspect and its manuality on the one hand and on the other hand from the widespread cynicism about its capabilities as a sort of spiritual vehicle. But how one would go about achieving, on the one hand, a redensification of the work of art and, on the other hand, a respiritualisation of it, I honestly don't know, but I hope I recognise it when I see it.

Tim Bowden

Historian, journalist, author and documentary maker, Bowden hosted the popular ABC-TV audience reaction show *Backchat* from 1986 to 1994, and that year was awarded an Order of Australia for services to public broadcasting. His books include *Changi Photographer*, about George Aspinall; *One Crowded Hour*, about war cameraman Neil Davis; *The Way My Father Tells It*, about his own father, and the major history *The Silence Calling: Australians in Antarctica 1947–1997*, which he also made into a television documentary series.

8 July 1997

In November 1994, while I was filming *Breaking the Ice* and *The Silence Calling* in Antarctica, I stood alone on top of an iceberg just off the coast of Princess Elizabeth Land, near Davis Station, the helicopters which landed me both flew away – you always fly in pairs down there for safety reasons – there was utter silence. The scene was absolutely breath-taking. To my left was the great tumbled mass of the Sørsdal Glacier, coming down the coast and breaking off as huge icebergs, one of which I was standing on; below me the sheer cliff of the iceberg plunged down into a frozen sea. In such an incredible location, I was gripped with a mix of exhilaration and raw fear. I have never felt so isolated and insignificant. A human speck in the vast emptiness of Antarctica.

And I had another thought – I hoped that they remembered which iceberg they had put me on when they came back to get me.

To get the chance to write the history of ANARE, Australian National Antarctic Research Expeditions, and to go down there to film for the ABC, was for me the ultimate assignment in a fairly long life in journalism. It is a story that has got the lot – exploration, drama and human emotion. As well there's science, history . . . the works, and I'm afraid that with this tome weighing in at just under two kilos, I may have failed the reading in bed test.

Human beings don't really belong in Antarctica. We go there like astronauts going into outer space, because we've got to take everything with us for survival. We've got to take our housing, food, fuel, everything we need to survive. And every visitor to the Antarctic continent is a transient. We're all visitors. Even the expeditioners who go there only stay a year or 14 months. No one lives there permanently.

I find it quite extraordinary that as late as the 1950s the geography and main physical features of the continent of Antarctica were largely unknown – including the Australian sector, the 42 per cent we rather ambitiously claim of Antarctica. The coast was a dotted line where they thought it might be; the great inland features, like the Lambert Glacier, the biggest glacier in the world, the Prince Charles Mountains which are to the south-east of Mawson, were unknown.

"I hoped that they remembered which iceberg they had put me on when they came back to get me."

I think that Australians have always seen themselves as frontier people, but our frontiers have tended to be inland Australia or the Northern Territory or perhaps even Papua New Guinea; Antarctica is however an Australian frontier and it is in many ways a forgotten frontier. But I wonder how many Australians would know the names of Phil Law, John Béchervaise, Syd Kirkby, Doug Leckie, Peter Crohn or Peter Clemence. One of the effects that I hope this book will have is to make the stories of those pioneers more apparent to the Australian people.

Our claim of 42 per cent goes back to the days of that great Australian explorer Sir Douglas Mawson, in the early part of the century. But what I think is not so generally known is that after the war – and of course all Antarctic activity closed down during World War II – it was Sir Douglas Mawson who kept nagging the Australian Government to actually do something about this ambitious claim. It is all very well claiming territory but you've actually got to lay a glove on the place – you've got to fish off its coast, probably whaling in those days, you've got to do some science or in fact just get there. The problem was that there were no suitable ships.

First they tried the improbably named *Wyatt Earp* which was actually a wooden Norwegian fishing trawler with sails. But it was quite hopeless and eventually had to come back without really achieving anything. The other ship they went down on – all they could do, by the way, at this stage was go to the sub-Antarctic Heard and Macquarie Islands, which are roughly halfway to Antarctica – was the LST3501, later renamed the *Labuan*, which was a landing ship tank. It was really a sort of cargo hold with an engine on the back. It was utterly unsuitable for going to the Southern Ocean. And those who went down in it still speak in awe of this – it was 300 feet long – and as it went over the huge swells the sides apparently would go 'clonk, clonk, clonk, clonk', like a flexing tobacco tin, and a ripple would run along the steel deck and throw you off your feet if you didn't keep a lookout.

It was remarkable that the thing got there at all and in fact it fell to bits in 1951, fortunately only three days out of Fremantle. Water got into the fuel, the condensers packed it in, the engine stopped, it was a dead ship and they towed it back in and it never sailed again. So they were very, very lucky to get away with it.

For the people that went down to those sub-Antarctic islands it was really a very basic life. They had World War II cast-off clothing, the food was hard tack – bully beef, tinned peaches and tinned butter and so on – and they had to put huts up to live in. Some of the ones for Heard Island that were sent down were actually designed for the tropics and they had louvred windows to let in the cool evening breezes, which had to be adapted.

On Heard Island in 1948 they put their year's meat supply in the local glacier but of course, being a sub-Antarctic island, it wasn't cold enough and after about three weeks their entire year's meat supply turned into a brown stain in the ice. So unfortunately – it sounds terrible in this day and age – they had to eat the wildlife, and penguin breast and elephant seal steaks became part of the menu. But the cook, Norm Jones, who was a very traditional Aussie cook, refused to cook the local tucker (he was happy to serve up the bully beef) and so on the cook's day off the scientists used to have a go at preparing skua stew or omelette de penguin.

One of the things that was immediately apparent about the Heard Island operation was the value of the meteorological data that they sent back, because for the first time Australian forecasters had some knowledge of where the weather was actually coming from, i.e. Antarctica. Although the grinding routine of sending the radio reports on Morse key every three hours did take its toll, the strong tradition of practical joking that is a thread through the ANARE history, came through. For example, on one occasion Swampy Compton, one of the radio operators, peed in the rain gauge and then had to confess later about the strangely inflated reading. His colleagues were very cross and had to radio corrections back to the mainland.

In 1954 they found a suitable ship, the *Kista Dan*, an ice-strengthened Danish ship, which was chartered by the Australian Government, and at long last they were able to break through the pack ice and reach the coast and set up Australia's first station, appropriately named after Sir Douglas Mawson, although it is on the western side of the Australian claim, not to the east where Commonwealth Bay and Mawson's Hut are.

All this was directed by the Antarctic Division's first director, Phillip Law, who was really Mr Antarctica for that period. He drove the whole program forward, he was director for 17 years, he personally led 28 expeditions down there each summer, where they would combine resupplying the stations with basic exploration of this unknown coastline – even though he was chronically seasick and these ice-strengthened ships were abominable in the open ocean because they have rounded hulls. It was said of the *Wyatt Earp*, for instance, that she'd roll on wet grass.

The men – and there were no women in those days – who were left on the fringes of this great continent were aware of the excitement and the luck, if you like, that history and fate had placed them in this unique position. Syd Kirkby, who was one of the early surveyors, said: 'We'd climb a mountain peak and look out and say, wow, in all time certainly no human being and no creature has ever seen it. It's a funny feeling. It's not a possessive feeling, it's a privileged sort of feeling. How did I get this lucky?'

The arrival of aircraft there enabled the exploration to be much more afield. The RAAF sent a flight down in 1956 and built a hangar at Mawson,

"These mountains seemed to be moving suspiciously quickly in relation to them and they worked out that they were actually looking at husky turds on a snow bank about 50 metres away."

which was the first hangar in Antarctica and it may still be the only hangar in Antarctica.

But not all the discoveries were great ones and the Antarctic light could sometimes play some very deceptive tricks. One morning Syd Kirkby and Peter Crohn, who was a geologist, came out of their tent in a white-out, they were in a kind of a bowl of opaque white, and noticed to their excitement a great range of mountains that they hadn't noticed the previous day, stretching across the horizon to the west, black and brown peaks. Wow, they thought, and they couldn't wait to get packed and get the husky dogs in their traces, and off they went. But these mountains seemed to be moving suspiciously quickly in relation to them and they worked out that they were actually looking at husky turds on a snow bank about 50 metres away.

So what's it like to live there? Well, Phillip Law was very keen in the early days to make sure that the Antarctic stations were not bastions of Ockerdom and he wanted people to live in a civilised fashion down there and right from the very first years there was a good polar library and a library of general books, there were gramophone records, classical and popular, feature films that had been brought down to 16 millimetre that they could show every Saturday night and wine. Now these were not wine drinking days, the '50s and '60s, and Phil used to give these earnest lectures to people about what wine they should drink with what food. One day on Heard Island he was doing this and the diesel mechanic up the back said, 'Eh, Phil, what wine do you drink with bully beef?'.

The films, as the videos of today do, could sometimes take over a station, literally. In 1950 on Macquarie Island, *Pride and Prejudice* was the cult movie and they played it perhaps a hundred times. They all knew the dialogue off by heart. When Phillip Law arrived at the end of 1950 to collect them, he found the whole station had adopted the courtly language of Jane Austen's 19th-century England – somebody would pass the butter and they'd say, 'Such graciousness, such affability, you overwhelm me'.

Women didn't go to the continent until 1981 although they did go down on summer visits before that. And Zöe Gardner was the first wintering doctor – you can't have a station without a doctor and that was the breakthrough – on Macquarie Island in 1976.

People often ask how you pee in a blizzard and the answer is, of course, quickly. But the lanyard-operated zip flies on Antarctic trousers aren't terribly useful for women and other arrangements had to be found. Denise Allen told me that she wanted to go running with the dogs when she was at Mawson Station in 1984, and she called on the ingenuity of the 27 men sharing her wintering year to help solve her difficulty. So they came up with a device that was a plastic eyepiece with a doctor's surgical glove attached to the bottom of it, and it worked wonderfully providing she didn't overflow it.

Let me leave you with a quote from the head of polar medicine in the Antarctic Division, Des Lugg, who reminds us that: 'When the darkness of the Antarctic winter comes down, the Australian stations remain as isolated as were the classic expeditions of Scott, Shackleton and Mawson, and the Antarctic remains an extremely dangerous place to live and work.'

! ?

SPEAKER: I believe there's a foundation been recently established to maintain and preserve the Mawson huts?

TIM BOWDEN: Mawson's Hut is around on the eastern sector of the Australian claim, it's towards the Ross Sea, and it's really remarkable there's anything left there at all after 85 years. The hut is in danger of collapsing and AAP, Australian Associated Press, has formed a foundation to raise $2,000,000 to try and do something about this. The Antarctic Division have tried on a couple of occasions over the years to do something but Mawson happened to build that particular hut in the windiest place in the world, as he soon discovered, so it's difficult to get there. You need some, as they say in the parlance of today, 'serious money' in order to be able to do this. Anyone interested should contact the AAP Foundation. Also, excitingly, people can actually pay good money, for a good cause, to go down on the ship that will begin the restoration work this year.

SPEAKER: I heard when I myself was down in the Antarctic that the huskies were getting very inbred and that they were taking them for this thousand-mile trip to Minnesota in America. Do you think that that is doing anything for the future of the huskies?

TIM BOWDEN: The huskies had been down there in isolation since 1954 – they did have some fresh stock brought down from time to time, by the way, so they weren't completely inbred. However, the decision to take them out in 1991 was a political one. Australia and France led the charge to have the mining ban put on Antarctica, it was called the Madrid Protocol on the Antarctic Environment and that was signed in 1991 and a condition of that was all introduced species should come out. And so the huskies had to come out. But sadly, because they were completely unprotected from viruses, being isolated down there for so long, many of those dogs have since died.

SPEAKER: I wondered if perhaps you could tell us about some of the scientific discoveries that were made by scientists down in the Antarctic?

TIM BOWDEN: The Australian scientists have been on the cutting edge of Antarctic science since the '40s and '50s. One of the important fields is, of course, marine biology – they've only recently, for instance, been able to put little transmitters, and even cameras, on the backs of penguins and seals and just see where they go and how they feed and what they do. Fascinating information. Elephant seals, those great big sleeping bags of blubber, dive down to – just imagine this – 2000 metres, two kilometres down, to get their food, and even the Emperor penguins go down to 1400 metres.

One of the most exciting fields today is microbiology. Because the Antarctic continent has been isolated from the rest of the world for many millions of years, all the organisms there have developed in isolation and they've found that a spoonful of Antarctic 'soil' yields umpteen new antibiotics and very interesting micro-organisms.

The big issue being investigated by ANARE scientists now is climate change. There are all kinds of interesting things happening with the sea ice because that is far more influenced by global warming and could be the greatest area of concern. The sea ice each winter doubles the surface area of Antarctica, so it reflects an enormous amount of heat back into the atmosphere and also contains the comparatively warmer oceans. And since the Antarctic Division has had its own research and resupply ship, the *Aurora Australis*, which is capable of actually breaking into the pack ice in winter, they've found that there are areas of ice which are much thinner and huge areas of open water there which were previously not known. So clearly the warming of the world by a few degrees could have quite a dramatic effect on this control of this heat and it could exacerbate the greenhouse effect.

The study of the upper atmosphere began initially in the '40s because of people's fascination with the Aurora Australis, these wonderful southern lights. And here's a wonderful example of the victory of pure science over practicality: in the 1950s there was an instrument developed called the Dobson Photospectrometer, which analyses the upper atmosphere including how much ozone is there; Phillip Law didn't really know what this was going to lead to but he sent one of them down to Macquarie Island and then later to the continent so that we have readings of the ozone content of the atmosphere from Antarctica from that time. The so-called hole in the ozone layer wasn't discovered until the early '80s, so I think that's a very good example of how sometimes you have to spend money on science even if you don't know what's going to come from it.

They are just some of the things that are going on.

SPEAKER: Can you tell me what effect the global warming has had on the wildlife?

TIM BOWDEN: You must understand that any changes in Antarctica are long term and this is why it's important to keep scientific programs going, because you don't really notice changes until you can measure them against 20, 30, even 40 years. There is some evidence that some of the catastrophic failures of penguin colonies in recent years might be associated with the fact that the krill are not getting to areas where they did before – or is this just one of nature's cyclic things?

Certainly the elephant seal population on Macquarie Island is in decline. It came back after the sealing of the early part of the century but is now only up to about 50 per cent of what it was and barely holding and scientists are still trying to work out why. It may be, for example, because the oceans are warming and the krill or the squid or whatever it is they feed on aren't coming up to such high latitudes as much as they used to. It's very difficult to give a categorical answer to your question except that there are some worrying signs that global warming may indeed be affecting some of the Antarctic wildlife.

Minette Walters

Fascinated by murder stories since she was a child, British writer Walters has explored the psychology of evil in her popular novels, many of them successfully translated to television. They include *The Ice House* (1991), *The Scold's Bridle* (1994), *The Dark Room* (1995) and *The Echo* (1997), about a rich woman and a homeless man found dead in her garage.

26 July 1997

The first publicity event I ever did was connected with the publication of *The Ice House*, almost five years ago today. My publishers in Britain had asked me if I was prepared to assist them in selling this novel; would I do publicity? It seemed to me only fair – one wanted to do one's bit even though they had paid me absolute peanuts, I have to say. However, there was a slightly flattering quality and I said, yes great, and expected reams of invitations, the *Times*, the *Telegraph, Guardian, Observer,* the *Sunday Times*, all wanting to interview me. Needless to say, nothing, nothing at all.

Finally a girl phoned through and she said, 'Minette, we have got you a radio interview. They are terribly keen, real fans of *The Ice House*. It is 11 o'clock next Tuesday.' Well, of course, I was thinking in terms of Radio 4, the Home Service, and I was thinking 11 o'clock must be women's hour and I was frightfully pleased about this because I had been a listener of women's hour for years. So I said, 'Okay, so what, London? What time should I be there? Sort of 10 o'clock in the morning in order to be ready?' 'No,' she said, 'it is 11 o'clock at night and it is Portsmouth local radio.' I live in

Romsey, between Winchester and Southampton. So I left a 10 o'clock; I was there outside the studio door by 10.15 and I was far too embarrassed to go in. So I thought, what do you do in these circumstances? Well, you can find a pub; this seems to be a reasonable thing, buy yourself a gin and tonic and relax. When you are very nervous you can drink a gin and tonic in approximately two seconds. So what do you do? You have another gin and tonic, and drink that one in two seconds as well.

I then thought, I have got to drive home, and we have very severe drink driving laws in Britain now, so scrap that. So I smoked 20 cigarettes instead. By this time it was only about 20 past 10. I knew I was not going to be able to speak, my throat was like something that Raymond Chandler described rather well and I thought, I cannot have anything more to drink. So I twiddled my thumbs but finally it got to the time and I presented myself at the studio door at five to 11 and went in to discover that the person who was supposed to be interviewing me was sick so I got the stand-in. He was even more nervous than I was and when I arrived he had two cigarettes in his mouth and he said, 'Do feel free to smoke, I am.' So I had another one. There was nobody there except him and me and so I wasn't offered any water or anything. I was just plonked in front of a microphone and he said, 'Okay, I am playing this bit of music and then we will start.'

He played the music and then he asked me the most peculiar question which I could not follow at all. I had not a clue what he was talking about and, on top of that, by this time my entire mouth was sticking together. I have made a tape of this and I listen to it occasionally because it is incredibly funny – every time I say something there is this terrible noise and it got worse and worse. I have to say, and believe me I am being complimentary to this man, he was a complete and utter plonker. He had not read the book, he had not got a clue who I was. He did not even know what kind of fiction it was plus no-one was listening to this program. This became patently clear because he kept saying, anybody who would like to phone in and ask Minette Walters a question, do feel free. This was because he could not think of any questions to ask me and in fact he kept complimenting me on my brooch. We really had hit rock bottom.

Needless to say, nobody phoned in and so we carried on this simply diabolical conversation between the two of us. As we approached the end of this hour-long program he came up with what he regarded as a brilliant wheeze – he would offer a signed copy of *The Ice House*, this being the copy that had been sent to him that he had never read, to whomever rang in with the correct answer to a question I set. I realised if anyone was listening this question was going to have to be phenomenally easy. So I abandoned things like who is Prime Minister of England at the moment and asked them about a television program, terribly simple question and nobody phoned in. So this scurrilous scumbag then said that the phones had broken, blamed British Telecom. But then somebody did phone. Her name, I will never forget it, was Ruby from Portsmouth and she needed a little assistance with the answer to the question but by dint of kind of giving it to her she gave it back.

He said, 'Do you know, Ruby, you are so lucky, BT has just mended the phones.' This being approximately three minutes to midnight and you can just imagine that an engineer had rushed out and in three minutes mended them. Anyway, she gave the answer and won a signed first edition of *The Ice House* one of which actually was sold in New York – approximately three or four months ago – for $2500. So she actually did win something rather good. My only problem is I do not think she knows the value of what she has won.

But how did I get there – what was I doing in this studio, what had taken me there? My career began with a cold cream feature. My mother did not like the fact that I was working as a barmaid. I thought it was rather a good job and I enjoyed it but my mother took against this and she decided it was time I had a proper job and she saw this advertisement for a sub-editor for the *Women's Weekly*. So I applied. I had nothing to lose. I thought I would show her that it is all very well, she might like me to do a proper job, but there was no guarantee I would ever get it. But I did.

For my first job, I was given 10 pots of cold cream all by different makers and I was told to go away and evaluate them and write an interesting piece on the subject of cold cream. Of course, I tried the scientific method, one always starts at least with the scientific method. I went home and I put one, two, three all over my face in a blob and when I woke up the next morning I couldn't see any difference at all. It did not appear to have either done any good or any harm. So I then went for the unscientific method which is you put all the numbers in a bag and draw them out – so number one was the best and down the line. All I am saying about this is please do not believe anything you ever read in newspapers or magazines because it is likely to be the same kind of writing.

"I then was moved on to doing celebrity interviews. I think I saw the death of a number of careers so I have always felt very badly about that."

I then was moved on to doing celebrity interviews. I have to say they were not great celebrities when I interviewed them. They certainly have never been celebrities since. I think I saw the death of a number of careers so I have always felt very badly about that. I have never heard of any of them ever again and I fear it must be something to do with what I wrote about them. At this point I was beginning to recognise that I was not desperately interested in writing factual stuff so, with enormous optimism, I applied for a job as editor of the hospital romance section of Women's Weekly Library romances and I got that job as well. I think it is something to do with I am quite a good interviewee, largely because I tend to interview people and they find this exciting until they employ me and then they think, God, that was a mistake. My job as editor of hospital romances was to find eight titles a month. Some of you might know these books. They are pink and very, very thin with tiny type, 30,000-word-long novelettes. So wouldn't you think this was easy, I have only got to find eight a month?

I used to read 400 manuscripts or attempt to read 400 manuscripts to find eight good titles. Truly, I would say every month there were two good ones written by professionals. There were two that with some work passed muster. You then had to choose the least bad of the rest of the 396 and rewrite them. That is what the sub-editors on hospital romances did and I sat there and I moaned, and I moaned. I had a colleague sitting next to me who was editor of general romances, the difference being as you will understand, I had doctors and nurses, he did not. He had to read 800 manuscripts a month. People were more inclined to write about non-doctors and nurses. Anyway, I moaned and moaned and moaned. In the end he challenged me to write one myself. He said, 'Come on you are always complaining. You ought to try one yourself and see how difficult it is.' I thought he was right. This is what I must do.

In a way it was incredibly exciting to discover I could, that I actually did have a talent for this. I think that one took me about four weeks to write, in the evenings as I was working during the daytime. It just proves that I am a very ethical person because you have to understand that I had 10 pseudonyms in the end and I was the purchasing editor. I could have been buying my own work over and over again. No-one would have known. I also used to sign the cheques but however I felt it would be entirely unethical to do that so I put it through to my publisher and asked him to read it with the pseudonym in place. I asked, 'Is this the kind of thing I should be buying?'. He read it and came out to me and said, 'Yes, it is very good, what's the problem? Why did you ask me if it's what you should be buying?' I said, 'Because I wrote it.' So we agreed from then on that if ever I wrote one I would pass it through. I should say at this stage he was not a great romantic fiction reader. He preferred Hammond Innes and Alistair McLean.

What I am going to do is describe to you the discipline that existed in that kind of romantic fiction writing. It was 30,000 words long and you had six chapters. Each chapter was 5000 words. You could have 10 less or 10 more each chapter but you could not go over that because otherwise the words did not fit properly into the page structure. So, that is it, six chapters, each one of 5000 words. On top of that are house style sheets. There are about 10 of them, it was a big package we sent out to would-be authors. I am not going into all the rules but the most important thing that was not allowed was sex, absolutely no sex, no kissing - bearing in mind we are talking about a romance here, no kissing except on the last page because kissing was viewed as sex and so they had to conduct their relationship with no kissing. Strong drink was absolutely forbidden. The strongest drink these people were allowed to have was cocoa. Never, under pain of death, were you allowed to mention balls or tits.

"The strongest drink these people were allowed to have was cocoa. Never, under pain of death, were you allowed to mention balls or tits."

I had a story sent to me where there was a child kicking a ball in the garden and I said, this is all right isn't it? No, balls are forbidden. You could not have bluetits, pecking away at milk bottles. Any word that had a double meaning was not allowed. So you could imagine half of this house style sheet, several pages of it, were the forbidden words, verboten, verboten, and I cannot tell you how many there were. You had to write a story with these impossible ingredients and a romance, after all, is supposed to be romantic. It is supposed to be incredibly attractive. The male hero has got to be knee-wobbly gorgeous and appeal to all the women who read the story – and by and large it is mostly women who read them. And this guy is not even allowed to kiss the woman he is interested in. All I can say to you is this: if you can write a believable fantasy with these ingredients then you have learnt the craft of writing. You can then, in my view, go on and write anything you want to because the minute you are allowed to have sex, balls, all the rest of it, my God, the sky is the limit.

People say to me, how did you make that extraordinary jump from romantic fiction to dark, psychological crime? Apart from the very flippant answer that if you had read as many romantic manuscripts as I have done you too would be dying to write dark, bleak, psychological crime, it is the fact that you are going from one disciplined structure to another highly disciplined structure. Structure is very attractive to writers. I think that is why some very unlikely writers choose to write crime because it has an ending. You have probably read general fiction books where it is quite clear the author has had trouble deciding where to end the novel. Because in a sense you can keep going and going and going. Where is an obvious end? The crime novel always has an obvious end. It is what you are working to from the moment you start writing.

I expect most of you know I am a prison visitor. This, people find very odd. My children love it and they say, 'Mummy goes to prison every Monday', which has thrown one or two people, most notably their house masters at school who looked at me somewhat askance when I turned up on their first speech days. But people assume I do it in order to get material for my books. In fact I do not. I started prison visiting before I became a crime writer. The prisoners all know who I am and in fact they are my best customers because somebody found out that *The Ice House* was worth a lot of money so they now all buy my first editions. Some of my longest signings are in Winchester Prison. They are very supportive although I have a long way to go before I reach Wilbur Smith's standing. He is Winchester Prison's favourite writer and I come second.

I am going to take you back now to the first piece of publicity I did for *The Sculptress* when that came out – tell you, in other words, my second piece of publicity because nobody else ever asked me to do any publicity for *The Ice House*. I was doing it for Spa FM which is Salisbury local radio. I was told that a bloke called John Green would be interviewing me. The night before he was supposed to be interviewing me, he phoned me up at home and said, 'Minette, the most awful thing's happened. My wife is your biggest fan. She's flown to America and she's taken both your books with her and I haven't been able to read them.' I thought, you scumbag. This has to be the lie of all lies. I am sure his wife was sitting at home listening.

So I said, 'So what, you want to cancel?' 'No, no,' he said, 'no, no. Look, you know, just to make it easy, make it much easier, could you write the questions for me? You write the questions and I will read them out tomorrow and then you can give the answers.' So I said, 'How many do you want?' He said, 'Fifteen, just jot the questions down and you give the answers.' I put the phone down and actually I got to seven because there really is a limit as to how many times you can pat yourself on the back without being sick. The questions went something like this. 'Minette, I just cannot believe your books. They are absolutely amazing. How do you keep the pace, the suspense, the mystery? You know, every book you've written, you're going to win prizes all round the world.'

He read every single one. I will just tell you that the answers all began in exactly the same way. They all began, 'Oh, John, you are sweet!' So I repeat, never believe what you hear.

#!?

SPEAKER: You spoke about going to see the prisoners. What did you get from them? What research do you get from them?

MINETTE WALTERS: In fact, they helped me on two books. *The Sculptress* very obviously because I had the atmosphere of the prison and Olive was based on a new prisoner I was given one week. I am not going to give you his real name because I never give their names away but we will call him Robert Redford – he had the name of a very famous film actor. The man who manages the prison visitors' book phoned me up and said, 'Minette, I'm going to give you the best-looking man in the prison.' And I said, 'Well, it's about bloody time. I seem to be getting the dogs.' He said, 'His name is Robert Redford' and he laughed. And I thought, oh God, I know what's coming.

So I turned up at the prison and I asked for Robert Redford at the correct wing and the prison officer was quite worried. He really was big, he was about six and a half feet and wide and he was covered in tattoos. He was also rather smelly. He was wearing a sort of string vest and he was entirely black because he had so many tattoos on him. He gave me Olive because I wanted somebody very intimidating and I suddenly realised just how intimidating sheer size can be, particularly when it is coupled with a nasty crime. He had been charged with an unpleasant crime. I hate to malign this man, he really was a very charming person. He was a gipsy and there was a feud going on between two gipsy families over a wedding that one family wanted and the other one did not. He and his two brothers, who were just as big as he was, had had spurious charges laid against them in order to have them locked up in prison while the feud was settled – in fact while the wedding took place because they were worried that the boys would kill other members of the gipsy families. He kept saying to me, don't worry, I'm completely harmless, and he was.

They were so brilliant with *The Echo*, the blokes I was seeing at the time, because I was asking them for sort of street jargon. About 90 per cent of what they gave me I was unable to use but 10 per cent I could and it was very helpful. By and large I never use their stories although they quite like me to, but they would never make a crime story or a murder story. I mostly see burglars. They always, every single man I have ever seen and I have probably seen about 300 by now, they always give me their backgrounds and the tragedy is that the backgrounds are so similar.

SPEAKER: Minette, I would very much like to know if your mother now thinks you have a proper job?

MINETTE WALTERS: She was a little worried about *The Ice House* because she thought there was an awful lot of rude words in it and she said that she thought my headmistress would be deeply upset by the book. My headmistress is now 94 – at that time she would have been 89 – and I said, 'You know, Mum, with the best will in the world, I did not write the story for Miss Engledow'. But Miss Engledow did read it. She wrote me a letter saying she thought it was wonderful, but then, you see, Jilly Cooper was also at Godolphin and I think Miss Engledow has been a little worried about Jilly Cooper so my books are positively okay by comparison. Godolphin is an interesting school because Jilly and I both had the same English teacher and before us Antonia Fraser was there, so clearly the school has a fine literary tradition.

Peter Carey

Melbourne-born Carey worked as an advertising copywriter before turning to fiction more than 20 years ago. His work has shown a surreal imagination and a curiosity about what it means to be Australian since his first collection of stories, *The Fat Man in History* (1974). His novels include *Bliss*, *Illywacker*, and *Oscar and Lucinda*, which won the 1988 Booker Prize. *Jack Maggs*, a loose retelling of Dickens' *Great Expectations*, won the 1998 Commonwealth Writers Prize and Miles Franklin Award and is being filmed by Fred Schepisi. Now living in New York, Carey is writing a novel about Ned Kelly.

12 August 1997

I thought I'd talk a little bit about writing *Jack Maggs*. There's a sort of a state of intellectual and emotional exhaustion which comes at the end of every book I've ever written and in the final stages of writing a novel I become less of a writer and more of a mechanic or a cabinet-maker, that is, there's no longer all that much art but a great deal of craft. And my days are spent worrying about whether two sentences might swap position or a minor character should change her name or whether the sun should shine in a window a paragraph earlier than previously. An adverb might be sawn off or a pause sandpapered away to nothing.

Sandpapering is not an occupation that engages the emotions a great deal and I think this is why I can emerge from a three-year struggle with the most passionate novel, one that I would have said grew out of the very roots of my soul, and feel a good deal less than I think I should. Probably I'm exhausted and all I feel is – well, not very much.

To experience this lack of affect in my own work is naturally very disturbing and unnerving. It can make me feel that I've failed and that my readers will experience the book in the same horrible disconnected way. This is really, I suppose, a rather uninteresting condition but I have suffered from it at the completion of all of my books.

However, the unease I felt about *Oscar and Lucinda*, the first book of mine to be set at least in part in a foreign country, was complicated by more vigorous, active emotions and doubts about my ability to successfully write about England and the English past. Here I was presuming to write about a country of which I was neither a resident nor a citizen, to which you may reasonably respond, 'So what?' To write any work of fiction you have to write about things you've never done. Novelists daily invent countries, imagine murder, arson, ghosts, talking cats, all without too much worry about whether they've had first-hand experience of these things.

"The empire, as Salman Rushdie would say, was about to write back."

In my own case I had no trouble turning a young man named Crabbs into a tow-truck or describing the out-of-body experience of a fellow called Harry Joy. Had I ever been a tow-truck? No. Had I ever had an out-of-body experience? I'm sorry, no. So why did writing about the English past seem to me at that time dangerous, almost impossible. I suppose I was overwhelmed by a feeling that that particular past did not belong to me.

It seems to me now in retrospect, although actually I would have become very angry with you if you'd said so at the time, that this is a very colonial state of mind. Here I was, I was a passionate nationalist, almost obsessed with defining my own country, but here I was believing that they might imaginatively possess us but that we might not imaginatively possess them. And this of course is not only embarrassing but also wrong.

Even in the most personal way the English past belongs to me. My grandmother was a Cockney from Bow and my great-grandfather – well, he may not actually have gone walking with Wordsworth, which is what the family story says, and I guess I'll never know whether that's true or not – but there's no doubt at all that he came from the Lake District.

However, embarrassing or not, the feeling was there. It was very hard for me to imagine taking charge of England and English history. But – and I'm talking about *Oscar and Lucinda* still – I had an idea for a novel and the idea would not let me escape. I had no more choice than poor Oscar had. I had to deal with the past like he had to deal with his fear of water. The empire, as Salman Rushdie would say, was about to write back.

So I began to create an English past in *Oscar and Lucinda*. There was so damn much of it. I thought I could never know enough. I tried with all my might to invent peculiar little corners which only I could own and I really would have done anything to avoid having to invent Oxford University but there was no choice, Oscar must take holy orders or there could be no book and so he had to go to Oxford – and I did too.

I arrived at Oriel College one summer morning. I knew I wasn't really meant to be there and I sensed that I might be at any moment discovered and sent away, or worse, and so I rushed across the lawn and entered the first staircase I came to. I knocked on some poor student's room, declared myself to be from the BBC and apologised for the intrusion. Then I took out my notebook and while he watched, with some justifiable degree of suspicion, I made intensive notes about his room, including, as I recall, the fact that he had left a grey sock as a bookmark in his copy of *Pride and Prejudice.*

I have a copy of all this stuff somewhere, although the only thing I really finally got out of that visit was the successive coats of paint which had made the panelling on the doors look like melted chocolate, something really I could have made up without leaving Sydney.

This constant neurotic research went on for three years and although I often had a wonderful time writing, when the end came, when the sandpapering was done, I really was sure that I'd failed to really convey the England of the 1860s. And even when the London critics finally assured me that the past I'd created was also their past, I still took a good time to settle down and to accept that I'd probably succeeded in doing what I set out to do.

Let me tell you, I didn't enjoy all of the anxiety and when it was all over I vowed, out loud, to my wife that I would never, never again take a voyage into the foreign past. And that's why I immediately sat down and wrote *The Tax Inspector*, set in Sydney.

Having made that vow, I'm a little astonished to be here today because I've damn well done it again and I've written a novel set in the English past, in London in 1837, about 30 years earlier than *Oscar and Lucinda*. Once again I was led there by an idea and the idea would not permit me to site the story anywhere else. The idea was born, as 16 reviewers have said in the last three days, out of Charles Dickens' *Great Expectations*. You remember how Magwitch was the convict who returned home to claim the boy he had adopted and how the son, Pip, was horrified to find the source of his wealth was not Miss Haversham but a convict from Australia.

So I thought I might re-invent Magwitch or create a character which was a riff on Magwitch, a shadow or a mirror of Magwitch. Dickens' Magwitch is foul and dark and frightening and murderous. But he was my idea and it would not go away. Magwitch was my ancestor. He was the first Australian to go back to London and find he was not really wanted. And I really wanted to write his story.

"The London of 1837 may seem murky to us now but it was a very bright place to a man who had just come from New South Wales."

I needed to, I wanted to re-invent him and to possess him. I didn't want to diminish his darkness or his danger but I also wanted to give him all that love and tender sympathy that Dickens' first person narrative gives his English hero, Pip. And I had a few other thoughts as well about mesmerism or animal magnetism and other things that I hope will intrigue you as much as they've intrigued me.

When I began to map out this book, I imagined I would dramatise Jack Maggs's life somewhere in the penal colony, to look at what he had suffered and to see how in spite of all the tortures he'd endured, at the orders of English officers, he still wished, against all commonsense, to raise an English gentleman and call him a son. But the story, as it turned out, had a pretty fierce and furious engine and I found myself flat out shovelling coal into its furnace and no time to think about changing continents.

So although all of those contradictions inherent in Jack Maggs's passions are firmly dealt with and are what the book is about, the action of the novel almost never leaves London. To write about London in the 19th century you have other issues than ones of culture and colonialism to make you nervous. When you enter 19th-century London you are entering, as a writer, very well-travelled streets and there is nothing in the least neurotic about being nervous about it. You are entering the territory of Dickens or Thackeray or Wilkie Collins. If you go to these great writers for information you will end up as nothing more than a plagiarist and a thief. Yet you must somehow, to put it bluntly, invade their territory and repossess it. How can this be possible? Well, first you need really good information. You need maps, charts, you need spies, agents, correspondents from the past.

Foreign spies are always best. They see things that the English themselves will never tell you. Only a foreigner for instance could write this:

> *The slices of bread and butter given to you with tea are as thin as poppy leaves but there is a way of roasting slices of buttered bread before the fire which is incomparable. One slice after another is taken and held to the fire with a fork until the butter is melted. Then the following one will always be laid upon it so that the butter soaks through the whole pile of slices. This is called toast.*

That was Carl Philip Moritz, a German who went on a walking tour of England in 1782. He demonstrates really well that wonderful quality that foreigners have, he can see what is happening. Can you imagine an English writer writing that? But that is the sort of stuff I needed. I have no toast in *Jack Maggs*, or actually none that Carl Philip Moritz would have thought worthy of his attention, but the toast does, I think, illustrate the point that the eyes of outsiders are the ones that can show us a foreign England. All fresh and new and waiting to be put at the service of a 20th-century novel. It is here that one sees what new wealth one can beg and borrow and also one begins to understand the degree to which one can quietly invent.

Fortunately the New York Public Library is filled to bursting with accounts of 19th-century visitors, mostly Americans, who are very keen to tell the folks at home exactly how things work and look in England. Those of you who are students of history will know that there were two sorts of gaslight. The first one we think of as rather dim and the second considerably brighter. You will know that the period I am writing about is the dim period, black, dark, sooty London. Yet to read about this London from the point of view of someone who has come from another place, say, New York or Moscow or Sydney, it might be like this. This is from this first chapter of *Jack Maggs*:

> *The man with the red waistcoat set off into the night. His cane tapping on the cobblestones and straight up into the Haymarket with his chin up and the orbs of his eyes everywhere reflecting an unearthly flare and glare. The light had shone all the way from Elephant and Castle. Gaslight blazing and streaming like great torches. Sausages illuminated, fish and ice gleaming. Chemist shops aglow like caves with their variegated vases illuminated from within. The city had become a fairground and as the stranger crossed the river at Westminster he saw that even the bridges of the Thames were illuminated.*

The London of 1837 may seem murky to us now but it was a very bright place to a man who had just come from New South Wales. It was with the aid of this gaslight that I was able to see how I might conquer London – well, at least for a few weeks. Of course, by the time I had finally completed *Jack Maggs*, by the time I had thrown out the last adverb and shifted the final comma and thrown out that anachronistic gavel which I had placed in the judge's hand, I was pretty much convinced that I had failed. But this time I recognised the feeling and that cheered me up no end.

! ?

SPEAKER: One of the interesting pieces of dialogue in *Jack Maggs* has Jack say that he would rather be a bad smell in England than a frigging rose in New South Wales. I wonder if this at all reflects your view as an expatriate now living in New York looking back at Australia.

PETER CAREY: No, the simple answer is I share almost nothing with Jack Maggs and certainly not that feeling. The thing about Jack Maggs's whole quest is to return to England and to return to the place where he had this horrible childhood, to the home of the people who were responsible for torturing him and with his heart full of love and need. He really would rather be a bad smell there than a frigging rose in New South Wales and the book is indeed the story of how Jack Maggs finally, ultimately and happily became a frigging rose in New South Wales. In no way do they represent my feelings.

SPEAKER: The beginning of your book seems like the beginning of *Moby Dick*. Did you have some of that same feeling about a search for something greater that you had to understand?

PETER CAREY: I am flattered, of course, but how to confess this? I have a brand new copy of *Moby Dick* sitting on my bookshelf and I was looking forward to some time in the northern summer reading it and it did not happen. So I really cannot comment on *Moby Dick* and I am sorry.

SPEAKER: I am worried that *Oscar and Lucinda* is a book that is almost impossible to make into a movie. I wonder how you feel about that?

PETER CAREY: At the moment I am adapting a friend's book for the movies and this is by way of answering your question. I am adapting Paul Auster's novel *The Locked Room*. This is not only a novel I like but it is also the novel of a really dear friend who was nice enough to suggest that I be the one to do it and it is a pretty weird process, believe me. All writers secretly want to rewrite their friend's book but they do not then imagine they are going to have to show the friend what they did. I always believed that the only way to properly adapt a novel is to treat it like a beautiful clay pot and that is you pick it up, throw it on the ground, jump on it and grind it back to clay and then you build it again. In other words you have to destroy it. Once you have done that you have two different objects. The book is the book – there is not a movie on earth that can alter a single word of *Oscar and Lucinda*. Anybody who has read it has that in their mind. They will go to the movie, maybe as a bad member of the audience, because they are not prepared to relinquish their private contract that they have made with those words.

I am not all that fussed about it. I am really honoured, to tell you the truth. If some other artists want to make something based on what I have done, then I am just pleased.

SPEAKER: I am one of many people who think that possibly they have got a book in them and would one day do a creative writing course. What tips could you give me and all of the others about how to choose a teacher?

PETER CAREY: People often ask me about creative writing courses and the undercurrent of the question is normally how can you possibly teach writing, what a lot of garbage and what an American's wank. I must confess that when I first arrived in the United States I had a job at NYU without which I would not have been able to stay in the country at all and so I was happy to take on this thing. I taught there for the first semester and nobody got any better, nor any worse, and I said to Alison, this is a bit of a wank this creative writing thing, because nobody got any better. I had to do it all a bit longer than that because the US immigration takes forever so I taught the next semester and the semester after that. The interesting thing that happened is that I started to get a bit better. Then miraculously the students started to get better. Then I discovered maybe it was not a wank after all and maybe you could actually teach something.

Certainly you cannot give anybody talent and if people have not got any stuff to write about you cannot invent it for them and if they are mad at their mummy and their daddy you cannot solve that. There is a whole lot of things that you cannot do but on the other hand there are things that you really can teach. In fact people are continually complaining that there are no more editors left any more and nothing is edited and so on. Ultimately a creative writing teacher to a large degree can work like an editor and there are various things you can encourage people to do. Believe it or not, you actually can teach someone to tell a story and you can teach them to follow an argument and you can encourage them and begin to have them think about looking at the world and seeing the world and they will have the aptitude for that or not.

People think writers are really good at looking at everybody and seeing into people's hearts and knowing what they feel. Really writers are the most self-absorbed people you have ever met. A group of writing students are all full of how they feel. You can see on the page that it is all about how they feel because they cannot see anybody else, they cannot see anything as the characters mostly do not have faces. So one of the things you are going to start to encourage them to do is to think about their characters and the world physically.

So I think, firstly, there are good teachers of creative writing – some of them will be famous writers and some of them will be just people who are wonderful teachers. The only way you know is by talking to people who have taken their classes.

I think books are possibly the best teachers of all and that writing every day is probably the single most important thing and after that if you have a good teacher then maybe the good teacher will save you a couple of years. Ultimately you are going to do it by yourself.

SPEAKER: When did you know that you were a writer?

PETER CAREY: I often think that if I had been really well-read when I began I would not have dared to begin writing; if I had really understood the arena that I was walking out into I would not have dared do it. I was very young and poorly read, amazed by everything and taught myself to be very clever. I certainly could not write and did not know very much but I had a lot of enthusiasm and had this blunt blind faith in myself. I never doubted that I could. I had no reason to really think that I could do it. I failed at university, I had to get a job, I went to an advertising agency; it was full of all these people who were writing and I thought, if they can do it, I can do it. There was nothing to support this but I am very stubborn and I did keep on at it and finally I did teach myself. I was not troubled by lack of faith in myself and I was guided and aided by a sort of useful stupidity, I guess.

Frank McCourt

Angela's Ashes **turned McCourt from a retired New York schoolteacher into a best-selling author and winner of the 1997 Pulitzer Prize and National Book Award. Urged by his pupils to write down the stories he told them about his poor Catholic childhood in Brooklyn and Limerick, he produced a heart-breaking and funny story, narrated in the natural voice of a young boy, and is now working on the sequel, *'Tis*.**

13 October 1997

One of the lovely things about going around like this with *Angela's Ashes* is meeting people from my past. There are two ladies here formerly of the O'Halloran family in Limerick, Mary and Sue, and they walked up here and greeted me and it is as if apparitions had appeared.

It was an illustrious member of their family who delivered about 90 per cent of the children of Limerick, Nurse O'Halloran, whom we all regarded with great awe. When I was small I knew she was Nurse O'Halloran, I knew she was something called a midwife, but I did not quite know quite what she did. A midwife. I thought she was somebody maybe who replaced wives when the wife went away. That would have been an enviable occupation. A kind of a consort, a concubine. This is how I grappled with the English language.

I was always grappling with the English language in one way or another. Somebody asked me recently what were the books that influenced me. And I started trotting out names like Dickens and so on but then I remembered the first book in my life that influenced me – there were two, but the first one was the catechism. That is the first major

"I made my way through the seven deadly sins and the ten commandments and the virtues and everything else."

book. Not only did you have to read it, and we were only six or seven years old getting ready for first confession and first communion, but there were questions that we had to memorise. All they said to me around the USA where everything is obsolete in two minutes was, how do you remember all of this stuff? I said, how could you not remember all of this stuff?

A columnist wrote a piece in the *New York Times* Book Review saying, 'I cannot for the life of me understand how Frank McCourt could remember looking in the mirror at 14 and finding himself less than appealing. I cannot understand how he could remember that at the age of 10 he had a sore between his eyes.' How could you not remember these things? And I wanted to write her a letter of consolation and console her for the poor state of her memory. How could you be a writer and not remember everything?

So the catechism was the first thing. And I owe the Catholic Church a lot for the rigour and sometimes the powerful discipline of school masters in Limerick. We had to be examined by the priest before we went to first confession and first communion. There was a little green catechism that cost threepence. Then later on for confirmation there was what I call the big red catechism which was thicker and that cost sixpence. And when I was a small guy I used to look at the confirmation boys and their big red catechism and I could not wait to grow up and be 10 and get the big red catechism.

The little green catechism began with the most powerful question of all: Who made the world? God. Who is God? God is the creator and sovereign Lord of Heaven and Earth and of all things. Then next question: Why did God make the world? I blew it one day. I had not memorised the answer and of course the master said, 'McCourt, why did God make the world?' 'So we'd all have something to stand on, sir.' That was one of my first bitter encounters with theology.

So I made my way through the seven deadly sins and the ten commandments and the virtues and everything else. At the age of six or seven, we became theologians. We realised most of all the value of mystery because as soon as you asked the question it is a mystery; you had to believe in it, because we were theologians, we were little Jesuits. They would tell us about God and how there were three persons in God. Well, I did not care if there were three persons in God, but they made it significant because if you did not care they would take you out and knock the hell out of you. The Father, the Son and the Holy Ghost. We wondered as we sat on the playground near the school how there can be three persons in one.

Then the other awful mystery that we were to believe in. The Virgin birth. We did not know what a virgin was and we hardly knew what a birth was and the two together mystified us completely but we trotted out the proper responses in the catechism anyway. Later on I found out what a virgin was. In a book.

These were all intellectual adventures in Leamy's School. Leamy's was what they call a national high school in Ireland. There were also Christian Brothers schools in the Ireland of my time. There is a school in Dublin, a Christian Brothers school, which is famed for producing the likes of Brendan Behan and Milo O'Shea and Jim Sheridan, the film maker. There are a lot of famous people from over there but we were not lucky enough in the lanes of Limerick to go to the Christian Brothers. We went to what they call a national school which is the lowest in the hierarchy of schools of the educational system.

We were sent there because we came from particular places. There was a hierarchy of addresses. The highest address you could live in in Limerick was an avenue. Oh, if you lived in an avenue. You probably had a maid that had a little white cap on her and a little white thing tied onto her waist. Then there was a road or a place. The lowest, at the bottom of all, was the lane. The lane was something built by Queen Victoria and her gang. They were called artisans' dwellings.

If you stood in the lane and straddled the gutter that ran down the middle of the lane that was called a channel and put your arms out you could touch the houses on both sides. Artisans' dwellings if you do not mind. And this was Her Majesty's way of taking care of the working classes of Ireland.

So we grew up in those lanes and because you came from a lane you were not going to go to the Christian Brothers, and never mind the Jesuits, only the upper classes with maids went to the Jesuits, so we went to Leamy's National School. The minute you walked into Leamy's National School you knew or we knew, everybody knew, we did know, we were only little children, that you were going to finish by the time you were 13 or 14, that you became a messenger boy – national schools supplied the messenger boys – or that you would be unemployed or you would go to England. Over the door of Leamy's National School they should have had a sign, Abandon Hope All Ye Who Enter Here.

We envied the boys who went to the Christian Brothers and the Jesuits. No, we did not envy the boys who went to the Jesuits, we went in awe of them, because we knew they were the ones who would rule the world. So when I went to Leamy's National School I learned that I was not going to go very far in the world. And everything was memorised. We memorised Irish history, the dates and the battles. When I finally arrived in America and started to look at American history I was very bored because everything simply had to do with legislation. People dumping tea into Boston Harbour over a Stamp Act. Who cared?

"The word 'informer' is the most reviled word in the Irish-English language."

There were no heroes like Irish history. And the main thing about Irish history, we were told, was the Irish were always on the verge of winning, over 800 years of Irish noble fighting. Always. No matter what the battle. The Siege of Limerick, the Battle of Kinsale, whatever it was, always about to win. But there was always the most hideous creature in Ireland, an informer, who always gave away our battle plans. That is why the word 'informer' is the most reviled word in the Irish-English language.

So we had to memorise. And it was not just the facts of history. We had to memorise the songs. With every Irish event there is a song. Every Irish county has a song. Practically every crossroads has a song. We knew the songs. At the end of every day – this is what makes me sad about American education – at the end of every day in Leamy's National School the last hour was devoted to singing. We would have to gather with a man named Mr Tom Scanlon and stand in two rows and sing. He'd give us a different song every week, whether it was in Irish or in English. So we learned all of these songs and he would encourage us to sing by rapping us on the head.

"They were only upper class and middle class and they had nothing to write about."

Then there was the poetry. We have to thank the English in many ways for invading us because if they had not invaded us look what the world would have been deprived of in the matter of literature or poetry and song. We would have had nothing to wail about and we wailed, baby, we wailed. So, the English by their presence and by their tyranny and everything else and sentencing our young men to be hanged gave us many songs – I mean, how could the world live without Kevin Barry or Roddy McCorley goes to die on the bridge of Toome today?

In addition to that, many hundreds of young men mostly were sentenced to die for rising up against the English. And English judges used to make a big mistake. They would say to a young patriot like Robert Emmet before they passed sentence, does the prisoner have anything to say? Never say that to an Irishman about to be hanged. The man known as the hanging judge, Lord North, had to tell Robert Emmet to shut up. It was time for dinner. So he had to be taken off and hanged in the morning.

We were required to memorise the dying speeches of many an Irish patriot. My father knew them. My father knew Robert Emmett's speech from beginning to end:

> *Until Ireland takes her place among the races of the earth then and not 'til then shall my epitaph be written.*

We knew them all. We knew the poetry:

> *In far foreign fields from Dunkirk to Belgrade lie the soldiers and chiefs of the Irish brigade.*

That was glorious. Everything was glorious. But the other line was:

> *They went forth to battle and they always fell.*

That was the sad line. This is the background that I think I have called on to write this book *Angela's Ashes.*

I have said a few negative things, I suppose, in the book about the church but still the church was our window on Europe, our window on whatever we knew of European culture. There was the architecture, all the bleak gothic or byzantine it might be, and then you stepped inside of the church and looked around and you saw the Stations of the Cross, there are paintings on the walls depicting the trial and execution of Jesus, the stained-glass windows, and then on the altar, the magnificent high altars, the liturgy, the ritual, the incense, the flowers, the candles and the slow movement of the priest through the mass. And the mystery of everything.

We were constantly told everything is a mystery which was all right by me because in the long run nobody knows anything. And that is what I got from the church; that in the long run it is all faith, baby.

But I think the mass itself, that is the second piece of literature, I think. The catechism first of all and then the missal. There was a little book came into our area, it was an American thing called *Father Steadman's Sunday Missal*, and on the left side they had the Latin and on the right side it had the English and it had little passages in red to denote where the priest was doing whatever the priest had to do in mass. So I think we absorbed Latin in the way that you do not do it when you have to conjugate verbs in school. We were able to move back and forth between the two pages.

And then there were the hymns, all the Latin hymns we had to know in school and in the churches, in the Confraternity of the Sacred Heart of Jesus of the Holy Family, in Limerick. So we moved all the time between three languages, Irish, English and Latin, and I think that was a very rich experience because I think it gave us a sense of language that you do not get anywhere else in world, considering the power of the church which reached into every corner of our lives.

We would sing hymns the way American kids sing rock music. We would go home and sing 'Faith of Our Fathers' just to enjoy ourselves. It was music. And recently somebody sent me a CD from Ireland with all the great hymns of our childhood and I cannot get them out of my head, 'Oh Sacred Heart of Jesus'. You will find me in the middle of the night singing this stuff.

These are the ingredients of a childhood and that is what I was trying to get at when I was teaching high school in New York City when they gave me writing classes, 16 year olds and 17 year olds. You cannot teach writing, you can only exhort them and help them find the material which is always under their noses. They would say things about my rich childhood. My rich childhood! They were only upper class and middle class and they had nothing to write about. They were comfortable. Nothing happened. And you, they said, you had a rich childhood, you have plenty to write about and you should write a book. And I did.

I suggested to these teenagers in New York that if you want to draw from your life there are ingredients. What are you? Are you a Jewish kid from the upper west side of Manhattan? The chances are your father or your grandfather or grandmother or mother was in a concentration camp or had certain adventures. Chinese kids whose mothers and fathers worked in Chinatown as dish washers, worked in sweatshops in the lower regions of Manhattan. There were stories everywhere which they tended to just think, oh, as I did my own story.

I was not going to write about a slum in Limerick and about growing up there because it was too sad. Who would want to know about a family that grew up with a lavatory outside their door shared by 11 other families? The other day in Auckland in New Zealand another lady from my past called me up, Mary Downs, who lived across from us, who would testify against some people in Limerick who said these things never happened. There was never a situation in Limerick where 11 people shared the lavatory. I could tell them there were situations in Limerick where 11 families shared no lavatory.

In addition to the certain ingredients that I used to talk to my students about if they wanted to draw from their own lives we had the church, poverty, the history – history was always there – the singing. There was another major ingredient in Irish life and that was the fags, cigarettes. Everybody smoked. And they smoked, my father, my mother and everybody else, a vile cigarette known as the Wild Woodbine which is concocted from the dung of a passing camel, I think.

Everybody in Limerick was hacking and hacking and hacking. In addition to the fact that

Limerick was a damp city and half the population had TB, in addition to that it did not matter, it did not occur to them maybe they should give up the fags. In addition to that I do not remember in my childhood approaching my teeth with a toothbrush. I do not know what our teeth looked like. I think they were a fine shade of green. Forty shades of green. There were no toothbrushes, no toothpaste, we just ignored them. In addition to that we were all mad for any kind of sugar. I think it had something to do with our diet which was mainly tea and bread, bread and tea, solid and liquid. What more do you want? A balanced diet. Teeth.

And finally into the world of work. When I finished school at 14 I had to get a job and the first job I had was in the post office in Limerick delivering telegrams and this is the day, a scene from my telegram boy days:

> *There are slow days at the post office and we sit on the bench and talk. We can talk but we're not to laugh. Miss Barry says we should be grateful we're getting paid to sit there, bunch of idles and street boys that we are, and that there's to be no laughing. Getting paid for sitting and chatting is no laughing matter and the first titter out of any of us and out we go 'til we come to our senses and if the tittering continues we'll be reported to the proper authorities. The boys talk about it under their breath. Toby Mackey says, what that old bitch needs is a good rub with a relic. Her mother was a street-walking flag hopper and her father escaped from a lunatic asylum with bunions on his balls and warts on his wank.*
>
> *There's laughing along the bench and Miss Barry calls to us, I warned ye against the laughing. Mackey, what is it you're prattling about over there? I said we'd all be better off out in the fresh air on this fine day delivering telegrams, Miss Barry. I'm sure you did, Mackey. Your mouth is a lavatory. Did you hear me? I did, Miss Barry. You'll be hurled down the stairs, Mackey. Yes, Miss Barry. Shut up, Mackey. I will, Miss Barry. Not another word, Mackey. No, Miss Barry. I said shut up, Mackey. All right, Miss Barry. That's the end of it, Mackey. Don't try me. I won't, Miss Barry. Mother of God give me patience. Yes, Miss Barry. That's the last word, Mackey, take it, take it, take. I will, Miss Barry.*

Michael Palin

From being beloved as a comedian in *The Monty Python Show* on television and in movies such as *Monty Python and the Holy Grail*, *The Life of Brian* and *A Fish Called Wanda*, Palin has reinvented himself as a novelist (his first novel was *Hemingway's Chair* in 1995), and as a travel writer and documentary maker. His BBC series and books include *Great Railway Journeys*, *Around the World in 80 Days*, *Pole to Pole* and, in 1997, *Full Circle*, which took him around the Pacific Rim and to Australia.

6 November 1997

It's a little over 18 months ago since our crew of seven came through Sydney on our circumnavigation of the Pacific and it is about six months ago that I came through here to publicise *Fierce Creatures*, a film made by John Cleese. First of all, let me give you a few facts about *Full Circle*, and then the fictions.

It's the longest of the three mega-journeys that I've made for the BBC over the last nine years. In fact, the ground we covered this time, about 50,000 miles, is more than the total mileage of *Pole to Pole* and *80 Days* put together. I decided after the mad rush of *80 Days* and the rigours of *Pole to Pole* to hang up my travelling clogs forever. But memory is a very fickle thing, and two years and a few good lunches after we returned from the South Pole and the gangrene had cured and new fingers had been transplanted, Clem Valance, the series producer, and myself started looking at maps again, and I found myself falling into temptation. You must never buy a diary with maps at the end, that is my problem.

What we found was that one glaring omission from all the itineraries up to that time had been the Pacific. Over the last few years everyone has been talking very knowledgeably about the Pacific Rim.

We are told it is the economic power house of the future, that the Mediterranean/Atlantic axis that has dominated the world for so long is now exhausted, in decline, but next century is the Pacific century. I have to admit I just nodded and said I'm sure you're absolutely right, but if anyone had actually even asked me to name the countries of the Pacific Rim . . .

So it was that after several bottles of wine and a few brandies we decided to go on the road again and attempt a full circle around the Pacific Rim. The sheer size of the Pacific was intimidating – it is a third of the world's surface, it widens out from being just 50 miles across in the Bering Strait to over 11,000 miles across between Vietnam and Mexico. Our route would pass through 18 countries, among them some of the most physically volatile on earth, bubbling with volcanoes, quivering with earthquakes, and it would take a very long time. As it was, we travelled and filmed for 270 days of one year, returning home occasionally to do our laundry and save our marriages. And have a damn good bath.

The longest single continuous period away on the journey was a voyage up from Cape Horn to the Bering Strait, up the American side of the Pacific, when we were away for three months. Our crew consisted of six people, including myself, and both the directors as well as our cameramen and sound recordists were old Pole to Pole hands. Things didn't start very promisingly. Little Diomede Island, which was our starting and hopefully our finishing point, might be a treeless rock at the end of the earth cut off from the world by pack ice for six months of the year, but it didn't stop a small group of Eskimos pointing at me with interest as we prepared to leave in one of their whaleskin boats and eventually asking me, 'Aren't you the guy from *Monty Python and the Holy Grail*?' Even the headhunters we met in Borneo had heard of the BBC. In fact they were still awaiting payment for the last time they had been used in a documentary. 'Send me the head of BBC 1,' they said. I promised I would.

As early as day six, we were marooned by fog in a bear sanctuary on the island of Kodiak off Alaska missing an important and what seemed at the time vital connection by the US coastguards down the Aleutian Islands; but then our luck turned, and within a week I was at a Siberian gulag and 10 days later being attacked with a stick by Japanese monks whilst meditating. Things were looking up. Though *Full Circle* turned out to be a very memorable journey, and certainly much more diverse and more demanding, more rewarding than anything I've done so far, there were certain anxious moments along the way.

The ship owner who ran the ferry that plied the dangerous Sulu Seas between the Philippines and Borneo was rather like the character I played in *Monty Python* who sold John Cleese a dead parrot. Whenever we asked about the ferry he said, 'Yes, it'll be there tomorrow. Yeah, no problem, it'll be

"After several bottles of wine and a few brandies we decided to go on the road again and attempt a full circle around the Pacific Rim."

there in the morning.' After five days the ferry still hadn't arrived. Then someone found out that it was laid up in a bay further up the coast with the engine room burnt out. So we asked him about that. He said, 'Oh, that ferry! Oh, that ferry! No, that ferry won't be going, not that ferry. You mean the one with the engine room burnt out?' 'Yes, that's the one, up the road.' 'No, that one won't be going, no, I've got another one just like it.'

"The maggots were crispy, fried, quite palatable, as were the baby grasshoppers which went with them."

The other ferry turned out to be just as demised. It was an elderly Japanese vessel built for inland lakes with a flat bottom and its bow doors wide enough to squeeze an iceberg through. 'It's all right,' he said, 'no, the Sulu Sea is flat calm this time of year, you'll be all right.' Within four hours we'd run into the worst storm of the entire journey. The boat just rocked up and down, up and down, and I most say in the whole of the journey I never felt my life in danger quite as much as on that Sulu Sea. I looked around for the ship owner but of course he hadn't taken the ferry with us, he was safe at home.

No more reassuring, I have to say, was our guide down the Urubamba River in Peru. The Urubamba River is a river that flows down out of the Andes and eventually becomes part of the Amazon. There are some very serious rapids there and we were spinning down these rapids virtually out of control, accelerating around vicious rocks and the backwaves were coming, a lot of spray, a lot of white water, suddenly a huge black rock was looming up ahead of us and our guide was looking around saying, 'This is fantastic, this is incredible.' I said, 'Well, you must have seen this plenty of times.' 'No, never been here before in my life, all new to me.'

This was the same guide who reassured me that first night when we camped by the river before I took a dip that piranha fish would not attack me. 'No,' he said, 'their predatoriness is a complete myth, a complete myth, they're the most misunderstood fish in the world. No-one ever got stripped to the bone in seven seconds by a piranha fish.' Okay, I say, that's fine, and I jumped into the water, splashed about, just in time to hear him shout, 'There is another fish'. I stopped and froze for a moment. 'Yes, it's attracted by a urine stream, it swims up your penis and starts to eat you from inside.' I was out of that water like a rocket and reduced to cleaning myself with Quickwipes for the next eight days. After a week or so I smelled of stale lemon.

As you might imagine on a journey of this length, the food and drink on offer was rich and varied. In Mexico City, I ate a plate of maggots. They were crispy, fried, quite palatable, as were the baby grasshoppers which went with them and the armadillo and beans that followed. The restaurant was run by a man who was a student of pre-Hispanic food. This was the food that the Aztecs ate before the Spaniards came and brought with them pigs and cows and hamburgers and all that other stuff.

There were other things that I ate that I didn't know I'd eaten and I'm rather glad I didn't know. In a town on the Yangtze River, we were given this rather strange chewy stuff in a brown sauce, and so I ate it because it's very important that you do eat the food. I noticed some of the crew at the other end of the table nudging each other. At the end of the meal as I was walking away, the sound man came up to me and said, 'That was jolly brave. I wouldn't have eaten bull's penis.' I said, 'Neither would I if I'd known, especially raw.'

"I discovered the three most important words any traveller needs to know, 'Sorry, I'm English'."

In an Indian village in the Amazon, I drank a large wooden bowlful of slightly bitter but to me very strong palm wine. Our interpreter pointed out that it was fermented, very high level, very strong because they used the sugar that grew around most of the villages. He said not all villages have sugar and if they don't have sugar it's fermented by the saliva from the old women. Nothing wrong with old women's saliva, so I said, 'Has this village we're in now got sugar growing anywhere around here?' He said, 'No, not around here.' So if you want a cocktail in the Amazon, just say, 'Palm wine, hold the saliva.'

Language proved to be as ever a rich source of confusion and experiment. In China after I had knocked back another very strong local beverage, they told me proudly, 'This is only for our most extinguished guests', which I thought was absolutely right. Another very serious Chinese student thought that Englishmen were very preserved, which I liked a lot, and in a hotel in a remote part of Japan, the privacy sign read, 'Do not disturd'. So of course I didn't. Not that I was going to anyway. We may be preserved but at least we've got manners.

But for sheer joyous incomprehension, this English translation of Spanish instructions on how to make a telephone call from a hotel room in Peru takes some beating and I read it as I found it on this card beside the phone when I was about to ring my wife from Puno in Peru. It read:

> *Mr Passing, if it did not obtain you response until the third stamp, I will serve you to cut the call and return to attempted, thus avoided you the unnecessarily collection of their/its/your/his call since telephony system registered the call as of stamped quarter though may not have been obtained response. Thanks.*

It was the 'Thanks' I was particularly fond of. If you go to an English language school in Puno, make sure they don't charge you too much.

I learned something new on almost every day of the journey: how to pick tea in Java, what it's like to share the same bed as Mao Tse Tung in China. I stayed at a guest house where Mao Tse Tung used to go on holiday and stayed in his room as used by Mao Tse Tung, so I slept on his bed, which was rather strange. Mao Tse Tung apparently slept very little, because he was very constipated and used to pace up and down all night long, restless and cross. Which I've decided is what makes dictators, they don't get a good night's sleep, they've got constipation and they get really pissed off and they're going to take it out on as many people as possible. Mao took it out on an awful lot of people.

I discovered what to do when rocks are thrown at your car in Bogota, Colombia – just smile at people – how to ask for a bath plug in Russia and the three most important words any traveller needs to know, 'Sorry, I'm English'. But I don't think I learned as much anywhere as I did in Australia. Thanks to my director's adventurous choice of subjects, I now have a passing knowledge of dog castration, crocodile hatching, riding cows and mustering camels. That was only in Sydney. The camel mustering which I underwent near Alice Springs was the most physically demanding and exhausting day's filming I have ever had in my life, and that includes filming *Monty Python and the Holy Grail* when I played a character which never actually made it onto film, which is more of a terrible irony.

The character was Mud-Eater. All I had to do was to crawl through mud and eat some of it when I got to a certain point whilst John Cleese swanned by playing a king or something like that. The props people said, 'Don't worry, Mike, we've got some chocolate that looks like mud.' Brilliant, you walk for about 100 yards, can you tell chocolate from mud? So I just used to scoop up a handful of something that was just very lightly, gently chocolate flavoured mud. At the end of the day – I don't know why I'm digressing – at the end of the day, at the end of the Mud-Eater sequence, we were filming in the Scottish Highlands and people realised that actually I'd been eating something truly unpleasant and the mud had been contaminated – pigs peed in the area, and all that.

So they took me to this little Scottish doctor. We knocked at his door at about 6 o'clock, thinking I should get some injection or something like that, and this little man appears. He's obviously on the third or fourth dram, 'Yesh, surgery's at five.' 'We've got a problem here.' 'Yes, what's the problem?' 'It's Mr Palin here, he may need a tetanus jab.' 'Aye, well, come in.' Eventually someone had to explain to him, 'Well, he's been eating mud'. 'I'll have another wee dram and we'll attend to that later on, here's mud in your eye.'

Ruth Cracknell

Australia's most loved actress, named a National Living Treasure by the National Trust, has spent almost 50 years in radio, theatre, film and television. In her 1997 book, *A Biased Memoir*, Cracknell covered it all, from the Phillip Street revues to the birth of the Sydney Theatre Company, the long-running television series *Mother and Son*, the film *Lilian's Story* based on Kate Grenville's novel, and recent stage performances in *Three Tall Women*, *Vita and Virginia* and the musical *A Little Night Music*.

14 November 1997

It was two years from the time I signed the contract with my publisher to the date when I had to hand the manuscript over, and I thought, that's fine, that's plenty of time. But the first year there was no way I was able to do anything because I was very, very busy with a play and a film – *Three Tall Women* and *Lilian's Story* – as well as many other things. However, thoughts for the book were with me all the time. When I was not actually writing, the manuscript was there in recollection, and mostly very happy recollection of the parts of the book that gave me the greatest joy to write – my childhood, my growing up. I was born in Maitland and I left when I was four – with my family, I took them with me – and then I was in Sydney.

I discovered how much I loved Sydney, and as I went to school and then later as I was working in the city, I knew that Sydney was very much my town. It still is; I think it's the most fantastic place. Recalling the Sydney that I knew in the '40s and '50s and even perhaps a bit – yes, a bit in the '30s – was particularly enjoyable. And I hope my account evokes a few memories for people who are old enough to remember Sydney then. And, for those who are not old enough to remember it, I hope it brings back the Sydney to them with the same clarity and particular love that I had for it then as one who walked through its narrow streets and alleys. A very, very interesting city it was, full of eccentrics –

"I think it's a particular quality of Sydney – that it does bring out a rather charming eccentricity along with everything else."

and I guess they're still here. I call them angels – you do see some very interesting angels in Sydney, flying about, sometimes just a bit off the ground, in wonderful sort of tutus and things. I think it's a particular quality of Sydney – that it does bring out a rather charming eccentricity along with everything else.

So, how did I start? I knew that what I was going to do was to write in depth about one play and one film because I thought it might be interesting for readers to know what the whole process (which is my least favourite word but I have used it now) of putting a play on is like, and what it is like making a film from the time you go along to the first rehearsal on day one. I did that with *Three Tall Women* and *Lilian's Story*.

The other thing I knew I wanted to do was not to write in just a strict chronological, linear way; I wanted to dart backwards and forwards and forwards and backwards, and as I'd read Gore Vidal's book, *Palimpsest*, I thought, yes, that's the way to go. Okay, I'm not Gore Vidal, but never mind. For me it was a very natural way to allow the pen or the word processor to disappear back 20, 30 or 40 years or 50 years when I was writing about something that happened that very day. So, that's the way I did it and I've delved into my experiences of theatre, television, radio and, of course, I've mentioned the one 'live' television piece that everybody seems to know me for.

I did start writing in longhand; I love writing in longhand, for me it's the most satisfying way of writing, but when you write in longhand and then transpose it to a word processor you know you're doing things twice and that's pretty senseless. But all the additional writing that I did in Melbourne whilst playing in *A Little Night Music* at night was done by hand, and in some ways I think these passages are some of the nicest parts of the book – if any of it's nice, that's up to you.

! ?

SPEAKER: Why have you never, with all your experience, taken up directing?

RUTH CRACKNELL: I'd be really, really terrible. I am not a very patient person and I want things to happen very quickly. That's my problem when I am rehearsing; I don't always enjoy rehearsals, I can't wait to be shot of them and get in front of people.

SPEAKER: I first fell in love with you in the days of *A Cup of Tea, a Bex and a Good Lie Down*. Remember those days when we had coffee, Cahill's caramel cake and ice cream?

RUTH CRACKNELL: Yes, I remember it all. Some of it was good and some of it was hideous.

SPEAKER: I read in an article that your wonderful coat in *Mother and Son* was a tweed from 1974. Do you collect memorabilia from different shows?

RUTH CRACKNELL: No, not at all, that just happened because the ABC wardrobe department was getting absolutely desperate for a coat, and anything that they presented to me was quite unsuitable. So I remembered that, 10, 12 years before in London I had bought an A-line hound's-tooth coat which was by then decidedly unfashionable, and that became the perfect coat for Maggie Bear. The ABC still has it and I'm not going to ask for it back because we all know what financial problems they're having at the moment.

SPEAKER: Which aspect of the arts do you feel most comfortable in – the theatre, film, radio, television or now writing?

RUTH CRACKNELL: I felt very comfortable writing, except when I was feeling a bit depressed as I delved into some of my bleaker memories. Writing is something you can do without any interruption, and that is lovely for a person who is a bit reclusive and getting more so by the minute.

Other areas of the arts each have their own particular joys. Nothing ever replaces the sheer electricity of what happens between an audience and somebody up on a stage, but the downside of that, of course, is that you have to do eight performances per week and that is, if you are playing a large role, a very, very exhausting way to spend your life.

Film I love – I just love the intimacy of it and the difference of it, the technicalities of it. Radio, just lovely. They are all good, and television we won't talk about. My bit on television was very special but it was a combination of being in the theatre and doing television because it was taped in front of a live audience. So it was a bit different from a lot of television.

SPEAKER: Do you remember playing the part of Mrs de Winter in the Modern Theatre Players production of *Rebecca* and I played the part of the colonel?

RUTH CRACKNELL: Good heavens, old romances! Isn't that wonderful. *Rebecca* had been a film with Joan Fontaine playing Mrs de Winter and I gave an unconscious but pretty good imitation of Joan Fontaine. Everybody was extremely kind, if uncritical. Yes, I do remember that, and that is an eternity ago.

SPEAKER: Do you know that you are now a topic of study on the HSC drama course? My drama students feel that theatre seems to be very patriarchal and so you are great heroine in many ways to many young women. They would like to know how you feel about the patriarchy of the theatre.

RUTH CRACKNELL: I don't think I ever gave it any thought. I was aware that in the days when I began the proportion of male to female roles was perhaps two women to six men. It didn't occur to me to question that for a while. No, I don't think I did question it, if I happened to be playing one of the female roles.

I guess I have been very lucky – extremely tenacious, I know. When I went to England in the '50s, it was to make my career there. I would have stayed in England, and at the time I left I was just at the beginning of what would have been hopefully a career there. What brought me back to Australia was a tragic circumstance – and the fact that I came back and that theatre here gradually started to be taken seriously from that moment was quite extraordinary.

I think these days you will find that young women in theatre have as good a run as the guys.

SPEAKER: Have you enjoyed any production any better than any others?

RUTH CRACKNELL: In the book I pluck out a few which seem to me to have been special for particular reasons. One of them was *Nicholas Nickleby* because it had a very particular shine to it; another was *Oedipus*. They were very, very particular and major productions and they were a bit different. If you're talking about a favourite role, then for me it is always the role I have just played. So at the moment my favourite role is Virginia Woolf [in *Vita and Virginia*] and I'm here to say I don't think that any role I play will exceed my feeling for Virginia. I've become very, very attached to her.

SPEAKER: When I was about six years old I saw you in *The Duenna*, and I enjoyed it though only a little girl. I have also enjoyed your performances as an adult and I want to say thank you. I enjoy you enjoying your craft.

RUTH CRACKNELL: Thank you very much. It is worth pointing out that *The Duenna* in some ways changed my professional life because up till then I'd never played comedy at all, not really – apart from some light comedy on radio. An English director came out and he cast me in *The Duenna*. To this day I'll never know why, but it changed my life because people began to realise that I could do comedy, and once that is discovered that's it. So I went straight from *The Duenna* to the Phillip Street revues.

"I don't always enjoy rehearsals, I can't wait to be shot of them and get in front of people."

Dickie Bird

Bird began playing cricket for Yorkshire at 19 and moved into a legendary 24-year career as an umpire. He retired from international cricket in 1996 after a record 66 Test matches, three World Cup finals and 92 one-day internationals. *Dickie Bird: My Autobiography* gave a rare and entertaining look into the passions and tensions of the cricket pitch.

17 November 1997

I think that characters are going out of all sports, which is very, very sad. A vast amount of money is coming to the game; the characters are slowly going out of the game. Nobody smiles any more on the field, do they? They are all miserable. I have always said, sport is to be enjoyed. Do not get me wrong – we all like to win, but sport is to be enjoyed.

Two great characters who have left the test match scene were Ian Botham and Alan Lamb. They always took the mickey out of me in test matches. There was always something happening. We always had a laugh and that helped to break the tension.

Then there was Geoffrey Boycott. He is a miserable man. I am the only man he talks to – he has not got a friend in the world. I have known him since he was 13 and he is the biggest miser I have ever met in my life. He will be at home at the moment and he will be counting his money and watching videos of himself batting. I have told him, 'Geoffrey, you cannot take your money with you', but he will. He will make sure he gets it in that coffin when they bury him and I have told him, 'I hope I'm still around because I will dig it up. '

He has run a lot of players out in his career, but there was one man who ran him out in a test match – the only man ever to run Boycott out. Ian Botham tells the story of how England was playing New Zealand at Wellington and the New Zealand captain left England a very, very fair declaration. The England captain, Bob Willis, called a meeting in the England dressing room as Boycott and Luckhurst were padding up to go to bat. He said, 'Gentlemen, we're going for these runs. This is a very, very good declaration. Now, then Geoffrey, I want you to play a few shots.' 'I'm playing my own game,' he said. 'Nobody is going to tell me how I'm going to play. I will be 120-odd not out at close of play.' Willis said, 'I want you to play shots because we can win this test match.'

Luckhurst and Boycott went out to open the innings for England and Boycott put England well behind the clock. So Bob Willis called for another meeting in the England dressing room. He said, 'Gentlemen, I want a volunteer to pad up and go in next and run Boycott out.' Botham said, 'Captain, I volunteer.' 'Is that right, Both? Put your pads on and go in next.' Luckhurst got out and Botham went in next man and all the England players said, 'Good luck, Both.'

'Leave it to me,' said Botham. He went out to the middle and said to Boycott, 'Now look here. This is instructions from the England cap and the England captain. You have put us well behind the clock. You have got to play shots. We have got to get up with the clock. We can win this test match.' 'I was playing my own game. I will be 120-odd not out at close of play.' Botham said, 'Will you? Anyway, good luck, Geoffrey.'

Botham got down to face his first delivery. In came the bowler, delivered the ball, Botham shook the ball to cover point and shouted to Boycott 'Come on!', and Boycott charged down the wicket and when he got to Botham's end, Botham was still sitting on his bat. He said, 'I'm sorry, Geoffrey, I'm not coming.' Boycott turned round. He was run out by the length of the field. He has not spoken to Botham since that day.

As I said, I am the only bloke he talks to. I have known him since he was a schoolboy and I started at Bowsie Cricket Club – I opened with Michael Parkinson who has done the foreword to my autobiography and we had this young schoolboy, Geoffrey Boycott, who batted at number six. He was only a kid of 13 and I remember him saying to me then, 'Dickie, by the time I am 23, I shall have the full white rose of Yorkshire on my cap and I shall have the three lions of England on my chest', and by God, he did it. I have never met anyone like him for that and to bat for my life I would go for Boycott.

I did play county cricket. A lot of people do not realise that, but I was not a very good player. I played for Yorkshire and Leicestershire and while I was at Leicestershire in 1963, the West Indies were touring England, Frankie Worrell's West Indies side. It was a great side because they had so many great players. They had Sir Garfield Sobers, to me the greatest all-round cricketer that I have ever seen. In that 1963 side were two great fast bowlers, Wesley Hall and Charlie Griffiths, and they were fast, I will tell you.

I was having a terrible time at Leicester in 1963, I could not get a run. I was in the second team and we were due to play the West Indies at Leicester and the Leicestershire selection committee – there were 39 of them on that committee – decided to bring me back into the team. Now, that was a big mistake because I was in terrible form. I thought, well, I have got to go out there tomorrow morning and face two of the world's fastest bowlers, Wesley Hall and Charlie Griffiths.

So I arrived at the ground at 7 o'clock in the morning for an 11.30 start. I could not get in. All the gates were locked. So I threw my bags over the wall and I climbed over the wall and I went out to the middle to have a look at the pitch that we were playing on. I thought, I hope it is flat, and when I saw this pitch, I could not believe it. Our groundsman had left the grass on it, and when he arrived I said, 'Hey, get this grass off, shave it all off, make it as flat as you possibly can. I have got to go out there and face two of the world's fastest bowlers.'

"Then there was Geoffrey Boycott. He is a miserable man. He will be at home at the moment and he will be counting his money and watching videos of himself batting."

He said, 'I'm not going to touch it. I want to see some excitement today.' I said, 'They'll see some excitement if they don't get this grass off.' But he wouldn't touch it, so when our captain, Maurice Hallam, arrived, I said, 'Hey, Maurice, if you win the toss, shove the West Indies in.' He said, 'I'm going to, don't worry about that. I've seen the pitch and I don't fancy playing against Wes Hall and Charlie Griffiths on that.'

The two captains went out, Frank Worrell of the West Indies and our captain, Maurice Hallam. Up went the coin, down it came and after all I had told him, he won the toss, our captain, and he decided to bat first. That was big mistake. In those days we did not have helmets and those big chest protectors and big arm guards. My protection was my handkerchief, that is all I had. All I had was my handkerchief, that was my thigh pad, and I went out that Saturday morning to face the two world's fastest bowlers. I thought, well, I will try and do my best. I remember I took leg stump guard from the umpire and it is a good job I did because if I had taken off from the middle, I do not think I would have been here this lunchtime.

I saw Wesley Hall marking his run about at the pavilion end and I thought, where is he going? I thought he might be going to move the sidescreen, but he was not. He was marking his run about at the side of the sign. I looked in front of me and I could not see any fielders. I thought, that is funny, he has no fielders, and I looked over my right shoulder and 30 yards back he had got nine slips.

I saw Wesley Hall racing in. He had this big gold medallion he was waving, I could feel that as he came in and I saw nothing. I think I pushed forward, no I played back. I cannot remember what I did, and I looked up and I saw the West Indies players running around him and hugging him, 'Well, bowled, Wes, well bowled.' I thought, 'Well bowled, that's funny' and I looked down and there no off and middle stumps there.

I played for Yorkshire with a great fast bowler called Freddie Trueman. There has only been one better for me and that is Dennis Lillee of Australia. But Trueman was a great bowler and I was honoured and privileged to play with him. Not only was he a great fast bowler, he was a tremendous character. I have said to Fred many a time, 'Fred, this fellow Lillee must go down in history as the greatest fast bowler the world has ever seen.' 'Thou what?' he says, 'I thought thou were a mate of mine. I can still bowl better now off five paces than he ever could' – and he believes he can.

Fred was great to be in the dressing room with. Before a match started, we would get changed slowly in the Yorkshire dressing room. Fred was never in our room before the match started. He always went to see the visitors, and he did not knock on the door of the visitors' dressing room – he used to just smash it open and say, 'Now then, lads, I'm here and I'm ready for you today. I can see you're looking a little bit uneasy. I might have eight or nine wickets of you I think today. Oh, there's my old friend from last season. He were by square leg umpire when I bowled him. That's one wicket I've got for a start. Anyway, lads, all the best to you. I'll be ready for you in that middle when we get out there, I shall be ready for you.' He came back into our room and said, 'Lads, I've got eight or nine wickets here and they're a bit shaky in that other room.'

If we had lost the toss and happened to be fielding, we would be out in the middle with the two umpires. Where is Fred? We would look round and Fred would be standing by the pavilion gate. He used to wait for the opposition opening batsmen to come out and as they came through the gate, he used to say to them, 'Don't close that gate, because you won't be long out here.'

I would have liked to have compared the fast bowlers of old with your Lillees and your Thomsons, your Holdings and Roberts and Tysons and people like this, but you cannot go back in history. I would have liked to see Larwood and Voss bowl. They both played for Nottinghamshire. At one time they were playing Northamptonshire and the Northamptonshire side had a fast bowler called Nobby Clark, a left arm over the wicket. They tell me he was very fast and he was letting the Nottinghamshire batsmen have everything, bouncers, beamers, the lot. They were all ducking and weaving. The Northamptonshire players as they were fielding went up to Nobby and said, 'Nobby, don't you think you ought to cool it a little bit? We've got to go into bat and they've got two of the world's fastest bowlers, Larwood and Voss.' 'I am not frightened of Larwood and Voss, they do not frighten me. What is the matter with you? They do not frighten me.'

Nobby Clark just ran through the Nottinghamshire batsmen and Lol Larwood came in at number nine. In the first bowl Nobby Clark let him have a vicious bouncer, straight at his head and Lol Larwood just got out the way of it. He said, 'Nobby, it will soon be my turn.' Nobby said, 'Yes, and I shall be ready for you. When I come into bat for Northamptonshire, Lol, if you pitch them in my half, I'll hit you straight back over your head. If you bowl them short, I'll hook you straight out of Northampton.' Larwood said, 'We'll see about that, Nobby.'

Northamptonshire went into bat and they tell me they have never seen bowling as quick as they saw that day from Larwood and Voss. They just ran through them and Nobby came in to bat at number nine and as he was taking guard off the umpire, Lol Larwood said, 'Now then, Nobby, it's my turn' and Nobby said, 'Yes, and I'm ready for you. You pitch them in my half, I going to hit you straight back over your head, Lol. You bowl them short, I'm going to hook you straight out of Northampton.'

Nobby got down to face Larwood who bowled him a vicious bouncer straight at his head. Nobby just swayed out of the way of it and as it went past, he flashed at it and got a thick edge and the ball flew to third slip who caught it after it had bounced two yards in front of him. Everybody looked at Nobby – gloves off, bat under arm, he is walking back to the pavilion. 'Come back and fight,' said Larwood, 'come back and fight.' 'Well bowled, Lol,' said Nobby, 'well bowled.' The umpire said,

'Come back, Mr Clark, the ball bounced two yards in front of third slip before he caught it.' 'I am satisfied it was a fair catch, Mr Umpire.'

I am going back now to 1976. The West Indies were touring England and the England captain in those days was a chap called Tony Greig. Before that test series started, Tony Greig said on television and in the press, 'I shall make the West Indies grovel.' I said, 'Greggie, you've made a big mistake there.' He said, 'Do you think so?' I said, 'Yes', because the West Indies had four cannons bowling, Holding, Roberts, Garner and Croft, and England had three pea shooters.

"Holding said to me, 'Dickie, I can do this man Greig for a pastime'."

I umpired three tests that series. I was umpiring the last test match at the Oval where Michael Holding had bowled magnificently. It was one of the finest pieces of fast bowling I have ever seen in a test match because he beat the English batsmen by sheer pace through the air because it was a beautiful pitch to bat on. I think he took seven wickets in the first innings and seven in the second. In the second innings Holding was bowling from my end and he got the first four English wickets very quickly and Tony Greig came out to bat at number six.

As he walked down the members' enclosure out to the middle, Holding was standing at the side of me waiting for Tony Greig to come out. Holding said to me, 'Dickie, I can do this man Greig for a pastime.' I said, 'Michael, I have noticed that throughout the series.' Greig got out to the middle and he took leg stump guard off me, and in came Holding. He just bowled him a medium-pace half volley on the line of the off stump and Greig lent over, had his shoulder left leg onto the line of the ball and with the full face of the bat, hit it through the off side for four.

It was a magnificent shot and all the English supporters at the Oval were on their feet chanting 'Greig, Greig, Greig, Greig, Greig!' As Holding walked past me polishing the ball, he said, 'Dickie, get ready, this ball' and he went back many a mile. When he came past me I've never seen a ball as quick in all my life. I was frightened to death – stood there as the umpire, frightened. By the time Greig's bat came down, his leg middle stumps were cartwheeling past the wicket keeper. Now, it was the turn of the West Indies supporters. It was the last test that won the series and Holding had bowled Greig and they were throwing the Bacardi Rum bottles and the Coca Cola cans all over the Oval. We were all ducking and weaving in the middle and they come on the field in their thousands and thousands. You could not see a blade of grass. You could not see the pitch we were playing on for Bacardi Rum bottles, Coca Cola cans, West Indies supporters. They were all over the Oval.

I thought, what do we do here? One big West Indies supporter came through all this lot and he put his arm around me. He was a big West Indian. He said, 'Mr Dickie Bird, Professor of Cricket?' I said, 'That's me, man.' He felt in his pocket and he brought out a wad of notes, reeled 50 quid off. He said, 'I want you to give this £50 to Michael Holding for bowling Greig.' I said, 'Thank you very much, man', and I shoved it in my back pocket. No, it's not still there, no, like a true Yorkshireman, that is now invested in the Halifax Building Society in Barnsley.

I have had a wonderful career. I have had a

chance to see the world. I have had a chance to meet some wonderful people. The public throughout the world, the cricketing public, have been marvellous to me and I would just like to say this: the Australians especially, they have been wonderful to me throughout my career and that means more to me than anything in life and it means more to me than all the money in the world.

! ?

SPEAKER: A few years ago they introduced a third umpire and the video replay. Was that an initiative of the umpires or if not, how was it received by the umpires?

DICKIE BIRD: I am a big believer, this is only my view, of leaving it to the umpire – accept the umpire's decisions and get on with the game, that is what I believe, but I am afraid in this day and age that they are wanting perfect decisions and you will never, never get perfect decisions and you can have all the electronic aids in the world.

I think it is good for the close run outs and it is probably good for the close stumpings at the wicket but I would not like to see it go any further than that and I cannot see how an electronic aid or a device, a third umpire, can help you with l.b.w. decisions, caught behinds and back pads. I think that is impossible because you have so many things to take into consideration. Also, I think if you brought any more electronic aids in or other things, umpires will lose confidence in making decisions.

SPEAKER: Apart from Thomson and Lillee, I have not heard you make any comment about great Australian cricketers that have crossed your path.

DICKIE BIRD: Well, I could have. I could have mentioned the Australian sides in the early '70s. I mentioned I thought that was a great side, Ian Chappell's side, when he had Jeff Thomson, Dougie Walters, Maxie Walker, Rodney Marsh, Greg Chappell who I think is one of the greatest batsmen that I have ever seen, Greg Chappell. So was Ian Chappell and if I was in a war, in the trenches, I would want Ian Chappell on my right side and I would want Steve Waugh on my left side.

David Suzuki

Canadian geneticist, environmentalist, broadcaster and author Suzuki is internationally known as a provocative public speaker, and for his award-winning television series *The Nature of Things*, as well as for many books, including *Genethics, Inventing the Future, The Japan We Never Knew, A Matter of Survival* and *The Sacred Balance: Rediscovering Our Place in Nature*. A regular visitor to Australia, he spoke at a literary luncheon on his way to the 1997 Kyoto convention on climate control.

26 November 1997

Years ago when my daughter, who is now 17, was 8 years old, she looked up at me as I was putting her to bed one night and said, 'Daddy, we're trying to stop the logging in the Stein Valley because we're right, aren't we?' Like all my other children, she had been deeply involved in many protests, marches and demonstrations as we fought against nuclear plants and clear-cut logging of important watersheds. I said 'Yes, of course, sweetheart, we are right' and she said 'But, Daddy, the forest companies and the loggers, they think they're right too, don't they?' I said, 'Yes, I guess they do' and she said, 'Then, Daddy, how do we know we're really right?'

Her question went right to the heart of the dilemma that we face and for years it niggled at me. I gave her a very glib answer at the time. I said, 'Sweetheart, if we stop the logging and it turns out we were wrong, if 20 years from now we find there is no crisis in biodiversity, the trees will still be there, they can cut them down then, but if we lose and they do cut the trees down and 20 years from now we discover that there is an ecological crisis, it will be too late, they'll be gone.'

It was a hedge to tell her, a hedge against the

uncertainty into the future, but her question nevertheless had pierced me very deeply because it is clear that as we battle, as we fight, as we struggle, we tend to demonise the people that we are fighting against. They're the bad guys. They're stupid, they're greedy, they're selfish and, of course, we're the good guys, we're thoughtful, we're caring, we're far-sighted. But her question indicated that those people on the other side to us are mothers and dads, they're concerned about their future and their jobs and security the way that we are and so the world doesn't divide easily into black and white, into the good guys and the bad guys.

It seemed to me increasingly in the battles that we were involved in, that every time there was a victory there was always a loser and when we're talking about a future for our grandchildren or about the very things on the planet that support our lives, we cannot afford to have losers any longer. So the challenge that was posed to me by my foundation, the David Suzuki Foundation, was whether it is possible to define a set of fundamental needs about which everyone would have to come together and agree, yes, we absolutely need these things for our very survival, to give us a quality of life that we would say makes living worthwhile and if we could all then agree that those must be the basis on which we build a sustainable future.

That was a challenge the foundation set to me. I wrote this book, *The Sacred Balance*, as a gift to the foundation.

Before I begin defining some of those fundamental needs, let me state where I and Amanda McConnell, who helped me write this book, started from. What was the state of the world that we assumed as we wrote this document? To indicate what the foundation of our position is, I have to remind you that in June of 1992 the largest gathering of heads of state ever in human history occurred in Rio at the Earth Summit. Four months after the Earth Summit a remarkable document was released called *World Scientists' Warning to Humanity*. It was signed by more than 1600 senior scientists from 71 countries in the world, including more than half of all Nobel Prize winners at that time. Let me give you an idea of what this document said:

> *Human beings and the natural world are on a collision course. Human activities inflict harsh and often irreversible damage on the environment and on critical resources. If not checked, many of our current practices put at serious risk the future that we wish for human society and may so alter the living world that it will be unable to support life in the manner that we know. Fundamental changes are urgent if we are to avoid the collision our present course will bring about.*

Now, scientists as a group tend to be incredibly cautious and conservative in the kinds of statements they make to the general public. For an eminent group of scientists to make such a strong statement was without precedent and if you think that is sobering, consider what they say later on in the document:

> *No more than one or a few decades remain before the chance to avert the threats we now confront will be lost and the prospects for humanity immeasurably diminished. We, the undersigned senior members of the world scientific community, hereby warn all of humanity of what lies ahead. A great change in our stewardship of the Earth and the life on it is required if vast human misery is to be avoided and our global home on this planet is not to be irretrievably mutilated.*

That's a pretty stunning statement to come from these scientists. The response of the media around the world was even more stunning – there was no response at all.

In February of 1994, 58 of the world academies of science, representing essentially all of the top scientists in the world, simultaneously released a document in anticipation of the global conference on population to be held in Cairo that reiterated the warning to humanity of four months before.

"When we flush the toilet or put the garbage out on the kerb, we never wonder where it goes."

In December of 1995, 2500 climatologists from around the world vetoed a document by the United Nations Inter-Governmental Panel on Climate Change and signed the document that concluded, after examining more than 20,000 scientific articles on climate, that the evidence was in that said that global warming is occurring and that human activity is a major contributor. On September 30th of this year, 1997, more than half of all Nobel Prize winners signed another document called *World Scientists Call for Action at Kyoto* and it was presented in person to President Clinton urging him to make a strong commitment to limiting greenhouse gas emissions when he went to Kyoto in December. It concluded: 'There is only one responsible choice – act now.'

My point in reciting all of this is to make it clear that there is no scientific controversy over the dimensions of the global environmental crisis. The best minds on this planet in science are telling us that we are on a catastrophic course in agriculture, in forestry, in fisheries, in the atmosphere and so on. It is not, as one of the environment ministers in Canada said a few years ago, drug-crazed hippies. It is not, as our national newspaper said, eco-terrorists, fuzzy-headed do-gooders and neo-Luddites who are warning us of the crisis we face, it is the leading scientists of the world.

So when I come to Australia and read that the coal industry is able to trot out these scientists who are claiming that global warming is not yet supported or proved, I just wonder where the hell these people are coming from and of course you have to ask where is their money coming from. Because, as a scientist, one of the most humiliating aspects of the last 20 years was the way the tobacco industry was able to deny the overwhelming scientific opinion that smoking and cancer were linked and exactly the same thing is going on now with the claims of the energy sector.

We live in a world that has become so fragmented that we no longer see how the way that we live interacts with the very things that keep us alive. If you or I were to get in a car and drive three blocks instead of walking, very few of us would think, uh-oh, I've really done something stupid and I've contributed to weather change or global warming.

Canada is a northern country and yet when we're up to our ass in snow in February Canadians go and buy fresh strawberries and lettuce and tomatoes without ever wondering, gee, where the hell are they growing this in Canada at this time of the year? When we flush the toilet or put the garbage out on the kerb, we never wonder where it goes. When we turn on the lights or take a drink from the tap, we never wonder where it comes from. We fail to understand the way that these services that we take for granted come ultimately from the biosphere itself and if we no longer see the connections between our lifestyle and the Earth, it becomes easy to understand why we begin to accept our leaders when they say those are services brought to you by a strong, healthy economy – if you don't have a growing, strong economy, you can't afford a clean environment.

I was told this in fact the first time I ever came to Australia by a group of economists who said, 'Guys like you, you're irresponsible because you want to do things before the economy. You can't afford it. If you don't have a good economy, you can't afford these changes you want.' But it is the Earth itself that delivers us all of these services. Everything in this room from the air to the glass to the energy to the plastics to the wood to the metal, everything in this room has come from the Earth and because the planet has been so provident it is possible for humanity to survive and to develop an economy. Without that, we don't live and we don't have the opportunity for an economy and yet we have this absolutely crazy notion of flipping at 180 degrees and saying it's the economy that delivers all of these services to us.

The challenge, I believe, is to rediscover the interconnectedness, the fact of our deep embeddedness in the natural world. What I believe is needed goes far beyond electing the right party to office who are going to enact the proper legislation and laws that will govern the way we behave.

The first time I ever went to China was in 1976 to do some films and at one point we were filming in a hospital and I was sitting in the waiting room and there were dozens of people sitting in that room and I was shocked to find that people were spitting on the floor – and I'm talking about a great, big, hacking gob right on the floor – and I thought, wow, that's amazing, apart from wanting to throw up on the spot. Now in Canada we don't have any laws that say, 'Don't spit on the floor'. We don't have any signs saying, 'You will be fined and thrown into jail if you gob on the floor'. We don't have spit police that go around making sure you don't spit on the floor. We just take it for granted. It's a part of our fundamental value system in Canada, and I hope in Australia, that you don't spit on the floor.

That's what we need in terms of the kind of basic needs I'm going to describe now, where everyone of us understands in a very profound way,

"My air here comes out and is fused right to your air that goes into your lungs."

these are the things that keep us alive and give us a rich life and you don't mess with them. Once we all have that understanding, it doesn't matter whether you elect Pauline Hanson or John Howard or Bob Brown, the level has been raised so that everybody in our society takes it for granted.

I believe that there are three levels of basic needs that must be protected as the foundation of our sustainable future. The first is based on our biological needs, the second is based on our social needs and the third on our spiritual needs. Today I'm only going to be able to cover the first level, that is our basic biological needs.

We forget, at our peril, that we have emerged out of the web of living things as another species. We are, above all, animals. As animals we have fundamental needs which, if they are not met, we die. It's as simple as that and the first basic need is that which we need from the moment we leave our mother's body at birth. From the infant's first breath that announces its arrival in the world to the very last gasp on our deathbed, we are pumping air into our bodies every minute. Basically our lungs are acting as a giant filter for the air that surrounds us. We take, on average when you're young, 40 breaths a minute. When you get older, like me, we're taking between 17 and 20 breaths a minute. So let's say on an average, in a lifetime, we've been breathing about 30 times a minute. When you're as old as I am, you've taken hundreds of millions of breaths.

One of the books of which I'm most proud is a book I wrote for children called *If We Could See the Air*. If we could see the air, we would think about it much more seriously. You can't draw a line and say the air ends here and you begin here. We are literally fused to the air. We are the air, it is always in us, a part of us, and if you could see it, you would see that the air I exhaust goes out in a little jet and it goes straight up your nose and there would be jets of air going all over the place and we're all pumping air into us that was once a part of everybody else. Air isn't a vacuum or empty space. Air is a physical substance that links all of us together. My air here comes out and is fused right to your air that goes into your lungs. We are embedded in this matrix of air, not only with each other but with trees and birds and snakes and worms that are all sharing that air with us.

There's a wonderful exercise that the American astronomer, Harlow Shapley, performed a few years ago. He said, 'If you look at air, 99 per cent of it is oxygen and nitrogen.' The reason we breath air in and need it is the oxygen which is a fuel for our metabolic fires. Nitrogen is mildly reactive, oxygen is very reactive. But one per cent of the air we breath in is a compound called argon. If you know any chemistry, argon is called an inert gas, it doesn't react with anything. You breathe it in, you breathe it out, it doesn't do anything in the body. So he said, 'We can follow the argon as it comes out of our body and around the world.' How many atoms of argon are there in that one breath of air that we've imagined? It turns out there are 3 times 10^{19}, that's a 3 followed by 19 zeros, of argon atoms in that one breath of air. So the minute that breath comes out of my nose, you're breathing in gazillions of argon atoms that were in my body and vice versa and when you open the door, out that air rushes, argon atoms rush across Sydney, Australia, around the world and one year later, if we all came back into this room, Shapley says on average, every breath we take would have 15 argon atoms from that one original breath we took a year earlier.

Now listen to what Shapley says:

> *Your next breath will contain more than 400,000 of the argon atoms that Gandhi breathed in his long life. Argon atoms are here from the conversations at the Last Supper, from the arguments of diplomats at Yalta and from the recitations of the classic poets. We have argon from the sighs and pledges of ancient lovers, from the battle cries at Waterloo, even from last year's argonic output by the writer of these lines, who personally has had already more than 300 million breathing experiences.*

It's a wonderful way at looking at air and I think once you think about it that way, then it becomes folly, it becomes almost ludicrous, that we treat a substance that should be regarded as sacred in such a destructive way by using it essentially as a sewer to dump the most toxic chemicals ever invented in massive quantities. This air that we depend on for our survival is a gift of life itself.

If we were to get into a time capsule and go back in time to before there was any life on this Earth, if we didn't have any breathing apparatus and opened the door to get out into the atmosphere, we would die in a matter of minutes. Why? Because the original atmosphere had no oxygen in it and it was rich in carbon dioxide. It was poisonous for human beings. It was life itself that began to remove the carbon dioxide out of the atmosphere and began to pump a pollutant into the air called oxygen. So life transformed the atmosphere into the oxygen rich one that we depend on and life continues to be the medium whereby this air is replenished with oxygen and carbon dioxide is removed. So not only is air, I believe, a sacred element, but the living skin of life, the diversity of living things is what confers it to us.

I could do the same kind of lyrical look at water. We're all basically a big blob of water. Over 60 per cent of us is water, by weight, and that water has come from around the world. Life itself cleanses it in the process of taking water up and transpiring it into the atmosphere. Water is created by living things and the same thing with soil. Soil gives us every bit of our nutrition. You and I are basically compost heaps for the carcasses of plants and animals that we've consumed for our existence. Every bit of the nutrition that goes into making our bodies was once alive and it has all come, ultimately, from the Earth and the soil of the Earth is a creation of life itself. Before life arose, there was no soil anywhere on the planet. Life created soil.

So the point I'm trying to make to you is clean air, clean water, clean soil and biodiversity are the very things that make it possible to live on this plant. Surely to God if that's true, and it is true, then that must be at the very basis of any consideration of what we do into the future. Not economic priorities and globalisation. They must be based on the assumption that none of this activity compromises in any ways these sacred needs. If we don't do that, it seems to me we would be absolutely suicidal.

There are other levels of needs that we have, we have social needs in which the fundamental need is love. If we don't have children who grow up with love, we have fundamentally, psychically and physically damaged individuals and how you maximise the opportunity for love is by stabilising communities. We have spiritual needs as well. But the biological ones are the basic needs. These must be the non-negotiable bottom line and they must be accepted by all people who've traditionally been battling over environmental issues. We must come together because as animals, social animals and spiritual animals, these are the things that make us human and that give us a rich, full life. That's the challenge into the next millennium.

Bryce Courtenay

An immigrant from South Africa in the 1950s, Courtenay is now in the *Guinness Book of Records* as Australia's most popular author. A former advertising executive, he had a huge bestseller in 1989 with his first novel, *The Power of One*, set against the background of South African apartheid. Among the books that have followed are *April Fool's Day*, about the death of his hemophiliac son from AIDS, and the Australian historical series which began with *The Potato Factory* in 1995 and continued with *Tommo & Hawk* in 1997.

5 December 1997

I often get asked, 'How do you write books, Bryce? Particularly a historical novel which requires an enormous amount of research?' And I remember asking William Boyd, the famous English writer, the same question. 'Well, Bryce, it is quite obvious,' he said. 'You do your research, that generally takes a year or 18 months; then you map out all your chapter headlines; then you write under each heading 150 words about what is in the chapter; then you divide all your research notes into that; then you do a synopsis of the whole book; and then you sit down and you write it.'

I thought, oh, shit! I just start on a wet Thursday and say, here we go, and a year later I come out of this dark tunnel and there is a book. That is how I write it. So I am awfully sorry I cannot help any of you would-be writers because the only thing I can tell you about writing is bum glue. Glue your bum onto a chair and that is it and keep going until it is finished because it is a discipline and you cannot do it without a discipline. Writing *Tommo & Hawk* required an enormous amount of research and I am fortunate that I was able to afford some very talented researchers to do the work, but one of the joys of writing this trilogy is that we are so rich in a history that has been untold.

Australian history is vastly, vastly under-written. I once met a professor from Harvard who told me that if you stacked all the American historical novels 12 foot high they would stretch for 127 miles. But if you did the same thing for Australian historical novels they would be 12 foot by some 27 feet. In essence, there is not a huge difference in the length these two countries have existed and yet they have this huge historical genre and we have this really very small one.

I think the answer lies in the fact that during the 19th century and certainly the first half of the 20th century people were reluctant to write our history because readers did not want to read it. Somehow we were ashamed of our past. It has only been in the last 20 years, in my experience, that people have been very, very proud of the fact that we came from where we came from and the circumstances in which we were settled. So, in effect, all of the books that should have been written in the 19th century and perhaps up to the 1960s in the 20th century just never got written and the only way people learn their history is via novels.

They do not learn it in history books and most of you here will remember that at school the history you were taught was the history of Britain which is astonishing when you think about it. Our own history was totally neglected. So we are a people who do not know intimately where we came from and for that matter who we are. When I started to write these books, when I opened the back door and looked into the backyard of the past, I absolutely could not believe how rich and wonderful this history was. It has not been a question of digging for alluvial gold – it has all been on the surface, all this wonderful stuff.

Tommo & Hawk is a book which is seminal in a sense because the 1850s, 1860s and early 1870s were a time in which we became, in a sense, a unique people. Sure, we were an Anglo-Celtic people, but we had become a unique people. There was such a thing as an Australian. No longer surrogate Englishmen, Welshmen, Scots or Irishmen, but an Australian. Somebody who spoke this peculiar language called Australian and it is a peculiar language and let me explain why that is so.

When the convicts came out to Van Diemen's Land and to New South Wales they came from disparate centres, from Belfast, from Edinburgh, from Birmingham, Manchester and London and each of these were entirely different tribes. They spoke virtually a different language. They even had different diets. They certainly had a totally different argot and they could not understand each other. The first place they actually coalesced or met was either in Van Diemen's Land or in New South Wales and so suddenly these disparate tribes of people had to form a new language and they formed the language called Australian. One in every five words was a brand new word to describe something that had never existed before. So that by 1815 and certainly in the 1830s Englishmen were referring to people as speaking Australian, this new language.

But it was not until about 1850 with the gold rush coming in and this large mass of new migrations that suddenly people who were not convicts outnumbered people who were convicts and we had a second generation of young Australians. It all suddenly came together and we became, in a sense, a nation.

The crucible in which a nation is formed is a hugely important idea – whether it be war or revolution, for example. With us it was a peaceable crucible, but it was a crucible where a lot of the attitudes which we have today started to form. There were riots in Lambing Flat against the Chinese. There was a huge feeling against Asian migration at that particular time. Our attitudes

"So we are a people who do not know intimately where we came from and for that matter who we are."

towards the indigenous people – because the pastoralists had now, in a very large sense, gained their land and gained the properties that they wanted – were formed then.

We are far from a reconciled nation yet. But we have to seek reconciliation. We are not just an ordinary Anglo-Celtic people. We are an astonishing people in so many senses. There have been four large English-speaking migrations or migrations from the mother land, England and Ireland, over the past two and a half centuries.

The first one, of course, was the pilgrim fathers. They were religious dissidents, middle-class people who built stout little ships and sailed across the Atlantic and discovered this astonishing place where the snow came down as it always had done in a great white doona and when the spring was there this great multi-coloured quilt came up and the top soil was five foot deep and the rivers teamed with fish and the forests with game. These people prospered mightily and became the greatest nation in the 20th century. The second one was to Canada where they discovered the prairies where even today when the wheat is ripe it changes the colour of the sky. Canada is thought to be potentially the richest nation on earth and they too, as an English-speaking people, prospered enormously.

Then there were those who went to Africa. William of Orange had acceded the Cape to the English throne and the English men and women who arrived there found that, indeed, the vines had tender grapes and a little later as they moved up to Natal to form a new British colony the grass was green and the cattle grew sleek and the black men bore their burdens and they too prospered mightily as an English-speaking migration.

But we were dragged kicking and screaming from the dungeons of Newgate and from the hulks on the Thames and put into leaky ships and sailed as far from our antecedent beginnings as it is possible to get onto the driest continent in earth, the burning shore and they threw us on the shore and said, 'Die, you bastards' and we all were bastards because that's just how it happened to be at the time – the whores and the pimps and the hopeless and the useless and the people nobody wanted, the white trash. They had found this antipodean rubbish heap where they hoped we would all go away and die and we picked ourselves up and we dusted the sand from our skirts and our pants and in 200 years we have built a society which sociologists call the most sophisticated ever to have been built in that period of time.

As far from its antecedent beginnings as it is possible to get, with the exception of New Zealand, of course, and we did this without any ghettos. We did this without any race riots. We did this as the most integrated egalitarian people on earth. By 1904 we had the highest standard of living on earth. This land that promised nothing, we had made it work for us. We were the second country to give women the franchise to vote and we were people who really made trade unionism work in the best possible way. This astonishing place has been an example to the world of how a people can survive under the most extraordinary circumstances.

The only sore, the only festering sore, is how we have treated our Aboriginal people and we have to seek reconciliation. Before we go into the 21st century I believe we have to seek reconciliation with our indigenous people. I do not think, for instance, that Wik is automatically right. I am sure there is compromise needed, but we have, at some stage, to say sorry. Until we do that I fear for the beloved country.

This is a beloved country. In 1950 we turned around and we said, 'Ooh, this Anglo-Celtic blood is getting a bit thin, I'll tell you what we'll do, we'll invite all the hopeless and useless back again.' We said, 'Anybody hopeless and useless out there you can come here, we've done this before.' And we invited everybody nobody wanted. We even invited the Poms back. In they came by their tens of thousands and today Australia is the most polyglot nation on earth. The blood and the brains of every nation on earth pulses through our veins. We have an astonishing future if we would use it correctly.

I came to this country 40 years ago. I was thrown out of my own. I can remember it was 7 o'clock in the morning and I came on deck and we were passing through these great sandstone cliffs and the boat was cutting a swathe through the harbour. The harbour was like a mill pond – like all of Sydney was contained in a crystal bowl and the sky just rose higher and higher and higher and higher. I knew that I had found the place I wanted to spend the rest of my life. I had just been to London where I had finished my education and for the four years I was there the skies sat on my shoulders and it weighed me down.

I got tired of the smell of damp coats and suddenly here rose this great antipodes and the great south land sky and I knew that I could never ever leave this place. It has been extraordinarily good to me. It has given me a beautiful wife, three wonderful children and a home. I remember this little boat going choo! choo! through into the harbour and we passed Parsley Bay and there was this large white house with a brilliant splash of bougainvillea on it. It took me 17 years to buy that house.

I look back at how fortunate I have been as a human being in this country and how my beginnings were. I was born deep in the heart of the Lebombo Mountains – hillbilly country, the deep north of southern Africa. My grandfather was a botanist and in England he had created a new genus of rose which he had called the Imperial Sunset. He had a brilliant career ahead of him. Except for one thing. The rose had no perfume. It was useless. So he gave up his job and searched the world and, so help me, he found the perfect place deep in the heart of the Lebombo mountains in this little town of die-hard Boers. There must have been a travelling salesman or something that came up one Saturday night because nine months later, much to her enormous surprise, my mother gave birth to a small infant and the preacher stood up at the pulpit that Sunday and said, 'There is born among us rotten seed of the womb' and that was me.

They gave me hell. I had a very rough upbringing, but fortunately my mother's surprise was so enormous that she immediately handed me into the arms of a large black woman and I suckled on her

"By 1904 we had the highest standard of living on earth. This land that promised nothing, we had made it work for us."

breasts for three years and as far as I was concerned this was my mother. The first language I spoke was Zulu and then Swazi and a little later Khosa and then finally English and Afrikaans. The greatest disappointment in my life was when I was handed back at the age of five before my mother put me in a rather dreadful boarding school which you may have read of in *The Power of One*.

I only had one question to ask of this fairly strange woman who I was supposed to call mother. I said, 'Could you just answer this question please, when am I turning black?' and without doubt the most disappointing moment of my life was when she told me that I never was going to be black. My friends were all black kids because I got hell from everybody else and when I went to school all the kids of seven years old were already about 6'5" and they used to beat the hell out of me.

Until one day I said, 'Hey, wait a minute, fellows, wait a minute, I'll tell you a story' and they said 'Ach, man, it had better be a good story because if it's not a good story I'm going to donner you.' I sat under a tree with about half a dozen kids and I told them a story. This got to the point where the whole school, every break, would sit under a tree and I would tell them a story. Because there were no radio, no newspapers, nothing in this little town, I swear I thought I had invented the serial, but I never would tell them the end of the story.

I would say, 'That is for tomorrow. If anybody beats me up you do not hear the end.' That was when I finally knew that I was a story-teller, that that was what I did best. I told 700 episodes of the same story and when my kids were born I started a story called 'Mr Puppet, the Wooden Spoon and the Yellow Aeroplane'. I told that every night of their lives until they were 17 or 18 – it just got more and more sophisticated.

At the age of 11 I won a scholarship to go to one of the poshest schools in South Africa. At school one day, I think I was in Form 2, one of the Africans working on the cricket pitch had approached me. I spoke to all the Africans at school because I could speak their languages. It is astonishing that after 300 years only two per cent of white South Africans speak an African language. This boy approached me and said, 'Sahbona InKosi', which literally translates as 'G'day, God' because whites required blacks at that time to call them God. 'Please will you teach me to read and write?' he asked. I said that I would and so with about half a dozen other kids at school who spoke Fanagzlo, which is like a lingua franca, we started in the school hall on Saturday nights and Sundays and after one month we had 600 Africans coming on the weekends to be taught how to read and write.

It was wonderful because they were so anxious to learn and they would come in their absolute Sunday best and all scrubbed and beautiful and wonderful with their slates and they would listen to every word. Then, of course, the police raided it and said I was a communist – I would have had a lot of trouble knowing there were two 'm's' in communist. They disallowed the school and we tried it somewhere else and they raided that and the headmaster told me that if I continued I would be expelled. And when I got a scholarship to go overseas I got a note from the Commissioner of Police which said, 'If you return to South Africa we will put you under house arrest'.

So I had to find a new country. I met Benita in London and she said, 'Have I got a country for you.' She was so right, because there has not been one second of the 40 years that I have been here that I have resented. It is almost as though I got born in the wrong place and somehow I crawled in the dark until I found this astonishing place.

Arundhati Roy

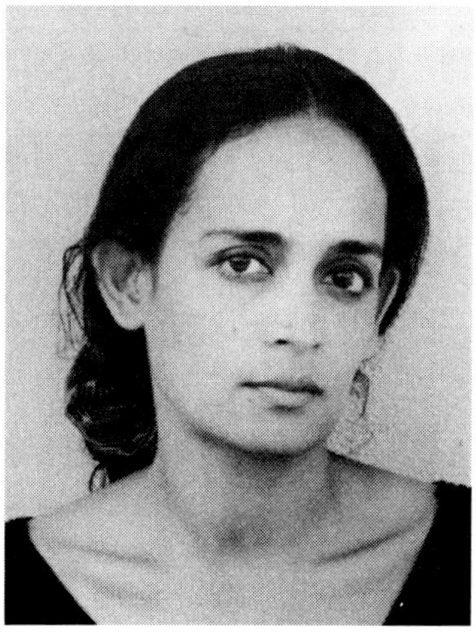

Roy sprang onto the international scene with her first novel, *The God of Small Things*, which was passed on by an Indian editor to a London agent, who flew straight to New Delhi and sold the book to publishers for more than a million dollars. As well as selling large numbers in 34 languages, the novel won the 1997 Booker Prize. The story of twin children and their Syrian-Christian mother's tragic affair with an untouchable is set in Roy's homeland, the Southern Indian Communist-ruled state of Kerala, where she grew up at the family pickle factory. This talk took the form of an interview with Susan Wyndham, Literary Editor of the *Sydney Morning Herald*.

6 April 1998

SUSAN WYNDHAM: Arundhati Roy is already a truly confident and sophisticated writer. This is not your average first novel. Yet she has only been a writer for five years. She did several other things beforehand – trained as an architect, baked cakes and sold them on a beach, acted in a film, wrote two screenplays, worked as a production designer. I wonder, Arundhati, what led you back to the old-fashioned craft of writing a novel?

ARUNDHATI ROY: Truthfully, the other things were just digressions because ever since I was a child if there was one thing I knew that if I could do, would do, it was write a book. But when I was in my teenage years, it was the last thing that I would ever have the luxury of being able to do and so the other things were really just ways of keeping my head above water. I didn't study architecture initially because I had any interest in the subject but because I just wanted to be able to support myself and earn my living. It is only when I joined college that I got very involved with it, extremely involved with it and now I see that all writers should study architecture first.

"This keeps the channels between your adulthood and your childhood open and I think it makes you a very adult child and a very childish adult."

SUSAN WYNDHAM: In fact I think architecture gave you the framework for the book, didn't it? It has a marvellous and very complex structure that unfolds the story piece by piece; it is layered and the revelations come slowly with repetitions. Were you thinking as an architect as you wrote?

ARUNDHATI ROY: When I started I was very aware of the fact that I was writing to some kind of structure but it eluded me. I didn't know exactly what I was doing. About two and a half years into the writing I remember making this series of graphic drawings – I drew the structure of the book out. I didn't start at the beginning of the book, just the way you don't start with the entrance when you design a building. But you use these design motifs throughout. So there is that sense of repetition, telling the reader: look, you are safe in my hands, I am taking you somewhere. It's like a chorus that reassures you or it's like having a homogeneity – when you design a door there has to be a link between the building and the door. In that sense I felt that I had to keep repeating motifs.

SUSAN WYNDHAM: The book is told largely from the point of view of the twins, Estha and Rahel, and you have a fabulous ability to get inside a child's mind. What are you memories of your own childhood like and how did you use them?

ARUNDHATI ROY: The book is set in the village that I grew up in and it is about a world that I know. I grew up on the edge of a very parochial, very traditional, very wealthy community called the Syrian Christians. My mother married outside the community and then was divorced when I was very young and we came back to live in the village. It was made very clear to me that these people were not willing to offer me the assurances that they would offer someone who belonged to them. What happens if you are an unprotected child or a person, let's say, whose protector is almost more vulnerable than yourself, is that you grow up trying to anticipate what the world is about to do to you. You are always anxious to try and understand it and why are people behaving in this way. When you grow up out of that you can never shrug it off because there was so much effort involved in that effort to understand. I think this keeps the channels between your adulthood and your childhood open and I think it makes you a very adult child and a very childish adult.

SUSAN WYNDHAM: You seem to have been just as strongly influenced by Western popular culture as you were by Indian culture. There is a whole chapter about the movie *The Sound of Music* and there are references to Elvis Presley, television and so on. Do you feel as though you are part of these two cultures equally?

ARUNDHATI ROY: Absolutely. Until a couple of years ago I had never been outside of India, but remember that for 300 years we were colonised so of course everything that you read, the language that you speak, the films that you see, is part of Western culture – there isn't any such thing as a sealed-off area that is purely Indian any more. So I often get stuck, caught in the cross-fire. In India there are sort of intellectuals, whom I call the religious secularists but the cultural bigots, who say, 'You're not authentically Indian.' I don't know what it is to be authentically Indian because I am an authentically colonised subject. I'm a product of my history.

SUSAN WYNDHAM: There is even an Australian character in this book. Tell us about Miss Mitten.

ARUNDHATI ROY: Miss Mitten was my teacher when I was five years old and she was responsible for the first coherent sentence that I wrote. Miss Mitten used to tell me with alarming regularity that she could see Satan in my eyes and that began because she was teaching us sums. We had always done sums up to 10 only, so it was 8 plus 2, 9 take away 7, and then without warning she slipped in 7 plus 8 and so we didn't know what to do. She happened to go out of the class, so I took off my shoes and counted on my toes. When she came back she asked, 'How did you do this sum?' For some reason I thought that it was a sin to admit to having taken off my shoes so I said I did it in my head. She said, 'No, you didn't' and so this began this whole Satan thing. The first sentence that I ever wrote, which my mother preserved and gave me recently, was: 'I hate Miss Mitten, and I think her knickers are torn.'

SUSAN WYNDHAM: The other major character in the book is the children's mother who becomes a social outcast for crossing lines of caste, colour, religion and education. From reading your book it would seem to many people that India, at least Kerala, is a seething mass of snobbery and prejudice. Is that fair?

ARUNDHATI ROY: It is, but let me know of any society that isn't. I think that human society since the dawn of time has found ways of dividing itself up, of making war across these divisions, making love across these divisions. There are always those who make them and those who argue against them. I would say that India lives in both the 7th and the 20th centuries simultaneously, so you have people who barely know what caste they belong to and at the same time you can read a story of someone who has been beheaded in a village for having married outside their caste. It's a very strange society in that sense. Everything is true about India.

SUSAN WYNDHAM: Can you tell us a little bit more about the reaction to the book in India and particularly in Kerala?

ARUNDHATI ROY: What has been delightful is that the book, despite a few things like the court case, has been received in India almost exactly in the same way that it has been received in Estonia and Finland and Australia and America. It has been an incredibly human response to it. The case again me for corrupting public morality isn't as horrible as it sounds. It's not like the whole country is hunting me down. It's a lawyer, a Syrian Christian lawyer, who has filed this case against me. When the case is accepted by the court it becomes the State of Kerala versus me, but the High Court has stayed

"I don't know what it is to be authentically Indian because I am an authentically colonised subject."

the proceedings until they hear it further. That is a very good sign which means they don't think there's much of a case there. There is so much violence there that things could be much worse. Writers and painters and artists and all kinds of people have had a much harder time so I'm almost grateful that it's just this.

"So I wrote a series of articles called 'The Great Indian Rape Trick'."

SUSAN WYNDHAM: Is the reaction of the Marxists likely to flare into something more?

ARUNDHATI ROY: Actually that's a much more frightening thing than the court case. The government that is in power in Kerala is Marxist but there is something faintly ridiculous about it. I am only saying this because I am so far away. In India whenever journalists ask me if I have a response, I say, 'Yes, have you got your pen ready? My response is, "Could not be reached".' They've said things like, 'There cannot be a character like Comrade Pillau in the Communist party', and they proceed to say almost verbatim the things that Comrade Pillau says in the book. For example, this is a statement issued by the 89-year-old leader of the Marxist party there, 'Arundhati Roy is a sexual anarchist, she shows a woman having illicit sex with a common labourer, and if she thinks that sexual anarchy is the way to revolution then I'm not a revolutionary because I'm not a womaniser.' It's the non sequitur of all time.

In fact, a lot of it began with a misunderstanding, a misreading of the book. I refer often to a particular area as 'the heart of darkness', a place across the river where there is this old abandoned house in which the children play. When they grow up and return to Ayemenem, they find that a five-star hotel has been built over the house of darkness; they have bought little wooden houses, ancestral homes, all over Kerala and re-assembled them here. I call them toy histories for rich tourists to play with. The hotel people liked to claim that it belonged to Comrade Namudhripad who is the elderly Marxist leader that I am talking about. Now I had written, 'So now old communists have become fawning bearers who stoop slightly behind their trays of drinks', and people claimed that I had said that Namudhripad was running a hotel and forcing old communists to work as bearers. So it started off from there and just got more and more strident. I hope that it's blown over. Actually it's very funny but that's the kind of thing that can go very horribly wrong for a writer.

SUSAN WYNDHAM: You've never been frightened though of being outspoken have you? You got into some trouble when you criticised the film *The Bandit Queen* on feminist grounds.

ARUNDHATI ROY: Yes, that was actually a big fight because this film was made by what I call the three leading feminists of India who all happen to be men. They made this film about Poolan Devi, a bandit who roamed the ravines of Uttar Pradesh for many years. The police couldn't catch her and finally she surrendered. When I went to see the film, I noticed Devi wasn't there, at this screening for all the beautiful people. They hadn't invited her. The film turned India's most famous bandit into India's most famous victim of rape. They had not only explicit rape scenes, but they had invented a few more rapes and there was no scene where she was a bandit. She was always being told what to do, where to sit, where to stand, how to walk.

Occasionally she did have a few foul-mouthed lines of dialogue but that's not feminism. Then I found they had no contract with her. I read the book on which they claim the film had been based; it was very hard to see where these connections came from. Then she started speaking to the press and saying, 'They refused to show me the film, it's like being re-raped.' So I wrote a series of articles called 'The Great Indian Rape Trick'.

SUSAN WYNDHAM: Whether you like it or not, you are going to be seen as part of the line-up of recent Indian writers who have been lauded worldwide – Salman Rushdie, Vikram Seth, and so on. Do you see yourself as part of a tradition of Indian writing? Are you influenced by them in any way?

ARUNDHATI ROY: I think one of the reasons why there is this excitement about Indian writers is that there isn't a tradition of Indian novels, it's being created, being moulded, just now. So sometimes as a writer you might be reacting against the way someone else writes but that still doesn't mean you're not influenced by that person. The only thing I would point out is that most of the big names that you find mentioned are men and most of them are people who have been educated in Cambridge and Oxford. I am not part of that and I think the difference is that for men politics begins outside the house, whereas for women, for me, it begins much closer. So you find that men writers are much more snug within the family than I am. For me it's a cool place, it's a frightening place, there isn't any safety there whereas for them it's more comfortable. For example, if a man writes about Partition or some political situation, in the background his mother will be warming the milk for him. That's something which I find hard to take.

"If you were to ask me if there was one thing that I believed in fiercely and unwaveringly, the answer would be in my own inconsequence."

SUSAN WYNDHAM: I've certainly been impressed by your coolness in winning the Booker Prize, having all this fame and success and money pouring your way. What is your reaction to it all?

ARUNDHATI ROY: If you were to ask me if there was one thing that I believed in fiercely and unwaveringly, the answer would be in my own inconsequence. I don't think there's any reason for anybody to get all pompous about these things – they just come and go and it would be foolish to take it very seriously.

Index of authors

Jeffrey Archer	121
Margaret Atwood	203
John Berendt	160
Maeve Binchy	137
Dickie Bird	252
Tim Bowden	219
Melvyn Bragg	192
Bill Bryson	198
Michael Caine	65
Peter Carey	231
Judy Cassab	166
Jung Chang	70
Gordon Chater	177
Bryce Courtenay	264
Ruth Cracknell	248
Roald Dahl	1
Blanche d'Alpuget	94
Nicholas Evans	181
Susan Faludi	52
Ranulph Fiennes	105
Frederick Forsyth	111
Kate Grenville	116
Josephine Hart	173
Robert Hughes	214
Barry Humphries	59
Elizabeth Jolley	22
Frank McCourt	237
Colleen McCullough	28
Adeline Yen Mah	210
David Malouf	82
David Marr	34
James Michener	40
Frank Moorhouse	150
Jan Morris	48
Michael Palin	243
E. Annie Proulx	127
Ruth Rendell	155
Graham Richardson	132
Arundhati Roy	269
June Salter	145
Vikram Seth	89
Wilbur Smith	16
Anne Summers	99
David Suzuki	258
Paul Theroux	6
Joanna Trollope	186
Desmond Tutu	142
Minette Walters	225
Fay Weldon	12
Morris West	75